THE MIND OF JESUS

THE MIND OF JESUS

William Barclay

1817

HARPER & ROW · PUBLISHERS

New York, Hagerstown, San Francisco, London

THE MIND OF JESUS

Copyright © 1960, 1961 by SCM Press Ltd

Printed in the United States of America

First Harper & Row paperback edition published in 1976.

This book is published in Great Britain
in two volumes entitled *The Mind of Jesus* and
Crucified and Crowned.

Grateful acknowledgement is made to the following for special permission to
reprint copyrighted material from the works indicated:

The Viking Press, New York: lines from 'The Creation', in *God's Trombones:
Some Negro Sermons in Verse* by James Weldon Johnson, copyright 1927 by
The Viking Press, Inc., 1955 by Grace Nail Johnson

Andrew Dakers Ltd, London: lines from 'The Carpenter', in *Collected
Poems*, by William Soutar, copyright 1948

E. P. Dutton & Co. Inc., New York: 'The Donkey', from *The Wild Knight
and Other Poems* by G. K. Chesterton

Sidgwick & Jackson, London: 'To and Fro About the City', from *Collected
Poems of John Drinkwater*

LIBRARY OF CONGRESS CATALOG CARD NUMBER: 61–7332

ISBN: 0-06-060451-4

82 83 84 85 86   10 9 8 7

CONTENTS

Contents

PREFACE

The substance of the chapters of this book first appeared in the form of a series of articles in *The British Weekly,* although it is true to say that the material has been so extensively rewritten that the book bears little relation to the original articles. I wish to begin by thanking the Rev. Denis Duncan, B.D., the editor of *The British Weekly,* for giving me permission to republish the articles in this form.

There are certain things which I would wish to say to those who will read this book.

The aim of the book is to try to make it possible to understand the mind, the work, and the meaning of Jesus a little better. The material on which this book is based is the material in the first three Gospels in the New Testament, and only very occasionally have I gone beyond that material. It is my own personal conviction that in these three Gospels we have a reliable account of the ministry and of the teaching of Jesus. I know well that we do not possess the material to write a biography of Jesus, but nevertheless I am convinced, and the more I study them the more I am convinced, that in these three Gospels we have material on which we can rely to reconstruct the basic events of Jesus' life, to understand his teaching, and at least to some extent to enter into his mind.

In this book I have not wished to argue; I have simply wished to set down the picture of Jesus as I see it, and to set out what he means to me. I am well aware that there are those who will differ from the point of view of this book to the point of violence, and who will think that some of the things in it are mistaken and misguided. I can only say to them that in the Jesus of this book I have found the Jesus who is the Saviour of men and who is my Saviour.

In the latter part of this book I have written about the Death and the Resurrection of Jesus, and about the meaning of the Cross. Anyone who writes about these events must have a strange feeling in his mind. He knows that he is writing about the greatest things in all the world, and yet he is conscious that all the time he is walking in a realm of controversy, a battle-ground of opposing theologies, an area in which the words heretic, liberal, modernist, conservative, radical, fundamentalist, have been hurled by one set of thinkers at another. I am quite sure that a man, without disregarding and without attacking the beliefs of others, must witness to his own. That is what I have tried to do. There are those who will think that I am wrong and sometimes even dangerously wrong, but I can only say that this is what I believe, and this is how there came into my life the new relationship with God which is the very essence of the Christian faith and of the work of Jesus Christ. 'There are as many ways to the stars as there are men to climb them', and what may seem to another mistaken and wrong has been very precious to me.

I do not think that there is anything new in this book, and its debts are many, and I have tried to acknowledge them in their own places. But I should like particularly to acknowledge two debts in connection with the chapter entitled 'Looking at the Cross'. In this chapter I have drawn largely on David Smith's *The Atonement in the Light of History and the Modern Spirit,* and on H. E. W. Turner's *The Patristic Doctrine of Redemption.* It is not so much that I have been in any way dependent on the thought and the conclusions of these books as that I have allowed myself freely to draw on the material which they provide, although I have always checked and investigated that material in its original sources.

I should like to acknowledge certain special debts. Originally this book was published by the Student Christian Movement Press in England and it owes much to the help and the encouragement, the criticism and the guidance of the Rev. David L. Edwards, the editor of that press; and it also owes much to the painstaking scholarship of Miss Jean Cunningham who originally prepared the manuscript for printing. Finally, I should like to thank Harper & Brothers and all in their editorial and production departments who have given me so much help and courtesy in the preparation of this edition of this book.

I shall be well content if this book does a little to enable its readers not to argue about Jesus and his work but to see a little more of the love of God in him.

WILLIAM BARCLAY.

Trinity College,
Glasgow.

THE MIND OF JESUS

1

THE GREAT DISCOVERY

It may be said that there are two great beginnings in the life of every man who has left his mark upon history. There is the day when he is born into the world; and there is the day when he discovers why he was born into the world. There was a day in the life of Jesus when he made that great discovery.

The greatest festival of the Jews was the festival of the Passover. On that day the Jews have always remembered, and still remember, how the hand of God delivered them from their bondage in the land of Egypt. It fell on 15th Nisan, in the middle of April, and it was kept in Jerusalem. It was one of the three obligatory festivals—the others were Pentecost and Tabernacles—to which every adult male Jew who lived within fifteen miles of Jerusalem was bound by the law to come. But such was the sanctity of this festival that Jews from all over the world gathered in Jerusalem to celebrate it, and a Jew of the Dispersion would save for a lifetime to keep one Passover in the Holy City.

The most careful preparations were made for the Passover. The roads were levelled and the bridges were repaired; the wayside tombs were whitewashed, lest any traveller should accidentally touch one of them, and, because of his contact with a dead body, become unclean (Num. 19.11). For six weeks before the festival it was the story and the meaning of the Passover which formed the subject of teaching in every school and of preaching in every synagogue. No one in Palestine could be unaware that the Passover was near. To any seriously-minded boy, to any boy with a sense of history and of country and an awareness of God, the day when he attended his first Passover in Jerusalem was bound to be a day of days.

So the day came when the boy Jesus was to attend his first Passover festival in Jerusalem (Luke 2.41–52). Everything on the roads, in the school, in the synagogue had for weeks been saying: 'The Passover is at hand!' And now the time had come.

It is the better part of a hundred miles from Nazareth to Jerusalem. It would take a week for the slow caravan to make its long journey. All the time of the journey Jesus was thinking of the Passover, and of how God had once delivered his people, and with every step of the way his expectation was kindled to a brighter flame.

A city that is set on a hill cannot be hid, and the astonishing sight of Jerusalem appeared to Jesus' eyes. Josephus describes the wonder of the Temple. 'The outward face of the Temple in its front wanted nothing that was likely to surprise either men's minds or their eyes; for it was covered all over with plates of gold of great weight, and, at the first rising of the sun, reflected back a very fiery splendour, and made those who forced themselves to look upon it to turn away their eyes, just as they would have done at the sun's own rays. The Temple appeared to strangers, when they were at a distance, like a mountain covered with snow, for those parts of it that were not gilt were exceeding white.'[1] There was a thrill in the mind of the boy Jesus as he saw the gleaming Temple ahead, and as he climbed Mount Sion with the Passover pilgrims, singing, as generations of pilgrims had sung: 'I was glad when they said to me, Let us go to the house of the Lord' (Ps. 122.1). He was sure that the Passover was going to give him the greatest experience in his life—and it did, although not in the way that he had expected it. So Jesus came to Jerusalem with expectation in his heart, and something happened.

On the afternoon of the day in the evening of which the Passover was observed the Passover lambs were killed. The lamb was not simply the main dish at the Passover meal; the lamb was a sacrifice; and, therefore, the lamb had to be slain in the Temple courts. There was one part of every slain beast which belonged to God, the blood. The Jews identified the blood of a living creature with the life of the creature. It was a natural identification, for as the blood flows away the life flows away. To God alone life belongs, and, therefore, to God alone the blood of every slain creature belongs, and it must be offered to him. So Joseph with Jesus took the lamb to the Temple to be slain so that the blood might be offered to God.

The *Mishnah*, the codified law of the Jews, describes the regula-

---

[1] Josephus, *Wars of the Jews* 5.5.6, Whiston's translation.

tions for the killing of the lamb and the offering of the blood. 'The priests stood in rows, and in their hands were basons of silver and gold. In one row all the basons were of silver and in another row all the basons were of gold. They were not mixed up together. Nor had the basons bases, lest the priests should set them down and the blood congeal. An Israelite slaughtered his own offering, and the priest caught the blood. The priest passed the bason to his fellow, and he to his fellow, each receiving a full bason and giving back an empty one. The priest nearest to the Altar tossed the blood in one action against the base of the Altar.'[1]

Let us think what this means. On one occasion in the reign of Nero the governor Cestius took a census of the number of lambs slain, in order to show Nero how many Jews attended the Passover festival. The number slain was 256,500.[2] Even if the figure is an exaggeration, as so many ancient figures are, the number must certainly have been immense.

Let us try to visualize the scene in the Temple courts on the afternoon before the evening of the Passover meal. The hundreds of thousands of worshippers, each one of them slitting the throat of the lamb and allowing the blood to drain away, the long line of the priests leading to the altar, the bowls of blood being passed from hand to hand finally to be dashed against the base of the altar, the odour and the reek of blood, the marble pavements of the Temple slippery with the blood of the lambs, the atmosphere of a vast slaughter house and butcher's shop—that is what Jesus saw. And in the mind of the young Jesus there arose the beginning of a great disillusionment. The Passover festival was intended to bring men closer to God. How could this welter of blood do that? Already, young as he was, Jesus knew God as his Father, and in Jerusalem at the Passover festival, he had expected to encounter God as never before—and now this. The expectation was turned to bewilderment; and the expected thrill became the unexpected disillusionment. In all this welter of blood there was no God for a wounded conscience, a contrite spirit and a seeking mind.

But to Jesus there was left still another hope. The supreme court of the Jews, embodying the highest wisdom of the nation, was the

---

[1] *Mishnah*, Pesahim 5.5f., Danby's translation.
[2] Josephus, *Wars of the Jews* 6.9.3.

Sanhedrin with its seventy members, presided over by the High Priest. Normally the Sanhedrin met in private in its own Hall of Hewn Stone, and there it discussed the matters of the law. But during the Passover time the Sanhedrin met in public, and any who wished might listen to the discussions of the learned men. Already Jesus was steeped in the prophets; Hosea and Isaiah were his familiar friends. Already he moved familiarly amidst the laws of Deuteronomy. Now he would go and hear the wisdom of the wise, and, even if the priestly ritual had been a grim disillusionment, surely here he would find the closer contact with God for which he was seeking. And once again bewilderment came to him. It was not of justice and mercy; love and holiness that they were talking. They were talking of the Sabbath law. The Sabbath law forbade work on the Sabbath day. To carry a burden was to work. Yes, but what constituted a burden? Could, or could not, a man go out on the Sabbath with nails in his shoes or sandals? Could, or could not, a man wear a false tooth on the Sabbath? If a cripple went out with a wooden leg was he carrying a burden? A man might not lift and carry and throw a stone on the Sabbath day. But did that apply to a stone big enough to fling at a bird, or big enough to throw at cattle? A man might not write on the Sabbath day; but did that apply, if he wrote in some fluid which left no permanent mark? These are all questions which are actually discussed in the *Mishnah* (Shabbath 6.2–5,8; 8.4–6). So they discussed the minutiae of the law, the legalistic details which for the scribes and Pharisees constituted religion. And there was no way to God there, no way to heal a broken heart, no way to assure a man of forgiveness for his sins, no way to make a man feel certain that God is his Father in heaven.

Jesus had come to Jerusalem with the most eager hopes and expectations. His heart had thrilled when he saw the Holy City gleaming in the distance. He had looked forward to the Passover festival with all his heart. And he had discovered that the way of the priests was completely unavailing. What had this butchery of lambs to do with bringing a man nearer to God, and what had this welter of blood to say about the God whose name is Father? He had discovered that the way of the wise men was unavailing. What had these petty legalistic details to do with justice and mercy and love? What had these arid discussions about the Sabbath law to do with a man who had known the tears of things, and who was bitterly conscious that he was soiled with sin? He had suddenly discovered that the whole paraphernalia of sacrifice was a vast irrelevance, and the whole apparatus of the law a barrier to God.

Somewhere Jewish religion had gone wrong, and had lost the way. Sacrifice had meant the giving of one's best to God, and what is one's best but oneself? But sacrifice had become a ritual slaughter of beasts instead of a self-dedication to God. The law had been meant to be a thing in which a man might find his delight, the basis of a life lived in reverence to God and in respect for men and for human personality, and instead it had become an unending collection of petty rules and regulations. It was not so much that Jesus felt the need to break with Jewish religion; it was rather that he felt the need to rediscover Jewish religion. It was not that he wished to destroy Jewish religion; he wished rather to fulfil it, and to rescue it from the shallows and the byways in which it had got lost.

And then out of the disillusionment there came to Jesus the voice and the revelation of God. There came the voice of the God whom he knew, as none other had ever known, as his Father. And God was saying: 'The priests have lost me; the wise men have lost me; the people seek me, and cannot find me. *It is your task to tell men of me and to bring them to my love.*'

On that day in the Temple Jesus had a unique experience of God as his Father; and he had a unique realization that it was his life's work to bring men to God and to bring God to men, in a way that neither priest nor rabbi could ever do. It was to be many a long year before he could set out on his task, but from that day his task was clear to him. He knew why he had come into the world.

2

WAITING FOR THE CALL

Even when a man discovers the task for which God has sent him into the world, he has still another problem to solve, the problem of when to begin upon it. If he begins too soon, he will begin without the necessary preparation and equipment for the task. If he waits until too late, he may never begin at all. If he chooses the wrong moment, his work may be foredoomed to failure even before he begins.

In the Temple Jesus had realized the futility of human ways of seeking for God, and he had made the great discovery that he had been sent into the world to bring all men to God; and now he had to await the call from God to set out upon his work. And Jesus waited long. He was twelve when the revelation in the Temple came to him (Luke 2.42); he was thirty when he left Nazareth to begin upon his work (Luke 3.23). Eighteen years is a long time to wait; but the silent years were not the wasted years, for they were years of preparation for the task that no one else in the world could do. Throughout the years Jesus was learning all the time.

He was learning the basic knowledge and the basic skills which are every man's equipment for life. As Luke tells us, he increased in wisdom and in stature (Luke 2.52). He learned to read, for we know that the day was to come when he was to read the lesson from the prophets in the synagogue in Nazareth (Luke 4.16). He learned to write, which in those days was a much rarer accomplishment. In the story of the woman taken in adultery, we are told that Jesus stooped down and wrote on the ground (John 8.8). In that passage an Armenian manuscript dating to AD 989 makes the curious addition that it was the sins of the woman's accusers which Jesus wrote on the ground, and that is why they slipped silently away. 'He himself, bowing his head, was writing with his finger on the earth, to declare their sins; and they were seeing their several sins on the stones.' Jesus was learning the skills which every boy must learn. There was a village school in Nazareth; to that village school Jesus must have gone. In that village school there was a nameless village schoolmaster, whose name no man will ever know, and yet that schoolmaster taught the Son of God. Many a teacher is doing a work far greater than he knows.

He was learning to do a good day's work, for it was as the carpenter of Nazareth that men know him (Mark 6.3). Jesus was the good craftsman. Justin Martyr tells us: 'He was in the habit of working as a carpenter when he was among men, making ploughs and yokes',[1] and there is a legend that Jesus of Nazareth made the best ox-yokes in all Galilee, and that men came from far and near to buy the yokes that Jesus made. Then as now craftsmen hung their trade sign and their slogan above their shops. Once Jesus said: 'My yoke is easy' (Matt. 11.30). The Greek word for *easy* is *chrēstos,* which means *well-fitting,* and some one has imagined that the sign above the door of the carpenter's shop in Nazareth was an ox-yoke with the words painted on it: 'My yokes fit well.'

It is, indeed, significant to note what the New Testament actually calls Jesus; it calls him a *tektōn* (Mark 6.3). A *tektōn* was more than a carpenter; he was a craftsman who could build a wall or a house, construct a boat, or make a table or a chair, or throw a bridge across a little stream. In the old days—and even now in the country places—there were men who, with the minimum of technical equipment and the maximum of the craftsman's inborn skill, could turn their hands to any job. In their hands wood and metal and stones become obedient, and such was Jesus. William Soutar, the Scots poet, wrote a poem about the craftsman's hands of Jesus:

> Glaidly he dressed the rochest deal
> To mak a kist or door;
> Strauchtly he drave the langest nail
> Wi' little sturt or stour.
>
> Monie a man as he gaed by,
> And monie a kintra wench,
> Wad watch the strang and souple hands
> That wrocht abune the bench.

[1] *Dialogue with Trypho* 88.

> And aye sae true, sae tenderly,
> Sae trysted wud they move
> As they had been a lover's hands
> That blindly kent their love.

In Nazareth Jesus got to himself the craftsman's strong and gentle hands.

He was winning the physical manhood to enable him to do his task. The time was to come when Jesus was to walk the roads of Palestine, and when he was to tell a would-be follower that the foxes had their holes and the birds of the air their nests, but that he had nowhere to lay his head (Luke 9.58). Jesus could never have lived the life he did live had he not been physically equipped for it. In those days a carpenter did not buy his wood from the saw-mill or from the wholesaler. He went out to the hill-side, chose his young tree, swung his axe, cut it down and carried it home on his shoulder. Certainly Jesus was no weak and anaemic person; he must have been bronzed and weather-beaten, in the perfection of physical manhood.

One of the great gaps in our knowledge of Jesus is that we do not know what in physical appearance he was like. In regard to this, tradition was divided into two. One line of thought began with Isaiah's picture of the Suffering Servant. 'His appearance was so marred, beyond human semblance' (Isa. 52.14). 'He had no form nor comeliness that we should look at him, and no beauty that we should desire him' (Isa. 53.2). Arguing from this, Irenaeus said that Jesus was weak, inglorious and without grace.[1] Origen said he was small, ill-favoured, and insignificant.[2] Cyril of Alexandria even went the length of saying that he was 'the ugliest of the children of men'. The other line of thought stemmed from Ps. 45.2: 'You are the fairest of the sons of men.' This line of thought painted Jesus in words and in pictures in the beauty of the Olympian gods.

The most famous of all descriptions is in the *Letter of Lentulus,* who purports to be governor of Jerusalem:

There has appeared here in our time, and still lives here, a man of great power named Jesus Christ. The people call him a prophet of truth, and

---

[1] *Against Heresies* 4.33.12.
[2] *Against Celsus* 6.75.

his disciples the Son of God. He raises the dead and cures the sick. He is in stature a man of middle height and well proportioned. He has a venerable face, of a sort to arouse both fear and love in those who see him. His hair is the colour of ripe chestnuts, smooth almost to the ears, but above them waving and curling, with a slightly bluish radiance, and it flows over his shoulders. It is parted in the middle on the top of his head, after the fashion of the people of Nazareth. His brow is smooth and very calm, with a face without wrinkle or blemish, lightly tinged with red. His nose and mouth are faultless. His beard is luxuriant and unclipped, of the same colour as his hair, not long but parted at the chin. His eyes are expressive and brilliant. He is terrible in reproof, sweet and gentle in admonition, cheerful without ceasing to be grave. He has never been seen to laugh, but often to weep. His figure is slender and erect; his hands and arms are beautiful to see. His conversation is serious, sparing and modest. He is the fairest of the children of men.

There are those who go the length of believing that this is nothing less than the police description of Jesus at the time of his arrest. But it is quite certain that the *Letter of Lentulus* is a forgery, although even then it is not impossible that it does embody a genuine tradition. It may be that we have to say of the appearance of Jesus, with Augustine, 'We are utterly ignorant.'[1] But this we can say, that in the silent years in Nazareth Jesus was building up the physical manhood without which he could not have faced or completed his task.

Throughout the silent years Jesus was learning the meaning of family life. The name for God which came most naturally to the lips of Jesus was Father; and the very use of that word is itself a very beautiful compliment to Joseph. It was said of Martin Luther that he hesitated to pray the Lord's Prayer and to say 'Our Father', because his own father had been so stern, so unbending, so unsympathetic that the word 'father' was not a word which he loved. To Jesus the name 'father' was the most natural and the most precious name for God, and it was in the home at Nazareth that he must have learned the meaning of that word.

There were words which Jesus heard in the home in Nazareth which lingered in his mind all his days. Once he came to a little girl whom all others thought to be dead, and said softly: '*Talitha, cumi*', which means, as we might say, 'Little lamb, get up!' (Mark

---

[1] *Concerning the Trinity* 8.4f.

5.41). Where did Jesus hear a child called 'Little lamb'? Surely these were the words which he had heard the gentle Mary croon over himself and over his brothers and sisters, when they were very young. Throughout the years Jesus was discovering that it was God indeed who had set the solitary in families (Ps. 68.6). He was no monkish ascetic; he grew up within a home.

The work in the shop and the life in the family were both parts of the essential education and preparation of Jesus for his task, for through them his full identity with men was established. In the shop he knew the problem and the anxiety of making a living for a household. He knew the problem of dealing with unreasonable people. He learned to see men at their best and at their worst and as they were. In the home he had to solve the universal problem of living together. Jesus did not live a secluded, isolated, protected life, on which the wind was not allowed to blow. He knew the life of the men whom he had come to save.

Throughout the silent years Jesus learned to love God's world, and to see God in creation and in common things. Jesus grew to manhood in the loveliest part of Palestine. Around the Sea of Galilee there was the Plain of Gennesareth, and the Jews sometimes said that the word Gennesareth meant Prince of Gardens. They called that plain 'the unequalled garden of God'. They called the country-side around Sepphoris 'a land flowing with milk and honey'. There was a Jewish proverbial saying that it was easier to raise a legion of olive trees in Galilee than to bring up one child in the rest of Palestine. Merrill in his book on Galilee lists the trees which grew there in the time of Jesus—the vine, the olive, the fig, the oak, the walnut, the terebinth, the palm, the cedar, the cypress, the balsam, the fir-tree, the pine, the sycamore, the bay-tree, the myrtle, the almond, the pomegranate, the citron, the oleander. In Galilee, said Josephus, trees which would not grow together elsewhere grew in the same place, as if nature were doing violence to herself.[1]

It was in this land of loveliness that Jesus grew up. He learned to love the sight of the sower sowing his seed (Matt. 13.1–8); of the corn field ripening steadily under God's sun (Mark 4.26–29); of the mustard bush with the birds clustering round to steal the little black seeds (Mark 4.30–32); of the scarlet poppies and anemones bloom·

[1] *Wars of the Jews* 3.10.8.

ing their one day on the hillside in raiment such as Solomon in his glory never wore (Matt. 6.28,29). Throughout the years Jesus was learning to look on the world as 'the garment of the living God'.

He was learning to use the common actions and happenings of life as windows through which to catch a glimpse of the truth and the glory of God. He watched his mother Mary using the leaven when she baked the bread (Matt. 13.33). He marked the frenzied search when a woman lost a silver coin amidst the rushes on the cottage floor (Luke 15.8f.). He knew what happened when some one carelessly put new wine into old bottles whose skins had lost their elasticity, and how a new patch on an old garment could leave things worse than ever (Matt. 9.16f.). He knew the joy of a village wedding feast (Matt. 9.15); he watched the fishermen with their nets (Matt. 13.47); he was moved by the care of the shepherd for his sheep (Luke 15.4–6). He watched the children playing at weddings and funerals in the village street (Matt. 11.16f.).

Few great teachers have had their feet so firmly planted on the ground as Jesus had. In these early years he was learning every day how to get from 'the here and now' to 'the there and then'. He was learning how near eternity is to time, and how to see God in the life and the actions and the things of every day.

Throughout the silent years Jesus was learning to dream. Nazareth itself is tucked away in a hollow of the hills, a secluded little town. But the extraordinary thing about Nazareth was that the world passed almost by its door. It has been said that Judaea was on the way to nowhere and Galilee was on the way to everywhere, for the great roads of the East passed through Galilee. Jesus had only to climb the hilltop above the cup-like hollow of Nazareth and the passing world was at his feet. From there he could look down on the great Road of the Sea, the road which went from Damascus to Egypt, one of the greatest highways in the world with its merchantmen and its caravans. From there he could see the strategic Road of the East which went out from the Mediterranean coast to Parthia and to the eastern bounds of the Roman Empire with its Arab traders and its Roman legions clanking on their way. From there, if he looked westwards, he could see the blue waters of the Mediterranean, with the sails of the ships and the cargoes of those who do business in great waters.

So Jesus could climb the hilltop behind Nazareth, and from there he could see the roads coming and going to the ends of the earth. It was there that he must have dreamed his dreams, and it may be that it was there that something first said to him: 'I, when I am lifted up from the earth, will draw all men to myself' (John 12.32).

It was in the silent years that Jesus learned to pray. When he went out upon his task, it was his custom to take eveything to God; again and again he withdrew from men to be alone with God. When he was in his last agony on the Cross, he prayed: 'Father, into thy hand I commit my spirit' (Luke 23.46). That is a quotation from Ps. 31.5 with the one word 'Father' added. But more, that was the first prayer which every Jewish mother taught her child to say, when he lay down to sleep at night, before the dark came down. It was with a prayer that he had learned at Nazareth on his lips that Jesus ended his agony and finished his task.

One thing more is to be added. Eighteen years is a long time to wait, and it may be that there was a very special reason for that delay. After the story of the birth of Jesus Joseph vanishes from the narrative. Even as early as the marriage feast at Cana of Galilee there is no word of Joseph being there (John 2.1–11). By far the most likely explanation is that Joseph was dead, and that the young Jesus had to take upon his shoulders the family business and the support of his mother Mary and of his younger brothers and sisters (Mark 6.3), and that he had to stay in Nazareth until there was some one in the family old enough to take over the carpenter's shop and to earn a living for the family. The day was to come when Jesus was to tell a story about a servant who because he had been faithful in a few things was made master over many things (Matt. 25.21–23). In that story Jesus was telling his own story, for it is quite certain that, if Jesus had not been faithful in the simple and the elementary duties of the home, God could never have given him the task of being the Saviour of the world. Throughout the silent years Jesus was learning many things; and in the performance of the simple duties he was proving himself for the task which God was to give him to do.

Let no man despise the simple duties of the home and the tasks which lie to his hand, for therein, for him as for Jesus, there is the purpose of God. Rabindranath Tagore, the Indian mystic, has a poem:

At midnight the would-be ascetic announced: 'This is the time to give up my home and seek for God. Ah, who has held me so long in delusion here?' God whispered, 'I', but the ears of the man were stopped. With a baby asleep at her breast lay his wife, peacefully sleeping on one side of the bed. The man said: 'Who are ye that have fooled me so long?' The voice said again: 'They are God,' but he heard it not. The baby cried out in his dream, nestling closer to his mother. God commanded: 'Stop, fool; leave not thy home,' but he heard not. God sighed and complained: 'Why does my servant wander to seek me, forsaking me?'

The Son of God, when he came into this world, prepared himself to save the world by serving in a home.

3

THE HOUR STRIKES

Throughout the years of preparation Jesus was waiting for the sign which was to tell him that he must go out to begin the work for which he had come into the world. It was when he was thirty years of age (Luke 3.23) that the sign came and the hour unmistakably struck.

It was then that John the Baptizer burst upon the scene in Palestine. John was related to Jesus, for he was the son of Elisabeth, the kinswoman of Mary (Luke 1.36). He had been born to Zacharias, the priest, and to Elisabeth in the days of their old age, when all hope and expectation of a child had gone (Luke 1.5–25, 57–80). It was clear to his parents that John was no ordinary child, and that he had been sent into the world for no ordinary task, and it was in the solitudes of the desert and in the lonely places that John grew to manhood (Luke 1.80).

John appears on the scene, as it were, full grown. We know of his birth; we know of his sojourn in the desert; we know that he emerges as the baptizer of crowds of people in the River Jordan; but what training he had, where he found his message, and whence he took his rite of baptism we do not know. Although we have no certain knowledge, can we deduce anything about the origins of the message and the baptism of John? Let us begin by examining the possible sources of John's rite of baptism.

The pagan world was well acquainted with baptism. Baptism was the gateway through which the initiate entered many of the mystery religions. It was through baptism, as Tertullian notes, that the initiate entered into the worship of Isis, Mithra and the famous Eleusinian mysteries.[1] Clement of Alexandria tells us that lustrations, that is, washings, 'held the premier place' in the mystery

[1] *Concerning Baptism* 5.

ceremonies.¹ The worshipper of Dionysos experienced 'the pure washing', as Livy calls it.² When Apuleius tells of his own initiation, he tells that the officiating priest brought him to the baths, and, demanding pardon of the gods, washed him and purified his body, according to the custom.³ Quite certainly the pagan world was familiar with baptism as an entry to the mystery religions in which the worshippers sought to find God. But it is very unlikely that John knew anything about these things, although there must have been at least some amongst those who came to him who knew, or had heard, about such baptisms.

The Jewish world knew about baptism, for the three necessary elements through which a proselyte entered the Jewish faith were circumcision, baptism and sacrifice. So prominent a place did baptism hold in the reception of converts to Judaism, that Rabbi Joshua argued that it alone was necessary, although he was confuted by Rabbi Eliezer.

Jewish proselyte baptism was carried out in the presence of three witnesses, if possible members of the Sanhedrin. The nails and the hair of the candidate were cut; he was stripped naked; he was completely immersed in water, so that his whole body was totally covered; the essence of the law was read to him, and he was warned of the difficulties and the dangers and the possible persecution which lay ahead; he confessed his sins to the men who were known as 'the fathers of baptism', and who correspond to godparents; then after blessings and exhortations he emerged a Jew. This process was held to effect in him the most radical change. He was said to emerge as 'a little child just born', 'a child of one day'. So completely was he a new man that it was theoretically argued that a proselyte who had been baptized might marry his own sister or his own mother, because for him the connection with the past was completely broken. Jewish proselyte baptism was no doubt founded on the many washings which the Jewish law laid down for the purposes of purification (cf. Lev. 15.5,8,13,16; 16.26,28). If washings were necessary for a Jew to cleanse the defilements he might have contracted, how much more was washing necessary for a Gentile coming from the polluted

¹ *Stromateis* 5.11.
² *Livy* 39.9.
³ *The Metamorphoses* or *Golden Ass* 11.23.

pagan world? That baptism of proselytes did exist in the time of John is proved by the record of the controversy between the famous Rabbis Hillel and Shammai. Shammai held that a proselyte who was baptized on the eve of the Passover might share in the Passover Feast, while Hillel held that so quick an entry to the sacred meal was impossible. Certainly John would know of proselyte baptism, although, as we shall later see, no such baptism had ever been undergone by Jews themselves.

It is not difficult to find antecedents for John's practice of baptism. It is not suggested that John was dependent on any of them, but it is certain that John came into a situation in which baptism was known and practised. But can we go further and can we find any antecedents for John himself?

When Josephus was describing the great Jewish sects and parties, he described the Pharisees and the Sadducees, and then he described what he called the third of the Jewish sects, the Essenes. Our information regarding these Essenes comes from three sources, from Philo's *Quad omnis probus liber* 12,13, from the elder Pliny's *Natural History* 15.17, from Josephus' *Wars of the Jews* 2.8.2–13, and from his *Antiquities* 13.5.9; 15.10.4,5; 18.1.5.

It is in fact hardly right to class the Essenes as parallel with the Pharisees and the Sadducees. The Pharisees and the Sadducees were by no means withdrawn from the world, and they were, at least to some extent, political parties as well as religious sects, but, as Schürer rightly says in *The Jewish People in the Time of Christ,* the Essenes were rather a monastic order. They seem to have come into being somewhere midway through the second century BC. They could be found in small groups in the villages and in the towns, but they found their real life and their real flowering living in communities, closely disciplined and closely organized. The main site of their community life was in the Desert of Engedi near the Dead Sea. To enter an Essene community was an act of spontaneous and deliberate choice. The candidate was first on a year's probation; he was then admitted to their washings and lustrations; he had another two years' probation; he was then admitted to the common meal, which was a feature of their communal life, and he then took the terrible and awe-inspiring oath that his whole life would be open to the brethren, but absolutely secret to the outsider.

Their communities were ascetic and their discipline was very strict. They practised absolute community of goods, so that amongst them, as Josephus says, there was neither 'the humiliation of poverty or the superfluity of wealth'. Even the desire to have anything of one's own did not exist among them. Thus sickness and old age lost their terrors among the Essenes, for the ill and the aged received from the common pool all that they needed.

Their way of life was very simple. Their work lay mainly in agriculture. They knew the healing properties of plants and stones. All trading was forbidden, for trading, so they said, leads to covetousness; they were pledged to make no weapons of warfare and to make nothing which could be used to harm anyone else. They were famous for the goodness of their lives, 'abstemious, simple, unpretending', as Schürer describes them.

They possessed no slaves. They took no oaths. They used no anointing oil. They wore white garments. They were meticulously careful in what we would now call matters of hygiene. They were extraordinarily modest in regard to the display of the naked body. They were celibate. They made no animal sacrifices, although, it is said, they sent incense to the Temple. All their meals were common meals; all were prepared by a priest; and before all meals there were careful washings and purificatory rites. They had a kind of passion for cleanliness. The most characteristic thing about their practices was their numerous washings. They bathed themselves in cold water before every meal; they bathed always after the performance of their natural functions; they bathed always after any contact with anyone less meticulous than themselves.

They had a strong belief in providence, or even in fate. They read and studied the Scriptures, and used them at their worship, at which they delighted in allegorical interpretations. They had a supreme reverence for the law and for Moses, the law-giver.

They had certain practices and beliefs which were curiously unJewish. First thing in the morning they prayed facing the sun, as if somewhere in their history and beliefs there had been some admixture of sun worship. They believed in the immortality of the soul, but not of the body; for they believed the soul to be pre-existent, and to be imprisoned in the prison house of the body. Thus death was the liberation of the soul, and the destruction of the body, for those who had lived and worshipped aright. This dualism of body and soul is not Jewish, and may have come to them from the East.

It has been suggested that it was from these Essenes that John the Baptizer came. They had their principal community in the very wilderness in which he must have grown up. Josephus (*Wars of the Jews* 2.8.2) says of the Essenes: 'Marriage they disdain, but they adopt other men's children, while yet pliable and docile, and regard them as their kin, and mould them in accordance with their principles.' The suggestion has been made that the Essene community adopted John while he was still a child. His parents were aged when he was born (Luke 1.7), and John may well have been left an orphan very young. So it is suggested that John may have grown up amongst these simple, ascetic, disciplined, pious people, who lived in their daily ritual of cleansing washings, and that it may have been from them that he took his uncompromising ethical demand, and also the cleansing washing of his baptism.

The connection of John with the Essenes is no new idea, but recent discoveries have revived and intensified the idea of this connection. It was in 1947 that there happened the accidental discovery of the first batch of these ancient documents popularly known as the Dead Sea Scrolls. They represent the books and the libraries of a community, perhaps four thousand in number, who lived in the ravine of Qumran at the north end of the Dead Sea. This community bears the strongest possible resemblance to the Essenes; in fact they may well be identified with the Essenes. This community believed that the covenant between God and Israel had always throughout history been preserved and maintained by some faithful remnant. They had withdrawn themselves from ordinary life, for they believed themselves to be the faithful remnant, who alone understood the true meaning of the law, a meaning which had been passed down to them through a series of Right-teachers or Teachers of Righteousness, who were also priests. They were awaiting the new Prophet and Teacher who would announce the new and golden age in which there would come to men God's anointed Priest and God's anointed King.

What we are here concerned with, and what we must here confine ourselves to, is the possible connection of John the Baptizer with this Qumran community. There are certain striking resemblances—and equally striking differences within the resemblances—between John and the Qumran community as their beliefs and practices and ideals are set out in their *Manual of Discipline,* which is one of the documents which have been discovered. We quote this in the version of Theodor H. Gaster, entitled *The Scriptures of the Dead Sea Sect.* The members of this community are to sever their connection with ordinary men 'to the end that they may indeed "go into the wilderness to prepare the way", i.e. do what Scripture enjoins when it says, "Prepare in the wilderness the way . . . make straight in the desert a highway for our God" (Isa. 40.3). The reference is to the study of the Law which God commanded Moses to the end that, as occasion arises, all things may be done in accordance with what is revealed therein and with what the prophets have revealed through God's holy spirit.'[1] The extraordinary fact is that the aim of this Qumran community is expressed in the very words of Isaiah which the New Testament writers use to describe the function of John the Baptizer (Matt. 3.3; Mark 1.3; Luke 3.4).

But with the resemblance there is a difference. It was for *themselves* that the Qumran community were preparing the way; they had deliberately separated themselves from men in order to prepare the way. If John was connected with them, he must have grown discontented with this narrow, confined, and even selfish preparation, and must have left them to strike out on the preparation, not of a sect or a community, but of a nation.

Further, in the *Manual of Discipline* there is the closest possible connection between the idea of cleansing ritually by water and the amendment of life. It is more than once insisted that the ritual cleansing is useless unless moral cleansing accompanies it. So it is said of the man who insists on walking 'in the stubbornness of his heart':

He cannot be cleared by mere ceremonies of atonement, nor cleansed by any waters of ablution, nor sanctified by immersion in lakes or rivers, nor purified by any bath. Unclean, unclean he remains so long as he rejects the government of God, and refuses the discipline of communion with him. For it is only through the spiritual apprehension of God's truth that man's ways can be properly directed. Only thus can all his iniquities be shriven so that he can gaze on the true light of life. Only through the holy spirit

[1] *Manual of Discipline* 8.13ff.

can he achieve union with God's truth and be purged of all his iniquities. Only by a spirit of uprightness and humility can his sin be atoned. Only by the submission of his soul to all the ordinances of God can his flesh be made clean. Only thus can it be sprinkled with waters of ablution.[1]

It is said of God in the recreated age: 'Like waters of purification God will sprinkle upon him (the good man) the spirit of truth.'[2] It is laid down: 'No one is to go into water in order to attain the purity of holy men. For men cannot be purified except they repent their evil.'[3] There is the closest connection between the demand of the Qumran community for holiness and the ethical demand of John.

It may well be that John had some connection with the Essenes, and that he even had some connection with the Qumran community. If he had, like so many great men he surpassed the origins from which he came. If he had not, it at least remains true that John delivered his message to men who had been at least to some extent prepared to understand it by the teaching of the Essenes and of men who lived in the life and held the belief of such communities as the community of Qumran.

However these things may be, the day came when John emerged from the desert with a message which was a shock to Jewish ears. He came with a *summons to repentance* (Mark 1.4; Matt. 3.2; Luke 3.3). The reign of God was about to invade the earth, and men must repent and be cleansed before the irruption of eternity into time. He came to summon sinners to repentance. He came with a *summons to preparation.* As the prophet Isaiah had done long ago (Isa. 40.3), he came with a summons to men to prepare the way of the Lord (Matt. 3.3; Mark 1.3; Luke 3.4–6). In the ancient days all roads were 'the king's highway'. When a ruler intended to go upon a journey or to visit a district, he sent ahead messengers with orders that the roads by which he intended to travel should be smoothed and repaired, for unsurfaced roads soon degenerated into rutted tracks, and would be allowed to remain so unless the king was to come. It was John's message that the King was on the way, and the road must be prepared for him. John's message was a message which pointed beyond himself to the one whose herald he was.

[1] *Manual* 3.4ff.
[2] *Manual* 4.21.
[3] *Manual* 5.13.

He came with an *uncompromising ethical demand*. His message struck at the very roots of comfortable Jewish orthodoxy. The Jews never lost the conviction that they were the chosen people, but they interpreted their chosenness in terms of privilege rather than in terms of responsibility. There were many who held that physical descent from Abraham was enough to ensure for a man the favour of God and salvation and the right of entry into heaven, no matter what kind of life he had lived. They could actually say that at the gate of hell there was stationed a kind of guardian angel to turn back any Jew who had the mark of circumcision in his flesh, and who had in error strayed there. Descent from Abraham was the passport to the favour of God. That was a belief on which John poured a withering scorn (Matt. 3.7–9; Luke 3.7f.). He insisted that what mattered was a man's character, and therefore he came with his absolute ethical demand. The rich must share with the poor; the tax-collector must be an honest man; the soldier must be a man under honouraole discipline; a man must live the good life wherever God had set him (Luke 3.10–14). And so in the end John came with a *threat*. The Greater One was coming; the axe was poised to smite the fruitless tree; the chaff was to be winnowed from the grain; the time of judgment was on the way (Matt. 3.11f.; Luke 3.9,16f.).

The message of John swept across the minds of the people like a blast of wind from heaven, because there were certain unique characteristics in it. Four things stood out in the message and the personality of John.

(i) In him the prophetic voice spoke again. The Jews wistfully and regretfully acknowledged that for three hundred years the voice of prophecy had been silent. The priest might sacrifice; the rabbi might teach and expound the law; but the authentic voice of prophecy spoke no more. But in John men recognized once again that accent and that authority with which the prophets had spoken.

(ii) John's summons was a summons to repentance. The Jews themselves had a saying: 'If Israel repent but for a single day, forthwith the Redeemer will come.' Here was the summons to that godly sorrow and that cleansing of life which were the essential prelude to the coming of the King.

(iii) It was a fixed par. of Jewish belief—and still is—that Elijah would return to be the herald of the coming of the Messiah and of the last times. Malachi heard the voice of God saying: 'Behold, I will send you Elijah the prophet, before the great and terrible day of the Lord comes' (Mal. 4.5). John's very clothes were the clothes which Elijah had worn (Mark 1.6; Matt. 3.4; II Kings 1.8). The accent of his voice was the accent of Elijah. Men could not but see in John the coming again of Elijah as the herald of the end.

(iv) But there was one completely unique feature of the ministry of John. John summoned the people to repent and to be baptized in order to receive forgiveness for their sins. *Never in history had a Jew been baptized.* Baptism was something not for Jew but for a Gentile. It was true that, when a Gentile came into Judaism as a proselyte, then he was baptized, for he needed to be washed and cleansed from the evil of his Gentile ways. That was natural and necessary for a Gentile, but no one had ever conceived that a Jew should need baptism, and that a member of the chosen people should need to submit to a cleansing process such as that. As Plummer puts it: 'John had excommunicated the whole nation.' John's summons was to men as sinners, who, even if they were Jews, desperately needed and passionately desired the cleansing which God alone could give. The unique fact about John was that John summoned the Jews to undergo baptism for their cleansing from sin, an unheard of thing for a Jew to do—and the Jews came in their hundreds to accept John's demand.

So when John emerged from the desert with his summons to repentance and to baptism, and when the people flocked out to the Jordan to be baptized, Jesus came too, because Jesus knew that for him the hour had struck. Here there is a problem which has exercised the minds of men ever since they began to study the New Testament. Why should Jesus be baptized? John's baptism was very definitely and very directly a mark of repentance, and it was designed for the cleansing of men so that their sins might be forgiven. What need of repentance had Jesus, the sinless one? What need had he of a baptism which was the mark of repentance, and the symbol of cleansing from sin, in order that men might be forgiven?

Even in the narratives of the four Gospels this difficulty and this problem lurk beneath the surface. John omits the story of the baptism altogether. For Mark the problem has not yet arisen. Mark

describes John's baptism as 'a baptism of repentance for the forgiveness of sins' (1.4), and goes on simply to say that Jesus came from
Nazareth of Galilee and was baptized by John in the Jordan (1.9).
Luke also describes John's baptism as 'a baptism of repentance for
the forgiveness of sins' (3.3); he tells how Jesus came to be baptized
and was baptized (3.21), but he takes care to make John bear
witness to the absolute supremacy of Jesus (3.15f.). But it is
Matthew who feels the problem most acutely. He tells us that John
came with the summons to repent for the Kingdom of God is at
hand, but he does not mention that the baptism was for the remission of sins (3.1). He cannot bring himself to connect such a
baptism with Jesus. He goes on to tell how Jesus came and how John
at first refused to baptize him, and how Jesus said that all righteousness must be fulfilled (3.13–15). The very way in which the Gospel
writers tell the story show how difficult Matthew especially found
the baptism of Jesus by John to be. Let us then look at some of
the explanations which have been suggested.

The oldest explanation is found in two writings of the early
Church. It is that Jesus was baptized, almost against his will, and to
please his mother and his family. Jerome[1] preserves a brief fragment
of the lost *Gospel according to the Hebrews;* 'Behold, the mother of
the Lord and his brothers said to him: John the Baptizer baptizes
unto the remission of sins; let us go and be baptized by him. But he
said to them: Wherein have I sinned, that I should go and be
baptized by him? unless perhaps this very thing that I have said is a
sin of ignorance.' An anonymous writer tells us that the lost *Preaching of Paul* speaks of 'Christ, the only man who was altogether without fault, both making confession respecting his own sin, and driven
against his will by his mother Mary to accept the baptism of John'.[2]
There may possibly be something in this, to which we shall return,
but these two ancient accounts show us Jesus accepting baptism to
please his family, and almost against his will.

It has been suggested that Jesus was baptized by John as the
representative of mankind. This is how Justin Martyr saw the
baptism: 'We know that he did not go to the river because he stood
in need of baptism, or of the descent of the Spirit like a dove; even

[1] *Dialogue against Pelagius* 3.2.
[2] *Tractate on Rebaptism* 17.

as he submitted to be born and to be crucified, not because he needed such things, but because of the human race, which from Adam had fallen under the power of death and the guile of the serpent, and each one of which had committed personal transgression.'[1] This view sees Jesus as making an act of repentance and of submission to God as the representative of all mankind. It is as if he brought to God for all men a perfect penitence and a perfect obedience.

It has been suggested that the baptism of Jesus was a fulfilment of prophecy. In Isaiah (11.2) we read of the promised King, 'The Spirit of the Lord shall rest upon him,' and the events of the baptism may be taken as a fulfilment of that prophecy. There was a Jewish tradition that the Messiah would not know himself and would not have any power until Elijah came to anoint him. It is possible to see in the baptism the fulfilment of the events which the prophets had foretold about the chosen one of God.

There may be truth in all these views, but we believe that the real meaning of the baptism is that for Jesus it was a deliberate act of self-identification with men. In the baptism Jesus identified himself with men in four different ways.

(i) He identified himself with men in their search for righteousness. When John refused at first to baptize him, Jesus told him to do so in order to fulfil all righteousness (Matt. 3.15). Those who came to be baptized were earnestly seeking to do God's will, and with that seeking Jesus identified himself.

(ii) He identified himself with men in their preparation for the breaking-in of God. For the Jews baptism by John was an act of preparation for the coming of the Kingdom, and Jesus joined in that preparatiton, for he was to bring the Kingdom.

(iii) He identified himself with men in their search for God. It was because men heard in John the voice of God that they flocked out to the Jordan to him. This crowd of people were searchers after God, and Jesus identified himself with them.

(iv) But we have not yet come to the deepest level of the meaning of the baptism. In the baptism Jesus identified himself with the sin and the sorrow of mankind. These Jews came to John as sinners; they came because a sense of sin drove them, and because they were

[1] *Dialogue with Trypho* 88.

made to feel as never before their need of God and their need of the forgiveness of God, and it was precisely with sinful men that Jesus identified himself. He made, as it has been put, 'common cause with all men in life in the mortal dilemma'. George A. Buttrick quotes the story of a man who in the time of his wife's infidelity, when he was in no way to blame, came to her and said: 'Since you and I have done this . . .' Such was his love that, even when the sin was not his own, he identified himself with the sinner, with the penitence and with the sorrow. In the baptism Jesus the sinless identified himself with sinful men. He took upon himself their sorrow, their contrition, their search for God; he became one in heart with the men whom he had come to save; he became, as Irenaeus put it, what we are to make us what he is.[1]

For Jesus himself the event of the baptism was a great occasion. There is little doubt that for Jesus the baptism was far more a private and personal experience than it was a public demonstration. The words of the voice at the baptism are given in two forms. Matthew has: '*This* is my beloved Son' (Matt. 3.17), as if Jesus was being pointed out by the divine voice to all who were there to see. But both Mark and Luke have: '*Thou* art my beloved Son' (Mark 1.11; Luke 3.22), as if to say that the words came to Jesus and to Jesus alone. The events of the baptism did not happen for the sake of the crowd; they happened for the sake of Jesus himself. So, then, for Jesus the baptism was certain quite definite things.

It was for him *the moment of decision*. As Rawlinson puts it: 'Jesus recognized his appointed hour.' It was the moment when he decided once and for all to cut the cables and to launch out into the deep. The prologue gave place to the main act of the drama; the preparation was ended and the task had begun.

It was for Jesus *the moment of assurance*. Deep within his inmost being he received the ultimate and unshakable certainty that he was, as no man had ever been or could ever be, the Son of God. Now here is where there may well be some kind of hint of truth behind the very early stories which tell of Jesus as being unwilling to go to John, and as going under pressure from his family. We have already seen the account of what happened which is in the *Gospel according to the Hebrews*. In that Gospel Jesus' words are: 'Wherein

[1] *Against Heresies,* Prologue to Book 5.

have I sinned, that I should go and be baptized by John? unless peradventure this very thing that I have said is a sin of ignorance.' The strange thing is that in that saying of Jesus there is a lurking doubt and uncertainty; Jesus in it recognizes the possibility that he may be mistaken. Two things are clear, and these two things must be set side by side. First, Jesus so identified himself with men that he entered absolutely and completely into the human situation. Second, a part of the human situation, which no one who has set his hand to some great task fully escapes, is self-doubt. To every man there comes the moment or moments when in his heart and soul there is a little shiver of doubt, a faint question mark, the terrible feeling that maybe he may be mistaken, the grim realization of the possibility that he may be on the wrong road. If these two facts are so, then Jesus did not fully enter into the human situation, unless at some time there were deep in his heart the self-doubtings and the self-questionings which are part of the heritage of the human spirit. The baptism was the moment when the last of these doubts perished for ever. In that moment there came to him such an experience of the fatherhood of God and of his own sonship, such an utter conviction of the approval of God, such a certainty of God's will for him, that he never doubted himself or his task again.

It so happens that certain of the Greek manuscripts have in Luke a variant reading in the sentence which contains the words of God. The best manuscripts all read: 'Thou art my beloved Son; with thee I am well pleased.' But the so-called Western Text reads: 'Thou art my beloved Son; *today I have begotten thee,*' which is indeed the full text of Ps. 2.7. If that were the true reading, it would mean that in that moment the man Jesus was fully and finally chosen for the work which God brought him into the world to do; it would mean that all through the long thirty years of preparation Jesus had so proved and prepared himself that now in this tremendous moment God was adopting him into unique sonship for a unique task; it would mean that in that moment God offered and Jesus accepted the supreme task of being the Saviour of the world.

In any event, the one thing that is certain is that for Jesus the baptism was the moment of assurance, when there came to him the utter certainty that the way ahead was clear.

It was for him *the moment of equipment.* In the most unique way the Holy Spirit of God came upon him (Mark 1.10; Matt. 3.16; Luke 3.22). Once again the implication of the narrative is that this was an experience which was personal and private to Jesus. Here is something that a Jew could understand. Again and again the coming of the Spirit of God was the preparation and the equipment of a man for some great task. It was so with Othniel (Judg. 3.10); with Gideon (Judg. 6.34); with Jephthah (Judg. 11.29); with Samson (Judg. 13.25); with Saul (I Sam. 10.10); with the king anointed by God (Isa. 11.2); with the Servant of God (Isa. 42.1). But in the case of Jesus there was a difference. In the case of the others the coming of the Spirit was the preparation for *a special task*; it was, so to speak, a temporary equipment; the tide of the Spirit flowed but the tide of the Spirit also ebbed; the flame blazed and the flame flickered. But in the case of Jesus the coming of the Spirit was an equipment *for life*; it was the permanent indwelling of the Spirit in him. A surviving fragment of the *Gospel according to the Hebrews*, preserved by Jerome in his commentary on Isa. 11.2, seems to seize upon this very point: 'And it came to pass, when the Lord was come up out of the water, *the whole fount of the Holy Spirit descended and rested upon him,* and said unto him: My Son, in all the prophets was I waiting for thee that thou shouldst come, and *I might rest in thee*. For thou art my rest, thou art my first-begotten Son, that reignest for ever.' It was no portion of the Spirit which came upon Jesus; it was the very fountain of the Spirit. It was no temporary gift of the Spirit; it was the permanent abiding of the Spirit in him. In the moment of the baptism Jesus was divinely equipped for his task.

Great as these things are, the baptism had a significance for Jesus which was still greater and still deeper. For him it was at one and the same time *the moment of enlightenment* and *the moment of self-dedication*. The voice which came to Jesus said: 'Thou art my beloved Son; with thee I am well pleased' (Mark 1.11; Matt. 3.17; Luke 3.22). That saying is composed of two sayings from the Old Testament. 'Thou art my beloved Son' is a quotation from Ps. 2.7. Ps. 2 is a description of a testing time in the life of the king of the holy nation. The heathen rage and rebel; but the king can have perfect confidence, because God has taken him as his son, and his cause is safe in the hands and in the power and in the promise of

God. Not only will his own realm be safe and his own throne secure
and his immediate enemies conquered and subdued; the day will
come when God will extend his kingdom to the ends of the earth.
No doubt when that psalm was first composed and sung it was
meant for a definite situation in history when the throne of Israel
was in peril; but, as the days went on, that psalm came to be regarded as a messianic psalm and as a prophecy and foretelling of the
triumph of the Messiah, the anointed King of God. So, then, when
Jesus heard this voice, he knew himself to be the Messiah, the King
sent by God to be the Lord of men and the ruler of the earth. Here
is the forecast of ultimate victory and of universal triumph.

But there was a second clause in the words which came to Jesus
in the divine voice—'with thee I am well pleased.' That is a quotation from Isa. 42.1 : 'Behold my servant, whom I uphold, my chosen,
in whom my soul delights.' That is part of the picture of the Servant
of the Lord, of the great and mysterious figure whose portrait culminates in Isa. 53, of the one who was wounded for our trans-
gressions and bruised for our iniquities, the one on whom the
chastisement of our peace fell, the one who was to be like a sheep
dumb before its shearers. When Jesus heard these words, he must
have realized with blinding certainty that his ultimate victory was
certain, but that the way to it was the way of sorrow, of suffering, of
sacrificial service, of self-dedication as an offering for the sins of
men.

So when Jesus heard the voice, he knew that he was God's chosen
Messiah, but he also knew that the way for him was the way of the
Cross.

In the baptism we see the self-identification of Jesus with men
and the self-dedication of Jesus to the purposes of God.

In Justin Martyr's account of the baptism there is one strange
addition to the story. Justin says: 'And then, when Jesus had gone
to the river Jordan, where John was baptizing, and when he had
stepped into the water, a fire was kindled in Jordan.'[1] This fire is
also mentioned in the *Gospel according to the Hebrews.* Where
Justin and that Gospel got the story we do not know and we cannot
tell. But the story is symbolically true, for in that moment of the
baptism there was kindled in the heart of Jesus a flame of sacrificial
love which nothing in time or in eternity could ever extinguish.

[1] *Dialogue with Trypho* 88.

4

CHOOSING HIS WAY

There have been those who have dismissed the story of the
temptations of Jesus as completely unhistorical. Guignebert, for
instance, describes it as 'completely legendary', 'sheer hagiographical
imagination', 'all too obvious fiction'. But the plain fact is that,
whatever may be said about the form of the temptation story, its
events are absolutely necessary, if we are to make sense of the life of
Jesus. It represents an essential step in the line of his life.

For years Jesus had waited in Nazareth, undergoing the long
preparation for his task. With the emergence of John the Baptizer
he knew that for him the hour had struck, and the time to begin had
come. In the moment of the baptism Jesus received assurance,
equipment, enlightenment to go on. And thereupon one decision
was necessarily forced upon Jesus. He knew now what his task was;
he knew what he had come into the world to do. He was the
Messiah, the Chosen One of God; he must bring to men the Kingdom of God. And the immediate question was—*How?* How was he
to set about this task? What methods was he to use? What way was
he to pursue? It is to these questions that Jesus found his answer in
the events of the temptation story. To be given a task is to be
obliged to find a method to carry it out. Jesus had been given his
task; and now in the events of his temptation he decided on the
method which he must follow. For Jesus this decision was all the
more necessary and all the more difficult in that there already
existed a popular picture of the Messiah as the triumphant liberator
of the Jewish people, the conqueror of Rome, and victorious over-
lord of all the earth. The choice before Jesus was whether he
was to fit himself into the popular messianic pattern or strike out
upon a way that was his own. It was to make that choice that Jesus
went into the lonely places to fight his personal battle with the

voices which called him to the wrong way. Before we begin to study
the meaning for Jesus of the events of the temptation story, there
are certain general facts which we must note.

We must be clear as to the meaning of the word *temptation* as it
is used in this story and in the Bible generally. For the most part we
regard temptation as a deliberate and malevolent attempt to seduce
a man into sin. But in the New Testament the word (*peirazein*)
means much more 'to test' than 'to tempt'. In this story of the
temptations of Jesus the Gospel writers are unanimous that it was
the Holy Spirit who led Jesus into the desert places (Mark 1.12;
Matt. 4.1; Luke 4.1). If we regard temptation simply as an attempt
to seduce a man into sin, that would mean that the Holy Spirit was
actually a partner in an assault on the purity and the goodness of
Jesus. In the Old Testament story which tells of Abraham and Isaac
we read: 'And it came to pass after these things that God did
tempt Abraham' (Gen. 22.1, AV). If we take the word 'tempt' in
nothing more than the sense of seduction into sin, we are left with
an incredible situation in which God sought to persuade Abraham
to sin. The difficulty vanishes immediately when we substitute the
word 'test' for the word 'tempt'. God was *testing* Abraham. The
temptation of Jesus was the *testing* of Jesus. Temptation is always a
testing; it is not meant to make a man fall; it is meant to test him
and to try him, so that out of the testing situation he will emerge
stronger and finer and purer, like a metal that is tested and tried in
the fire.

The temptation story is the strongest proof that Jesus was conscious of possessing special and wonderful powers. It would be no
temptation to an ordinary person to change stones into bread or to
leap down unharmed from the Temple pinnacle. Unless his mind
was unhinged with the delusion of grandeur, he would know that
he could not do these things. The temptation story is the story of a
person who was aware that he possessed special powers, and who
was faced with the suggestion that he should use these powers in the
wrong way.

The method of the tempter is very revealing. None of the courses
which he suggested was obviously evil. There is surely nothing obviously wrong in turning stones into bread; there is surely nothing
wrong in demonstrating the care of God for his own by taking some

adventurous and dangerous course of action; there is surely nothing wrong in an action which will win over the whole world. If temptation was obviously evil, if the result of falling to temptation was obviously disastrous, no one would ever fall. In the old story of the temptation in the Garden of Eden the forbidden fruit which the tempter urged Eve to eat was good for food, pleasant to the eyes, and to be desired to make one wise (Gen. 3.6). The subtlety of temptation is that it suggests a course of action which is on the face of it attractive and advantageous. The power of temptation lies in the fact that so often evil can look like good—to him who takes only the short-term view of life.

When we think of the temptation story, and when we think of what was happening to Jesus, we must not think in terms of a series of external scenes. We must think of a struggle that was going on in the inmost heart and being and soul of Jesus, an inner agony of choice and decision. It is true that there are some—Bengel was one —who thought that Satan always works through human agencies, and who imagined that what happened was that some emissary or some deputation of the Sanhedrin followed Jesus out into the desert, and attempted to persuade him to embark upon the role of the conquering Messiah, and so to fulfil popular expectation and gain popular support. That is not what we are to think of. We are to think of a long struggle in the deeps of the being of Jesus, going on continuously until for the time being he gained the victory. Nor are we to think of this as a final victory. Luke tells us at the end of the story that the devil departed for a season (4.13,AV), until an opportune time (RSV). The whole story is a vivid way of describing the inner battle in the heart and mind and soul of Jesus, a battle which lasted until the end of the day.

There is one fact which sets this story in a class by itself among Gospel stories. The story can have had only one source; it can have come from none other than Jesus himself. He was alone in the desert; it was his own private and personal and inmost struggle; and the story of it can have come from nowhere else than from his own lips. The day must have come when he told it to his disciples for their warning, their comfort and their strengthening. This story is, therefore, one of the most sacred in the whole Gospel narrative.

There remains one other thing which it is essential to say. The tempting of Jesus was a real tempting. To put it in technical terms, there is an old argument as to whether we are to think of Jesus in terms of *non posse peccare* or *posse non peccare;* that is to say, whether we are to say that it was *not possible for him to sin,* or that it was *possible for him not to sin.* There have always been some who in a mistaken reverence have held that there was no possibility of Jesus falling to temptation, that he was of such complete goodness and purity, that he was, so to speak, so much God that he could not possibly have fallen to temptation. To believe that is to make the temptation story quite unreal, and to reduce it to a kind of play-acting. We must have no doubt of the utter reality of the temptation of Jesus; and, when we realize this, the temptation story becomes one of the most dramatic stories in history, for in those days when Jesus was tempted and tested, the fate of God's plan of salvation was literally swinging in the balance. It is further true that Jesus was not tempted less but more than any other person. In the case of ordinary men like ourselves, the tempter never has to put out his full power; we fall long before that; but in the case of Jesus the tempter put forth every effort he could, and Jesus overcame them all. To Jesus there came a strength and violence of temptation which no one else has ever known—and he overcame.

So, then, Jesus had come to the all-important moment when he had to choose how he would approach the work which God had given him to do. Jesus sought no human advice; he went away to be alone to settle the problem and to think the matter out. It was into 'the wilderness' that he went.

The wilderness was the Wilderness of Judaea, which stretches from the hill country south of Jerusalem down to the Dead Sea. It covers an area of thirty-five by fifteen miles, and in the Old Testament its name is Jeshimmon, which means 'The Devastation'. Sir George Adam Smith describes it in *The Historical Geography of the Holy Land:* 'The strata were contorted; ridges ran in all directions; distant hills to north and south looked like gigantic dust-heaps; those near we could see to be torn as if by waterspouts. When we were not stepping on detritus, the limestone was blistered and peeling. Often the ground sounded hollow; sometimes rock and sand slipped in large quantities from the tread of the horses; sometimes the living rock was bare and jagged, especially in the frequent gullies, that therefore glowed and beat with heat like furnaces.' It was into that grim and bleak loneliness that Jesus went to make his great decision.

For forty days Jesus was alone (Mark 1.13; Matt. 4.2; Luke 4.2). The forty days is not to be taken with time-table-like literalness. It was for forty days that the rains preceded the Flood (Gen. 7.12); it was for forty days that Moses was on Mount Sinai (Ex. 24.18), and that Elijah was in the wilderness (I Kings 19.8). It is to be taken simply as expressing a long period of time.

Mark (1.13) tells us that Jesus was with the wild beasts. It may be that Mark adds this detail to add further grim loneliness to the scene, as if painting a picture of a wilderness in which no human foot trod and there were only the beasts. But it also may be that Mark is thinking of the new covenant in which man and the beasts will be fearless friends together (Hos. 2.18), and that he is thinking of the beasts, not as threatening Jesus, but as being his companions in the wilderness loneliness, in which case the picture would be a picture of loveliness and not of terror.

During this time Jesus was fasting (Matt. 4.2; Luke 4.2), and a time of fasting like that necessarily heightens a man's mental and spiritual perceptiveness and awareness.

The story of the temptations is told in Mark 1.12f., Matt. 4.1–11 and Luke 4.1–13. Mark gives us no detail at all. In Matthew and Luke the order of the temptations is different. In Matthew the order is, first, to turn the stones into bread; second, to leap down unharmed from the pinnacle of the Temple; third, to worship Satan and so to gain the lordship of the kingdoms of the world. In Luke the order of the second and third temptations is reversed. It does not make any real difference, and we shall use Matthew's order as the basis of our study. Let us first look at the actual temptations themselves before we seek to study their meaning and their significance for Jesus.

The first temptation was the temptation to turn the stones into bread (Matt. 4.3f.; Luke 4.3f.). What temptation could be more natural to a man who had fasted for forty days, especially when the little pieces of limestone rock with which the desert was covered were exactly like little round loaves of bread? Had not God said: 'I will rain bread from heaven for you' (Ex. 16.4)? Was not the promise: 'They shall not hunger or thirst' (Isa. 49.10)? But Jesus

countered this temptation with the words of the law: 'Man does
not live by bread alone, but by every word that proceeds from the
mouth of God' (Deut. 8.3).

In the second temptation Jesus in imagination saw himself on 'the
pinnacle of the Temple', and the temptation was to leap down, and
to land at the foot of it unharmed (Luke 4.9–12; Matt. 4.5–7). 'The
pinnacle of the Temple' may be either of two places. On the south
side of the Temple rose the Royal Porch. The outer wall of the
Royal Porch rose straight up from the side of the hill on which
Jerusalem and the Temple were built. There was a sheer drop of
four hundred and fifty feet to the Kedron valley below, a drop so
famous and notorious that Josephus tells us that no one could look
down it without being overcome with dizziness.[1] Edersheim has
another suggestion to make. The first great event of the Temple day
was the morning sacrifice which had to be made as soon as dawn
came. There was a tall tower in the Temple, on the top of which a
priest was stationed with a silver trumpet to sound the blast upon
it when the first streaks of dawn came across the hills, and so to
tell all men that the time of sacrifice had come. At such a time
the Temple court would be thronged with expectant worshippers,
with their eyes fixed on the priest who waited to give the signal that
the dawn had come. If Jesus chose to leap down from the top of
that tower at that moment he would indeed have an audience for
his miracle of sensation.

This, then, was the second temptation which came to Jesus. Had
not God promised: 'He will give his angels charge of you,' and, 'On
their hands they will bear you up, lest you strike your foot against a
stone' (Ps. 91.11f.)? But once again Jesus countered temptation
with a word from the law: 'You shall not tempt the Lord your
God' (Deut. 6.16).

In the third temptation Jesus saw himself on a high mountain
from which all the kingdoms of the earth could be seen. Of course
there is no mountain from which the whole world may be seen;
but here the *Gospel according to the Hebrews* has an interesting
addition. It identifies the mountain as Mount Tabor, the very
mountain from whose summit Jesus may well have looked on the
world and its roads, when he was a boy.

[1] *Antiquities* 15.11.5.

Was not the promise of God: 'Ask of me, and I will make the nations your heritage, and the ends of the earth your possession' (Ps. 2.8)? So the tempter tempted Jesus to strike a bargain with him, and all these nations would be his. But again Jesus countered temptation with a word from the law: 'You shall worship the Lord your God and him only shall you serve' (Deut. 6.13).

So Jesus vanquished temptation; but the battle was not over. As Luke has it, the tempter, though defeated on this occasion, departed from him until an opportune time (Luke 4.13). For Jesus, as for all men, the battle with the tempter is never wholly won until the very end of the day.

Before we examine the three temptations in detail, we must note that in them the tempter made one basic attack on Jesus. He attacked Jesus' consciousness of himself and of his task. 'If you are the Son of God,' he began (Matt. 4.3,5; Luke 4.3,9). This was an attack which was to return even when Jesus was on the cross. 'If you are the Son of God,' said his enemies, 'come down from the cross' (Matt. 27.40; Luke 23.35–37). Here is the temptation to Jesus to distrust himself, to doubt his call, to question his task and his ability and equipment for it. It is as if the tempter said: 'How can you, a penniless, uneducated, Galilean carpenter, possibly be the Messiah of God? Who ever conceived of a Messiah starving in a wilderness? Who ever thought of a Messiah on the way to a cross?' There is nothing so paralysing as doubt; there can be no decisive and effective action without certainty. Jesus well knew the traditional and conventional ideas of what the Messiah ought to be; and he well knew that the way he was called upon to choose was a complete and revolutionary contradiction of them. The tempter began by seeking to make Jesus doubt his own call from God, but Jesus was so sure of God, and of his own relationship to God, that the attack failed.

Let us now take each temptation by itself and study its meaning.

(i) There was the temptation to turn the stones into bread. There were two temptations there.

(*a*) It was the temptation to use his power selfishly. After all, Jesus might well say: 'My response to the summons of God has lost me my job and my living. I was once a reasonably well-to-do carpenter, and now I am a homeless wanderer. Why should I not use my powers to satisfy my own needs?' Here was the temptation to use power for himself and not for others.

(*b*) It was the temptation to attempt to win men by material gifts, and so to bribe them into becoming his followers, a temptation which was all the more acute because of the dreams of prosperity and plenty which did attach themselves to the messianic age. But Jesus well knew that men whose loyalty can be bought by the bribe of material gifts can just as easily be lured from their loyalty by some one who bids for their support with the offer of still more munificent gifts. *E.g. Many left when he Taught about bread*

(ii) There was the temptation to leap down from the Temple pinnacle. Again there were two temptations there.

—(*a*) There was the temptation to dazzle men with sensations. Men can always be temporarily dazzled into following a leader; but Jesus well knew that today's wonder can very easily become tomorrow's commonplace; and he who proposes to win men by sensations is committed to a course in which he must find ever more and more marvels to offer, or his followers will drift and dwindle away.

(*b*) But this in point of fact was a temptation which was typical of a whole attitude of mind. It was the temptation to become the kind of messianic leader who rose in Palestine again and again, the kind of leader whose one aim was to lead a sensational and successful rebellion against Rome. It is the grim fact that in Palestine between the years 67 and 37 BC no fewer than 100,000 men perished in abortive rebellions. The day was to come when Theudas was to persuade a great mass of the people to follow him out to the Jordan, with the claim that with a word he would cleave the waters in two and they would pass over dryshod,[1] only to have his followers annihilated by Cuspius Fadus, the Roman governor. The day was to come when an Egyptian impostor (Acts 21.38) was to lead hordes of the Jews out to the Mount of Olives with the promise that with a word he could cause the walls of Jerusalem to collapse, only to have his revolt crushed by Antonius Felix.[2] There had been, and were to come, any number of sensation-promising revolutionaries.

[1] Josephus, *Antiquities* 20.5.1.
[2] Josephus, *Antiquities* 20.8:6; *Wars of the Jews* 2.3.5.

They had never lacked a following and they never would lack one. Jesus was confronted with the temptation to take the way which so many would-be, self-styled saviours of their country had taken.

(iii)   There was the temptation to worship Satan, and so to enter into possession of the kingdoms of the world. That is the temptation to compromise. It is as if Satan said: 'Do not be so un-compromising; do not pitch your demands quite so high; allow men just a little more latitude; strike a bargain with me; and then they will follow you to the end.' But for Jesus there could be no compromise with anything that was less than the best, and with any-thing which was not completely subject to God.

The temptations which came to Jesus were the temptation to the selfish use of power, the temptation to set material benefits in the forefront of his programme, the temptation to seek for quick results by sensational means, the temptation to win popularity by compro-mise, and, perhaps more than anything else, the temptation to distrust himself and to doubt his call, and to accept traditional ex-pectations rather than to listen to the voice of God. And his method of dealing with temptation was to submit every desire and every inclination to the word and the will of God, and to obey the verdict that he found there.

5

THE BEGINNING OF THE CAMPAIGN

'Jesus came into Galilee preaching the gospel of God' (Mark 1.14). In that one sentence Mark sets down the beginning of the campaign of Jesus.

A wise commander has to decide not only *when* to begin but also *where* to begin. The *point* of attack is at least as important as the *time* of attack. It was in Galilee that Jesus began, and there are three reasons why Galilee was a wise choice.

Galilee was the territory which Jesus knew best. It was in Galilee that he had grown to manhood; it was in Galilee that he had learned as a schoolboy and worked as a man; it was in Galilee that he had worshipped in the synagogue and worked in the carpenter's shop. He could speak to the people of Galilee because he had lived their life and understood their thoughts and spoke their speech.

Galilee was easily the most populous part of Palestine. If Jesus wished to reach the greatest number of people within the most limited area and in the shortest time, then Galilee was the place to begin. Josephus was once military governor of Palestine, and, therefore, he speaks out of intimate and personal knowledge of the country. He tells us in his autobiography that in Galilee there were 204 towns and villages,[1] none with a population of fewer than 15,000 persons.[2] That is to say, there were at least 3,000,000 people in Galilee. He tells us that, in addition to putting garrisons in nineteen fortified towns, he was able to raise an army of more than 100,000 young men.[3] These statements may sound like exaggerations, but

[1] *Life* 45.
[2] *Wars of the Jews* 3.3.2.
[3] *Wars of the Jews* 2.20.6.

they are made by the man who was once governor of the country, and the first is made in a letter to those who are actually to supersede him in the command in Galilee, and it is scarcely likely that in such circumstances, when his words could be so easily disproved, Josephus would be deliberately inaccurate. Burton, in his book *Unexplored Syria*, tells of standing on a spur of Lebanon, and of looking at the country just north of Galilee, and he says that in ancient times 'the land in many places must have appeared to be one continuous town'. There was no part of Palestine which could have provided Jesus with so great an audience for the message which he had come to bring.

The character and temperament of the people of Galilee were such that they were of all the inhabitants of Palestine most likely to be receptive to a new teacher and a new teaching. Judaea is tucked away in inaccessibility; Galilee was traversed by the greatest roads in the ancient world; and therefore Galilee was far more open to new ways and to new ideas than Judaea could ever be. The Galilaeans were eager, forward-looking people. 'They were ever fond of innovations,' said Josephus, 'and by nature disposed to changes, and delighted in seditions.'[1] They were ever ready to follow a leader who would begin an insurrection. They were quick in temper and given to quarreling. 'The Galilaeans,' he said again, 'have never been destitute of courage.'[2] The Talmud says of them, 'They were ever more anxious for honour than for gain.'[3] There was a certain impulsive chivalry about the Galilaeans. Peter with all his shining virtues and with all his impulsive faults could well have sat for the portrait of a typical Galilaean. Amongst such a people Jesus would find men ready to listen and ready to thrill to a new message and a new call from God.

His own background, the number of the people, their character and their temperament and their history, made Galilee for Jesus the best of all places to open his campaign and to launch his mission among men.

The leader who will change the minds of men and who will

---

[1] *Life* 17.
[2] *Wars of the Jews* 3.3.2.
[3] *Jerusalem Talmud*, Kethuboth 4.12.

change the world in which he lives must wisely choose his time of attack and his place of attack, but he must also have something more. He must be able to put his message into one flashing sentence, which men will immediately and unmistakably understand, and which will at once penetrate into their minds and lodge in their hearts. That is what Jesus did. He came to men with a command and a statement, with an imperative and an indicative. 'Repent,' he said, 'for the kingdom of heaven is at hand' (Matt. 4.17; Mark 1.14f.). Let us look, then, first at the imperative and then at the indicative of Jesus.

The imperative of Jesus is *Repent!* The terrible sin of Bethsaida and Chorazin and Capernaum was that they had seen his mighty works and yet had not repented (Matt. 11.20f.; Luke 10.13–15). Men are confronted with the alternative, 'Repent or perish' (Luke 13.3,5). The disciples are sent out to bring to men the summons to repent (Mark 6.12). It is the repentance of the sinner which wakens the greatest joy in heaven (Luke 15.7,10). Clearly, if we are to understand the mind of Jesus, the meaning of this word *repent* must be fixed and defined.

In the New Testament the word for 'repentance' is *metanoia,* and the word for 'to repent' is *metanoein*. Both words are connected with *nous* which means 'the mind'. In this case the prefix *meta* means 'after', and *noia* means 'a thought'. Therefore, the basic meaning of *metanoia* is 'an afterthought'. The classical writers sometimes contrast *metanoia,* 'afterthought', with *pronoia,* 'forethought', saying that the wise man exercises forethought, *pronoia,* and has not to depend on afterthought, *maetanoia,* in order to mend mistakes which forethought would have avoided. But 'an afterthought' may very easily be *a changed thought*. In the light of the consequences, in the light of a new appreciation of the circumstances, in the light of new knowledge and new awareness a man's second thoughts may be very different from his first thoughts; and it is from this that *metanoia* comes to mean 'repentance'. If we begin from here, we can see that in all true repentance there must be four different elements.

(i) There must be the realization that one's actions were wrong. A man must come to realize that he was mistaken and on the wrong way.

(ii) There must be sorrow for his error, for his wrong-doing, for his sin.

(iii) There must come a changed attitude to life, to conduct and to action as a whole. Repentance does not simply mean that a man is sorry for the consequences of the thing which he did, or the course of action which he has taken. It means that he has come to see the wrongness of the whole attitude of mind, the whole view of life, which made him act as he did. To take an example, a man may live loosely and immorally in the sphere of sexual relationships; he may thereby injure his body and contract some disease. Repentance does not mean simply being sorry that this consequence of his own immorality has come upon him; it means the coming of the awareness that his whole view of life, his whole attitude to personal relationships, was wrong, and the awakening of bitter sorrow in his heart that he ever was the kind of man he was, and that he ever had the attitude to life he had. The godly sorrow of repentance must never be confused with sorrow for the consequences of a deed, although it is true that the sudden realization of the consequences may awaken true repentance in a man's heart.

(iv) There must follow a change of action to fit the change of mind. A change of life must accompany the change of heart. A man must bring forth fruits meet for repentance. This is well shown by another Greek word which very commonly accompanies *metanoia* and *metanoein*. This is the word *epistrephein,* which means 'to turn'. When the people of Lydda heard Peter, they *turned* to the Lord (Acts 9.35). In Antioch a great number believed and *turned* to the Lord (Acts 11.21). It is Paul's appeal to the people of Lystra that they should *turn* from earthly vanities to the living God (Acts 14.15). The Gentiles who have *turned* to God are to be admitted into the Church without more ado (Acts 15.19). Paul's commission is to *turn* men from darkness to light (Acts 26.18). Paul tells Agrippa how he preached that men should *repent* and *turn* to God (Acts 26.20).

The picture is that a man is facing in one direction—away from God—and in repentance he changes his direction—towards God. Repentance means a turning round and a facing in the opposite direction. There is a strange and cryptic saying of Jesus reported in the apocryphal *Acts of Peter:*

Except ye make the right hand as the left hand, and the left hand as the right hand, and that which is upwards as that which is downwards, that which is before as that which is behind, ye shall not know the Kingdom of God.

When does the right become the left, the left the right, and that which is before that which is behind? *Obviously when a man turns round.* When does that which is upwards become as that which is downwards? When a man is, so to speak, stood on his head, that is, when he begins to see the world the other way round, when his values are reversed, when the things he thought important become unimportant, and when the things he disregarded become the most important things in life. Repentance means the reversal of the direction of life in order to face God.

All these four elements must be present, or repentance is unreal. Without the realization of sin, repentance cannot even begin. Saul Kane discovers 'the harm I've done by being me'. But a man may be quite unaware of the error of his ways, quite blind to the ugliness of his life, quite insensitive to the grief and the pain which he is causing to other people. Or he may be well aware that he is doing wrong, but not be in the least sorry for it. He may in fact glory and take a pride in his ability to do as he likes, to get his own way, to break the laws of honesty and honour. Or he may cease from his wrong-doing, but his attitude to it may be in no way changed. He may cease simply from fear of the consequences, simply from lack of opportunity, and, if a way came to him whereby he might continue in his wrongdoing and escape the consequences or be able to hide it in secrecy, he would certainly take it. His view of life has in no way altered. Or he may be really sorry for his sin; his attitude to life may be truly altered; but at the same time his sin may have such a grip and a power over him that he cannot leave it. He may be powerless to break the self-forged chains which bind him.

And now we come to the final step in the matter. A man cannot take any of the steps of repentance *without the help of Jesus Christ.* A man cannot realize his own sin and the ugliness of his own life, until he sees goodness and compares himself with it. He must see his secret or open sins in the light of Jesus Christ's pure countenance. When a man sets his own life in the light of the life of the Lord of all good life, then he realizes his sin. A man cannot be truly sorry for sin until he sees the whole consequences of sin. In the Cross of Christ he is enabled to see what sin can do; he is enabled to see that sin can take the loveliest life the world ever saw and smash and break it on a cross. The cross shows every man the terrible destructive power of sin. A man cannot break the chains that bind him, he cannot turn his godly sorrow into an effective change of life, without the enabling power of Jesus Christ. It is only with and through Jesus Christ that he can make the change which repentance demands. Repentance is begun, continued and ended in Jesus Christ.

So, then, Jesus came with the imperative *Repent!* It was a word which men would immediately recognize. It was an ancient cry. It was with that summons that John the Baptizer had come (Mark 1.4; Matt. 3.2; Luke 3.3). It was a summons which had rung for ever through the teaching of the prophets. Jesus the prophet came to summon men to repentance; but he did more—he came to make the essential repentance possible, and only he could do that.

6

THE KINGDOM OF GOD

'Repent,' said Jesus, 'for the kingdom of heaven is at hand' (Matt. 4.17). We have looked at the imperative of Jesus—'*Repent!*' Now we must look at the indicative of Jesus—'*The kingdom of heaven is at hand.*'

We must begin by noting one minor point. The Gospels use two phrases, the Kingdom of God and the Kingdom of Heaven—and they mean exactly the same. The approximate figures for the usage of the two phrases in the Gospels are that Matthew speaks about the Kingdom of Heaven thirty times and of the Kingdom of God only three times: Mark and Luke speak about the Kingdom of God sixteen and thirty-two times respectively and do not use the phrase the Kingdom of Heaven at all. We may see the equivalence of the two phrases by comparing Matt. 19.23, Mark 10.23 and Luke 18.24. Matthew gives the saying of Jesus in the form: 'It will be hard for a rich man to enter *the kingdom of heaven.*' Mark and Luke give it in the form: 'How hard it will be for those who have riches to enter *the kingdom of God.*' Matthew himself in the very next verse (19.24) goes on to say: 'It is easier for a camel to go through the eye of a needle than for a rich man to enter *the kingdom of God.*' Clearly the two expressions are interchangeable.

The reason for the two forms is this. The name of God was so holy that no devout Jew would lightly take it on his lips. Such was his reverence for the sacred name that he always sought for some fitting way to avoid speaking it. One of the simplest ways to avoid the use of the name of God was to speak of heaven instead. Matthew is the most Jewish of all the Gospel writers. He therefore hesitates in reverence to use the name of God, and so, instead of speaking about the *Kingdom of God,* he habitually speaks about the *Kingdom of Heaven.*

A second and most important point to be noted is the meaning of the word 'Kingdom'. As it is commonly used in modern speech, a kingdom is a territory, an area of land. The Kingdom of Britain is the territory which belongs to Britain. But that is not what the word means in the New Testament. In the New Testament the Kingdom of God is not the area of territory which belongs to God; it is the sovereignty, the lordship, the rule and the reign of God. The Kingdom of God is not the territory over which God reigns as an earthly king reigns; it is the sovereignty of God, a state and condition of things in which God rules and reigns supreme.

The idea of the Kingdom of God, the sovereignty of God, was a conception which was central and basic to the message of Jesus. He emerged upon men with the message that the Kingdom was at hand (Matt. 4.17; Mark 1.15). To preach the Kingdom was an obligation that was laid upon him (Luke 4.43). It was with the message of the Kingdom that he went through the towns and the villages of Galilee (Luke 8.1). The announcement of the Kingdom was the central element in the teaching of Jesus.

The expression itself was familiar to Jewish ears. The Jewish rabbis and teachers drew a distinction and a contrast between the 'yoke of heavenly sovereignty' and 'the ungodly sovereignty' or 'the yoke of flesh and blood'. They held that God's sovereignty upon earth began with Abraham. 'Before our father Abraham came into the world,' they said, 'God was, as it were, only the King of heaven; but when Abraham came, Abraham made him to be King over heaven and earth.' To the rabbis the sovereignty of God was intimately connected with obedience to the law. The Gentile who became a proselyte and who submitted himself and his life to the law was said to 'take upon himself the sovereignty of heaven'. Every synagogue service began—and still begins—with the recital of the *Shema:* 'Hear, O Israel, The Lord our God is one Lord; and you shalt love the Lord your God with all your heart, and with all your soul, and with all your might' (Deut. 6.4–10); and every time a man shared in the recital of that essential creed of Israel he was said to take upon himself again the sovereignty of the yoke of God.

This sovereignty of God reigned within Israel, but the time was to come when it would reign and rule over all the people of the earth, and when all peoples would submit themselves to it, and when it would be as wide as the world. Since God, being God, is already the Lord of all the earth, although there are so many who have not yet accepted his lordship, the Jewish teachers spoke not so much of the *coming* of the sovereignty of God, as of the *manifestation* or the *appearing* of the sovereignty of God. They looked forward to the day, not when that sovereignty would begin, for it already existed, but when it would be accepted by all, and so manifested throughout the whole earth.

This idea of the sovereignty of God was conceivable in two different ways. There was the idea of popular Jewish thought. According to this idea, all time may be divided into two ages—this present age, and the age to come. This present age is wholly evil, beyond help and beyond hope and beyond cure, wholly given over to evil. The age to come is wholly good, the age in which the sovereignty of God will be a reality. No human means can turn the one age into the other; that must be done by the direct action of God and the direct breaking in of God into time and into this world. That will happen on the Day of the Lord, which will be the end of one age and the beginning of another. It will come with suddenness and unexpectedness; it will be a time of cosmic upheaval and of the shattering of the entire scheme of things as they are; it will be a time of terror and of judgment in which the world as it is will be destroyed; and then out of the chaos and the travail and the birthpangs will arise the new age in which God is supreme. But there was also another idea which obtained in at least some circles of rabbinic thought. It looked on the coming of the sovereignty of God as a slow process, in which more and more universally men submitted themselves to the yoke of the law, until in the end the sovereignty of God was accepted and admitted by all. The way to it might be different, but Jewish thought never for one moment abandoned the conception that in the end the sovereignty of God would be supreme.

When we turn to the teaching of Jesus about the Kingdom, as it is reported to us in the Gospels, we find a wealth of material, pointing apparently in more than one direction and leading apparently to more than one conclusion. It will, therefore, be better to set down the material as it comes, and so try to allow a pattern to emerge from it, than to begin with a preconceived pattern and to try to fit the material to it.

In the Gospels the Kingdom is often spoken of as something which has come, something which has not emerged from history but which has invaded time out of eternity, something which has not arisen on earth but which has descended from heaven, something which is in no sense an achievement or attainment of man but which is entirely the gift and the work of God.

When Jesus healed the demon-possessed man, he said: 'If it is by the finger of God that I cast out demons, then the Kingdom of God has come upon you' (Luke 11.20; Matt. 12.28). It is God's good pleasure to give Jesus' men the Kingdom (Luke 12.32). The Kingdom is *preached* (Matt. 4.23; 9.35; 24.14; Luke 9.2). The Kingdom is *proclaimed* (Luke 9.60). The good news of the Kingdom is *announced* (Luke 8.1). The Kingdom may be *received* (Mark 10.15; Luke 18.17). The Kingdom may be *entered* (Matt. 5.20; 18.3; 19.23; Mark 10.23–25; Luke 18.24f.). A man may *be not far from* the Kingdom (Mark 12.34). Only a reality which is already given and already present can be spoken of in such terms.

Further, this coming of the Kingdom, this entry of the Kingdom into the present world, is something entirely new, something literally epoch-making. Great as John the Baptizer is, the man who is least in the Kingdom is greater than he (Luke 7.28). Up to the time of John the law and the prophets existed—and none will question the greatness of either—but since John the Kingdom of God is preached (Luke 16.16). The Kingdom is something which by its emergence has put everything that went before it out of date. In the giving of the Kingdom God has done a new thing for men.

It is nevertheless also true that the Kingdom is of long and ancient standing. Abraham and Isaac and Jacob and all the prophets are in the Kingdom of God (Luke 13.28; Matt. 8.11). Even in their day it was possible for a man to enter the Kingdom. In this sense the Kingdom is no new thing but goes back to the beginning of man's search for and discovery of God.

In spite of all this it is nonetheless true that the Kingdom has still to come, that it is still in some sense in the future. Joseph of Arimathaea was waiting for the Kingdom (Mark 15.43; Luke 23.51). It is the promise of Jesus that the Kingdom will come with power within the lifetime of some of those who were actually listening to him (Mark 9.1; Matt. 16.28; Luke 9.27). It is the hope and the faith of Jesus that he will drink the cup new in his Father's Kingdom (Mark 14.25; Matt. 26.29). The coming of the Kingdom is an event for which Jesus taught his people to pray (Matt. 6.10; Luke 11.2), and men do not pray for that which they already possess.

And yet it still remains true that the Kingdom is a present reality. The Kingdom is within you, or among you (*entos humōn*) (Luke 17.21). It is necessary to find some explanation of the meaning of the Kingdom which will cover the fact that the Kingdom can be— and is—past, present and future at one and the same time, that the Kingdom goes back to the patriarchs and the prophets, and yet at the same time with the coming of Jesus is so near that men can feel the breath of it upon them (Matt. 4.17; 10.7; 12.28; Mark 1.15; Luke 10.9,11; 11.20).

We have already seen that the Kingdom is often spoken of as the work and the gift of God, as that which is given, as that which has come by the action of God to men. But in the Gospels there is another and equally strong line of thought about the Kingdom which relates the Kingdom to the most intense and strenuous effort of men.

Men are bidden to *seek* the Kingdom (Matt. 6.33; Luke 12.31). The word is *zētein,* and it has been well translated: 'Make the Kingdom the object of all your endeavour.' Men are said to *press* into the Kingdom (Matt. 11.12; Luke 16.16). The word is *biazesthai,* and it is the word used of attackers storming a city. Men must storm their way into the Kingdom. 'The Kingdom,' as Denney said, 'is not for the well-meaning but for the desperate.' To enter the Kingdom is *worth any sacrifice.* It is better surgically to cut off any member of the body which would hinder a man from entering the Kingdom than to preserve the body whole and to be shut out of the Kingdom (Matt. 5.29f.; Mark 9.43–48).

There are at least two passages in which by implication the Kingdom is equated with *life* itself. If we compare Mark 9.43,45,47, we shall see that in the first two verses it is *life* that is spoken of, and in the third it is the *Kingdom* that is spoken of, and the meaning is the same. In the story of the rich young ruler the request of the young man is for guidance as to how he is to find *eternal life* (Matt. 19.16; Mark 10.17; Luke 18.18); and, when he has made his tragic departure, the word of Jesus deals with how difficult it is for a rich man to enter the *Kingdom of God* (Matt. 19.23; Mark 10.23; Luke 18.24). By implication the Kingdom is nothing less than heaven, and nothing less than life.

Even if we regard the Kingdom as entirely given, as entirely the gift of God, it still remains true that the teaching of Jesus lays down certain very definite conditions regarding entry to the Kingdom. No man can enter the Kingdom without *the childlike spirit* (Matt. 18.3). No man can enter the Kingdom without *the forgiving spirit* (Matt. 18.23–35). No man can enter the Kingdom without a *certain attitude to his fellow-men* (Matt. 25.31–46). If his attitude to men is an insensitive unawareness of the needs and the sorrows of others, he is shut out from the Kingdom. If a man would enter the Kingdom, his life must be a demonstration of love, *agapē,* in action. No man can enter the Kingdom without *a certain standard of righteousness.* The Christian standard of righteousness must exceed the righteousness of the scribes and Pharisees, or there is no entry to the Kingdom (Matt. 5.20). The teaching of Jesus uncompromisingly lays down the conditions of entry into the Kingdom.

As there are certain conditions of entry to the Kingdom, so there are certain hindrances to entry into it. *Riches* are a grave hindrance to entry to the Kingdom; it is very hard for a rich man to enter the Kingdom of God (Matt. 19.23f.; Mark 10.23–25; Luke 18.24f.). Riches encourage a false independence in a man, making him feel that he can buy his way into, or buy his way out of, anything. When a man is rich, he has so big a stake in this earth that it is very difficult for him to see beyond it, or to contemplate leaving it. Riches are not a sin, but they are a very grave danger and threat to a man's entry to the Kingdom. *The inability to make a clear-cut decision* is a hindrance to entry to the Kingdom. If a man puts his hand to the plough, and looks back, he is not fit for entry to the Kingdom (Luke 9.61f.). There are things in life which conspire to keep a man out of the Kingdom.

There is a clear *element of judgment* in the Kingdom. The Kingdom involves a separation and a division between men. This is notably shown in the parables of the tares and of the dragnet (Matt. 13.24–30, 37–43, 47–50). Parable after parable involves a judgment on a man based on how he did or did not accept the opportunities and perform the duties of life. *The invitation to enter the Kingdom can be refused,* just as a man may foolishly and discourteously refuse an invitation to be the guest at a feast (Matt. 22.1–14; Luke 14.15–24). *The opportunity to enter the Kingdom can be lost,* just as the foolish bridesmaids lost their opportunity to share in the joy of the wedding festivities (Matt. 25.1–13). *The privilege of entering the Kingdom may be taken away,* as Jesus warned those who had consistently spurned the messengers of God, and those whose reaction to himself was without faith and without love (Matt. 8.11, 21.43; Luke 13.28).

There is no doubt that, even if the Kingdom is given independently of the action of men, a man of his own actions and reactions has much to do with his entry to it, or with his failure to enter it.

Having assembled our material we have now to ask if there is any general principle which emerges from it, and if there is any pattern into which all the varied ideas of the Kingdom can be fitted. We have the paradox that the Kingdom is at once past, present and future. It is something into which the prophets and the patriarchs entered; it is something which is here now within or among men; and it is something for which Jesus taught his disciples still to pray. We have the paradox that the Kingdom is something which is given, and which is the direct result of the personal action of God, and that yet at the same time it is something which is very much dependent on the action and the reaction of men.

The outstanding difficulty which confronts us in any study of the Kingdom is the fact that nowhere in the teaching of Jesus is the Kingdom defined. It is continuously illustrated by parable after parable. Its invitations, its demands, its paramount importance are consistently stressed. The danger and the terrible consequences of failure to enter it are again and again underlined. But no concise definition of it ever appears. Since that is so, we must try to deduce our own definition of it.

In the Lord's Prayer two petitions appear side by side (Matt. 6.10):

> Thy kingdom come,
> Thy will be done, on earth as it is in heaven.

By far the commonest feature of Hebrew style is *parallelism*. The repetition of a statement in a parallel form is a characteristic of

Jewish poetical style. In this repetition the second of the two parallel statements repeats, amplifies or explains the first. Almost any verse of the Psalms will illustrate this method of writing in action.

> The Lord of hosts is with us;
> The God of Jacob is our refuge (Ps. 46.7).

> He makes me lie down in green pastures,
> He leads me beside still waters (Ps. 23.2).

> The earth is the Lord's and the fulness thereof,
> The world and those who dwell therein (Ps. 24.1).

> The Lord is your keeper;
> The Lord is your shade
> On your right hand (Ps. 121.5).

In each case the parallel repeats the first statement in such a way as to amplify or to explain it. Let us again set down the two parallel phrases in the Lord's Prayer:

> Thy kingdom come,
> Thy will be done, on earth as it is in heaven (Matt. 6.10).

Now let us apply the principle of parallelism to these two phrases; let us assume that the second amplifies and explains the first. We then arrive at this definition of the Kingdom: *The Kingdom is a state of things on earth in which God's will is as perfectly done as it is in heaven.* If this definition is accepted, the pattern begins to fall into place.

(i) It is a natural definition of the Kingdom. To be a citizen of any kingdom is to accept and to obey its laws; therefore, to be a citizen of the Kingdom of God must be to accept and to obey the laws of God. If the Kingdom of God means the sovereignty of God, then no man can be within that Kingdom unless he submits himself to the lordship of God in perfect obedience to the will of God.

(ii) This conception of the Kingdom individualizes the Kingdom. Membership of the Kingdom now becomes a matter between each man and God, and involves the personal acceptance by each man of the will of God. The Kingdom becomes not a vague generality but a personal issue between a man and God. To enter the Kingdom means personally to accept the will of God. It must be clearly realized that, although this conception of the Kingdom individualizes the Kingdom, it does not turn the Kingdom into a selfish thing; for to accept the will of God is not only to be in a certain relationship to God, it is very definitely also to be in a certain relationship to men. No man can be oblivious to the claims of his fellow-men upon him and at the same time accept the will of God.

(iii) This conception of the Kingdom explains how the Kingdom can be at one and the same time past, present and future. Any man who in any age and generation accepted the will of God was within the Kingdom. Any man who today accepts the will of God is within the Kingdom. But two things are clear. The world is still very far from a condition in which all men accept the will of God; and the individual man is still not in a condition in which he consistently, constantly and uninterruptedly accepts the will of God. For most men the acceptance of the will of God is still spasmodic. The rebellion of the human heart, the resentment of the human spirit, and the instinctive independence of the human will are still far from being eradicated in us. Therefore, the full consummation of the Kingdom is still in the future, and must still be an object of man's prayers and man's endeavours.

(iv) This conception of the Kingdom enables us to understand the place of Jesus in the Kingdom. Through him the Kingdom had come and was to come. In him the new thing had entered into life and into the world so that the time which followed his coming was different from the time which preceded it. This is true for three reasons.

(*a*) In Jesus the Kingdom was embodied. He alone of all who had ever lived, or ever would live, perfectly and completely fulfilled the will of God. The very essence of his life is obedience to the will of God. At the beginning he met the tempter with a quotation from the word of God, thereby opposing the invitation to take the wrong way by setting over against it the will of God. In the end in Gethsemane he won his final battle before the Cross by saying: 'Thy will be done' (Matt. 26.36–46; Mark 14.32–42; Luke 22.39–46). All through his earthly life he had these times of retirement when he sought for himself the will of God. The Fourth Gospel depicts Jesus as saying: 'My food is to do the will of him who sent me, and to accomplish his work' (John 4.34). The whole picture of Jesus in the Gospels is the picture of one who began, continued and ended his life in complete and chosen obedience to the will of God. That is why it can be said that in and with Jesus the Kingdom came. He was the perfect embodiment and the perfect demonstration of the meaning of the Kingdom.

(*b*) The very fact that he rendered to God this complete obedience meant that through him there were unleashed in the world powers with which no other person could ever have been trusted and which no other person could ever possess. His unique obedience brought to him a unique power. If any ordinary person were to be entrusted with any kind of miraculous power, the certainty is that he would do with it far more damage than good. It was because of Jesus' perfect obedience that he came to possess his special power.

(*c*) Not only does Jesus within his own person demonstrate the Kingdom; he also enables others to enter into it. He removes the barrier between God and men. He cancels the power of past sin and by his Spirit and his presence enables men to overcome present sin. He thereby enables men also to accept and to obey the will of God, and so to enter the Kingdom of God.

It remains only to test out this conception of the Kingdom on typical Gospel passages. When we are bidden to seek the Kingdom (Matt. 6.33; Luke 12.31), it means that we are bidden all through life to make the acceptance of the will of God the object of all our endeavour, and then life will bring all its blessedness to us. When we are bidden to cut away anything that will hinder entry to the Kingdom (Mark 9.43–48), or when the Kingdom is likened to a man who finds some precious thing and sells his all to buy it (Matt. 13.44–46), it means that it is worth any sacrifice to accept and to do the will of God. When the childlike spirit is said to be a necessity of entry to the Kingdom (Matt. 18.3), it means that we must bring to God the obedience which a child owes and brings to his parents. When the forgiving spirit is said to be a condition of entry to the Kingdom (Matt. 18.23–35), and when a certain attitude to men is said to be necessary for entry to the Kingdom (Matt. 25.31–46), it means that we must forgive as God forgives and treat men as God treats men. When it is said that the Kingdom belongs to the poor in spirit (Matt. 5.3), it means that, when a man realizes his own utter helplessness and worthlessness and inadequacy, and submits his ignorance to God's wisdom, his weakness to God's power, his sin to God's mercy, then he enters the Kingdom of God.

To do the will of God and to be in the Kingdom of God are one and the same thing. Because Jesus did that, he is the embodiment of the Kingdom and in him the Kingdom came. Because he enables others to do that, he is the gateway to the Kingdom. Because the world as yet is very far from making this perfect submission to the will of God, the Kingdom has still to come in all its fulness; but in the end the plan and purpose of God will be realized in a state and condition of things in which his will is as perfectly done on earth and among mankind as it is in heaven and in Jesus Christ, for that is the Kingdom.

7

THE POINT OF ATTACK

A leader must not only choose the area in which he will launch his campaign; he must also choose the point within the area at which he will direct his initial attack. The problem which faced Jesus was the problem which faces every man with a message—the problem of communication. Already he had chosen Galilee as the area of his initial campaign. At what point within Galilee was he to make his beginning?

If today a man was convinced that he had a message from God, in what place would he most naturally seek to begin to deliver that message? Quite certainly such a man with such a message would begin in the Church. He would certainly feel that there his message would receive an interested and receptive audience.

In Palestine in the time of Jesus there were two places which correspond to the modern Church. There was the Temple. But the Temple was not the place in which Jesus could begin. In the whole land there was only one Temple, the Temple in Jerusalem. The one reason for the existence of the Temple was the offering of sacrifice. In the Temple there was no preaching and no instruction. There was sacrifice; there was prayer; there was music; and on certain occasions there was the reading of Scripture; but in the ritual and liturgy and services of the Temple there was no place for preaching and instruction, and no opportunity for the delivery of a message from God by word of mouth.

There was the synagogue. The case of the synagogue was quite different. There were synagogues in every town and village; the law was that, wherever there were ten Jewish families, a synagogue must be built. Sacrifice was no part of the synagogue worship. The synagogue was primarily and essentially a teaching institution. The synagogues have been described as 'the popular religious universities

57

of their day'. If a man had a message from God for the people, the synagogue was the place in which to deliver it.

Further, the order of service in the synagogue was such as to give the opportunity desired. The synagogue service consisted of three parts. It began with a time of prayer. It centred in a time for the reading of Scripture in which both the law and the prophets were read, with members of the congregation sharing in the reading. It was for this reading of Scripture that the synagogue really existed. It went on to a time of preaching and teaching. In the synagogue there was no one person to preach the sermon, give the address, or expound the teaching. The ruler or president of the synagogue was neither teacher or preacher; he was an administrative official whose business it was to see that the business of the synagogue was carried out with efficiency and the services with decency and order and reverence. It was the custom that any distinguished person present, anyone with a message, was invited to give his message and to address the congregation. Here, indeed, was the opportunity for any man with a message from God to give it. In every town and village where there were Jews he would find a synagogue, and in the synagogue service he would find an open opportunity to deliver his message.

Here, then, was the place for Jesus to begin. Here, at least at the beginning of his ministry, before he was branded as rebel and heretic, he would find a ready-made congregation and an opportunity to speak to them. So we find him in the synagogue in Capernaum (Mark 1.21). We find him going round Galilee teaching in the synagogues wherever he went (Matt. 4.23; 9.35; 12.9; Mark 1.39; 3.1; Luke 4.15; 4.44; 6.6; 13.10). It always has been, and still was, his custom to go into the synagogue on the Sabbath day (Luke 4.16). It was therefore in the synagogue that Jesus deliberately began to deliver his message.

What, then, was the message which Jesus brought to the congregations of the synagogues up and down Galilee? Luke gives us an account of Jesus' visit to the synagogue at Nazareth (Luke 4.16–30). As we have already seen, in the synagogue the congregation shared in the reading of Scripture. In Nazareth Jesus received the duty of reading the lesson from the prophets. It was from Isa. 61:

The Spirit of the Lord is upon me,
because he has anointed me to preach good news to the poor.
He has sent me to proclaim release to the captives
and recovering of sight to the blind,
to set at liberty those who are oppressed,
to proclaim the acceptable year of the Lord.

Clearly in that passage Jesus saw the picture of himself. 'Today,' he said, 'this scripture has been fulfilled in your hearing' (Luke 4.21). This is the essence of the message of Jesus, and, if that be so, we can at once tell certain things which he must have felt and believed about himself and about his task and about the message which he came to bring to men.

He regarded himself as under obedience and as under orders. He regarded himself as *sent* by God. It was at God's command that he had come, and it was the orders of God that he was carrying out. He was the envoy and apostle of God, as indeed the writer of the Letter to the Hebrews was later to call him (Heb. 3.1).

He regarded himself as equipped with the power of the Spirit. He regarded himself as *empowered* by God. He was who he was, he did what he did, he spoke as he spoke, because the Spirit was on him.

He regarded himself as the *fulfilment* of all that the prophets had said and dreamed. In him the visions of the prophets, the hopes of men, and the promises of God came true. As Paul was later to say: 'All the promises of God find their Yes in him' (II Cor. 1.20). He did not come to destroy the past, but to fulfil the past. He is the one for whom men throughout the centuries have been waiting.

He regarded himself as the messenger of *mercy*. There is a curious deliberate finality in the way in which Luke tells how Jesus read this passage. He read this great promise of the mercy of God, and then *he closed the book* (Luke 4.20). If that is so, then Jesus actually stopped in the middle of a verse as the verses are arranged in the English version of Isaiah. He stopped halfway through Isa. 61.2. And what follows? At what does Jesus stop? He stops at the words 'to proclaim . . . *the day of vengeance of our God.*' That part of the prophecy Jesus did not read. We can only think that he stopped there because he did not regard that as his task; it was mercy, not vengeance, that he come to offer men; it was love, not wrath. He is above and beyond all else the messenger of mercy.

The mercy which Jesus promised and brought was of *the most practical kind*. It was good news for the poor; it was liberty to the captives; it was sight to the blind; it was freedom for the oppressed; it was the mercy and the grace of God for which all had been waiting.

Here is the great characteristic of the message which Jesus brought. It was a promise, and not a threat. It was the offer of the mercy and the grace and the love of God, and not the threat of the wrath and the vengeance and the anger of God. He came above all to bring gifts to men.

Already in Nazareth the shadow of things to come fell across the path of Jesus. So far from welcoming his message, the people of Nazareth resented it. Did they not know his parents? Were his brothers and sisters not still living in the town? Had he not himself been the village carpenter before he left home? What right had he to speak like that? (Matt. 13.55–57; Mark 6.3–6; Luke 4.22–30.) Many motives were to combine to lead to the crucifying of Jesus. At the very beginning he met the simplest and the most human of them all—the inveterate prejudice of his fellow-men against the man who dares to be different and who fails to conform to the conventions of his environment. Men hate to be disturbed, especially by one of themselves.

8

CHOOSING HIS MEN

A leader may map out his campaign with the greatest care; he may choose his sphere of operations, his time and place of attack with the greatest skill and insight; but ultimately he is dependent on his men, and especially on his staff. 'One man,' said Field Marshal Montgomery, 'can lose me a battle.' Unless the leader has men on whom he can rely to accept his orders and to carry out his plans, all his own wisdom and foresight can go for nothing.

Douglas Blatherwick in *A Layman Speaks* tells how in the Champness Hall in Rochdale there was a concert by the Hallé Orchestra under Sir John Barbirolli. The hall was crowded to capacity. As the crowd was leaving the hall a man said to the minister: 'When are you going to have this place full on a Sunday evening?' The minister answered: 'I shall have this place full on a Sunday evening when, like Sir John Barbirolli, I have under me eighty trained and disciplined men.' Anyone leading a campaign must have a staff through whom he can act. And that was true of Jesus. So the time came when Jesus chose the men who were to be his twelve apostles. There were two great reasons why he chose them.

(i) Jesus chose his men *because his work had to go on.* Jesus never had any doubt that for himself there was a cross at the end of the road; he knew that in the end he must die. Already in Nazareth an attempt had been made on his life. There they had hustled him to the hilltop in order to hurl him down, but he had escaped from their hands (Luke 4.29). If his work was to go on, he had to gather round him an inner circle of men whom he could train to know him, to understand him at least in part, and to love him, who would come to know his purpose and his task, and who would carry it on when he had to leave the world in the body. For him his men had to be the living books on which he imprinted his message, the

living instruments through whom his purposes could be carried out.
In modern times, if a man wished to perpetuate his message, he
might write it in a book, and so commit it to posterity, but in the
days of Jesus there was no such thing as a printed book. Robertson
Smith writes of the eastern ideal in those days: 'The ideal of instruction is oral teaching, and the worthiest shrine of truths that must not
die is the memory and heart of the faithful disciple.' Jesus had to
have his own men, if his work was to go on.

(ii) He chose them *because his work must go out.* In his days in
the flesh Jesus was under all the limitations of space and time. His
presence could be in only one place at a time; his voice could reach
only a limited number of people. In that ancient world there were
no means of mass communication, such as print and newspapers and
wireless now provide. If any message had to be taken to men, it had
to be taken to them personally. So Jesus had to have men to go
where he could not go, and to speak where he could not speak.

In his book, *Then and Now,* Dr John Foster tells how an enquirer
from Hinduism came to an Indian bishop seeking baptism. The man
had read the New Testament without help and guidance, entirely
by himself, and he had seen the meaning of it. The picture of Jesus
in the Gospels fascinated him; and the Cross moved him to the
depths of his being.

Then he read on . . . and felt he had entered into a new world. In the
Gospels it was Jesus, his works and his suffering. In the Acts . . . what
the disciples did and thought and taught had taken the place that Christ
had occupied. The Church continued where Jesus left off at his death.
'Therefore,' said this man to me, 'I must belong to the Church that carries
on the life of Christ.'

Jesus needed his men so that through them his work might go
on and might go out. They were to be in a very real sense his body,
so that in them and through them he might continue his work and
extend it in time to all men.

There are three accounts of the choosing of the twelve—Mark
3.13–19; Matt. 10.1–4; Luke 6.13–16. Each of these accounts has
its own contribution to make to our understanding of the purpose
of Jesus in choosing the twelve.

(i) Jesus offered the twelve an *invitation.* As Mark has it: 'He *called* to him those whom he desired' (Mark 3.13). As Luke has it: 'He *called* his disciples' (Luke 6.13). The word for 'to call' is different in the two Gospels. In Mark it is *proskaleisthai,* which means rather 'to invite', and in Luke it is *prosphōnein,* which means rather 'to summon'. So, then, Jesus began with two things. He began with an *invitation.* An invitation is something which can be accepted or refused at the decision of him who receives it. It was volunteers, not conscripts, whom Jesus sought as his men. He began with a *challenge.* Jesus invited men neither to ease or to safety; he invited them neither to honour or to prestige; he invited them neither to financial gain or material advancement. There was little to be gained by attaching themselves to a penniless Galilaean wanderer, who was clearly on the way to a head-on clash with the religious authorities of the day. It was a challenge to leave all, to take up a cross, and to follow him. Jesus always challenged, and never bribed, men into allegiance to himself.

(ii) The invitation was in fact a *selection.* 'Jesus called his disciples, and chose from them twelve' (Luke 6.13). The word is *eklegesthai,* and it implies deliberate choice and selection. As John was later to put it, Jesus was in effect saying: 'You did not choose me, but I chose you' (John 15.19). Out of the crowds who were loosely attached to him these men were chosen to be indissolubly bound to him, to be his staff, his shock troops, his righthand men.

(iii) The invitation and the selection were in fact *an appointment* to a task and office. 'He appointed (*poiein*) twelve' (Mark 3.14). This was a setting apart for special service, an appointment for a special place in the plan and the purpose of God.

(iv) The invitation and selection were for certain great purposes. Jesus chose his men that *they should be with him* (Mark 3.14). They were to be with him for two reasons. They were to be with him *for his own sake.* Jesus, too, needed friends. 'A friend,' said Aristotle in a great phrase, 'is another self.' Jesus needed those to whom he could open his heart and reveal his mind. A man can bear many things in life, but the hardest of all things to bear is loneliness; a man can dispense with many things in life, but he cannot dispense with friendship. 'No longer,' Jesus was to say, 'do I call you servants . . . but I have called you friends' (John 15.15). It may well be said that the greatest of all Christian titles is 'the friend of Jesus'.

They were to be with him *for their sakes*. It is the simple and the obvious truth that no man can bring Jesus to others until he knows him himself. The Christian life must always be a two-way process, a coming in to Jesus and a going out to men. The Christian must live constantly *with* Christ, if he is to live *for* Christ among men.

(v) The object of this companying with Jesus can best of all be seen in one of the great names of the Christian—the name *disciple*. The *disciple* is in Greek the *mathētēs*, the learner. Confronted with the unsearchable riches of Christ (Eph. 3.8), the Christian must always be learning more and more about his Lord and about the way of Jesus. One of the greatest threats to a real Christian life is what might be called static Christianity. The great fact of sanctification must never be forgotten. In Greek sanctification is *hagiasmos*; Greek nouns which end in *-asmos* regularly denote and describe a process, and *hagiasmos*, sanctification, is *the road to holiness*. The Christian is the disciple, the learner, penetrating ever more deeply into the wonder of Jesus, because he lives with him.

(vi) But the object of this companying with Jesus is seen just as much in another great title for the twelve; they were the *apostles*. The word apostle means 'one who is sent out'. The kindred word *apostolē* can mean a naval squadron, and the word itself can mean an ambassador. 'He appointed twelve to be with him, and *to be sent out* to preach' (Mark 3.14). Both Matthew and Luke actually call the twelve the apostles (Matt. 10.2; Luke 6.13). The twelve were called to be with Christ that they might be sent out to be his heralds, his envoys and his ambassadors to men.

(vii) They were sent out with two main functions. They were sent out *to preach* and *to heal* (Mark 3.14f.; Matt. 10.7f.). The normal New Testament word for 'to preach' is *kērussein*, which is the verb of the noun *kērux*, which means 'a herald'. The twelve were to be the heralds of the King, bringing to men the announcement of the arrival of the King, and the proclamation of the message of the King. In their healing they were to bring to men, not a theoretical exposition, but a practical demonstration of the love of God.

Jesus described the work of his men in a special phrase, and he gave them a special title. He said that he would make them *fishers of men* (Matt. 4.19; Mark 1.17; Luke 5.10). In point of fact many of them were fishermen by trade, and this title is a one-word summary of the kind of men which they must be, and the way in which they must approach their work.

(i) The very circumstances of a fisherman's life and work compel him to live close to God. Any man who day by day faces the elemental forces of nature and their threats is bound to be aware of God. It is a common saying that there are no atheists among sailors. The very fact that their life was on the waters, amidst the storms and the waves, made them aware of God. Jesus chose to be his men those for whom God was already a very present reality.

(ii) They were necessarily men of courage. The seaman, perhaps more than any other man, constantly takes his life in his hands. The seaman prayed to whatever gods there be for protection: 'My boat is so small and the sea is so large.' Dr Johnson in one of his sweeping statements once said: 'No man will be a sailor who has contrivance enough to get himself into a jail; for being in a ship is being in a jail, with the chance of being drowned.' The twelve were men to whom taking a risk was part of the day's work. They were men to whom launching out into the deep was a daily experience.

(iii) They were necessarily men of patience and perseverance. There must be a certain undiscourageability about the man who will be a fisherman. Often he will have to wait long; often all his toil will be for nothing, and he will have to come home empty-handed, prepared to start all over again. The fisherman is already a man who has learned to work and to wait and to go on in face of apparent failure.

(iv) They were necessarily men of judgment. The fisherman must wisely choose his time, his place, his net, his bait. That too is the problem of the fisher of men. He must be wise enough to choose his time of approach, his method of approach, his way of presenting the offer of Christ to fit each individual case, or he may well lose more men than he will win.

Jesus chose his staff with wisdom. He chose men who had learned the lessons of life not in an academy or in a seminary but in the business of living. He chose men whom life had already moulded for his purposes. He chose them, first to be with him, then to be sent out as his ambassadors to men.

9

THE MIRACLES OF JESUS

We have already listened to Jesus' opening manifesto in the synagogue in Nazareth (Luke 4.18):

> The Spirit of the Lord is upon me,
> because he has anointed me to preach good news to the poor.
> He has sent me to proclaim release to the captives
> and recovering of sight to the blind,
> to set at liberty those who are oppressed,
> to proclaim the acceptable year of the Lord.

Therein there is outlined a programme of the most practical help, and the determination to accept the task of alleviating the sufferings and the sorrows of men. By that proclamation Jesus was committed to a life, not of words, but of actions. It is clear that he will go out on a campaign in which he will teach as much, and more, by his deeds as by his words.

No one can read the Gospels without being brought face to face with the miracles of Jesus. The miracles are not extras which may be excised and deleted from the story without injuring its structure and its framework. If we remove the stories of the miracles the whole framework of the Gospel story falls to pieces, and often even the teaching of Jesus is left without an occasion and a context. In the first chapter of Mark there are no fewer than six references to healing. In the synagogue in Capernaum Jesus healed the man with the unclean spirit (Mark 1.23). In the fisherman's cottage he healed Peter's wife's mother (Mark 1.31). In the open air he healed the crowds who came to him at evening time (Mark 1.32–34). He cast out devils from those who were demon-possessed (Mark 1.39). He healed a leper (Mark 1.40–44). The chapter ends with crowds flocking to him for the help and the healing which they were convinced that he could give to them (1.45). Mark opens his story with the picture of Jesus the healer of men.

When we read the Gospel narrative, we come from it with the impression that time and time again Jesus was the centre of a crowd of people eagerly clamouring for healing, and that he was able and willing to heal them all. Again and again we come on passages like this: 'They brought him all the sick, those afflicted with various diseases and pains, demoniacs, epileptics, and paralytics, and he healed them' (Matt. 4.24; cf. Matt. 8.16; 12.15; 14.14; 15.30f.; 19.2; Mark 1.34; 3.10; Luke 4.40; 6.18; 7.21). 'He healed them all' runs like an ever-recurring theme or chorus throughout the gospel narrative.

Very early Matthew lays down what may be called the pattern of the ministry of Jesus: 'He went about all Galilee, teaching in their synagogues and preaching the gospel of the kingdom and healing every disease and every infirmity among the people' (Matt. 4.23; cf. 9.35). Preaching, teaching, healing—that was the threefold pattern of the ministry of Jesus. It was a precisely similar scheme of activity that he laid down for his men when he sent them out on their mission for himself and for the Kingdom. He gave them power over unclean spirits and to heal every disease and infirmity; he sent them out to preach that the Kingdom was at hand, and to heal the sick, to raise the dead, to cleanse the lepers and to cast out demons (Matt. 10.1,7f.; Mark 6.13; Luke 9.1,6; 10.9). Healing was an inseparable part of the pattern of his work and of the pattern of the work of his apostles.

It was in fact over this very question of healing that there came his head-on clash with the orthodox religious authorities of his day. It was because he healed on the Sabbath day, and thereby broke the Pharisaic Sabbath law, that he was branded as a dangerous and heretical law-breaker, and as one who must be eliminated as quickly as possible. He clashed with the Pharisees over the healing on the Sabbath of the man with the withered hand (Matt. 12.9–14; Mark 3.1–6; Luke 6.6–11), the woman bent for eighteen years with her infirmity (Luke 13.10–17), the man with the dropsy (Luke 14.1–6). It would be impossible to remove Jesus' ministry of healing and to make sense of his whole career.

When we try to understand the miracles of Jesus, we are met with an initial difficulty, the difficulty of defining a miracle. That which would be a miracle in one age or in one society is a commonplace in another. Even fifty years ago people would have regarded it as a miracle to be able to sit in a room and look into a glass-fronted box and see plays being acted, games being played, events happening hundreds and even thousands of miles away. A Viking would have regarded an 80,000-ton ship speeding across the Atlantic as a miracle. A Roman charioteer would have regarded as a miracle a machine which can move through the air faster than sound can travel. Hippocrates or Galen or any other ancient physician would have regarded modern anaesthetics or modern surgical operations on the heart or lungs as a miracle. Julius Caesar or Hannibal, Napoleon or Wellington, would have regarded as a miracle—even if a devilish one—the devastation which one single atom bomb can cause.

We may put this in another way. The conception of *the possible* does not stay steady; it varies from age to age. Everyday we perform as a matter of course actions which previous generations would have regarded as fantastically impossible. We make a railway journey of four hundred and fifty miles at an average speed of sixty miles an hour. We reach a great city, effortlessly move down into the bowels of the earth on a moving staircase, travel through a man-made tunnel, and reach our destination by another moving staircase. We enter an hotel and are whisked up to the sixth floor in an elevator. We shave with an electric razor. We pick up a little instrument and carry on a conversation with some one hundreds of miles away as clearly as if he were in the same room. What would have been an impossibility in one century is a routine action in the next; and what would have been a miracle in one age of history is a commonplace in another. A vivid illustration of this is the simple fact that in the ancient world very few people had ever tasted fresh fish; Epicurus lists it as a luxurious and extravagant delicacy. It was impossible to transport it for any distance and to keep it fresh in transit. And now fish is a staple item of diet.

To define a miracle as something which is impossible is a quite inadequate definition, for who is to define the possible and the impossible in any way which is not relative to his own position in time and in progress?

If we are to understand the miracles of Jesus at all, we must see them against the mental and spiritual climate of the age in which they happened. Since that is so, certain facts about the age of the New Testament have to be taken into account.

That age had a completely different attitude to the miraculous. Modern man is suspicious of the miraculous; he dislikes anything that he cannot explain; and he thinks that he knows so much about the universe and its working that he can say roundly that miracles do not happen. The last thing which he expects is a miracle. On the other hand, the ancient world revelled in the miraculous. It looked for miracles; it expected miracles; and the result was that apparently miraculous events happened. To put it paradoxically and yet truly, the miraculous was a commonplace.

Tacitus and Suetonius are reputable historians, and both are essential sources for the history of the Roman Empire. Both relate an incident from the life of the Roman Emperor Vespasian. In Alexandria there came to Vespasian a man who was blind and who besought him to cure him by touching his eyes with his spittle, and a man who had a diseased hand, who besought him to heal it by touching it with the sole of his foot. At first Vespasian refused to grant the requests, for he had no belief that any cure would follow. Finally he was persuaded. 'He put on a smiling face, and amid an eagerly expectant crowd did what had been asked of him. The hand immediately recovered its power. The blind man saw once again. Both facts are attested to this day, when falsehood can bring no reward, by those who were present on the occasion.'[1] There is every reason to believe that these cures happened, and that they were not uncommon in the ancient world.

In the ancient world the god of healing was Aesculapius. The two great centres of his worship were Rome and Epidaurus. Epidaurus has been called the Lourdes of the ancient world. Sufferers came to these temples, and spent the night there in the darkness. The emblem of Aesculapius is the snake. Accordingly, tame and harmless snakes were let loose in the dormitories; when they touched the

[1] Tacitus, *Histories* 4.81; Suetonius, *Vespasian* 7.

people lying there, the people thought that it was the touch of the god, and they were healed.

There was a passage-way at Epidaurus which was covered with tablets erected by those who had undergone cures. There is a tablet erected by a certain Alketas. 'Though blind he saw the dream vision; the god seemed to come to him and to open his eyes with his fingers, and the first thing he saw was the trees which were in the temple. At daybreak he went away cured.' In the ruins of the temple of Aesculapius at Rome there are many such tablets. There was a certain Julianus who 'was spitting blood and who was given up as hopeless by everyone'. The god sent him a dream oracle. He was to take grains of corn from the altar and for three days he was to eat them with honey. This he did, 'and he was cured, and came and returned thanks publicly before the people.'

One thing is certain. No one goes to the trouble and expense of erecting a marble tablet to commemorate a cure that did not happen. These things happened in the temples of the ancient gods.

We may call it superstition; we may call it a kind of primitive religion; we may call it a childlike faith. The fact is that these people lived in an age which expected miracles. There is a kind of rationalism which kills wonder. When wonder is dead, wonderful things cease to happen. We might well receive more miracles, if we stopped insisting that miracles do not happen, and began expecting them to happen.

This expectancy in the ancient world came from its conviction of the universal nearness of the divine power. Men believed that the world was full of *daimons,* spirits who were intermediaries between the gods and men. Every person, every association of persons, every place had its *daimon.* Samuel Dill describes the mind and soul of that age in *Roman Society from Nero to Marcus Aurelius.* 'With gods in every grove and fountain, and on every mountain summit, with gods breathing in the winds and flashing in the lightning, or the ray of sun and star, heaving in the earthquake or the November storm in the Aegean, watching over every society of men congregated for any purpose, guarding the solitary hunter or traveller in the Alps or the Sahara, what is called miracle became as natural to the heathen as the rising of the sun. In fact, if the gods had not displayed their power in some startling way, their worshippers would have been shocked and forlorn. But the gods did not fail their votaries. Unquestioning and imperious faith of this kind is always rewarded, or can always explain its disappointments . . . The divine power was everywhere, and miracle was in the air.'

The tendency of modern man is to forget God unconsciously or to eliminate him deliberately, to live in a universe in which he never thinks of God. In the ancient world men lived in a universe where they never forgot the mysterious presence of divinity. Their awareness may have been more closely kin to superstition than to religion, but none the less things happened, because men would have been surprised if they did not happen. Men were open to wonder in a way that is not true of men today.

This belief in the intermingling and the interpenetration of the human and the divine showed itself in another feature of life in the ancient world; it showed itself in the belief in demon-possession. As we can see from the Gospel narratives, demon-possession was a very common phenomenon in the ancient world. Men believed that the air and atmosphere were crowded with demons, most of them malignant spirits waiting to work men harm. They believed that the air was so full of them that it was impossible to insert the point of a needle into the air without touching one. Some said that there were seven and a half million of them; some said that there were ten thousand on a man's right hand and ten thousand on his left. 'The whole world and the circumambient atmosphere,' as Harnack put it, 'were filled with devils.'

Various explanations were given of the existence of these demons. Some said that they had been there in the world since the beginning of time, always waiting to work men harm. Some said that they were the spirits of malignant people who had died, and whose spirits were still going on with their evil and malevolent work. The most common explanation was that they were the offspring and the descendants of the wicked angels, who in the old story descended from heaven and seduced mortal women (Gen. 6.1–8).

It was believed that they could eat and drink, and that they could beget children, and so propagate their own evil line. They lived in unclean places, such as tombs. They inhabited places like deserts where there was no cleansing water. In the lonely places their howling could be heard, and we still speak of *a howling desert*. They were specially dangerous in the midday heat, and between sunset and sunrise. They specially attacked women in childbirth, the newly-married bride and bridegroom, children who were out after dark, and travellers by night. After dark no one would greet anyone else on the road, lest the greeting be given to a demon. The male demons were known as *shedim* and the female ones, who had long hair, as *lilin* after Lilith. The female demons were specially dangerous to children, and that is why children have their guardian angels (Matt. 18.10).

These demons sought an entry into a man's body. Their commonest way of gaining an entry into a man was to hover around him while he ate and to settle on his food, and so to get inside him. All illness was ascribed to these demons. They entered into a man and seduced him into falling to temptation. They were responsible for mental illness, for madness and for insanity. They were equally responsible for physical illness. The Egyptians believed that there were thirty-six different parts of the human body, and that any of them could be invaded and inhabited by a demon. There were demons of blindness, of deafness, of leprosy, of heart disease, and of every kind of illness and trouble.

The strength of this belief may be seen in a practice cited by A. Rendle Short in his book *The Bible and Modern Medicine*. In many ancient burying-places skulls have been found which have been trepanned, that is to say, skulls which have a small hole bored through them. Clearly in a time when there were no anaesthetics and no real surgical instruments the making of such a hole must have been a very formidable operation. The hole is too small to be of any practical use. The proof that the hole was bored in the lifetime of the person involved is that there is often fresh bone formation round the edges of the hole. The purpose of the trepanning was to release the demon within the man through the hole. The fact that ancient man would submit to such an operation and that ancient doctors would carry it out is proof of how real and intense the belief in demons was in the ancient world. The Ebers Papyrus, discovered in Egypt in 1862, and dating back to 1550 BC, is one of the most ancient medical documents in the world. It has one hundred and eight sections of treatments and prescriptions for all diseases, amongst which there is a prayer to Isis that the patient may be delivered from 'demoniacal and deadly disease'. The treatment of demon-possession was even part of the medical textbooks in the ancient world.

This universal belief in demons had two results. First, if a man was convinced that he was possessed by a demon, that there was a demon settled in any part of his body, then inevitably the physical symptoms of illness would follow, for the belief of the mind always affects the health of the body. The belief and the conviction that he was occupied and possessed by a demon would quite easily make a man's mind mad or paralyse his body. In the ancient world a very great deal of illness was not physical and functional but mental and psychological, and was produced by the belief in the sufferer's mind that he was in the power of some demon. Second, if the belief that he was occupied and possessed by a demon was exorcised from the mind of such a person, then the physical symptoms would depart with the departure of the belief. So long as the man believed that he was possessed by a demon, nothing would cure him, and no treatment would be of any use. But, if his mind was liberated from the belief that he was in the power of a demon, his body and his mind would also at once be liberated from all their pains and their distress. Hence exorcism was a common practice in the ancient world. The belief in demon-possession produced illness, but it also made illness dramatically curable, if the patient could be liberated from the belief.

Two questions will immediately arise. First, is there any such thing as demon-possession? Is demon-possession a reality, or is it a complete delusion? There are those who are not so willing to dismiss demon-possession as nothing but an ancient superstition as once most people were. There are, for instance, types of epilepsy in which there is no morbid pathology of any kind; that is to say, there is no discernible physical reason either in the body or in the brain for the illness; and there are those who wonder if it may not be that there is such a thing as demon-possession after all. But the fact is that, in thinking about the miracles of Jesus, the reality or otherwise of demon-possession is really irrelevant. The one quite certain fact is that the sufferer himself was completely convinced that he was so possessed. Delusion it might be, nevertheless his belief in it was so complete and absolute that it produced all the symptoms and consequences of physical or mental illness. Demon-possession was an unquestionable reality for the man who believed himself to be suffering from it.

Second, did Jesus believe in demon-possession? To that question there are two answers. It is not in the least likely that the medical and scientific knowledge of Jesus was in any way in advance of his age; all the likelihood is that Jesus did so believe. Further, even if Jesus did not believe in demon-possession, even if he knew that it was a superstitious delusion, it was absolutely necessary for him to assume the patient's belief before he could effect a cure. It would have been pointless for Jesus to tell the sufferer that all his suffering was pure imagination, that the whole condition was a complete delusion, that the madness and the pain and the paralysis were quite unreal. For the patient they *were* real; and Jesus had to assume their reality in order to cure them, even if he himself did not believe in it.

The consequence of all this is that there is not the slightest difficulty for any modern man in believing in any of the miracles which involve the exorcism of demons. The missionary in primitive civilisations is still exorcising demons today. In almost every home we have seen an analogy to this. Illness comes; there is anxiety and alarm; the patient is afraid; those who have no medical knowledge are filled with fear and foreboding as they watch him and try to alleviate his distress. The doctor is sent for. If, as so often happens, the doctor is trusted and respected and even loved not only as physician but as family friend, then the moment the doctor enters the room a new calm comes with him. The fear subsides; the taut nerves relax; confidence returns; the man who can handle things has come. If that can happen with a man, how much more would it happen in the calm, strong presence of Jesus? Jesus' power over the mind of the demon-possessed is something which it is easy to understand. We may well believe that belief in demon-possession is no more than a delusion; we must believe that the symptoms it produced were absolutely real; we have no difficulty in believing that Jesus could restore a demon-possessed man or woman to health of mind and health of body.

Still another factor in the ancient situation was the belief that sin and suffering were indissolubly linked together. It was the firm belief of the Jews that there could be no suffering without some sin to account for it, and that there could be no sin without some suffering to follow from it. When Job was ill and tortured and agonized, his friend Eliphaz said bluntly and accusingly to him: 'Think now, who that was innocent ever perished?' (Job 4.7). This was a basic rabbinic principle, and in his commentary on the Synoptic Gospels C. G. Montefiore cites sayings of the rabbis which illustrate this. Rabbi Ammi said: 'There is no death without guilt, no suffering without sin.' Rabbi Alexandrai said: 'No man gets up from his sickness till God has forgiven all his sins.' Rabbi Hija ben Abba said: 'No sick person is cured from his sickness until all his sins are forgiven.'

There is a sense in which we might well agree with this. The suffering of the world is due to the sin of the world. But we would not make the linkage in the individual human life. We would not say that in every case the individual's suffering is due to the individual's sin. The children often suffer tragically for the sins of the fathers. No man is an isolated unit; we are all bound up together in the bundle of life; every man is involved in the human situation; and again and again his suffering is not due to his own sin but to the sin in which all mankind are involved.

But the Jews rigidly believed this. It is easy to see what could happen, especially in the case of a sensitive person with a tendency towards a kind of morbid self-examination. Such a man might sin; the memory of his sin, the consciousness of his sin, remorse for his sin might take complete possession of him, until it became nothing short of an obsession. He would well know the orthodox connection between sin and suffering. And it would almost inevitably happen that he would think himself, will himself, believe himself into serious illness in which distress would lodge in his mind and pain or paralysis within his body.

To cure such a man, the first thing essential would be to assure him of the forgiveness of his sins. Until he had that assurance, nothing would remove his physical or mental illness; once he had that assurance his mental or physical symptoms would vanish like the night before the dawn. That is precisely why Jesus began one of his most notable miracles by saying to the sufferer: 'My son, your sins are forgiven' (Mark 2.1–12; Matt. 9.1–8; Luke 5.18–26). The assurance of forgiveness was the one thing necessary to shatter the self-imposed bonds of pain which the conscience of the sufferer had imposed upon himself.

In this approach to the sufferer Jesus was entirely at one with modern medicine. Paul Tournier in *A Doctor's Case Book* quotes an illustration of this kind of thing from his own experience. One of his friends had as a patient a girl suffering from anaemia. No treatment had any success. He sent her to the medical officer of the district with a view to having her accepted as a patient in a mountain sanatorium. The medical officer granted the application, but he wrote to the doctor: 'On analysing the blood, however, I do not arrive at anything like the figures you quote.' The doctor did not doubt his own analysis; but he took a fresh sample of the blood, tested it in his own laboratory, and found to his astonishment that the blood count had completely changed. He knew that he had made no mistake in either this or his former tests. Why the change? He sent for the girl. 'Has anything out of the ordinary happened in your life,' he asked, 'since your last visit?' 'Yes, something has happened,' she replied. 'I have suddenly been able to forgive some one against whom I bore a nasty grudge; and all at once I felt as if I could at last say "Yes" to life!' Her mental attitude had changed her whole bodily condition. The removal of the resentment and the consequent removal of the subconscious feeling of guilt had changed the whole matter. The girl was now at peace with God and at peace with her fellow-human-beings—and health came back.

In any situation in which the idea of sin and the idea of suffering have become intertwined and dependent on each other, it is the sense of guilt which brings the illness, whether the illness be physical or mental; and, if the sense of guilt is removed, if the assurance of forgiveness is received, then the illness will disappear. It is easy to understand how Jesus was able to restore people to health and strength of body and of mind by assuring them of the forgiveness of sins.

It is of interest to note that a well-known psychiatrist has said that he seldom has Roman Catholics amongst his patients. Even if we admit that a Roman Catholic would sooner go to a priest than to a psychiatrist, the fact remains suggestive. The psychiatrist attributed this to the fact that the Roman Catholic is in the habit of confessing his sins and of then receiving absolution for them; and he suggested that the Protestant churches should not only condemn sin, should not only urge the confession of sin in prayer, but should also in no uncertain voice proclaim the fact that in Jesus Christ we *are* forgiven. If the prayer of confession ended with the proclamation of forgiveness, it might well relax the tension in many a mind and body distressed by the consciousness of sin.

When we are thinking of the stories of the miracles of Jesus, we must take into account still another characteristic of the Hebrew mind. The Hebrew seldom or never thought of things, or explained events, in terms of what we would call secondary causes. We would say that certain atmospheric conditions caused the thunder, the lightning or the rain; the Hebrew would simply say that God sent the thunder, the lightning or the rain. We would say that certain weather conditions caused the failure of crops. The Hebrew would say that God sent blasting and mildew and caused a famine. We would say that certain unhygienic practices and certain unsanitary conditions caused an epidemic of illness in a place. The Hebrew would say that God had sent a plague upon the people. We habitually ascribe events and conditions to secondary causes; the Hebrew just as habitually ascribed them to God.

It so happens that there is a piece of Hebrew history which is described from three different points of view by three different historians from three different countries. Few events in ancient history made such an impression on men's minds as the disastrous withdrawal of Sennacherib from his attack on Palestine and on Jerusalem. The Old Testament historian describes that event: 'And that night the angel of the Lord went forth, and slew an hundred and eighty-five thousand in the camp of the Assyrians, and when men arose early in the morning, behold these were all dead bodies. Then Sennacherib king of Assyria departed, and went home, and dwelt at Nineveh' (II Kings 19.35f.).

The Greek historian Herodotus[1] hands down the Egyptian version of the same story. The people were in terror. Sethos the priest prayed for deliverance. The god told the people not to fear and

[1] Herodotus 2.141.

said: 'Myself will send you a champion.' So, the story goes on, one night a multitude of fieldmice swarmed over the Assyrian encampment, and devoured their quivers and their bowstrings and the handles of their spears, and the enemy fled unarmed, and many perished. So, Herodotus goes on to say, to this day in the Temple of Hephaestus in Egypt there is a statue of the Egyptian king with a mouse in his hand with the words: 'Look on me and fear the gods.'

The third account of the same incident is in the work of Berosus, a Chaldaean historian, and it is handed down to us by Josephus.[1] He says quite simply that 'a pestilential distemper' came upon the army of the Assyrian king. The king was in great dread and terrible agony at this calamity, and in his fear he fled back to his own kingdom with his surviving forces.

Here, then, are the three accounts. The Hebrew account says that the angel of the Lord caused the destruction; the Egyptian account says that mice caused it; the Chaldaean account says that a terrible pestilence caused it. Which is right? All three are right. Rats and mice are notorious carriers of plague, especially of bubonic plague. What happened was that a terrible outbreak of plague fell upon the Assyrian armies, and they were forced all unexpectedly back to their own country. The Egyptian and the Chaldaean historians had some idea of secondary causes; the Hebrew historian described the event as the direct action of God.

It is quite clear that anyone who thought as the Hebrews thought would see God's hand in all kinds of events for which others would find a natural explanation. The Hebrew would not, for instance, ascribe the cure of a disease or an illness to a physician or a surgeon, but direct to God. And who shall say that the Hebrew was wrong, for did not a great doctor say, 'I only bandage men's wounds—God heals them'? It is clear that there is far more room for the conception of the miraculous in a world such as the Hebrew believed in than in the kind of world in which we believe. A miracle has been described as 'the will of God expressed in natural events'. It may be that the Hebrew was more right than we think, and that there are more miracles in this world than our earthbound philosophy recognizes.

[1] *Antiquities* 10.1.5.

In seeking to understand the miracles of Jesus there is one other factor which we must take into account. It must be obvious that we cannot see anything as some one else sees it, unless we see it from his standpoint and from his viewpoint. With the single exception of Luke all the New Testament writers were Jews; they, therefore, saw events through Jewish eyes. If, then, we try to interpret their writings in terms of modern Western thought we are bound to distort it. We must, as far as we can, think ourselves back to their position. When we do that, we come upon one consistent principle of Jewish writing and teaching. No Jewish teacher would ask of any story: 'Did this literally happen?' He would ask: 'What does this teach?' C. J. Ball sums up the rabbinic method of teaching and of interpretation:

We have to bear in mind a fact familiar enough to students of Talmudic and Midrashic literature . . . the inveterate tendency of Jewish teachers to convey their doctrine, not in the form of abstract discourse, but in a mode appealing directly to the imagination, and seeking to arouse the interest and sympathy of the man rather than the philosopher. The Rabbi embodies his lesson in a story, whether parable or allegory or seeming historical narrative; and the last thing he or his disciples would think of is to ask whether the selected persons, events and circumstances which so vividly suggest the doctrine are in themselves real or fictitious. The doctrine is everything; the mode of presentation has no independent value. To make the story the first consideration, and the doctrine it was intended to convey an afterthought as we, with our dry Western literalness, are predisposed to do, is to reverse the Jewish order of thinking, and to do unconscious injustice to the authors of many edifying narratives of antiquity.[1]

This is to say that Jewish teachers were more concerned with truth than with fact. They are not interested in the momentary historical events of any story; they are interested only in the eternal truth which the story is designed to illuminate and to convey.

We are not entirely unfamiliar with this way of thinking. When we read the *Pilgrim's Progress* we do not ask whether these persons literally lived, or whether the events happened at a given time in a given place in the world of space and time; we ask what is the

[1] Introduction to the Song of the Three Children, *Speaker's Commentary, Apocrypha*, Vol. II, p. 307.

eternal truth that this story is seeking to convey to us about God and man.

We must seek to read the miracle stories of the Gospels with the same eyes as those who wrote them. We must not apply to them the same standards as we would apply to the narrative of a modern Western historian or of a newspaper report. Unless we understand why and how they were written, we shall not understand what they were designed to teach us, and we shall often lose the precious kernel through over-concern for the husk.

The Greek words which are used for the miracles of Jesus are in themselves expressive of the character and the nature of the miracles. Three words are used for the miracles in the New Testament.

The miracles are called *dunameis,* which means 'works of power' (Matt. 11.20-23; 13.54,58; Mark 6.2,5; Luke 10.13; 19.37). It is said of Jesus that the power (*dunamis*) of the Lord was with him to heal (Luke 5.17). It is said that power (*dunamis*) came forth from him, and he healed them all (Luke 6.19). And this was a power of which Jesus was conscious, for, when he was touched in the crowd by the woman with the issue of blood, he was conscious that power had gone out of him (Mark 5.30; Luke 8.46). From this word we learn that the miracles are the irruption of divine power into the human situation for help and healing.

The word *teras* is used to describe the miracles, but it is never used alone. In the Gospels *teras* is not used at all of the miracles of Jesus, although it is used of the astonishing things that the false Christs would do (Matt. 24.24; Mark 13.22). *Teras* means something which produces wonder and amazement and astonishment. The word *teras* has no kind of moral quality. A conjuring trick could be a *teras,* for a *teras* is only something which produces amazement.

As we have said, *teras* is never used alone to describe the miracles of Jesus; when it is used, it is used along with *sēmeion,* which means 'a sign'. In Acts Jesus' miracles are said to be *signs and wonders* (Acts 2.22), and *signs and wonders* were frequent phenomena in the life of the early Church (Acts 2.43; 4.30; 5.12; 6.8; 14.3; 15.12). The word *sēmeion* is the characteristic word for the miracles of Jesus in the Fourth Gospel, although it is not used in the first three Gospels (John 2.11,23; 3.2; 4.54; 6.2; 7.31; 9.16; 11.47; 12.18; 20.30).

It is the word *sēmeion* which really describes the miracles of Jesus. A *sēmeion* is a sign; it is a significant event; it is an action which reveals the mind and character of the person who performs it; it is an outward action designed to allow him who sees it to see into the inner mind and heart of him who performs it. Above all the miracles were events which revealed the mind and the heart of Jesus, and, through him, the mind and heart of God.

Of what, then, are the miracles of Jesus the sign and the revelation? They are the revelation of two things. They are, as we have already seen, the revelation of *power*. In them we see in action a power which is able to deal with the human situation, a power through which pain and suffering can be defeated, a power through which sin, and the consequences of sin, can be overcome. They are the revelation of *pity*. Again and again it is said of Jesus that he was *moved with compassion,* either for the crowds or for some sufferer (Matt. 9.36; 14.14; 15.32; 20.34; Mark 1.41; 6.34; 8.2; Luke 7.13). The word is *splagchnizesthai,* which is the strongest word in Greek for the experience of pity and compassion. *Splagchna* are the bowels, and the word describes the pity and compassion which move a man to the depths of his being. The miracles, therefore, are the sign of power and pity in the heart of Jesus, and therefore in the heart of God. They are the sign that God cares, and that God can make his care effective. They are the sign that the power of God is used in pity, and that the pity of God is backed by power. In the miracles we see the power and the pity of God combine to deal with the human situation.

Having sketched the background against which the miracles of Jesus happened, and having accepted the basic fact that they are signs of the power and the pity of God, exercised in love for men, we can now go on to look at the miracles themselves. When we do so, we find that the miracles of Jesus fall into four different classes. There may sometimes be doubt and debate into which of these classes any individual miracle falls, but the four classes do cover the miracles.

(i) *There are acts and healings which are beyond our comprehension.* It is inevitable that that should be so. The unique quality of Jesus is his sinlessness. It may well be that *sinlessness* is an inade-

quate term in which to describe Jesus, for the word itself is a negative word rather than a positive one, and might well be interpreted
in terms of refraining from doing things rather than in terms of
positive action. But this remains true—if Jesus was sinless, it means
that in every decision and action of life he knew, accepted and acted
on the will of God; he rendered to God a continuous and a unique
obedience. If that is so, it is quite clear that Jesus could both develop
and be entrusted with powers such as ordinary persons cannot
possess. If an ordinary person were entrusted with the power of
working miracles, it is certain that he would do more harm than
good. He would be bound to use such power in ignorance, and
therefore unwisely. He would be bound to use it in essential human
selfishness, and therefore dangerously. The great problem of the
present human situation, in which men control powers which can
disintegrate the very universe, is in fact that men possess power
which they are neither spiritually nor morally fitted to control. Their
achievement in the world of science has outstripped their growth
in the world of the spirit.

The Greeks told their story of a good and simple man called
Gyges, who lived a kind and an upright and honest life. By chance
he entered into possession of the ring which gave him the power
of being invisible, and he straightway embarked on something very
like a career of crime. He had acquired a power which he was not
fit to use.

The fact that for Jesus there was no other rule of life than the
will of God made it possible for him to receive and to acquire
powers which would have been safe in the hands of no other person.

(ii) *There are miracle stories which must be interpreted in the
light of the vivid Eastern way of putting things, and which are in
fact stories of quite natural happenings told as an Oriental would
tell them.*

The best example of that type of story is the story of the coin
in the fish's mouth (Matt. 17.24–27). The time had come to pay
the Temple tax, which every Jew must pay. The tax was half a
shekel, which was equal to two drachmae, a sum equal to about
one shilling and sixpence. This sum must be evaluated against the
fact that a working man's wage in Palestine was about eight-pence
per day. For a Palestinian peasant half a shekel was a considerable

sum. So, as the story runs, Jesus said to Peter: 'Go and catch a fish. In the fish's mouth you will find a piece of money enough to pay our joint tax. Take it, and go and pay the Temple tax for yourself and for me.'

If we insist on taking that story literally, we are confronted with a series of difficulties. First, the whole event is a *teras;* it is simply an amazing and astonishing happening with no moral significance whatever. Second, it represents Jesus as doing what he never did, what he in fact absolutely refused to do, what in fact he rejected once and for all at the time of his temptations; it represents him as using his power for his own benefit and for his own convenience. If this story is to be taken literally, it is the one and only occasion on which Jesus used his power to profit himself. Third, if the story is taken literally, it tells of a very easy way out of a practical difficulty. Life would be very much easier, if we could pay our just and legitimate debts by finding coins in fishes' mouths. It would in fact be a quite immoral and unethical way in which to gain money, and would be an incentive to laziness and to shiftlessness. Fourth, if the story is to be taken literally, it has no point at all for us today. It sets us no example and brings us no challenge and establishes no Christian principle. It is simply a wonder story.

What, then, did happen? This we regard as an essential question, for we strongly believe that no miracle story is a baseless invention and fiction, but that every miracle story goes back to some actual event. We must remember the Eastern delight in vivid narration; and we must also remember that Jesus often taught with a smile and with a flash of humour, which clothed the truth in the sunshine of laughter. Surely what Jesus said was something like this: 'Peter, the Temple tax is due. We haven't any money, and we must pay it, for we must fulfil all our lawful obligations. Well, then, away back to the boats for a day! Get out the nets, the lines, the bait! We need the money, and you'll get it in the fishes' mouth!' This is Jesus saying with a wit that made the saying memorable: 'Meet your obligations from your day's work.'

Here there is something which is immediately relevant. If the story is taken literally as telling of the finding of a coin in a fish's mouth, whereby a just debt was paid, then the story has nothing to do with us, for we will never pay our debts that way, nor would it be good for us if we could; but if the story says to us, 'Pay your debts by doing an honest day's work,' then the story speaks to our situation.

It will mean that the shop assistant finds the necessary money for life in the work of the counter on which she serves; that the garage mechanic will find it in the cylinders and the pistons of the car that he is repairing or servicing; that the typist and the author will find pound notes in the keys of the typewriter; that the plumber will find silver in his blowlamp and in his solder; that the wireless engineer will find it amongst his valves and trans-formers and condensers. This story will say to us that Christian diligence and Christian efficiency are the way to pay our debts and to meet the needs of life. Taken with a crude and humourless and uncomprehending literalness, this is only a wonder story with nothing to say to us for life; taken with imagination and insight and an appreciation of the way in which the mind of an Eastern teacher works, this is a story which gives us a recipe for life and living.

(iii) *There are a large number of Jesus' miracles which, at least in principle, it is not difficult to understand; for it is difficult to see why anyone should have any great difficulty in accepting the healing miracles of Jesus.*

In a world in which illness was connected with demon-possession and with the consequences and the results of sin, it is easy to see how the impact of a calm strong personality could break the belief in demons, and how a word of grace and of authority could con-vince of forgiveness, and how health of body and of mind could thus be restored. We ourselves know well the peace and the calm which can come to us in trouble on the arrival of some one whom we respect and trust and love, and whom we know to be able to cope with the situation. We know, and are continually coming to know better, how closely body, mind and spirit are interconnected; we have experienced the power of the impact of an authoritative and beloved personality upon us; and we have no difficulty in understanding how the presence and the power of the personality of Jesus released men from the pains and distress of body and of mind which their own fears and superstitions had brought upon them. There are few things in the Gospel narrative easier to be lieve and to accept than the fact that Jesus healed the bodies and the minds of men.

(iv) *There are certain miracle stories—and they are the most precious and important of all—which are not so much designed to tell us the story of a single incident as to enshrine and to embody an eternal truth.* They are indeed *sēmeia,* signs which enable us to see, not so much what Jesus did, as what Jesus does. And, if it be insisted that such stories be taken with crude and stubborn literalism, then the greater part of their value and meaning is lost. To illustrate this, we shall take the greatest of these stories, the story of the raising of Lazarus (John 11.1–44).

If this story is taken as a literal account of a raising from the dead, we have to ask the question, Why did the other Gospel writers omit it, especially when John implies that it was the moving cause of the Crucifixion (John 11.47–54)? There can be no doubt that this story goes back to some notable event in the life and the ministry of Jesus—but to what?

The story clearly centres round one saying, for the sake of which the story exists: 'I am the resurrection and the life; he who believes in me, though he die, yet shall he live; and he that liveth and believeth in me shall never die' (John 11.25f.). The story is the casket which contains that gem; the story is the presentation of Jesus as the Resurrection and the Life. But nothing can be clearer than that the saying is not *physically and literally true.* 'He who believes in me, though he die, yet shall he live'—but he who believes in Jesus Christ does *not* come back to physical life within this world of space and time. 'Whoever lives and believes in me shall never die'—but death is *not* arrested for the man who believes in Jesus Christ; the hurrying years do not wait for him. Death in the physical and literal sense of the term comes to him as surely as it comes to every man. As Epicurus long ago had it, in regard to death we mortals all live in an unfortified city. Taken physically and literally, that great saying of Jesus is not true. If it be taken physically and literally Jesus is in fact promising something which he cannot and does not perform. But taken spiritually, this saying is blessedly and profoundly and gloriously true. Spiritually the Christian is abundantly armed against all death's endeavours. Spiritually the Christian is gloriously saved from the death of sin and raised to newness of life.

If this saying of Jesus must be taken in a spiritual sense, then it is clear that we must take the whole story in a spiritual sense. Surely what is meant is something like this. Lazarus had committed some terrible sin, a sin which had brought to the home at Bethany a grief like the grief for death, a sin which he would never have committed, if Jesus had been present, a sin which had made his name stink in the nostrils of men, a sin which had broken the hearts of his sisters, a sin which had left him spiritually dead, and even unable to repent. Then comes Jesus—and all is healed and all is changed. Lazarus is raised to life anew. Once again Jesus had shown himself the friend of sinners, to the amazed joy of Martha and Mary and Lazarus, and to the bitter resentment and cold criticism and venomous hatred of the orthodox good people of his day. Surely this is the supreme conversion story of the New Testament.

If we want some parallel to this, we get it in the words of Paul. 'For I through the law am dead to the law, that I might live unto God. I am crucified with Christ' (Gal. 2.19–21). We know that Paul was not *physically* dead; we know very well that he was not *literally* crucified; and we also know that it is gloriously true that out of the frustration and death of sin, he rose through Jesus Christ to the wonder and the glory of new life.

If this story is simply the story of the raising of a dead man in the village of Bethany somewhere about the year AD 28 or 29, then it has nothing to do with us; it cannot and it does not happen now; but if it is the story of the defeat of the death caused by sin, then it is telling of something which Jesus Christ can do, and does, every day in life.

In *The Bible Speaks to You,* Robert McAfee Brown tells how he was chaplain on a troopship on which 1,500 American Marines were returning to America from Japan for discharge. To his surprise and delight a group of them came to him with a request for Bible Study. Towards the end of the trip they were studying John 11. Professor Brown was thinking within himself: 'What are these men making of this, "I am the Resurrection and the Life"? The question is not, "Was a corpse reanimated in AD 30?" but, "Are these words true in AD 1946?"' At the end of the study a young marine came to him. He said something like this: 'Padre, everything in this story we have been studying today points to me.

I've been in hell for the last six months, and since I have heard this chapter I am just getting free.' He went on to explain. He had gone into the Marines straight from college, and had been sent overseas to Japan. He had been bored and had gone out to find amusement and had got into trouble, bad trouble. No one knew about it—*but God knew about it*. He had a terrible feeling of guilt. He felt that his life was ruined. He felt he could never again face his family, even if they never knew the wretched story. 'I've been a dead man,' he said, 'condemned by myself, condemned by my family, if they knew. But, after reading this chapter, I'm alive again.' He went on: 'The Resurrection and the Life that Jesus was talking about is the real thing here and now.' That lad had a hard job to get things put straight again, but he did it, for, when life seemed ended for him, and when he seemed a dead man, Jesus raised him to life anew, out of a life which sin had killed. And that is exactly what this story means.

Let no man think that such an approach to the miracles of Jesus is either negative or destructive. The aim is not to explain away the miracles; the aim is to appropriate the miracles. There is little use in a Jesus who *did* things almost two thousand years ago, but who has ceased to do them now. What we need is a Christ who still *does* things. There is little relevance in the story of a Jesus who raised a dead man to life in Bethany nineteen hundred years ago, but who never does that now; there is every relevance in a Christ who to this day daily raises men from the death of sin and liberates them to life eternal. There is little relevance in a Jesus who stilled a storm on the Sea of Galilee nineteen hundred years ago, and who stills no storms today, for there are those whose loved ones have been taken by the storms in spite of the most intense prayers; there is every relevance in a Christ who stills the storms which rise within the hearts of men today, and in whose presence today every storm becomes a calm within the heart. There is little relevance in a Jesus who turned water into wine nineteen hundred years ago, and who never does so today; there is every relevance in a Jesus in whose presence today there enters into life a new quality of radiance and joy and exhilaration which is like the turning of water into wine.

We believe that when these stories are read in a spirit of crude and unimaginative literalism, they lose almost all their value; we believe that many of them are not meant to describe literal happenings, but are meant to describe spiritual changes and experiences which are still triumphantly happening in the power of the risen Lord. They are presenting eternal truth in a picture, and they tell, not of things which *happened,* but of things which *happen.*

In the miracle stories we see demonstrated the power and the pity of God exercised in love for men, and by many of them we are intended to see, not, for instance, a storm stilled on the Sea of Galilee, but a storm stilled in the hearts of men even in the midst of a terrifying upheaval, the record not of an act of Jesus, but the sign of the continuing action of Christ, not the record of an event to be read about, but the record of an experience offered still to be enjoyed.

10

THE MASTER TEACHER

Even if Jesus had no other claim to be remembered, he would be remembered as one of the world's masters of the technique of teaching. 'Teacher' was a title which even his enemies were prepared to concede to him. When they came to him with a testing question, they began by saying: 'Teacher, we know that you are true, and teach the way of God truthfully' (Matt. 22.16; Mark 12.14; Luke 20.21).

The frequency with which Jesus was called *teacher* is concealed by the fact that the Authorized Version consistently translated the Greek word for teacher by the English word 'master', using 'master' in the sense in which we speak of a 'schoolmaster'. There are three titles applied to Jesus in the Gospels all of which describe him as a teacher. The commonest is *didaskalos,* which is used of him almost forty times. This is the word which the Authorized Version translates 'master'; to read the Gospels in the Revised Standard Version or in the Moffatt translation is to see how often the word 'teacher' is applied to Jesus. Luke uses the word *epistatēs* (Luke 5.5; 8.24,45; 9.33,49; 17.13). This is the word which would be used in secular Greek for a headmaster. Sometimes the Gospel writers retain the word *Rabbi* (Matt. 26.49; Mark 9.5; 10.51; 11.21; 14.45). *Rabbi* literally means 'My great one', and was the standard Jewish title for a distinguished and acknowledged teacher. It would be the word by which Jesus was most commonly addressed, and *didaskalos* and *epistatēs* are both translations into Greek of the title *Rabbi*. When we put the three titles together, and when we remember that they all represent and go back to the word *Rabbi,* the standard word for an accepted teacher, we find that in the narrow space of the Gospel narratives Jesus is called 'teacher' more than fifty times.

The New Testament presents us with the picture of Jesus as the teacher *par excellence*.

In the conditions in which he taught Jesus had certain problems to face, and the way in which he met the challenge of these problems is a demonstration of his greatness as a teacher.

(i) It is true that Jesus began his teaching in the synagogues of Galilee, but before long the opposition and the hatred of the orthodox religious authorities of his day had shut the door of the synagogue against him, and driven him out to the roads, and the hillside, and the seashore. By far the greater part of his teaching was done in the open air. It was field preaching. In the great early days of Methodism John Wesley could write: 'Our societies were formed from those who were wandering upon the dark mountains, that belonged to no Christian Church; but were awakened by the preaching of the Methodists, who had pursued them through the wilderness of this world to the Highways and the Hedges—to the Markets and the Fairs—to the Hills and the Dales—who set up the Standard of the Cross in the Streets and Lanes of the Cities, in the Villages, in the Barns, and Farmers' Kitchens etc.—and all this in such a way, and to such an extent, as never had been done before, since the Apostolic age.' That was a repetition of the preaching of Jesus.

All teaching which is done in the open air demands one outstanding quality—it must be *immediately arresting*. He who preaches in a pulpit, or lectures in a college, or teaches in a schoolroom, has one initial advantage. He has an audience who cannot get up and move away when they wish! But the teacher in the open air has first to persuade men to stop and then to persuade them to stay. His teaching must be immediately arresting, or he will never collect an audience, or, having collected an audience, he will never retain it.

(ii) He who would teach in the open air must have *a universal appeal*. In a church or a class room or a lecture hall the preacher or teacher will have a more or less homogeneous audience; but in the open air the hearers will be of every kind. One of the most amazing characteristics of Jesus as a teacher is the universality of his appeal. We find him teaching in the synagogues (Matt. 4.23; Luke 4.15). We find him teaching in the Temple at Jerusalem (Mark 14.49; Matt. 26.55; Luke 20.1). We find him engaged in technical arguments and discussion with the foremost scholars of his day (Matt. 22.23–46; Mark 12.13–44; Luke 20.19–44). We find him in the streets and on the roads, using a fishing-boat as a pulpit by the seashore, holding the crowds spellbound with his words (Matt. 11.1; Mark 2.13; 4.1; Luke 5.17). We find him teaching the intimate inner circle of the disciples (Matt. 5.1; Mark 8.31), and yet we find that amidst the crowds the common people heard him gladly (Mark 12.37).

This is extraordinary teaching. There is many a teacher who is very effective in the pulpit of a church but quite ineffective with a crowd at the gates of a shipyard or a factory. There is many a man quite at home on the rostrum of a class room but quite unable to make his message intelligible to the ordinary man and woman. There are men whom the crowds will gladly hear but who would be lost in the more rarified atmosphere of the academic world. There have been very few teachers who were equally at home and equally effective with any kind of audience—but Jesus was. As a teacher he had in a unique degree the quality of universal appeal.

(iii) He who would teach and preach to crowds in the open air must have the gift of being *immediately intelligible*. If a man is learning by reading a book, when he comes on a difficult sentence or on an idea or a passage that he does not immediately understand, he can halt and go back over it and linger on it until he has elucidated it and grasped its meaning. But he who is learning by listening cannot do that. If the hearer does not grasp immediately the meaning of what is being said, he loses the thread of the argument; or he begins to puzzle about the difficult sentence and its meaning, and so loses what follows, and cannot catch up again. The man who would teach crowds in the open air must have a limpid lucidity and a transparent simplicity which make it almost impossible to mistake what he is saying. One of the great characteristics of the teaching of Jesus is that, however much men might disagree with it, he never left anyone in any doubt what he was saying and demanding.

(iv) To be arresting, to be universal in appeal, to be immediately intelligible—these are demands made upon any open air preacher to mixed crowds. But Jesus was faced with still another problem. His message had to be *permanently memorable*. Jesus taught in times long before there was any such thing as a printed book, and when handwritten manuscripts were rare and expensive. In modern conditions a teacher may hope that, even if what he is saying is forgotten, it may always be recovered and rediscovered in the printed word. He can always hand to those whom he teaches a permanent record in print of that which he teaches. He can refer, and point his readers, to books which contain and explain what he has been saying. It was not possible for Jesus to do that. He had to teach in such a way that he immediately printed his message permanently and indelibly on the minds of his hearers. That is to say, he had not only to find a message, but he had to find an unforgettable form in which to express his message.

So, then, Jesus had to solve the problem of teaching in such a way that his message was immediately arresting, universally appealing, immediately intelligible and permanently memorable. Let us now see how he solved the problem.

(i) Jesus used *the unforgettable epigram,* the phrase which lodges in the mind and stays there, refusing to be forgotten, even when the mind would willingly forget it.

Whoever exalts himself will be humbled, and whoever humbles himself will be exalted (Matt. 23.12; Luke 18.14).
A man's life does not consist in the abundance of his possessions (Luke 12.15).
No one who puts his hand to the plough and looks back is fit for the kingdom of God (Luke 9.62).
Whoever would save his life will lose it, and whoever loses his life for my sake will find it (Matt. 16.25).
What will it profit a man, if he gains the whole world and forfeits his life? Or what shall a man give in return for his life? (Matt. 16.26).

Such sayings have the gadfly of truth in them. Their supreme quality is that they will not leave a man alone. He cannot forget them. Every now and then they flash unbidden into his mind. Even when he would willingly forget them, they flash across the screen of his memory and leave him thinking and wondering. Often Jesus taught in sayings which refuse to be forgotten.

(ii) Jesus used *the thought-provoking paradox.* He said things which on the face of it sounded incredible, but which somehow haunt the mind and the heart with the lurking suspicion that after all they may be true. This is specially true of the Beatitudes (Matt.

5.1–16; Luke 6.20–26). Blessed are the poor, the hungry, the sorrow-ful, the persecuted. Every one of them bluntly and flatly contradicts the world's standards and the world's measurements; here is a reversal of all that is accepted as worldly and prudential wisdom, a turning of life upside down. Unless a man becomes like a little child, he cannot enter the Kingdom of Heaven (Matt. 18.3). Herein all the worldly standards of greatness and of prestige are annihilated in a sentence.

The great value of these sayings is their long-term disturbing power. When a man first hears them, he may well dismiss them as fantastic and unreal and incredible and untrue. But something has been dropped into his mind which even against his will compels him to think, and, if he goes on thinking for long enough, conclusions will force themselves upon him, even if he does not wish them to be true. In many ways Jesus is the great disturber, and not least in these thought-compelling paradoxes which he dropped into the minds and hearts of men.

(iii) Jesus used the *vivid hyperbole*. There are times when men need shock treatment, if they are to see the truth. They must be taken and shaken out of their comfortable lethargy. 'If your right eye,' said Jesus, 'causes you to sin, pluck it out and throw it away. If your right hand is opening the way to temptation, cut it off and hurl it from you' (Matt. 5.29f.; Mark 9.43–48). 'If any man comes to me, and does not hate his own father and mother and wife and children and brothers and sisters, yes, and even his own life, he cannot be my disciple' (Luke 14.26). Literalism is here forbidden, for this is the language of poetry and of passion. Sometimes a pic-ture has to be overdrawn, if men are to see it at all. Jesus never hesitated to say the most shattering things in order to stab men broad awake, so that even against their will the light of the truth would banish the unseeing slumber from their eyes.

(iv) Jesus used *penetrating humour*. Horace, the Roman poet, in a famous phrase, spoke of speaking the truth with a smile.[1] Often truth spoken with a smile will penetrate the mind and reach the heart; the lesson strikes home without wounding because of the wit in the saying. It was this form of teaching that Jesus used when he was speaking of the folly of criticizing and finding fault with each

[1] *Ridentem dicere verum:* Horace, *Satires* 1.1.24.

other, and when he drew a picture of a man with a plank in his own eye seeking to extract a speck of dust from the eye of some one else (Matt. 7.1–5).

'Laughter,' said Thomas Hobbes, 'is nothing else but sudden glory.' 'Let your speech,' said Paul, 'always be gracious, seasoned with salt' (Col. 4.6). And C. F. D. Moule comments that this verse may well be 'a plea to Christians not to confuse loyal godliness with a dull, graceless insipidity'. It has been all too true that too often in Christian teaching laughter has been a heresy and seriousness has been identified with gloom. Jesus knew that often the way to the heart of an audience is through a smile; and he said things which at the moment made men laugh, but which, when they thought about them, left them face to face with the gravity of truth.

(v) The teaching instrument which is above all connected with the name of Jesus is the parable. To teach by parables is to teach by story-telling, for a parable may be well described as 'an earthly story with a heavenly meaning'. If Jesus had no other claim to fame, he would rank as one of the supreme constructors of the short story. As a teaching instrument the parable has three great advantages.

(a) The parable, the story, is the teaching instrument which all men know, and which the Jews especially used. From childhood men say: 'Tell me a story.' Sir Philip Sidney spoke of 'a tale which holdeth children from play and old men from the chimney corner'. In the Old Testament there is Nathan's courageous parable to warn David of his sin (II Sam. 12.1–7), and Isaiah's parable with the picture of the nation of Israel as the vineyard of the Lord (Isa. 5.1–7).

The Jewish rabbis knew and used the parable in their teaching. There is, for instance, a very beautiful rabbinic parable which tells why God chose Moses as the leader of his people. 'When Moses was feeding the sheep of his father-in-law in the wilderness, a young kid ran away. Moses followed it until it reached a ravine, where it found a well from which to drink. When Moses came up to it he said: "I did not know that you ran away because you were thirsty. Now you must be weary." So he took the kid on his shoulders and carried it back. Then God said: "Because you have shown pity to one of a flock belonging to a man, you shall lead my flock Israel." '

When Jesus used the parable, he was using the method of teaching which all men know from their childhood, and which the Jewish teachers had always known and loved.

(*b*) To teach in parables is to teach in pictures, and most men think in pictures. There are very few people who are capable of grasping abstract truth; for most men truth has to become concrete before it becomes intelligible. We might, for instance, labour long and ineffectively to define the abstract idea of beauty, but, if we can point at a person, and say, 'That is a beautiful person,' then the abstract idea becomes clear.

It is not only *The Word*, which must become flesh; every great idea must become flesh, every great word must become a person, before men can grasp and understand it. So, for instance, when Paul speaks about faith, he does not enter into a long and abstract discussion and definition. He draws the living picture of Abraham. In Abraham faith becomes flesh; the abstract becomes concrete; the idea becomes a picture and a person.

That is why the story is the most universal form of teaching— and Jesus was a master of that method without an equal.

(*c*) The parable has in it the characteristic approach of Jesus to teaching. The parable does not so much *tell* a man the truth as it enables a man to *discover* the truth for himself. The parable says to a man, 'It is like this . . . Think of it this way . . .' and then leaves him to draw his own conclusions and to make his own deductions. Truth which is merely told is quick to be forgotten; truth which is discovered lasts a lifetime. Truth can never be inserted into a man like a pill or an injection; truth is like a goal to which a man's mind under the guidance and the stimulus of God must journey in its own seeking.

The great value of the parable is that it does not impose truth on a man; it puts a man in a position in which he can go on to discover, or to realize, truth for himself. A parable has the double power of opening a man's mind to new truth, and of making him aware of truth which he already knows, but the relevance of which he has failed to see.

In all his teaching Jesus moved from 'the here and now' to 'the there and then'. He began on earth to reach heaven; he began in time to end in eternity; he began from where men are to lead men to where they ought to be. He began from the corn growing in the cornfield, from a woman baking in a cottage kitchen, from a coin lost in the rushes which strewed a living-room floor, from a sheep which had wandered away, from a son who had run away, from an everyday incident of assault and robbery on the Jerusalem to Jericho road. Jesus could do that because for him the world is 'the garment of the living God'. He knew that the visible things of this world were designed to enable us to see through them and beyond them to the invisible things (Rom. 1.20). As William Temple put it: 'Jesus taught men to see the operation of God in the regular and the normal—in the rising of the sun and the falling of the rain and the growth of the plant.' Everything in God's world was to him a road to lead men's thoughts to God.

(vi) We may finally note that in his teaching Jesus used three forms of logical argument, as W. A. Curtis has pointed out.

(*a*) He used the *reductio ad absurdum*. He was accused of casting out devils by the help of the prince of devils. His answer was: 'How can Satan cast out Satan? If a kingdom is divided against itself, that kingdom cannot stand. And if a house is divided against itself, that house will not be able to stand. And if Satan has risen up against himself and is divided, he cannot stand, but is coming to an end' (Mark 3.23–26). With one shrewd blow Jesus reduced the charge of his opponents to an absurdity.

(*b*) He used the *logical dilemma*. He did not break out in railing rebuke against those who brought to him the woman taken in adultery. He simply said quietly: 'Let him who is without sin among you be the first to throw a stone at her' (John 8.7). When they accused him of breaking the Sabbath day by healing on it, and when he knew that they were seeking to find a way in which to kill him, he faced them with the question: 'Is it lawful on the sabbath to do good or to do harm, to save a life or to kill?' (Mark 3.4). He silenced his opponents by impaling them on the horns of a dilemma.

(*c*) He used the *argument a fortiori*. 'If you then,' he said, 'who are evil, know how to give good gifts to your children, *how much more* will your Father who is in heaven give good things to those who ask him?' (Matt. 7.11). 'If,' he said, 'God so clothes the grass of the field, which today is alive and tomorrow is thrown into the oven, will he not *much more* clothe you, O men of little faith?' (Matt. 6.30).

There are many men who genuinely have something to say, and who have never learned how to say it effectively. There are many men who have truth to teach, but who have never succeeded in teaching it, because they never learned the technique and the method of teaching. Let no man despise the study of the technique of teaching! Jesus did not despise it. Jesus had something to say and he knew how to say it, and the teacher will still find in him the perfect model.

11

WHAT JESUS SAID ABOUT GOD

The distinguishing and differentiating characteristic of the message of Jesus is that it is a *gospel*. The word 'gospel' (*euaggelion*) means good news, and it was good news that Jesus came to bring. No one could have called the message of John the Baptizer good news: it was the message of a threat with the axe poised at the root of the tree, the fire about to descend, judgment and destruction to be launched upon the world. It was good news of great joy that the angelic host brought to the shepherds as they watched their flocks by night (Luke 2.10). Mark's title for his book is 'the beginning of the gospel of Jesus Christ' (Mark 1.1). It was to announce good news to the poor that Jesus came (Luke 4.18; 7.22). It was the good news of the Kingdom that he brought to men in the synagogue, in the open places, in the towns and villages, and in the Temple (Matt. 4.23; 9.35; Luke 8.1; 20.1). It was his initial summons to men that they should repent and believe the good news (Mark 1.14f.), and, when he sent out his twelve men, it was with good news that he sent them (Luke 9.6). Jesus' message to men is good news about God.

If, then, Jesus came to bring good news about God, it must mean that he came to tell men things about God that they did not know, or did not realize, before. We must therefore begin by examining the beliefs of men about God before Jesus came.

The Jewish conception of God can be summed up in one word, the word 'holy'. Again and again God is described as 'The Holy One of Israel' (II Kings 19.22; Ps. 89.18; Isa. 1.4; 5.24; 10.20; 30.11; 47.4; 60.9; Jer. 50.29; Hos. 11.9). In Isaiah alone God is described as 'The Holy One' no fewer than twenty-nine times. Again and again in the law a law is laid down as binding and obligatory because it is given by the God who is 'holy' (Lev. 19.2;

20.26; 21.8). God must be given exclusive service because he is a holy God (Josh. 24.19). In Hannah's prayer there is none as holy as the Lord (I Sam. 2.2). God, says the Psalmist, must be exalted because he is holy (Ps. 99.9). As Isaiah heard it, the cry of the seraphim is: 'Holy, holy, holy is the Lord of hosts' (Isa. 6.3). The holiness of God is the primary doctrine of Judaism.

In Hebrew the word for 'holy' is *qadosh,* which has as its root meaning 'different', 'separate', 'set apart'. The thing or the person described as holy is different, separate, set apart from other things or persons. The priest is holy because he is different from other men; the Temple is holy because it is different from other buildings; the Sabbath day is holy because it is different from other days. God is supremely holy because he is different from all other persons and beings; he belongs to a different scale and sphere of life; he is completely different from men; he is the 'wholly other', the one who is essentially different from men. Inevitably this conception, whose key-note is difference, has certain consequences.

(i) It issues in the conception of *the unapproachability of God.* Clearly the difference between God and man sets a vast and unbridgeable gulf between God and man. But to Jewish thought it did more than that. God is so different from men that to approach God at all is dangerous and even fatal. No man can enter into the nearer presence of God and escape with his life.

After the wrestling at Peniel, it is Jacob's astonished and incredulous cry: 'I have seen God face to face, and yet my life is preserved' (Gen. 32.30). As Moses heard it, God said to him: 'You cannot see my face; for man shall not see me and live' (Ex. 33.20). When Gideon realized who his visitor had been, he cried out in terror: 'Alas, O Lord God! For now I have seen the angel of the Lord face to face.' And God's answer was: 'Peace be to you; do not fear; you shall not die' (Judg. 6.22f.). When Manoah discovered that the messenger who had brought him news of the coming birth of a son was an angel of the Lord, his terrified reaction was: 'We shall surely die, for we have seen God' (Judg. 13.22). At this stage of things the idea is that God is so holy, so different, so unapproachable, that to see him is to die.

This essential difference between God and man is called *the transcendence of God;* and with the course of the centuries this idea of the transcendence of God was not lessened but intensified. In the Old Testament story of the giving of the law, the law was given to Moses directly from God. The people were amazed that God had that day talked with a man and that that man was still alive (Deut. 5.24). But twice in the New Testament we are told that the law was given, not directly from God, but through angelic intermediaries (Acts 7.53; 1 Th. 4.16). By New Testament times the idea was that God was so different and separate and apart from men, so transcendent, that any transaction between God and men could not be direct, but must be performed through some intermediary.

So, then, the idea of the holiness of God issued in the idea of the dangerous unapproachability of God. H. G. Wells in one of his novels tells of a man, near to mental and spiritual collapse under the stress and strain of things, who was told by his nerve specialist that his only hope lay in fellowship with God. The man's amazed answer was that he would as soon think of cooling his throat with the milky way or shaking hands with the stars as having fellowship with God. That is a parallel to the orthodox Jewish idea of God.

(ii) This idea of the holiness of God issues in the idea of what might be called *the unpredictability of God*. It is difficult to put this idea into actual words. In the Old Testament God is *King* far more than he is *Father*. In the ancient world the king was an absolute monarch, answerable and responsible to no one. Suetonius tells us how Caligula, the Roman Emperor, told his grandmother to remember that he could do anything he liked and do it to anyone. The idea is that in the presence of God man has no rights whatever, that there is no reason whatever why man should understand, or see any reason in, the acts of God as they affect either himself or the world.

There are two Old Testament passages which illustrate this absolute power of God. The first is Jeremiah's parable of the potter and the clay (Jer. 18.1–10). Jeremiah sees the potter work with the clay; it does not come off his wheel in the way in which the potter wants it to; he simply crushes it down and begins all over again. Then Jeremiah hears God say: 'O house of Israel, can I not do with you as this potter has done? Behold, like the clay in the potter's hand, so are you in mine hand, O house of Israel.' The more one thinks of that passage the more terrible it becomes. Men have no more rights in the presence of God than the clay in the hands of the potter; men have no more right to understand than the clay; God can take and make and break living, human personalities as the potter can take and make and break the clay.

The second passage is in Job 38 and 39. Job, the good man, is involved in disaster; he would state his case to God; and in these chapters is God's answer to him. From the point of view of magnificent and dramatic poetry they rank with the great literature of the world—but they are terrible chapters. 'Where were you when I laid the foundation of the earth? . . . Have you entered into the springs of the sea? . . . Have the gates of death been revealed to you? . . . Have you comprehended the expanse of the earth? . . . Do you know the ordinances of the heavens? . . . Can you send forth lightnings?' On and on goes this battery and bombardment of unanswerable questions, the whole essence of which is that God is saying: 'What right have you to speak to me? Who are you to claim to understand what I do? I am not answerable and responsible to you. My power and holiness give me the right to do as I like—even to smash you.' It is magnificent—but it is cold comfort for an agonized body and a broken heart. Here is the picture of the unpredictable God, the God whom a man cannot understand and is not meant to understand, the God before whom a man can only bow his head with all resistance broken.

(iii) Inevitably this idea of the holiness of God leads to another idea about God. God's holiness will necessarily affect his relationship with all men, but it is bound very specially to affect his relationship with the sinner. There are in the Old Testament voices, such as the voice of Hosea, which speak from hearts which have glimpsed the patient love and the infinite mercy of God; but in the main stream of Jewish orthodox thought God is the God whose aim is the destruction of the sinner.

'Let sinners be consumed from the earth,' says the Psalmist, 'and let the wicked be no more!' (Ps. 104.35). 'Rebels and sinners shall be destroyed together,' writes Isaiah, 'and those who forsake the Lord shall be consumed' (Isa. 1.28). 'The day of the Lord comes, cruel, with wrath and fierce anger, to make the earth a desolation, and to destroy its sinners from it' (Isa. 13.9). 'All the sinners of my people,' Amos hears God say, 'shall die by the sword' (Amos 9.10). There is a rabbinic saying: "There is joy before God when those who provoke him perish from the world.' The holy God is set on the destruction of the sinner.

Nowhere does this appear more vividly than in the words of Ps. 24. 'Who shall ascend the hill of the Lord? And who shall stand in his holy place? He who has clean hands and a pure heart, who does not lift up his soul to what is false and does not swear deceitfully. He will receive blessing from the Lord and vindication from the God of his salvation' (Ps. 24.3–5). That is often read at the beginning of a Christian service, and yet to any sensitive and thinking man the effect of it is to slam the door to God's presence in his face. This is the Jewish conception which thought of the holy God as absolutely hostile to sinners, and which filled the scribes and Pharisees with horror, when they saw Jesus eating with and befriending and companying with tax-gatherers and sinners.

Judaism stressed the holiness of God. That holiness stretched a great gulf between God and man; it surrounded God with a certain sublime unpredictability without any responsibility to men; it tended to make men think of God as the sworn enemy of the sinner.

Before very long in its history Christianity was to go out to the Greek and Roman world. What ideas of God would the Christian message encounter there? Would the Christian message of God be good news about God there also? What were the Greek and Roman ideas about God and about the gods?

(i) The oldest, the most primitive, and perhaps the commonest idea was the idea of *grudging gods*. There was an essential hostility and suspicion between gods and men. The gods grudged men everything they attained, achieved, or received. To be successful, prosperous or great was dangerous; mediocrity alone was safe. Herodotus found a parable in the fact that the tallest trees were most likely to be blasted by the lightning stroke; any man who raised himself out of the common ruck of men was in danger of being blasted by the gods.

The typical story is the story of Prometheus. Prometheus cared for men. He therefore stole fire from heaven, gave it to men, and taught them how to use it. Zeus, chief of the gods, was mightily angry. He caused Prometheus to be chained to a rock in Scythia;

he prepared a vulture to tear out Prometheus' liver every day, which ever grew again only to be torn out again, until in the end Hercules freed him from his torture.

Here is the essence of the matter. The gods were enraged that men should enter into any blessing. Man was not the child of the gods; he was rather the victim of the gods. There was an essential conflict of interests, an essential enmity between gods and men.

(ii) The gods were *the unknown and the unknowable gods.* It is true that in the great days of Greek thought men believed that the power of human thought could scale the heights of heaven and storm the citadels of the divine. But even then the discoveries could only be for the few, the very few. As Plato had it, it is difficult to find out about God, and when you have found out about him, it is impossible to tell anyone else about him. Discovery is difficult, communication impossible. Even the greatest men, as Plutarch had it, only see God when they have removed themselves from the body, and then only like a flash of light in thick darkness—a moment of illumination, and then the dark again. Never God and man can meet, as Plato said. 'To whom, then,' said Plutarch, 'shall I recite prayers? To whom tender vows? To whom slay victims? To whom shall I call to help the wretched, to favour the good, to counter the evil?' The gods were beyond the reach of men.

(iii) To the Greeks the gods were *detached from the world.* The actual government of the world was in the hands of the *daimons,* who were intermediaries between gods and men. The *daimons* were in charge of the natural forces and the day-to-day ordering of the world and its ways and affairs. As Glover put it: 'The One God is by common consent far from all direct contact with this or any other universe of becoming and perishing.' 'The Ultimate God rules through deputies,' but is himself completely detached from the world. If you remove the *daimons,* Plutarch held, you make confusion and disorder of everything, 'bringing God in among mortal passions and mortal affairs, fetching him down for our needs.' 'He who involves God in human needs does not spare his majesty, nor does he maintain the dignity and greatness of God's excellence.' The *daimons* are everywhere but God is nowhere among men. The idea of an incarnation would have been incredible to a Greek.

(iv) All this came to a head in the two great philosophies which were the religion of the world in New Testament times. These two great philosophies were Epicureanism and Stoicism. For the Epicurean the gods were beings without a care. For the Epicurean the end of life was *ataraxia,* absolute untroubled serenity, absence of pain of body and trouble of mind. The gods alone enjoy *ataraxia* in perfection, and, since that is so, they are bound to be completely detached from the world. If they were in the least interested in the world, if they were in the least involved in the world, it would mean that they were bound to know worry, anxiety, effort, care. The first sentence in the *Principal Doctrines* of Epicurus is: 'The blessed and immortal nature knows no trouble itself nor causes trouble to any other, so that it is never constrained by anger or favour. For all such things exist only in the weak.' Lucretius describes the gods: 'The very nature of divinity must necessarily enjoy immortal life in the deepest peace, far removed and separated from our troubles; for without any pain, without danger, itself mighty by its own resources, needing us not at all, it is neither propitiated with services, nor touched by wrath.' So the gods live in their remote majesty in 'their peaceful abodes, which no winds ever shake nor clouds besprinkle with rain, which no snow congealed by the bitter frost mars, but the air ever cloudless encompasses them and laughs with its light spread wide abroad. There moreover nature supplies everything, and nothing at any time impairs their peace of mind.'[1] It was thus that Tennyson, in 'The Lotos Eaters', drew his picture of the gods:

For they lie beside their nectar, and the bolts are hurl'd
Far below them in the valleys, and the clouds are lightly curl'd
Round their golden houses, girdled with the gleaming world:
Where they smile in secret, looking over wasted lands,
Blight and famine, plague and earthquake, roaring deeps and fiery sands,
Clanging fights, and flaming towns, and sinking ships, and praying hands.

This is the conception, not of gods who are hostile to men, but of gods who, because they are gods, are completely unaware of the existence of man and of the world.

The other great philosophy of the Greek world in the age to which the Christian message came was Stoicism. The aim of the Stoics was to attain perfect tranquillity, *eudaimonia,* a happiness

[1] Lucretius 1.646ff.; 3.18ff.

which is perfect peace. A state of perfect peace is a state in which
a man lives a life in which there is no such thing as an unsatisfied
desire. Therefore, the way to happiness in life is to eliminate deliberately every desire. Teach yourself to be absolutely indifferent, to
desire nothing. Not only must we desire *nothing;* we must also desire
no one. As Edwyn Bevan put it: 'Leave one small hole in a ship's
side and you let in the sea. The Stoics, I think, saw with perfect
truth that if you were going to allow any least entrance of love and
pity into the breast, you admitted something whose measure you
could not control, and might just as well give up the idea of inner
tranquillity at once.' To attain tranquillity, said the Stoic, you must
banish all emotion for ever and ever.

If that be true of men, it is still truer of God. If anyone can
feel love and pity, it means that some one else can have some
influence over him; it means that some one else can make him
sad or glad. Now, if some one else can make us sad or glad, it
means that for the moment that person can influence us, has
power over us, and is greater than we are. Clearly no one can be
greater than God; that means that no one can ever influence God;
that must mean that no one can ever make God sad or glad; no
one can move the feelings and emotions of God, or that person
would be, if only momentarily, greater than God. Therefore the
first essential in God is that he must be totally without feeling; he
cannot feel love or pity and remain God. The first and essential
attribute of God is what the Stoics called *apatheia,* which is not
apathy in the sense of indifference, but apathy in the sense of absolute incapability of all feeling.

To the Stoics God was *the God without a heart,* the God who
could not care, the God to whom pity and love were utterly impossible, just because he was God. In Epicureanism men are confronted
with gods who are not even aware of their existence; in Stoicism
men are confronted with a God who, because he is God, cannot
care; and it is hard to say which is worse for wounded hearts.

We must now go on to see the good news about God which
Jesus brought, and with which Christianity went out to meet the
human situation. To begin with, two things immediately stand out.
The fact that Jesus came is the proof that God is *a self-revealing*

God. The coming of Jesus is the proof that God is not the hidden and the unknowable God, but that his great desire is to be known by men. Further, this knowledge of God is not open only to the few, the philosopher, the theologian, the man of high intellectual stature and of great intellectual calibre. It is open to all, even to the simplest. The reason for this is that it is a knowledge which is based on love. Here is the difference between *knowing* a person and *knowing about* a person. *To know about* a person is an exercise of the mind, and such knowledge may be achieved without ever having met the person at all. For instance, we *know about* the great figures of past history, and we *know about* the great figures of the present day who move in a circle and a sphere into which we are never likely to penetrate. *To know* a person is essentially an exercise of the heart, and a personal relationship. We cannot really *know* either a person or a subject unless we love that person or that subject.

It is perfectly true that there are many questions about God, man, and the world, to answer which requires the most strenuous efforts of the greatest minds and the highest intellects. The systematization of Christian truth certainly requires the toil and labour of the mind. But to know God personally as companion, friend and lover of the souls of men is a knowledge which is open to all.

Paul Tournier, the great Christian doctor, declares that life, in order to be life, must necessarily be *dialogue*. No one can find life in any real sense of the term in isolation. He must find it in contact, in dialogue, with others. The supreme dialogue of life is the dialogue with God. Paul Tournier writes: 'Jesus Christ is the dialogue re-established. He is God coming to us because we cannot go to him.' Jesus came with the good news that God is not a God who hides himself, that God is not a God whom only the philosophers may know, that God is the God who at all costs desires to be known, and who in the most costly way has revealed himself to all men.

The second general fact which stands out in the message which Jesus brought is that *God is involved in the human situation.* It was precisely this that both Jew and Greek had come to deny. The Jews so stressed the holiness and the transcendence of God that they removed him from human contact altogether. They even, in popular thought, delegated to the archangels the duty of presenting the prayers of the faithful to God. Sometimes that was held to be the duty of Michael, sometimes of Raphael. 'I am Raphael,' says Raphael to Tobit, 'one of the seven holy angels, who present the prayers of the saints and enter into the presence of the glory of the Holy One' (Tobit 12.15). The Greeks considered it an insult to God, a complete misunderstanding of the nature and the being of God, to involve God in the world or in the human situation at all. The entry of Jesus into the world is the proof that God is involved in, identified with, the human situation. In Jesus the God who was afar off has indeed been brought near.

There is a third great fact about the Jewish and the Greek idea of God which includes the other two. Both the Jews and the Greeks really believed in a God who is essentially *a selfish God*. It is for the sake of the glory of God that sinners must be destroyed; the supremacy of God will brook no rival and no disobedience. The serenity and the tranquillity of the gods are all that matter; anything that would even tend to affect the peace of the gods must be eliminated. The idea of the pain and the sorrow of God is far removed from all that. But Jesus brought into the world the message of a *selfless God,* a God to whom men were so dear that he bore their sins and sorrows on his heart, and gave himself for them. It may be drawing the contrast too violently, but there is a certain truth in saying that before Jesus came men thought of a God who existed and ordered all things for his own sake; after Jesus came men were given the vision of a God who existed and ordered all things for the sake of men. The God of Jesus is love—and love is always selfless, when it is true love.

So Jesus came to men, and the Christian Church went out to the world, with the message of a self-revealing God, a God who is involved in the human situation, a God who is selfless in his love for men. It is from these great facts about God that everything else follows.

(i) Jesus came to tell men of an *inviting* God, a God who desires to be approached. One of the great characteristic words of Jesus is the word 'Come!'. He invited men to follow him in discipleship (Mark. 1.17; Matt. 4.19). He invited his own men to share his solitary prayer and communion with God (Mark 6.31). He invited the weary and the heavy-laden to come to him for rest and help (Matt. 11.28). He likened his own invitation to the invitation to a marriage feast (Matt. 22.4). He told in his parable of how, in the days to come, those who cared as he cared would be invited to share the glory that was prepared for them (Matt. 25.34). Continually on Jesus' lips there was an invitation.

It is difficult to imagine anyone holding an intimate and loving conversation with one of the Greek gods, or even with the holy God of the Old Testament; but, for the Christian, God is the God with an eternal invitation in his heart, and prayer is the acceptance of that invitation to speak with, and to listen to, God. H. V. Morton in *A Traveller in Rome* tells of a scene he watched in the Church of St. Clemente. A poor, old, ragged woman, like a little black ghost, came shuffling in in carpet slippers. 'She was like a bundle of old, dry leaves wrapped round with cobweb. First she knelt and told her beads, then she approached the crucifix, and, bending forward, kissed the feet, and placed her cheek against them, whispering all the time . . . She seemed to be holding a conversation with the crucifix, pausing as if for a reply, and then speaking again . . . I fancied from her manner that she was in the habit of talking to Christ like this, perhaps telling him her anxieties, and maybe the events in the tenement where she lived.' Here was a simple person conversing with God. It is the invitation to do that that Jesus brought.

The Synoptic Gospels all say that, at the moment Jesus died, the veil which shut off the Holy of Holies in the Temple was rent in two (Matt. 27.51; Mark 15.38; Luke 23.45). Into the Holy of Holies only one man could enter, and that only on one day in the year. Into the Holy of Holies only the High Priest could enter, and the one day on which he could enter was the Day of Atonement; and even on that day the time during which he might linger in the Holy of Holies was strictly limited. The instruction was that he must linger no longer than necessary, lest he put Israel in terror, and lest the people fear that God had smitten him dead. The rending of the veil is the symbolic statement of the fact that Jesus came to men with an invitation to approach the God to whose presence there were no barriers any more. Once it had been the belief that to see God is to die; Jesus came with the invitation to all men to enter into the presence of God with childlike confidence and boldness.

(ii) This invitation was not only an invitation to those who, as it were, deserved it, to those who were morally good, spiritually devout, perfectly righteous. It was an invitation to sinners, for Jesus came with the message of a *forgiving* God. Around him the taxgatherers and the sinners and the women of the streets gathered (Luke 15.1). He ate with them (Matt. 9.10; Mark 2.15; Luke 5.30), so that the righteous orthodox of his day called him the friend of publicans and sinners (Matt. 11.19; Luke 7.34). He said that he had come to call, not the righteous, but sinners to repentance (Matt. 9.13; Mark 2.17; Luke 5.32), and that he had come to seek and to save that which was lost (Matt. 18.11). He said that there was joy in heaven over one sinner who repents (Luke 15.7,10).

There is a world of difference here. The Pharisees and the orthodox Jews who kept the law avoided sinners as they avoided people with the plague. People who knew that they were sinners would never have dared to approach the scribes and the Pharisees, even if they had wished to. This is a far cry from the God who can only be approached by those who have clean hands and a pure heart (Ps. 24.4), and whose aim it is to obliterate the sinner.

Jesus came with the message of a God whose love not even sin could destroy, and whose heart's desire was that men should accept the offer of forgiveness which he was making to them, and, in being forgiven, should learn to mend their ways.

(iii) Jesus came with news of God even more startling than that God was an inviting and a forgiving God. The Jew would not have doubted that, if a sinner came creeping back to God in remorse, contrition and repentance, and if he humbly pleaded for forgiveness, he would be forgiven. God would accept the man who came humbly and penitently back to him. But Jesus came to tell of a *seeking God,* a God who did not wait for the sinner to come back, but who went out to seek and to search for him, and to appeal to him to come back.

This is the fact about Jesus which above all impressed C. G. Montefiore, the great Jewish liberal scholar. Again and again in his commentary on the Synoptic Gospels he returns to this idea of the seeking God as to something which was absolutely new. Commenting on Mark 2.17 he writes: 'Jesus sought to bring back into glad communion with God those whom sin, whether "moral" or "ceremonial" had driven away. For him sinners (at least certain types of sinners) were the subject not of condemnation or disdain, but of pity. He did not avoid sinners, but sought them out. They were still children of God. This was a new and sublime contribution to the development of religion and morality . . . To deny the greatness and originality of Jesus in this connection, to deny that he opened a new chapter in men's attitude to sin and sinners, is, I think, to beat the head against the wall.' Again, in commenting on Matt. 9.36, he writes: 'So far as we can tell, this pity for the sinner was a new note in religious history.' Again on Luke 15.1 he writes: 'The sinners drew near to hear him. Surely this is a new note, something which we have not yet heard in the Old Testament, or of its heroes, something we have not heard in the *Talmud,* or of its heroes. "The sinners drew near to hear him." His teaching did not repel them. It did not palter with, or make light of, sin, but yet it gave comfort to the sinner. The virtues of repentance are gloriously praised in the Rabbinical literature, but this direct search for, and appeal to the sinner are new and moving notes of high import and significance. The good shepherd who searches for the lost sheep and reclaims it, and rejoices over it, is a new figure which has never ceased to play its great part in the moral and religious development of the world.' Montefiore stresses the newness of the human side of this. In commenting on Matt. 18.10–14 he writes: 'What is new and striking in the teaching of Jesus is that this process of repentance takes an active turn. Man is bidden not merely to receive the penitent gladly, but to seek out the sinner, to try to redeem him, to make him penitent.'

To Montefiore the idea of the seeking God, the God pictured in terms of a woman seeking a lost coin, and a shepherd seeking a lost sheep (Luke 15.1–10) was something quite unparallelled and gloriously new.

It would be great if God accepted us back when we came to him in humble penitence; it would be precious that God should wait for the sinner to come back. But that God shouid go out and seek the sinner is something sublime, and something new. Here, indeed, is good news of God.

(iv) This truth of the seeking God has a necessary corollary. God is the God of *the individual love.* It is not *mankind* that God loves; it is *men*. The shepherd cannot be content with ninety-nine sheep while one is lost; the woman cannot be content with nine coins while one is lost; the one, the individual, matters intensely to God.

Paul Tournier is fascinated by what he calls the *personalism* of the Bible. God says to Moses: 'I know you *by name*' (Ex. 33.17). God says through Isaiah: 'It is I, the Lord, who call you by name' (Isa. 45.3). Paul Tournier tells of a girl who was one of his patients. She was the youngest daughter in a large family, the support of which was a sore problem to the father. One day she heard him mutter despairingly, referring to her: 'We could well have done without that one!' That is precisely what no one will ever hear God say. The love of God is at one and the same time completely universal and completely individual. As Augustine so beautifully expressed it: 'God loves each one of us as if there was only one of us to love.' With God there is no one who is lost in the crowd.

There is a saying of Jesus which appears in two forms and the variation in it may be the symbol of this individual love of God. Matthew reports Jesus as saying: 'Are not two sparrows sold for a farthing? And one of them shall not fall on the ground without your Father's will' (Matt. 10.29). Luke reports Jesus as saying: 'Are not five sparrows sold for two farthings? And not one of them is forgotten before God' (Luke 12.6). Jesus in all probability used both forms of the saying, and used them both at the same time. If a purchaser was prepared to spend one farthing, he received two sparrows; but, if he was prepared to spend two farthings, he received not four sparrows, but five, for one was thrown into the bargain, as if it was worth nothing at all. Not even the sparrow which in human eyes has no value at all is forgotten by God.

Even the individual who on human valuation is valueless is valuable to God. It is easy to see what such a message must have meant to the slaves of the Empire who were defined by law not as persons but as living tools, with no more rights than a tool.

(v) It may be that we dare to go on to something further yet. Other thinkers have called God by various names—The Supreme God, The First Cause, The Creative Energy, The Life Force. All these descriptions of God have one characteristic in common—they are *impersonal*. But Jesus always spoke and taught of a God who is a *person.* In all reverence we may draw a certain conclusion from that. No person can exist in isolation; personality and isolation are mutually contradictory. Every person needs other persons to complete himself. It is in communication and fellowship with other persons that personality is fulfilled and realized. We therefore come to the astonishing conclusion that *God needs men;* that in some mysterious sense creation was for God a necessity; that somehow God needs the world and men to complete himself. That is why God created men and the world; that is why God loves men with an everlasting love; and that is why God would go to any lengths of sacrifice to bring men back to himself.

A Negro poet, James Weldon Johnson, has put the matter in the way in which a child might put it. His poem is not theology—theology might well be shocked by it—but it has a childlike truth.

> And God stepped out on space,
> And he looked around, and said:
> 'I'm lonely—
> I'll make me a world.'
>
> Then God walked around,
> And God looked around
> On all that he had made.
> He looked at his sun,
> And he looked at his moon,
> And he looked at his little stars;
> He looked on his world
> With all its living things,
> And God said: 'I'm lonely still.'
> Then God sat down—
> On the side of a hill where he could think,
> By a deep, wide river he sat down,
> With his head in his hands,
> God thought and thought,
> Till he thought: 'I'll make me a man.'

There is a child's truth there, the truth that God needs man, because God is a person; and from that need there springs the forgiving, seeking, individual love of God. But that is something of which no one had dreamed till Jesus brought to men the good news of God.

All that Jesus came to say about God is summed up in the name by which he himself called God, and by which he taught others to call God, the name *Father*. The name Father as applied to God had a long history before Jesus came to give it a new meaning and a new content, for Jesus was by no means the first to call God Father.

The word 'father' can have behind it two spheres of meaning. It can be connected either with *paternity* or with *fatherhood*. When the word 'father' is connected with the idea of paternity, it means no more than the person who gave a child life, who begat him, who brought him into this world. It is perfectly possible that a father in this sense may never even set eyes on his child. The sole relationship between father and child in this sense of the term is the relationship of physical begetting, and father and child could live their lives and go through the world and never even meet. In the idea of paternity there is no necessary intimacy, fellowship, love. On the other hand when the word father is connected with the idea of fatherhood, it describes a relationship of closeness and intimacy and love. It describes a relationship in which day by day, so long as life and need last, the father cares for the child in body, mind and spirit, in which the father nourishes the child with food, guides the child with advice, surrounds and strengthens the child with continual love.

It was not until the coming of Jesus that men learned the full meaning of the fatherhood of God, although for many centuries they had been groping their way to it.

(i) Men began with the idea of God as father in the sense of *the progenitor of their race*. That is to say, they thought of the fatherhood of God in terms of paternity. It was he who had begotten their race, and it was to him that they owed their lives in the physical sense of the term. So we find Syrian names like Abibaal, which means son of Baal, and Benhadad, which means son of Hadad; Baal and Hadad were Syrian gods. So we find a tribe calling themselves 'sons of Hobal', and Hobal was their god. So we find the Greeks calling Zeus 'Father of gods and men', and meaning much what a modern man would mean, if he called God 'The First Cause', or 'The Life Force'. In this idea there is little or no thought of intimacy or fellowship; the idea is that of God as father in the sense of the physical giver of life.

(ii) The Jews had always a vivid sense of God as *the father of their nation*. So they can say:

> 'Do you thus requite the Lord,
> you foolish and senseless people?
> Is not he your father, who created you,
> who made you and established you?' (Deut. 32.6).

> 'Have we not all one father?
> Has not one God created us?
> Why then are we faithless to one another?' (Mal. 2.10).

At this stage there is a definite conviction that God is the father and founder and possessor of the nation, but so far the fatherhood of God is to the nation, not to the individual within it.

(iii) There is one exception to this. If God is the father of the nation, then it is not unnatural that in a special sense he may be called *the father of the king of the nation*. The promise of God to David regarding David's son is: 'I will be his father, and he shall be my son' (II Sam. 7.14). The coronation psalm says of the king: 'You are my son, today I have begotten you' (Ps. 2.7). But this very psalm shows that the sonship comes to the king as king; it is on the day that he becomes king that he becomes son. God becomes the king's father, not because the king is an individual man, but because the nation is personified and embodied in him. We have not yet reached a stage at which God is thought of as the father of the individual.

(iv) The nation of Israel is in a very special sense the child of God, and God is in a very special sense the father of Israel. God is the father of Israel in a sense in which he is not the father of any other nation. This must mean that *God has become the father of Israel by a special act of choice and of adoption.* Jeremiah hears God say: 'I am a father to Israel, and Ephraim is my first-born' (Jer. 31.9). Choice and adoption require some moment when the choice is made and when the adoption becomes effective. Very often the Jews saw the special adoption by God of their nation in the deliverance from Egypt. Then God stepped in, and in a special sense made Israel his nation. Hosea hears God say: 'When Israel was a child, I loved him, and out of Egypt I called my son' (Hos. 11.1). God's message through Moses to Pharaoh was: 'Israel is my firstborn son, and I say to you, "Let my son go that he may serve me" ' (Ex. 4.22). Once this act of choice and adoption had been made, it was carried out, confirmed and cemented in the events of history as they affected Israel for weal or for woe. In the wilderness Israel has seen 'how the Lord your God bore you, as a man bears his son' (Deut. 1.31). 'As a man disciplines his son, the Lord your God disciplines you' (Deut. 8.5). Isaiah hears God say: 'Sons have I reared and brought up, but they have rebelled against me' (Isa. 1.2). Still at this stage it is the nation which is in question, and God is not yet the father of the individual.

(v) But out of this stage there emerges a very important development. Any act of choice, any act of adoption, by the very fact that it is made, automatically demands a response. Quite clearly, all Israel has not made that response to God; many have been deaf to God's commands and have turned their backs on God's appeal. Only some have responded in love and in obedience to the choice and the adoption of God. It, therefore, follows that *God is the father of the good and of the righteous in a way in which he cannot be the father of the disobedient and the rebellious*. Often the commandments of God run like this: 'You are the sons of the Lord your God; therefore you shall not . . .' (e.g. Deut. 14.1). Sonship and obedience must go together. 'A son honours his father, and a servant his master. If then I am a father, where is my honour?' (Mal. 1.6). 'As a father pities his children, so the Lord pities *those who fear him*' (Ps. 103.13). Here we are at the first great step towards the individualizing of the fatherhood of God. The nation is still God's nation; but there is a quite different relationship between God and the obedient from that which exists between God and the rebellious.

(vi) Another way in which to express this is to say that man's sonship of God becomes *an ethical sonship*. This is an idea which gains strength all through the literature between the Testaments. In *Jubilees* God says: 'Their souls shall cleave to me and to all my commandments, and they will fulfil my commandments, and I will be their father and they will be my children' (*Jubilees* 1.24). 'He correcteth the righteous as a beloved son' (*Psalms of Solomon* 13.8). There is a rabbinic saying: 'Be strong as a leopard and swift as an eagle and fleet as a gazelle and brave as a lion to do the will of your father who is in heaven.'

There was within the Jewish nation a not unnatural reaction to this. An ethical sonship makes great demands on a man; it demands his love, his loyalty, his devotion, his obedience. There were Jews who insisted that God was so much the father of the nation of Israel that any Israelite was safe from all judgment simply because he was a son of Abraham, which indeed was the view that John the Baptizer attacked (Luke 3.8). 'A single Israelite,' says the *Talmud,* 'is worth more in God's sight than all the nations of the world.' Justin charges the Jewish teachers with teaching that an Israelite, just because he is of the seed of Abraham, will receive the Kingdom even if he is a sinner, faithless and disobedient.[1]

It is quite true that there was in not a few cases this degeneration of the idea of the fatherhood of God, but in the highest and the best Jewish thought the idea of sonship was acquiring an increasingly ethical quality, and that fact made the individualizing of the fatherhood of God an increasing reality.

(vii) Once a man realizes that true sonship and devoted and loving obedience go hand in hand, then the note of a personal, individual relationship enters in. True, the individualizing of the fatherhood of God is not yet common, but the Sage in his difficulties can pray: 'Lord, Father, and Master of my life' (Ecclus. 23.1). There the true individual note strikes.

Because of this there enters into Jewish thought, at least on rare occasions, a new tenderness and intimacy in the relationship between God and man. G. F. Moore in *Judaism* quotes a beautiful comment on Ex. 14.19 by Rabbi Judas ben Ila'i: 'The angel of God who went before the camp removed and went behind them. It is like a man who was walking in the way, and letting his son go on before him. Came robbers in front to take the boy captive, the father put him behind him. Came a wolf from behind, he put him in front. Came robbers in front, and wolves behind, he took him up in his arms. Did he begin to be troubled by the heat of the sun, his father stretched his garment over him. Was he hungry, he gave him food; thirsty, he gave him drink. Just so God did.'

Stage by stage, the individualizing of the idea of the fatherhood of God was coming about; and yet it had a long, long way to go

[1] *Dialogue with Trypho* 140.

before there could come into it the tenderness, the intimacy, the childlike confidence which Jesus was to bring.

(viii) When we come finally to examine Jesus' conception of the fatherhood of God, we meet with two most significant and illuminating facts.

(*a*) There is the *extraordinary rarity* with which Jesus uses the name 'Father', as applied to God, at all. In Mark, the earliest of the Gospels, Jesus only calls God 'Father' four times (Mark 8.38; 11.25; 13.32; 14.36). Further, in Mark Jesus does not call God 'Father' at all until after Peter's confession at Caesarea Philippi, and then he only does so within the circle of the disciples. There is only one conclusion to be drawn from this. To Jesus, to call God Father was no theological commonplace; it was something so sacred that he could hardly speak of it at all in public; and, when he did speak of it, it was only in the presence of those who, at least to some extent, understood.

(*b*) There is the *extraordinary intimacy* which Jesus put into the term. Jesus called God '*Abba,* Father' (Mark 14.36). As Jeremias point out there is not even the remotest parallel to this in all Jewish literature. *Abba,* like the modern Arabic *jaba,* is the word used by a young child to his father. It is the ordinary, everyday family word which a little child used in speaking to his father.[1] It is completely untranslatable. Any attempt to put it into English ends in bathos or grotesqueness. It is a word which no one had ever ventured to use in addressing God before.

For Jesus the fatherhood of God was something of almost inexpressible sacredness, and it was something of unsurpassable tender intimacy. In it is summed up everything that he came to say about God in his relationship with men.

When we set this conception of God as the Father, to whom a man may go with the same confidence and trust as a child goes to his earthly father, beside the Jewish conception of the remote transcendence of God and beside the Greek conceptions of the grudging God, the gods who are unaware of our existence, the god without a heart, we see that it is indeed true that Jesus brought to men good news about God.

[1] *The Parables of Jesus,* p. 134.

12

WHAT JESUS SAID ABOUT MAN AND SIN

It is not possible to move far amidst the sayings and the writings of the serious minds of any age without coming upon the essential paradox of manhood. On the one side we come upon passage after passage which speaks of the futility, the helplessness, the degradation, the degeneration, the sin of life. 'Men,' said Seneca, 'love their vices and hate them at the same time.'[1] 'The beginning of philosophy,' he says, 'is a consciousness of one's weakness in necessary things.' Man oscillates between right and wrong, unable to declare boldly and unequivocally for either. Glover summarizes the letter of Serenus to Seneca: 'I find myself not quite free, nor yet quite in bondage to the faults which I feared and hated. I am in a state, not the worst indeed, but very querulous and uncomfortable, neither well nor ill. It is a weakness of the mind that sways between the two, that will neither bravely turn to right nor to wrong. Things disturb me, though they do not alter my principles. I think of public life; something worries me, and I fall back into the life of leisure, to be pricked to the will to act by reading some brave words, or seeing some fine example. I beg you, if you have any remedy to stay my fluctuation of mind, count me worthy to owe you peace. To put what I endure into a simile, it is not the tempest that troubles me, but sea-sickness.'[2]

Sometimes the matter is worse than wavering oscillation; it is utter moral helplessness. Let the guilty see virtue, says Persius, and mourn that they have lost her for ever.[3] He speaks of filthy Natta 'benumbed by vice'. Epictetus demands: 'When a man is hardened

---

[1] *Letters* 112.3.
[2] *Concerning Tranquillity of Mind* 1.
[3] *Satires* 3.38.

like a stone, how shall we be able to deal with him by argument?'
Here is the picture of the man who, as Glover put it, is suffering
from necrosis of the soul. Seneca can call himself *homo non tolera-
bilis,* a man not to be tolerated.[1] Marcus Aurelius can speak with
a kind of contempt for manhood: 'Of man's life, his time is a
point, his existence a flux, his sensation clouded, his body's entire
composition corruptible, his vital spirit an eddy of breath, his
fortune hard to predict, his fame uncertain. Briefly, all the things
of the body are a river; all the things of the spirit, dream and
delirium' (2.17).

On the one side there are the voices of pessimism, of helplessness,
and of despair. But on the other side, often in the very same writers,
there emerges at least in flashes the conviction of the greatness of
man. The same Seneca, who is so conscious of frustration and of
sin, can write: 'God is near you, with you, within you. I say it,
Lucilius; a holy spirit sits within us, spectator of our evil and our
good, our guardian.'[2] Glover collects certain of the things which
Epictetus in his *Discourses* says of man. Man's part in life is to be
the spectator and interpreter of God (1.6); he is the son of God
(1.9); his duty is to attach himself to God (4.1), and like a soldier
to obey God's signals and commands. He is to look up to God and
to say: 'Use me henceforth for what thou wilt. I am of thy mind;
I am thine' (2.16).

As Samuel Angus has pointed out in *The Mystery Religions and
Christianity,* there is in Greek thought a strong strand which insists
on the essential connection between God and man. 'We are indeed
his offspring,' said Aratus, the Stoic poet, a saying which Paul was
to quote (Acts 17.28). Cicero says that man is a god because he has
the same clontrol over his body as God has over the universe,[3] and
that knowledge of the gods leaves us 'in no way inferior to the
celestials, except in immortality'.[4] And this is a line of thought
which the Christian writers repeat. 'The Logos,' said Clement of
Alexandria, 'became man that from man you might learn how man
may become God.'[5] Lactantius believes that the chaste man, who

[1] *Letters* 57.3.
[2] *Letters* 41.1.
[3] *Republic* 6.24.
[4] *Nature of the Gods* 2.61.
[5] *Protrepticus* 1.8.4.

has trampled all earthly things underfoot, will become 'identical in all respects with God' (*consimilis Deo*).[1] 'Every believer,' says Methodius, 'must through participation in Christ be born a Christ.'[2] And Athanasius says, 'He was made man that we might be made God.'[3]

On every side we meet the paradox of manhood, the fact that man is a helpless sinner, and the fact that man is somehow kin to God.

That paradox of manhood appears in all its sharpness in the teaching of Jesus and in his view of man. No teacher had ever a higher view of man than Jesus had. That is proved by his entire method of approach. No one ever flung such commands at men; no one ever launched such challenges at men; no one ever confronted men with such invitations. We have only to remember how much of Jesus' teaching and speaking consists of *imperatives,* culminating in the great imperative: 'You must be perfect, as your heavenly Father is perfect' (Matt. 5.48). There is no point in issuing commands, challenges and invitations, if there is no possibility of response. Jesus expected a response from men, for he worked on the assumption that every man has a sleeping hero in his soul. Jesus believed that man could make a response, even if it required his own death to make that response possible.

But this is not to say that Jesus thought lightly of sin. He did not see man through a golden and sentimental haze. The very fact that Jesus came into the world to live and die is the proof of the desperate case of man, entangled in his sin. As G. K. Chesterton once said, whatever else man is, he is not what he was meant to be. To Jesus, what mattered most was not the actualities of manhood but the potentialities of manhood. The important thing to him was not so much what man was, but what he could make him.

Bernard Falk, the famous editor, writes of the secret of the success of Lord Northcliffe. The secret was: 'He was never satisfied.' Today's results were only a foretaste of tomorrow's. 'You began your career with him every day. It was not what you had done that

---

[1] *Divine Institutes* 6.23.
[2] *Symposium* 8.8.
[3] *On the Incarnation* 54.

interested him, but what you were going to do.' Jesus was open-eyed
to the sin of man, but at the same time Jesus believed in man with
complete confidence, provided that man would accept the offer that
he was making. The problem of manhood is sin; and, as Jesus saw
it, sin operates within three spheres.

(i) There is sin *as it affects ourselves*. To Jesus sin is the failure
to be what we can be and what we ought to be. The commonest
word for sin in the New Testament is *hamartia*. *Hamartia* was not
originally an ethical word; it was a shooting word; and it means
'a missing of the target'. Sin is the missing of the target at which
life must aim, and which life ought to hit.

It is the man who failed to use his talent who is unsparingly condemned (Matt. 25.14–30). It is the salt which has ceased to be of
any use as salt that is fit for nothing but to be cast out and trampled
under foot (Matt. 5.13). It is the fig-tree which, in spite of every
advantage, stubbornly refuses to bear any crop, which is in danger
of complete destruction (Luke 13.6–9). It is the tree which does not
bring forth good fruit which is to be cut down and cast into the
fire (Matt. 7.18f.).

It is not suggested that men are equal in ability and that they can
be equal in achievement; to differing servants differing talents are
given (Matt. 25.14–30). But in one thing men can be equal—they
can be equal in effort, for no man can give to life more than he has
to give. Men are judged by how they use, and what they make of,
that which they have; and a first law of the Christian life is that
uselessness invites disaster. Sin is the determination to play selfishly
safe, to preserve and to husband life (Matt. 16.24–26), and therefore the failure to be what we can be. Dick Sheppard conceived
of judgment in terms of a man facing God, and God saying quietly:
'Well, what did you make of it?'; and that is indeed at least one of
the standards by which a man will be judged.

(ii) There is sin *as it affects others*. Sin is failure in personal
relationships in life.

(*a*) Sin is failure to respond to and to react to human need.
That is the great lesson of the parable of the sheep and the goats
(Matt. 25.31–46), and the parable of the good Samaritan (Luke
10.25–37). To see some one in need and to remain unmoved, or
to pass by on the other side, or to be so unaware of others as not

even to see their need, is sin. The human relationship should be a relationship of continual awareness issuing in continual help, and to fail in that responsibility is sin.

(*b*) Sin is failure in pity. The unforgiving servant, who had received pity from his master, had no pity for the fellow-servant who was indebted to him, and he was therefore condemned (Matt. 18.21–35). In the parable of the prodigal son the elder brother is implicitly condemned, and the reason for his condemnation is his lack of pity for the brother who had gone wrong (Luke 15.25–32). In the parable of Dives and Lazarus, Dives is sternly condemned, and the severity of the condemnation upon him is at least in part due to his callous acceptance of Lazarus as a part of the inevitable landscape of life, and his failure to see him as a person to be pitied and helped (Luke 16.19–31). As it has been well said, it was not what Dives *did* do that got him into gaol, it was what he *did not* do that got him into hell. Sin is the failure to reproduce in human life the divine pity of God.

(*c*) Sin is failure in respect for men. In the parable of the Pharisee and the tax-gatherer (Luke 18.9–14) the sin of the Pharisee was that he was completely certain of his own righteousness and arrogantly contemptuous of others. He was equally certain of his own goodness and of others' badness. To Jesus, contempt for a fellow-man is one of the most serious sins, and to be conscious of no sin is the greatest sin of all.

(*d*) Sin is failure in fellowship with men. It is separation where there should be togetherness. And the seriousness of such failure in fellowship with men is that it causes a breach not only between man and man, but also between man and God. No man can be at peace with God when he is not at peace with men. It is Jesus' instruction that, if a man is bringing a gift to the altar, and if he remembers, as he is bringing it, that there is an unhealed breach between himself and a fellow-man, he must leave the gift, go away and mend the breach, and only then come back and offer the gift, for only then will it be acceptable to God (Matt. 5.23f.). A man must be in fellowship with men before he can find the fellowship of God.

(*e*) To put it at its widest, sin is failure in love. The great characteristic of God is an undefeatable goodwill and an uncon-

querable benevolence to all men, good and bad alike. He makes
his sun to rise on the evil and the good, and sends his rain on the
just and the unjust. It is that undefeatable love that those who seek
to be the children of God must reproduce in their lives (Matt.
5.43-48). To fail to do so is to fall short of the perfection God
requires, and so is to sin. Sin is the absence of love.

In our thinking about sin in regard to others, we have so far
been thinking of it in terms of failure, that is, in negative terms.
But there is a positive aspect of sin in regard to others. Of no sin
does Jesus speak with greater severity than the sin of being the
cause of sin to others, Jesus most sternly condemns those who put a
stumbling-block in the way of others. The word which is used for
stumbling-block is a vivid word; it is the word *skandalon*. Originally
skandalon meant the bait-stick in a trap, the trigger on which the
animal stepped, and which snapped shut the jaws of the trap. Later
it came to have two general meanings. It meant anything which is
calculated to make a man trip up, like a stone set in his way, or
a rope stretched across his path. It meant a pit, cunningly dug, and
covered over with the merest skin of soil or branches, so that, when
the unwary victim stepped on it, it collapsed and engulfed him.
Jesus says that any fate is better than the fate of the man who has
caused another to stumble and fall (Matt. 18.6,7). When Robert
Burns was a young man, he went to Irvine to learn flax-dressing.
There he fell in with a man who introduced him to that way of life
which was to be his ruin. In the after days Burns said of him: 'His
friendship did me a mischief.' That is one of the most terrible of
verdicts. It is sin to ruin one's own life; it is doubly sin to ruin the
life of another. It is a terrible thing *to learn* to sin; it is a tragic
and disastrous thing *to teach* to sin.

(iii) There is sin *as it affects God*. The truth is that *all* sin
affects God; *all sin* is sin against God. The Psalmist lamented:
'Against thee, thee only, have I sinned' (Ps. 51.4). To Jesus, also,
that is the only true confession of sin.

(a) Sin is taking our way of things instead of God's way of
things, and doing so deliberately. Herein is the very essence of the
temptations of Jesus (Matt. 4.1-11; Luke 4.1-13). Jesus was confronted with a choice between two ways of attempting to carry
out his mission to men. There was the human way of bribing men

with gifts, dazzling them with wonders, striking a working compromise with the standards of the world, a way which might well have led to a spectacular, if impermanent, triumph. There was the way of sacrificial love and loyalty and service, the way of God, the way whose inevitable end was the agony of the Cross. Which way was he to take? The way of human impulse, or the way of divine command? The condemnation of the scribes and Pharisees is that they set their own human traditions above the commandments of God (Matt. 15.1–9). The tragedy at the heart of the story of the prodigal son is that the son thought that he knew better than the father; his one desire was to get away from home, to take life into his own hands, to be independent, to do what he wished. Sin is doing what we like instead of doing what God likes. Sin is allowing our will to take the place of God's will. Sin is the deliberate denial of the basic fact in life that God gave us wills that we might make them his, and that in doing his will is our peace.

(*b*) Sin is the setting of self in the middle of the picture. It is living life in the conviction that we are the most important people in the world. Jesus drew the picture of the man who gives alms, the man who fasts, the man who prays, with the object of being seen by men. His aim is to focus the eyes of men upon himself (Matt. 6.1–18). Jesus drew the picture of the scribes and Pharisees, who wore dress which was ostentatiously pious, who loved the chief seats at any function, who revelled in the flattery and the adulation of men (Matt. 23.1–12). Sin is the attempt, either deliberate or unconscious, to occupy the centre of the stage. It is walking looking unto ourselves, instead of looking unto Jesus. Sin is the enthronement of self on the throne which God alone ought to occupy.

(*c*) There is another way to put this. Since God is love, all sin is sin, not so much against law, as it is against love. Sin is not so much a breaking of God's law as it is a breaking of God's heart. Therefore, sin is the deliberate refusal of the invitation of God. In the parable of the great feast, the condemnation of the guests is that they preferred going about their own business to accepting the invitation of the king (Matt. 22.1–10; Luke 14.16–24). In the parable of the wise and the foolish builder, the wise builder is the man who erects life on the foundation which Jesus Christ offers; the foolish builder is the man who rejects the offer and the way of

Jesus Christ (Matt. 7.24–29). The condemnation of Capernaum and Chorazin and Bethsaida is that they had seen the mighty works of Jesus, they had seen God in action in Jesus, and had rejected him (Matt. 11.20–24). The condemnation of the generation of the Jews to whom Jesus preached is that they saw the wisdom of God full displayed in Jesus, and rejected it (Matt. 12.41f.).

Browning optimistically claimed: 'We needs must love the highest when we see it.' But the tragedy of the human situation rests in the very fact that that is not true. Men can see the highest and refuse it. They can be confronted with God's loving invitation, God's holy command, God's perfect truth, and they can deliberately refuse the invitation, reject the command, and remain blind to the truth—and therein is sin.

(*d*) This is the line of thought which brings us to the consideration of the most terrible of all sins, the sin against the Holy Spirit, the sin for which there is no forgiveness (Matt. 12.22–32; Mark 3.22–30; Luke 12.10). For the correct understanding of the meaning of this sin two initial things have to be remembered.

First, we must note the occasion on which Jesus said this. Jesus had cured a demon-possessed man; the scribes and Pharisees had not denied the cure—they could not; but they had ascribed it to the fact that Jesus was in league with the prince of the devils. That is to say, these scribes and Pharisees could look on the Son of God and see in him the ally of Satan; they could look on incarnate goodness and call it incarnate evil. Somehow or other they had contrived to get their spiritual standards reversed and upside down.

Second, we must be quite clear that when Jesus spoke of the Holy Spirit, he must have been using the term in its Jewish and not in its full Christian sense. The only sense in which his hearers could understand the Holy Spirit was in the Jewish sense of the term. Pentecost and the full glory and promise of the Spirit had not yet come. What, then, was the Jewish idea of the Holy Spirit? According to Jewish thought the Holy Spirit had two supreme functions. First, he brought God's truth to men. Second, he enabled men to recognize that truth when they were confronted with it. The Holy Spirit, so to speak, operated from *outside* by bringing God's truth to men, and operated from *inside* by enabling men to recognize that truth when it was brought.

To this we must now add a further fact of life. If for long enough a person refuses to use any faculty, in the end he will lose it. If a man does not use a physical skill, he will lose it. If a man refuses to use some accomplishment, he will lose it. If a man never uses some language of which once at school he had a smattering, he will forget even the little he knew. If a man reads nothing but trivial books, or listens to nothing but cheap music, in the end he will lose the ability to read good books or to listen to good music. If a man refuses to use any muscle in his body, it will in the end atrophy. When Darwin was a young man, he enjoyed reading poetry and listening to music, but, he tells us, he had so made his brain into a machine for recording biological data, that he never read poetry and never listened to music, and so he lost completely the power to appreciate them; and, he said, if he could start life over again, he would see to it that he kept the faculty of appreciation alive.

What is true of physical or aesthetic or intellectual faculties is also true of spiritual faculties. Let us, then, apply this rule here. If a man consistently enough and long enough refuses to accept and to listen to the guidance of the Holy Spirit, then in the end he will become quite unable to recognize that guidance when it comes. That is to say, he will be quite unable to recognize truth when he sees it. That is what had happened to these scribes and Pharisees. They had so long taken their way, they had so long refused God's way, they had so consistently rejected the guidance of the Spirit, that they had brought themselves into a condition that they were totally unable to recognize truth when they were confronted with it; they had come to a state when they could call good evil and evil good. That is the sin against the Holy Spirit, for it is the consequence of consistent and continuous refusal of the guidance of the Spirit.

But why should that be the sin for which there is no forgiveness? If a man has lost the power to recognize the good when he sees it, then he becomes unaware when he is doing wrong, and he becomes unable to feel the fascination of the good. He can neither feel remorse for sin nor desire for goodness. If that be so, *he cannot repent.* Penitence is an impossibility for the man who has lost the faculty to recognize the good. And without penitence there can be no forgiveness. Such a man has been shut out from forgiveness, not by

God, but by himself. There, therefore, remains the truth, which, if it had been recognized, might have saved many from an agony of soul and even from the collapse of their reason—the one man who cannot have committed the sin against the Holy Spirit is the man who fears that he has; for, if he had, the days of the possibility of remorse would be past.

The essence of sin is to dethrone God and to enthrone self; the essence of sin is to take our way instead of God's way; and the dreadful consequence is that, if a man does that for long enough, he comes to a stage when he cannot recognize God's voice when he hears it, and when he cannot recognize God when he is confronted with him.

We have still to see wherein Jesus' view of sin was new and original and far-reaching. To understand this we must first of all look at the three sins which Jesus most sternly condemned.

(i) Jesus sternly condemned *self-righteousness*. In the parable of the Pharisee and the tax-gatherer, the tax-gatherer who sorrowfully confessed his sin and who in humility acknowledged his unworthiness went away a forgiven man, while the Pharisee who thought of nothing but his own merits went away unforgiven (Luke 18.9–14). In the story of the woman who was a sinner, who anointed Jesus' feet in the house of Simon the Pharisee, the contrast is between the woman and Simon; and the contrast lies in the fact that the woman was vividly, intensely, bitterly conscious of her sin and of her need for forgiveness, while Simon was not conscious that he had any need for forgiveness at all (Luke 7.36–50). As Jesus saw it, to be conscious of no sin is in itself sin, and specially so when the consciousness of virtue brought with it contempt for those whom it regarded as sinners.

(ii) Jesus sternly condemned *externalism*. The Pharisees identified goodness with certain external acts, with the abstention from certain kinds of food, with elaborate and complicated rules of ritual washings, with a strict schedule and time-table of formal prayer, with the meticulous giving of tithes and the like. Jesus insisted that goodness has little to do with the physical condition of a man's hands but has everything to do with the spiritual condition of a man's heart (Mark 7.14–23). He likened the Pharisees to men who cleansed the outside of the cup but forgot about the inside; to white-washed tombs which gleamed white on the outside but which were inwardly full of decayed dead bodies and bones (Matt. 23.25–28). To Jesus no external act, least of all conventional religious actions, constituted goodness.

(iii) The sin which Jesus most often condemned was the sin of *hypocrisy* (Matt. 6.2,5,16; 7.5; 15.7; 16.3; 22.18; 23.13, 15, 25–27; 24.51). Fine words without fine performance were anathema to him; it was by its fruits that a tree was known and by his deeds that a man was known (Matt. 7.19,20). It is not those who say 'Lord, Lord' who enter the kingdom, but those who do the will of God (Matt. 7.21).

The word 'hypocrite' is a revealing word. It is almost a trans-literation of the Greek word *hupokritēs,* which means 'an actor'. A hypocrite is a man who acts a part, a man who presents the world with a version of himself which is in fact a lie, and it was precisely that sin that Jesus unsparingly condemned.

It is here that we come to the centre of Jesus' conception of sin. To Jesus sin is *an attitude of the heart.* It may be that a man's out-ward actions are beyond reproach, but that does not necessarily make him a good man; the deciding factor is the attitude of his heart.

The key passage is in Matt. 5.21–28. There Jesus takes two illustrations. The law says that we must not kill; Jesus says that we must not be angry with a brother man. The law says that we must not commit adultery; Jesus says that no forbidden desire must enter our hearts. Here was a moral and spiritual revolution. The ordinary view of sin was—and still is—that, if we abstain from certain forbidden deeds, we are good people. It is the teaching of Jesus that the thought and the desire are quite as important as the action and the deed. It is his teaching that we must not only not do the forbidden thing, but that *we must not even want to do it.* The test is not confined to a man's actions; the test includes the desires of a man's heart. This is new and revolutionary teaching, and immediately it lays down three great facts about sin.

(i) It brings all men under sin. We may well claim that we have never murdered anyone; we may well claim that we have never even struck anyone; but who can claim that he never experienced the emotion of anger, and who can claim that he never wished to strike anyone? We may well claim that we have never committed adultery; but who can claim that no forbidden desire has ever at any time entered his heart? It is Jesus' teaching that a man may abstain from these actions and from all such actions, and still be a sinner, if the desire to do them has been in his heart. The plain truth is that on many an occasion many a man has been kept from sinning by no higher motive than fear of the consequences. A. E. Housman wrote:

> More than I, if truth were told,
> Have stood and sweated hot and cold,
> And through their veins in ice and fire
> Fear contended with desire.

We may say: 'I am not a sinner, because I have not been guilty of any forbidden deed.' The question of Jesus is: 'Can you say that you have never *desired* to do any forbidden deed?' And that question means that all men are sinners.

(ii) This means—and it is a fact that runs all through Jesus' teaching—that the only person who can judge men is God, for God alone sees the secrets of the hearts of men. If we accept Jesus' teaching, it means that many a man confronts the world with an appearance of unimpeachable rectitude; he is full of good deeds; his attitude appears to be that of Christian charity and Christian forbearance; no one can mark in him an impure or an immoral deed. But beneath the surface, there smoulders a fire of concealed desire, of secret pride, of hidden bitterness, which God alone knows. A man can face the world with the face and even the conduct of a saint, while within him there is the heart of a devil. There can in any event be few men who would willingly allow anyone to see into the inner workings of their minds. In his book *The Meaning of Persons* Paul Tournier tells of the kind of thing which he is continually meeting in the course of his practice as a doctor. 'One man always acts with impeccable correctness, but only with great difficulty does he admit what his behaviour is like in secret. Another appears always extremely serious-minded, but has childish habits which he carefully hides. A devoutly religious man lays bare to me the intolerable tragedy of his life; he is generally thought of as an example of serene piety, whereas he is really haunted constantly by sexual obsessions.' Clearly God alone can judge this amazing complex of human nature.

Nor must it be forgotten that the other side of the matter is true. A man may appear to the world to be a constant and even a shameless sinner, and yet in his heart he may hate himself and his sin, and yearn for goodness. 'A man,' said H. G. Wells, 'may be a bad musician, and may yet be passionately in love with music.' God does not see only the evil desire; he sees the inward desire for that elusive goodness by which many and many a man is for ever haunted.

Only God can see the evil desires that are for ever kept on the leash, and only God can see the wistful yearnings which somehow never come to action; therefore, only God can judge.

(iii) If all this is true, it means that God is the only cure for sin. The plain truth of life is that a man may master his actions, but he can never by himself master his thoughts and his desires. The more he tries to do so, the worse his state becomes. For that he needs some power outside and beyond himself. In his autobiography, *The Living of these Days*, H. E. Fosdick tells of his experience when as a young man he had a serious physical and nervous breakdown: 'I learned to pray, not because I had adequately argued out prayer's rationality, but because I desperately needed help from a Power greater than my own. I learned that God, much more than a theological proposition, is an immediately available Resource.' The only cure for sin, the only solution to the paradox of manhood, is the indwelling power of God. A man becomes a man, a man reaches his true manhood, when he can say with Paul: 'It is no longer I who live; but Christ who lives in me' (Gal. 2.20).

13

WHAT JESUS SAID ABOUT HIMSELF

Before we begin to think about the teaching of Jesus about himself and about his work, it is necessary to start with a reminder. There is a tendency to think of Jesus' work entirely in terms of his death. But it must be remembered that the life of Jesus is every bit as important as the death of Jesus. It is quite clear that the death of Jesus would have had no value without the life which preceded it. To think of the work of Jesus without thinking about his life is just as serious an error as to think of the work of Jesus without thinking about his death. His work must be seen in terms of his life and his death.

There were three great descriptive titles by which Jesus was often addressed, and to which he would certainly have laid claim.

(i) Jesus regarded himself as a *preacher*. Early in his ministry he said to his disciples: 'Let us go on to the next towns that I may preach there also, for that is why I came out' (Mark 1.38). To preach was the primary object for which he came into the world.

The word which is used in Greek for 'to preach' is *kērussein;* this is the verb of the noun *kērux,* which means 'a herald'. The word *to preach* has in English come down in the world; it is a word which has acquired associations of dullness and conventionality without any thrill. But, when the word is used of Jesus, it means *a herald's proclamation*. It is a message from the King; it is the word of authority with no hesitations and apologies in it; it means that Jesus brought a proclamation and announcement from God to men. It is clear that Jesus regarded himself as having come to men with truth such as the world had never heard before. Jonah had been the most effective of preachers; Solomon had been the wisest of men, and had drawn visitors from distant places to listen to and to admire his wisdom; but with the coming of Jesus something greater than the supreme greatness of the past had arrived in the world (Matt. 12.41f.; Luke 11.31f.). Here was a message greater by far than the greatest message of the past. It is significant to see how this word *kērussein* is used of Jesus.

(*a*) Sometimes the word is used absolutely (Matt. 11.1; Mark 1.38; Luke 4.44). The message of Jesus is *the divine proclamation of God to men*. It was not an airing of doubts, nor was it a weaving of fine-spun arguments. It had the accent of certainty and of authority, as of one who was not expressing his own opinions but bringing God's indisputable and unanswerable truth to men.

(*b*) Most often the proclamation is *the proclamation of the Kingdom* (Mark 1.14; Matt. 4.23; 9.35; Luke 8.1). We have seen that the Kingdom is a society upon earth in which God's will is as perfectly done as it is in heaven. The preaching of Jesus was the announcement of the will of God; the life of Jesus was the demonstration of life lived in obedience to the will of God; the summons of Jesus was the summons to accept the will of God; the offer of Jesus was the offer of power to live according to the will of God; the message of Jesus was that the time when the will of God would be supreme is on the way. The claim of Jesus was that he could bring to men the will of God, as no one else had ever done and as no one else could ever do.

(*c*) The proclamation is characteristically and essentially *the proclamation of a gospel,* the accouncement of good news (Matt. 4.23; 9.35; Luke 4.18). It was the news that the will of God is the salvation of men; it was the news of a God who was reaching out to men in love far more than he was pursuing them in wrath. It was the offer of the supreme gift of God to those who would receive it.

(*d*) The proclamation of the good news was not unconditional, for it included *a demand for repentance* (Matt. 4.17; Mark 1.14f.). The offer of God is made to those who turn away from their past lives and who turn to him.

Jesus came to men as the herald of God's truth, God's will, God's love, God's demand upon men.

(ii) Jesus regarded himself as a *prophet*. In reference to himself he said that it was only in his own country and among his own countrymen that a prophet had no honour (Matt. 13.57; Mark 6.4; Luke 4.24). When he set his face to go to Jerusalem, he went saying that it was unthinkable that a prophet should perish outside Jerusalem (Luke 13.33). The place of the prophet in God's scheme of things is expressed most essentially by Amos: 'Surely the Lord God does nothing, without revealing his secret to his servants the prophets' (Amos 3.7). The prophet is not simply, or even mainly, a *foreteller* of future events; the prophet is a man who is within the counsels of God, and who, therefore, is able to *forthtell* the will of God to men. Jesus came as one uniquely knowing the mind of God, uniquely in the confidence of God, so that he might bring God and the will of God to men.

(iii) Jesus regarded himself as a *teacher*. There are three closely inter-related words used of Jesus; in fact they all most probably go back to the same Aramaic word.

(*a*) There is the word *Rabbi,* to which the other two words go back. Six times Jesus is called Rabbi, five of them by his disciples and the sixth by a blind man appealing for his sight (Mark 9.5; 10.51; 11.21; 14.45; Matt. 26.25; 26.49). *Rabbi* literally means 'My great one', and it was the title given by the Jews to the greatest and the wisest teachers. This was a title which Jesus was offered and which he accepted.

(*b*) There is the word *epistatēs*. Luke alone uses this word; Luke was a Gentile, and this is a characteristically Greek word, and Luke uses it as a Greek substitute for the Hebrew Rabbi. In Luke's Gospel it occurs six times, five times on the lips of the disciples, and once on the lips of a leper desiring to be healed (Luke 5.5; 8.24,45; 9.33,48). This is a great Greek word. It is the word in Greek for a headmaster, and in particular for the man who was in charge of the *ephebi,* the cadets who were engaged in their years of national service of their country. The duty of the *epistatēs* was defined as being 'to lead the souls of the young men on the path which leads to virtue and to every manly feeling'. Here again Jesus is regarded, and regards himself, as the master teacher.

(*c*) There is the word *didaskalos. Didaskalos* is the normal Greek word for 'teacher' and in the Synoptic Gospels it is used of Jesus more than thirty times, as is the kindred verb *didaskein* which means 'to teach'. It is the word by which all kinds of people addressed

Jesus. He is so addressed by his disciples (Mark 4.38; 10.35; 13.1);
by the Pharisees (Matt. 9.11; Mark 12.14); by the Sadducees
(Mark 12.19); by people who came to him with all kinds of requests
for help and for guidance (Mark 9.17; 10.17; Luke 8.49; 12.13).

The narrative of the Gospels shows Jesus teaching in all kinds
of places and under all kinds of conditions; in the synagogues
(Matt. 9.35; 13.54; Mark 1.21; 6.2; Luke 4.15,31; 5.17; 13.10);
in the Temple (Mark 11.17; 12.35; 14.49); in the cities and villages
(Matt. 11.1; Mark 6.6); by the seaside, with a fishing-boat for a
pulpit (Mark 2.13; 4.1; Luke 5.3); in the streets (Luke 13.26), and
in the inner circle of the disciples (Matt. 5.2; Mark 8.31; 9.31;
Luke 11.1).

Jesus was the teacher *par excellence,* and it was the title by which
towards the end he called himself. When he was making preparations for the last Passover meal, his instructions were to go to a
certain house in the city and to say: 'The Teacher says, My time is
at hand; I will keep the passover at your house with my disciples'
(Matt. 26.18; Mark 14.14; Luke 22.11). It was as if he knew that
that was the title by which he would be most easily recognized.

So, then, Jesus regarded himself as the preacher, the herald of
God; the prophet, the one within the secret confidence of God;
the teacher, the one who could bring men wisdom from heaven
to meet the problems of earth.

We have even more direct information about the teaching of
Jesus regarding his own work, for there is in the first three Gospels
a series of sayings in which Jesus stated what he came to do.

(i) He came to be *the Divine Physician of the sick souls of men.*
After the call of Matthew, Matthew made a feast to which Jesus
came. Matthew was a tax-gatherer, and his friends were in the eyes
of the orthodox as disreputable as himself, and to the feast he
invited these friends. At that feast Jesus also consented to be a
guest. The orthodox religious leaders were shocked that any re-
spectable man, and especially anyone who had any claims to be a
teacher, should keep such company. How could any decent person
be the fellow-guest of tax-gatherers and sinners? Jesus' answer was:
'Those who are well have no need of a physician, but those who are
sick . . . I came not to call the righteous, but sinners' (Matt.
9.9–13; Mark 2.14–17; Luke 5.27–32). Later Epicurus was to call

his teaching 'the medicines of salvation', and Epictetus was to call his lecture-room 'the hospital for the sick soul'. When Antisthenes, the founder of the Cynic philosophy, was asked why he was so severe with his pupils, he answered: 'Physicians are exactly the same with their patients.'

Jesus regarded himself as the Divine Physician who had come to enable men to be healed of the universal human disease of sin. That is to say, Jesus did not regard the sinner with loathing and with repulsion. A lay person might find himself disgusted and revolted and sickened by some terrible physical condition; a doctor would find in the same condition only a call to his compassion and a summons to his skill. Jesus did not regard the sinner as a damned man; he regarded the sinner as a sick man. Jesus came, not to shrink away in fastidious horror from the disease of sin, not complacently to shut his eyes to sin and to pretend that it did not exist, not to palliate and to excuse sin; he came to be the Divine Physician who has the cure for sin. The very fact that Jesus could think of himself in this way is the proof that the desire of God is not for the destruction but for the healing of the sinner.

(ii) He came to be *the Divine Servant of men*. There was an occasion when James and John and their mother Salome came near to precipitating a crisis in the company of the disciples. They came with the request that, when Jesus entered into his Kingdom, they should sit in the chief places of honour, one on his right hand and one on his left. The only throne which Jesus offered them was the throne of martyrdom. Very naturally the other disciples were angry that James and John had sought to steal a march upon them and to earmark the principal place of honour for themselves. It seemed for a moment that personal ambition and personal resentment were on the verge of wrecking the unity of the apostolic company. It was then that Jesus spoke to them of the only true royalty, the royalty of service, and ended his words by saying of himself: 'The Son of Man came, not to be served, but to serve' (Matt. 20.20–28; Mark 10.35–45).

Here is the proof that Jesus came into this world not so much to receive things from men as to give things to men; he came not for his own sake, but for the sake of men; he came not to dominate like a conqueror but to serve like a servant. It was a commonplace of ancient religion that men should sacrifice to God; but it was something completely new that God should sacrifice himself for men.

(iii) He came to be *the Seeker of the lost*. When Jesus passed through Jericho on his last journey to Jerusalem, he made the startling proposal that he would stay in the house of Zacchaeus. Zacchaeus was the chief of the tax-gatherers, and such a proposal would shock all patriotic and orthodox Jews to the core of their being. But Jesus laid down the principle on which he was acting: 'The Son of Man came to seek and to save the lost' (Luke 19.10).

It is essential to give to the word 'lost' its right meaning in a passage like this. It has not its theological sense of 'damned', condemned to destruction by God for ever and ever; it has its simple, human, sorrowful meaning of 'in the wrong place, going in the wrong direction, all astray'. Zacchaeus had set out on the wrong way to find real happiness and real success in life. In the journey of life he was lost—and there seemed no way back. Jesus came to find the men and women who were heading straight away from God, and who were, therefore, lost, and to turn them back to God, for the road to God is the only right road. He did not wish to annihilate sinners, he wished to find them.

There is here the closest possible connection with the idea of Jesus as the shepherd who seeks and finds the lost sheep (Luke 15.3–7). The Palestinian shepherds were expert trackers; they could follow the track of the sheep where no one else could even see a sign of it, until, often at the risk of their lives, and always at the expense of toil and weariness, they found the lost sheep and brought it back. Even so Jesus tracks down the sinner, the man who has taken the wrong road, the man who had got his life into the wrong place, the man who is lost, until he finds him, not to blast him with the divine wrath, but to bring him back within the circle of the divine love.

(iv) He came to be *the Fulfiller of all that was best in the past*. 'Think not', he said, 'that I have come to abolish the law and the prophets; I have come not to abolish them, but to fulfil them' (Matt. 5.17). Here is Jesus' claim that in him there are fulfilled the highest hopes and dreams of the past. Before his coming men glimpsed the truth; in him they could gaze on the full vision of the truth. Before his coming men heard faint echoes of the voice of

God; in him they heard clearly and unmistakably the voice of God. Before his coming they had their gropings towards that which life should be; in him they saw life and received life, and life more abundant. Before his coming men had a knowledge of God, of the will of God, and of goodness which was partial and fragmentary; in him there came to them the perfect knowledge of God and of God's will. In the old Joseph story there is a wistful text. Joseph in prison came upon the imprisoned servants of Pharaoh's household and they were troubled; and the reason of their trouble was in their own words: 'We have had dreams, and there is no one to interpret them' (Gen. 40.8). Jesus is the great interpreter and fulfiller of the dreams which haunt the minds and hearts of men.

(v) He came to be *the Divine Liberator of mankind*. 'The Son of Man,' he said, 'came . . . to give his life as a ransom for many' (Mark 10.45). Men were in the power of sin, captured by sin as a brigand captures a traveller on a journey, in servitude to sin as a man is a slave to a master from whom he cannot escape, a slave who can never pay the price of his own freedom, and by the work of Jesus man is liberated from the evil power which has him in its grip and from the fetters of sin which bind him. Jesus is the emancipator of mankind from the power of sin.

(vi) He came as *the Saviour of men*. There is one saying of Jesus which is entirely characteristic and peculiarly revealing. On the road to Jerusalem Jesus and his men came to a Samaritan village. They requested hospitality, and not surprisingly they were rebuffed. Thereupon James and John wished to call down fire from heaven and to obliterate the inhospitable village, but Jesus forbade it. 'The Son of Man,' he said, 'came not to destroy men's lives but to save them' (Luke 9.56). Therein is the very essence of the gospel. It was not for destruction but for salvation that Jesus came into the world. Even when men opposed him, his one desire was not to wipe them out, but even then to save them. His great aim was to save men both from the continued folly and the ultimate consequences of their sin.

Here then we have Jesus characterized in his own words—the Divine *Physician* come to cure men from the universal human disease of sin; the Divine *Servant* come to spend himself for others; the tireless *Seeker* searching for men who had got life into the wrong place and who were travelling on the wrong road in the wrong direction; the great *Fulfiller* of all the hopes and dreams and visions which have lodged within the hearts of men; the Divine *Liberator* come to set men free from the grip and the power of sin; the *Saviour* of men who would not even destroy his enemies, but who sought to the end to save them from their folly and from all that their folly would bring in time and in eternity.

But there is another side to this picture, and without the other side the picture would be but half drawn. To leave the picture there would be to leave a picture in which there is nothing but gentleness, but there is iron in the picture too.

(i) Jesus came with the demand for *implicit obedience.* He told the story of the wise and the foolish builders, of how the one chose for his house a foundation so strong that no storm could shake the house, and of how the other chose for his house a foundation so infirm that the storms shattered it into ruin (Matt. 7.24–27). The implication of this story is quite clear. The claim of Jesus is that he and his teaching are the only possible foundation for life, that the man who founds his life on him is certain of safety and that the man who refuses to found his life on him is certain of disaster. There are few men in history who have dared to say that obedience to them is the only foundation for life.

(ii) He came with the claim for *complete loyalty.* The claim of Jesus for loyalty is explicit and unique. 'He who loves father or mother more than me is not worthy of me, and he who loves son or daughter more than me is not worthy of me' (Matt. 10.37). 'If anyone comes to me and does not hate his own father and mother and wife and children and brothers and sisters, yes, and even his own life, he cannot be my disciple' (Luke 14.26). This is to say that it is the demand of Jesus that loyalty to him must take precedence of even the supreme human loyalties of life. He came with the demand that he must be given a place in a man's life which not even his nearest and dearest can share.

(iii) He came as *the great disturber.* 'Do not think,' he said, 'that I have come to bring peace on earth; I have not come to bring peace, but a sword' (Matt. 10.34). It was the plain fact of history that when Christianity first came into this world it frequently split families into two. One of the earliest charges levelled against the Christians was that they tampered with domestic relations. Most people wish nothing more than to be left alone, and, when Jesus enters a man's life, he shakes him out of his comfortable lethargy. No man can invite Jesus into his life and remain the way he is. It is true that Jesus offers peace, but it is the peace which only comes after a battle which may tear a man's heart out.

(iv) He came as *the agent of judgment*. 'I came,' he said, 'to cast fire on the earth; and would that it were already kindled!' (Luke 12.49). Fire is always the symbol of judgment in biblical language. Fire is that which burns out the alloy and leaves the metal pure. Jesus came to bring the cleansing fire of God in judgment upon sin.

(v) He came as *the touchstone of God*. It was his claim—and no claim can go any further—that a man's reaction to him settled that man's eternal destiny. 'Whoever is ashamed of me and of my words,' he said, 'of him will the Son of man be ashamed when he comes in his glory' (Luke 9.26; Mark 8.38). 'Everyone who acknowledges me before men, the Son of man also will acknowledge before the angels of God; but he who denies me before men will be denied before the angels of God' (Luke 12.8f.; Matt. 10.32f.). It is the claim of Jesus that response to him is the test which settles a man's eternal destiny.

So then Jesus came with the claim for absolute obedience, with the claim for complete loyalty, with the claim to have the right to disturb life, with the claim to be the agent of judgment, with the claim to be nothing less than the touchstone of God. If anyone makes a claim like that, he is either a deluded megalomaniac or the Son of God; he is either mad or divine. Which was Jesus?

14

THE SELF-CHOSEN TITLE OF JESUS

If we place any reliance at all upon the Gospel records of the life of Jesus, we are compelled to conclude that *Son of Man* was Jesus' own most personal and most deliberately chosen title for himself. The title Son of Man occurs in the New Testament about eighty-two times, and with a single exception all the occurrences are in the Gospels. The one exception is the saying of Stephen in Acts 7.56: 'Behold, I see the heavens opened, and the Son of man standing at the right hand of God.' Within the Gospels themselves the phrase never occurs except on the lips of Jesus with one exception, and that one exception is a quotation of the words of Jesus. The question of the crowd to Jesus is: 'How can you say that the Son of man must be lifted up? Who is this Son of man?' (John 12.34). If we accept the account of the Gospels, this is clearly Jesus' own title for himself. Paul never uses it; the General Epistles never use it. To all intents and purposes no one uses it but Jesus; no one ever even addresses Jesus by that title. It is uniquely his title for himself, and therefore we are bound to try to find out what it means.

Jesus normally spoke Aramaic; in Aramaic 'Son of Man' is *bar nasha;* and that is the Aramaic phrase simply for 'a man', a member of the human race. If a rabbi was beginning a story or a parable, he would begin: 'There was a *bar nasha,* there was a man.' This is also true of the Hebrew of the Old Testament, in which the phrase would be *ben adam,* and would mean simply 'a man'. Again and again in the Old Testament the phrase 'son of man' means quite simply 'a human being', and appears as an expression strictly parallel to 'a man'. 'God is not a man that he should lie,' said Balaam, 'or a son of man that he should repent' (Num. 23.19). 'Blessed is the man who does this,' said the prophet, 'and the son of man who holds it fast' (Isa. 56.2). 'Put not your trust in princes,' says the Psalmist, 'in a son of man, in whom there is no help' (Ps. 146.3). 'What is man that thou art mindful of him, and the son of man that thou dost care for him?' (Ps. 8.4). The phrase 'son of man' normally means simply 'a man'.

To this we must add Ezekiel's characteristic use of the term 'son of man'. In Ezekiel the term 'son of man' occurs more than ninety times as God's address to the prophet. 'Son of man, stand upon your feet, and I will speak with you' (Ezek. 2.1). 'Son of man, eat what is offered to you; eat this scroll, and go, speak to the house of Israel' (Ezek. 3.1). 'Son of man, go, get you to the house of Israel, and speak with my words to them' (Ezek. 3.4). In Ezekiel the phrase 'son of man' contrasts the weakness and the frailty of Ezekiel's humanity with the knowledge, the strength, and the glory of God.

It is along these lines that certain interpreters of the Bible have sought to explain Jesus' use of the title. Such explanations have taken four lines.

(*a*) It is suggested that when Jesus spoke as Son of Man he was speaking in terms of his human nature, and that when he spoke as Son of God he was speaking in terms of his divine nature. That view is in serious danger of turning Jesus into a split personality and of forgetting that in his one person the two natures were fused into one.

(*b*) E. F. Scott in *The Kingdom and the Messiah* quotes two other explanations. It has been suggested that, when Jesus used the title Son of Man, he was thinking of himself in terms of The Man, The Representative Man, The Man in whom humanity finds its perfect expression, its perfect example, its consummation, and its peak. F. W. Robertson wrote of Jesus: 'There was in Jesus no national peculiarity or individual idiosyncrasy. He was not the Son of the Jew, or the Son of the Carpenter; nor the offspring of the modes of living and thinking of that particular century. He was The Son of Man.' That suggestion fails on two grounds. First, it is too abstract. Second, as we shall go on to see, it does not fit the facts, for it is with the title Son of Man that Jesus in fact makes, not his most human claims, but the claims that are most super-human and divine.

(*c*) E. A. Abbott thought that Jesus used this phrase against two backgrounds, against the background of Ezekiel and of Ps. 8. We have already seen that in Ezekiel 'son of man' expresses human weakness, frailty and ignorance. But what of Ps. 8? That psalm very uniquely combines the idea of man's humiliation and weakness and the idea of man's likeness to God. 'What is man that thou art mindful of him, and the son of man that thou dost care for him?' There speaks the frailty of man. 'Yet thou hast made him little less than God, and dost crown him with glory and honour. Thou hast given him dominion over the works of thy hands; thou hast put all things under his feet' (Ps. 8.4–6). There speaks the divine destiny of man. The Psalmist shows man's *present humiliation* and man's *infinite potentiality*. So Abbott believed that 'by his adoption of the expressive title Son of Man Jesus sought to intimate that he stood for the divine potentiality in human nature. He was the Man in whom God revealed himself, and whose victory would deliver all men from their bondage.'[1] The objection to that view is simply its complicated nature. If Jesus did use the title Son of Man in that way, it is almost impossible that anyone could have grasped his meaning when he spoke.

(*d*) It has been suggested that, when Jesus used this title, he was deliberately contrasting himself with the visions of a Messiah who was a supernatural, apocalyptic, wonder-working figure, that he was deliberately disowning all such ideas, and that he was speaking of himself as humble and simple, a complete antithesis of the popular ideas of the Messiah. The objection to that view is that, as we shall see, Son of Man was in fact a messianic title, and a messianic title of the most superhuman and supramundane kind. The one thing that the title Son of Man would never convey to a Jew was the idea of humility and simplicity.

Each of these interpretations has its truth and its beauty, but we shall clearly have to turn in some other direction to explain Jesus' choice and use of this title.

There is one other view at which we must look before we come fully to grips with what we believe to be the right interpretation of this title. It has been suggested that, when Jesus spoke of the Son of Man, he was not speaking of himself, but of some one to

[1] *Notes on New Testament Criticism*, pp. 140 ff.

whom he was looking forward, and for whom he was preparing the way. When he sent out his twelve apostles, he said: 'You will not have gone through all the towns of Israel, before the Son of man comes' (Matt. 10.23). That could certainly be taken to mean that the Son of Man was some one whom Jesus was expecting in the immediate future. When Jesus was speaking of the final destiny of men, as Luke reports it, he said: 'Everyone who acknowledges me before men, the Son of man will also acknowledge before the angels of God' (Luke 12.8). That again could be interpreted as differentiating betweeen Jesus and the Son of Man. But the fact is that, if we had only these two passages to work on, we could argue that Jesus looked forward to the coming of the Son of Man as some one other than himself; but against these passages we have to set more than eighty passages in which it is clear that Jesus is speaking of himself. There are, indeed, differing versions of the same saying of Jesus, which make it certain that Jesus was speaking of himself when he spoke of the Son of Man. In Luke 6.22 we read: 'Blessed are you when men hate you, and when they exclude you and revile you, and cast out your name as evil, *on account of the Son of man!*' In Matt. 5.11 we read: 'Blessed are you when men revile you and persecute you and utter all kinds of evil against you falsely *on my account.*' It is clear that, in these two versions of this saying of Jesus, *on account of the Son of Man* and *on my account* mean the same thing. We may confidently disregard the suggestion that Jesus thought of the Son of Man as some one other than himself.

It will greatly help us to understand Jesus' use of the term Son of Man, if we understand the problem which faced him. Jesus' problem was the problem of communication; but in his case that which he desired to communicate was not so much a message in words as himself. It would, therefore, be of the greatest value to him, if he could find a compendious phrase which would be a summing up of himself, and which would enter into and lodge in men's minds. In his search for such a title he might do any of three things. He might invent a completely new title which had never been used before. That he did not do, because Son of Man is not a new title and certainly had been used before. Second, he might appropriate a title which existed, but which was colourless and vague, and fill it with a new content, and so use it for his own purposes. That again he did not do, for, as we shall see, there is no more vivid title in certain aspects of Jewish thought between the Old and New Testaments than the title Son of Man. Third, he might take a title which was known, and which painted a recognizable picture, and he might use it in a way so new, so unparalleled, so startling, that men would be shocked and jolted into attention. Nothing awakens interest like the completely new use and application of a well-known thing. We believe that this is what Jesus was doing, when he took the title Son of Man as his self-chosen title for himself. What, then, was the lineage of this title?

Without doubt the origin of the title Son of Man is to be found in the Book of Daniel. In Dan. 7 the seer has a vision of the great empires which have hitherto held world power and world dominion. He sees these empires in terms of wild beasts. They have been so savage, so cruel, so callous, so bestial that they cannot be typified in any other way. There is the lion with eagles' wings (v. 4), which stands for Babylon. There is the bear with three ribs in its mouth (v. 5), which stands for Assyria. There is the leopard with four wings and four heads (v. 6), which stands for Persia. There is the fourth nameless beast, with iron teeth, dreadful, terrible and exceedingly strong (v. 7), which probably stands for the all-conquering might of the empire of Alexander the Great. These are the powers which have hitherto held the world in thrall, and they are describable only in terms of monstrous beasts. But now their power is broken and their day is ended. So the writer goes on:

'I ·aw in the night visions,
and, behold, with the clouds of heaven there came one like a son of man,[1]
and he came to the Ancient of Days and was presented before him.
And to him was given dominion and glory and kingdom,
that all peoples, nations and languages should serve him;
his dominion is an everlasting dominion, which shall not pass away,
and his kingdom one that shall not be destroyed' (Dan. 7.13f.).

The power which is to receive the kingdom is further defined: 'But the saints of the Most High shall receive the kingdom, and possess the kingdom for ever, for ever and ever' (Dan. 7.18).

The point is that the new power which is to inherit the ever-

---

[1] So all the modern translations; the AV 'like the Son of man' is wrong.

lasting kingdom is gentle and humane; as the previous world empires could only be typified as savage beasts, so this empire of God can be typified as a son of man. Further, the power which is to inherit the kingdom is identified as the saints of the Most High, that is, the Chosen People, the nation of God, the people of Israel. The prophecy of Daniel is a prophecy of the exaltation of Israel and the coming of a world power which is gentle and humane as the preceding world powers were savage and bestial; and just as the previous powers were doomed to destruction this new power is destined to last for ever.

Even in their darkest days, even when they were a captive and subject nation, the Jews never lost the sense of being the Chosen People, and never lost the confidence that soon or late the kingdom would belong to them and to God. To that end they never ceased to expect the Messiah who was to be God's agent and instrument in the liberation of his people and the bringing in of his kingdom. It was only natural that they should nourish their hearts on passages of prophecy like the Daniel passage. The Daniel passage said that the kingdom would be given to one like unto a son of man. It was, therefore, a very natural step that the Messiah, the delivering one, should come to be known as the Son of Man. If there had been nothing but the Daniel passage, the idea of the Messiah Son of Man might well have developed into the picture of one who was gentle and humane and kind, and quite unlike the savage world rulers who had gone before; but perhaps about 70 BC there emerged a book which spoke much about that Son of Man, and which sharpened and intensified the picture. There are many passages in Enoch which describe that Son of Man, and in all of them the Son of Man is a divine, superhuman, pre-existent figure waiting beside the throne of God to be unleashed with victorious power against the enemies of God. He has been hidden and preserved in the presence of God from the beginning. Before the sun and the signs of the Zodiac were created, and before the stars of heaven were made, he was named before the Lord of Spirits. He will come from God, and when he comes it is true that he will be a staff whereon the righteous may lean and stay themselves, and a light to the Gentiles. But he will mightily destroy the enemies of God and of the people of God. He will put down the kings and the mighty from their seats, and the strong from their thrones; he will break the teeth of sinners; as for those who will not acknowledge him, darkness shall be their dwelling and worms shall be their bed. Terror and pain shall seize men when they see this Son of Man. They shall plead for mercy; their faces will be filled with darkness and shame; the sword shall abide before his face; as straw in fire God's enemies will burn before him, and as lead in the water they shall sink before the face of the righteous and no trace of them will ever again be found. He will sit in judgment, and his word will go forth and be strong (Enoch 46.2–6; 48.2–9; 62.5–9; 63.11; 69.26–29). So, then, in Enoch the Son of Man became a divine, superhuman, apocalyptic figure, ready to descend in victorious power from heaven, breathing out slaughter and destruction, exalting the righteous but smashing the enemies of God, and bringing in the end all things to judgment. This was the picture of the Son of Man which the Jews knew, and this was the picture that title would paint in their minds; and it was not unnaturally a popular picture in days of national misfortune and distress.

Now let us turn directly to Jesus' use of this title. We can distinguish various ways in which Jesus according to the Gospels used this title.

(i) He used the title Son of Man as a substitute for 'I'. 'Foxes have holes,' he said, 'and birds of the air have nests; but the Son of man has nowhere to lay his head' (Luke 9.58; cp. Matt. 11.19; 16.13; Luke 6.22; 7.34).

(ii) He specially used the title when he was making great claims or declarations. 'The Son of man came to seek and save the lost' (Luke 19.10). 'The Son of man came not to be served but to serve, and to give his life as a ransom for many' (Matt. 20.28; Mark 10.45; cp. Luke 9.56; 11.30).

(iii) He used it in connection with the Resurrection. After the experience on the Mount of Transfiguration, his instructions to his disciples were: 'Tell no one the vision, until the Son of man is raised from the dead' (Matt. 17.9; Mark 9.9).

(iv) He used it in connection with the glory which was to come, and into which he would enter. 'Hereafter,' he said at his trial, 'you will see the Son of man seated at the right hand of Power, and coming on the clouds of heaven' (Matt. 26.64; Mark 14.62;

Luke 22.69; cp. Matt. 19.28; Matt. 24.30; Mark 13.26; Luke 21. 27).

(v) He used it in connection with his coming again. 'There are some standing here who will not taste death before they see the Son of man coming in his kingdom' (Matt. 16.28). 'The Son of man is coming at an hour you do not expect' (Matt. 24.44; Luke 12.40; cp. Matt. 24.27,30,37,39; Luke 17.24,26,30; Luke 18.8).

(vi) He used it in connection with the coming judgment. 'The Son of man will send his angels, and they will gather out of his kingdom all causes of sin and all evildoers' (Matt. 13.41; 16.27; 25.31; Mark 8.38; Luke 9.26; 21.36).

We are not claiming that every Gospel word that we have cited is a verbatim report of the words of Jesus. The salient and significant fact is that the Gospel writers, when they wished to report or depict Jesus speaking about such subjects, naturally thought of him as using the term Son of Man. If we pause here, we see that there is nothing in these uses of the term Son of Man which does not fit into the picture which we have already found in Enoch. This was a way of speaking of the Son of Man which was perfectly intelligible to popular Jewish thought. The majestic glory, the stern judgment, the ultimate triumph could all have come straight from the picture in Enoch.

(vii) But *Jesus repeatedly used the term Son of Man in connection with his sufferings and his death.* 'The Son of man will be delivered to the chief priests and scribes, and they will condemn him to death, and deliver him to the Gentiles to be mocked and scourged and crucified, and he will be raised on the third day' (Matt. 20.18; Mark 10.33; Luke 9.44; 18.31f.). 'The Son of Man must suffer many things' (Mark 8.31; 9.12; Luke 9.22; cp. Matt. 17.12,22; 26.2, 24,45; Mark 9.31; 14.41; Luke 22.22,37; 24.7).

Here is something completely new; here is something which had never before been even remotely connected with the Son of Man; here is something which would leave the hearers of Jesus shocked and incredulous and wondering if they had heard aright. And here is something which explains a whole series of problems which are otherwise inexplicable.

(i) It explains the reaction of Peter at Caesarea Philippi. At Caesarea Philippi the sequence of events was that Peter made his

great discovery; Jesus thereupon went on to teach his disciples that
he must go to Jerusalem to suffer and to die; and to this teaching
the reaction of Peter was violent: 'God forbid, Lord! This shall
never happen to you' (Matt. 16.21f.; Mark 8.31f.; Luke 9.22).
Peter's reaction was more than the reaction of appalled and horrified love. It was due to the fact that he was totally incapable of
effecting any connection between the idea of the Son of Man and
the idea of suffering, let alone the idea of death. To him such a
connection was a contradiction in terms, something which was incredible, incomprehensible and impossible.

(ii) It also explains the violence of the reaction of Jesus to
Peter's outburst. 'Get behind me, Satan!' Jesus said. 'You are a
hindrance to me; for you are not on the side of God, but of men'
(Matt. 16.23; Mark 8.33). Jesus, too, knew the idea of the Son of
Man in Enoch. In his temptations he had been faced with the
temptation to become that kind of Son of Man; and in this moment
at Caesarea Philippi Peter was facing Jesus again with that very
same temptation which had faced him in the wilderness at the
beginning of his ministry, a temptation which was now all the more
acute with the Cross looming ahead.

(iii) It explains one of the most puzzling situations in the whole
story of the Gospels. We have seen that Jesus repeatedly foretold
his sufferings and his death. *Why then were the disciples so utterly
unprepared for them?* Why was it that the Cross came to the
disciples as such a devastating shock? The reason is quite simple.
They regarded Jesus as the Son of Man, and to the end of the
day they never succeeded in effecting any connection in their minds
between the Son of Man and suffering. It is one of the habits of the
human mind that it shuts itself to that which it does not wish to
hear. By a curious kind of selective process it accepts what it wishes
to accept and rejects what is either frightening, disturbing or incomprehensible to it. The connection of the Son of Man with suffering was so revolutionary, so contradictory of every received and
accepted belief, that the minds of the disciples could not cope with
it, and never assimilated it. Majesty, glory, judgment, triumph,
they could understand, but not all the warnings of Jesus could
penetrate minds shackled to conventional beliefs.

(iv) It explains the paramount importance of the Resurrection in the belief of the early Church, and especially in the belief of the Jewish section of the Church. It has been well said that the Resurrection was the 'star in the firmament' of the early Church. It was the Resurrection which vindicated Jesus as Son of Man. If his career had ended on a cross, it would have been impossible to see in him the consummation of the idea of the Son of Man; but the triumph of the Resurrection clothed Jesus with the ultimate victorious majesty which was necessary for the completing of the picture.

It remains to ask one question. When did Jesus import this new and startling connection with suffering into the idea of the Son of Man? It is a notable fact that apart from two instances in Mark 2 Jesus did not use the term Son of Man until after Caesarea Philippi; that is to say, this title belongs to the closing act of his ministry. It has been suggested that Jesus set out with the highest hopes of winning men, and that only bit by bit was he forced to the conclusion that he would be despised and rejected and would end on the cross. This would mean that Jesus, so to speak, began with the Enoch idea of the Son of Man and only modified it to include suffering under the compulsion of circumstances. We have already produced our evidence that this is not so in our discussion of the baptism of Jesus. At his baptism he heard the voice which told him that he was at one and the same time the Messianic King and the Suffering Servant. From the beginning he saw both the Cross and the glory.

Jesus took and used the term Son of Man, not because he wished to enact and fulfil it as men understood it; not because it was so colourless that he could insert any meaning he chose into it. He took it that he might use it in such a way that those who heard him might be shocked and startled into listening and thinking. Even then it required the events of the Cross and the Resurrection to interpret it to the dull minds of men. But by his use of it Jesus expressed his own certainty that as the Suffering Servant he must accept the Cross, and that as the Messianic King he must enter into glory.

15

THE MEN AGAINST JESUS

When we read the Gospels, it is very difficult for us to under-stand the implacable hostility and the envenomed hatred which could not rest until they had driven Jesus to the Cross. We find it almost impossible to understand why anyone who lived a life of such love and service and kindness and sympathy should have in-curred such savage opposition. The opposition was quick to arise. As early as the second chapter of Mark's Gospel we find the sus-picion and the criticism of the scribes and Pharisees in action. We find the opposition to Jesus centred in three groups of people— the scribes and the Pharisees, who together form one group, the Sadducees, and the priests. Let us take these groups one by one, and let us try to see why they hated Jesus so much that they strained every nerve and were prepared to use any means to eliminate him.

(i) The opposition to Jesus is consistently connected with *the scribes and Pharisees* (Matt. 12.2,14; Mark 2.16; 3.6; Luke 6.2,7; 14.3). The scribes and Pharisees cannot be understood apart from the Jewish conception of the law. In Judaism the word law is used in three senses. First, it is used of the Ten Commandments, which are the law *par excellence*. Second, it is used of the Pentateuch, the Five Rolls, the first five books of the Bible, which are the law as contrasted with the prophets and the writings which constitute the rest of the Old Testament. Third, it is used of what is known as the scribal or the oral law. Clearly the third was the last to come into being, but in the eyes of the scribes and Pharisees it was the most important and the most binding of all.

To the Jew there was nothing in this world so sacred as the law. 'The law,' they said, 'is holy and has been given by God.' They believed that the law had been created two thousand years before the world had been created, and that it would last for ever after the world had come to an end. They said that Adam had been created on the day before the Sabbath in order that he might begin life with an act of the observance of the Sabbath law. They even went the length of saying that God himself studies the law. 'There are twelve hours in a day,' the saying ran, 'and during the first three the Holy One sits down and occupies himself with the law.' It was believed that every single syllable and letter of the law was holy and divine. It was believed that the law contained the whole will of God, fully and finally stated, that nothing could be added to it, or subtracted from it, and that there was no appeal against its ordinances and verdicts.

Here we come upon the whole principle upon which the scribes and Pharisees thought and lived. If the law is the complete will of God, it must contain everything that is necessary for the good life. But, when we go to the law, what we find is a series of great principles. For the scribes and Pharisees this was not enough. They desired to find a series of rules and regulations which would govern every action and every situation which could possibly arise in life. If the law is absolutely final and complete, then it must follow that anything necessary for the good life which is not *explicit* in it must be *implicit*. So, then, throughout the centuries the scribes made it their business and their life work to deduce from the great moral principles of the law an unending series of rules and regulations to meet every possible individual action and situation in life. In the hands of the scribes the comparatively few supreme moral principles were turned into an infinity of petty rules and regulations.

This mass of rules and regulations is what is known as the scribal or the oral law, or the tradition of the elders (Mark 7.3; Matt. 15.2). And the day was to come when this mass of scribal regulations was regarded as even more sacred and binding than the actual word of Scripture itself, so that it could be said: 'It is more culpable to teach contrary to the precepts of the scribes than contrary to the law itself.'

For many centuries this mass of material was never committed to writing. It was lodged in the memories of the scribes, who were the experts in the law, and passed down by word of mouth from generation to generation of rabbis. Midway through the third

Christian century a summary of all this scribal law was written down. The name of that summary is the *Mishnah,* which consists of 63 tractates on various sections of the oral law, and which in English makes a book of almost 800 pages. Not content with this, scribal scholarship embarked on the task of making commentaries on the tractates of the *Mishnah.* These commentaries are embodied in the *Talmuds.* There are two *Talmuds;* the *Jerusalem Talmud* runs to 12 printed volumes, and the *Babylonian Talmud* to 60 printed volumes. To put it in a summary way, the law of the Ten Commandments under scribal development had finished up as a library—for ever unfinished—of rules and regulations.

It is necessary to see this scribal method in action, because it was Jesus' head-on collision with this whole conception of religion which was the immediate cause of his crucifixion. We can see this process at work in the development of the Sabbath law. In the Old Testament itself the Sabbath law is very simple: 'Remember the sabbath day to keep it holy. Six days you shall labour and do all your work, but the seventh day is a sabbath to the Lord your God; in it you shall not do any work, you, or your son, or your daughter, your manservant, or your maidservant, or your cattle, or the sojourner who is within your gates; for in six days the Lord made heaven and earth, the sea, and all that is in them, and rested the seventh day; therefore the Lord blessed the sabbath day and hallowed it' (Ex. 20.8–11). Here there is laid down a great religious principle, conserving the rights of God and of man. But this was not enough for the scribes; this had to be worked out in hundreds and hundreds of rules and regulations about what could, and what could not, be done on the Sabbath day. In the *Mishnah* the regulations about the Sabbath run to 24 chapters, on one of which a certain famous rabbi spent two and a half years in detailed study. In the *Jerusalem Talmud* the section on the Sabbath runs to sixty-four and a half columns, and in the *Babylonian Talmud* it occupies a hundred and fifty-six double folio pages.

How, then, did the scribes proceed? The commandment says that there must be no work on the Sabbath. The scribe immediately asks: 'What is work?' Work is then defined under thirty-nine different heads which are called 'fathers of work'. One of the things which are forbidden is the carrying of a burden. Immediately the

scribe asks: 'What is a burden?' So in the *Mishnah* there is definition after definition of what constitutes a burden—milk enough for
a gulp, honey enough to put on a sore, oil enough to anoint the
smallest member (which is further defined as the little toe of a
child one day old), water enough to rub off an eye-plaster, leather
enough to make an amulet, ink enough to write two letters of the
alphabet, coarse sand enough to cover a plasterer's trowel, reed
enough to make a pen, a pebble big enough to throw at a bird, anything which weighs as much as two dried figs. On and on go the
regulations.

It was the scribes who worked out all these rules and regulations; it was the Pharisees who devoted their whole lives to the
keeping of them. The word *Pharisee* means either 'interpreter', in
the sense of skilled expert in the Law, or perhaps more likely 'separated one', in the sense of a man who has separated himself from
all ordinary people and from all ordinary activities to concentrate
on the keeping of these innumerable legal regulations. This
to the scribes and Pharisees was goodness; this, they believed, was
what God desired. To keep these rules and regulations was to serve
God.

Let us take another example. Certain ritual cleansings and washings were laid down. Before a man might eat, he must wash his
hands in a certain way. He must take at least a quarter of a log
of water, that is, a measure equal to one and a half eggshells of
water. He must hold the hands with the finger-tips upwards and
pour the water over them until it ran down to the wrists; he must
then cleanse the palm of each hand with the fist of the other; he
must then hold the hands with the finger-tips pointing downwards
and pour water on them from the wrists downwards so that it ran
off at the finger-tips. This was not a matter of hygiene; it was a
matter of ritual; even if the hands were spotless, it must be done.
To do it was to please God, to fail to do it was to sin.

It can easily be seen that the identification of true religion with
this kind of thing has certain inevitable consequences. Religion
became *legalism;* it became the meticulous keeping of a mass of
rules and regulations. Religion became *externalism;* so long as a
man went through the right actions and the right ritual he was a
good man, no matter what his heart and thoughts were like, and

no matter how hard and unsympathetic he might be towards·his fellowmen. Religion could very easily become a matter of *pride*. A man might spend his whole life keeping these rules and regulations, which were obviously impossible for ordinary people, and might then thank God that he was not as other men are (Luke 18.9–14). There were never more than six thousand Pharisees; and it was inevitable that many of them were proud and arrogant and contemptuous of the common man. In fairness to the Pharisees it must be remembered that they were completely in earnest. To undertake this mass of rules and regulations must have been a tremendous task, yet in that law there was their delight; they loved the discipline of it; in it all they saw the service of God. Even if they were misguided in their whole method and outlook they were none the less fanatical in their desire to serve God. The scribes and Pharisees clashed with Jesus on three main grounds.

(*a*) It is quite clear that under this system religion became the affair of the expert. Only the scribes knew the immense ramifications of the oral law; only the Pharisees could keep them. Obviously all this put true religion out of reach of the ordinary working man. He could not engage in the ordinary working activities of the world and keep the law. To keep the law was in itself a whole-time occupation. Religion in its higher reaches became the preserve of the expert and of the professional.

Here was the first objection of the scribes and Pharisees to Jesus. He had never been to a rabbinic college; he was not a trained scribe and a professional rabbi; he was a mere layman, a carpenter from Nazareth. What possible right had he to set up as a teacher and to presume to talk to men about God and about life? 'How is it that this man has learning, when he has never studied?' (John 7.15). 'What is this? A new teaching!' (Mark 1.27). 'Is not this the carpenter's son? Do we not know his mother and his brother and his sisters? Where did this fellow get these things he is talking about?' (Matt. 13.54–58; Mark 6.1–5; Luke 4.22–24). These experts in religion were horrified, scandalized, insulted that this untrained Galilaean should invade their territory and should dare to teach. This was accentuated by the respect and adulation which these scribes and Pharisees claimed and received. The very name *Rabbi* means 'My Great One'. 'Let your esteem for your friend,' they said, 'border on your esteem for your teacher, and let your respect for your teacher border on your reverence for God.' They laid it down that the claims of a teacher went beyond the claims of a father—for instance, if it came to a choice between ransoming a father and a teacher from captivity, the teacher must be ransomed first—for a man's father only brought him into this life, while his teacher brought him into the life of the world to come.

Into this world of religious privilege, religious precedence, religious prestige there strode this young Galilaean with his revolutionary teaching—and the scribes and Pharisees were shocked and offended. What right had any common man to talk about God? The religious professionals have never granted to the common man the right to speak about God, and the religious professionals of Palestine were determined to silence Jesus of Nazareth.

(*b*) There was worse to come. From the point of view of the scribes and Pharisees evidence began to pile up that Jesus was himself a consistent and deliberate breaker of the law, that he consented to others breaking it, and that he even incited them to do so.

In the story of the Gospels there is a dramatic development in the idea of Jesus as a deliberate breaker of the Sabbath law. When he first healed a man on the Sabbath in the synagogue at Capernaum, there was astonishment and amazement (Mark 1.21–27). Such a thing could not be done in a corner and hidden away (Mark 1.28), and soon there developed a Pharisaic system of espionage in which the emissaries of the Pharisees deliberately followed Jesus to watch him and to accumulate more and more evidence that he was an inveterate and deliberate and blasphemous Sabbath-breaker. The matter began with the incident of the disciples plucking and eating the ears of corn as they passed through the cornfield on the Sabbath day (Matt. 12.1–8; Mark 2.23–28; Luke 6.1–5). There was no question as to the legality of the plucking itself; the law expressly laid it down that a man might pluck the ears of corn as he passed through a field, so long as he did not use a sickle (Deut. 23.25). But, when this was done on the Sabbath, it technically broke no fewer than four scribal Sabbath laws. To pluck the ears of corn was technically *to reap* on the Sabbath; to separate the husks from the grain was technically *to winnow;* to rub the grain between the palms of the hands was technically *to grind;* and the whole process was technically *to prepare food for use.* The simple act of the disciples was a fourfold breach of the oral law.

In the eyes of the scribes and the Pharisees the matter became rapidly worse. The plucking of the ears of corn might be regarded as a private matter; but Jesus began publicly to heal on the Sabbath day. The Jewish law on Sabbath healing was quite clear. To heal on the Sabbath day was to work on the Sabbath day, and was, therefore, forbidden. There were certain necessary exceptions. Medical attention was permissible when life was actually in danger, as, for instance, in the case of diseases of the nose, throat, eyes and ears. But, even in such cases it was lawful only to take steps to keep a man from becoming worse, and not to make him any better. The trouble might be arrested, but not cured. So, it was lawful to put a plain bandage on a wound, but not a medicated bandage; it was lawful to put plain cotton wool in the ear, but not medicated material. Unless life was in danger, the oral law definitely and distinctly forbade healing on the Sabbath day.

This was a law which Jesus knowingly and deliberately broke. When Jesus entered into the synagogue where the man with the withered hand was worshipping, the emissaries of the scribes and Pharisees were there deliberately to see if he would heal in order that they might have evidence on which to accuse him, and, when he did, they went out and laid their plans to destroy him (Matt. 12.10–14; Mark 3.1–6; Luke 6.6–11). Here was open declaration of war: the scribes and Pharisees were there to watch; and Jesus in their presence deliberately broke their law. Here was calculated defiance. Nor did Jesus stop there. He healed the bowed woman (Luke 13.11–17), the man with the dropsy (Luke 14.1–6), the man who was born blind (John 9), and all on the Sabbath day.

Jesus' point of view was quite simple. He believed that human need takes precedence of any ritual rule or regulation. It was quite true that the life of none of these people was in actual danger; as far as their lives were concerned the matter might well have waited until the next day; but it was Jesus' conviction that no human being must suffer for an hour longer than was necessary in order to keep a ritual law. He cited the example of David who in the extremity of hunger and of need had taken the shewbread which none but the priests might eat (Matt. 12.3f.; Mark 2.25f.; Luke 6.3f.). He cited the fact that the law permitted that an animal which had fallen into a pit might be helped on the Sabbath day. How much more must a human being, a child of God, be helped (Matt. 12.11f.; Luke 13.15; 14.5)?

Here was a head-on clash. The scribes and Pharisees saw religion in terms of obedience to rules and regulations, to rituals and to ceremonies; Jesus saw religion in terms of love to God and love to man. The scribes and Pharisees were perfectly sincere. To them Jesus was a law-breaker, a blasphemer, a bad man, an underminer of the very foundations of religion. It was absolutely necessary to destroy him before he did any more disastrous damage to Jewish religion. It is one of the supreme tragedies of the death of Jesus that he was hounded to his death by the most fanatically religious people of his day, by men who genuinely believed that they were serving God and protecting the rights of God by killing him.

(c) There was one final difference between Jesus and the scribes and Pharisees. To the scribes and Pharisees the attitude of Jesus to sinful men and women was shocking and incomprehensible. He well knew that they contemptuously called him the friend of tax-gatherers and sinners (Matt. 11.19; Luke 7.34). When Jesus went to be a guest at the feast that Matthew gave after his call, the Pharisees demanded of Jesus' disciples how their master could bear to eat with tax-gatherers and sinners (Matt. 9.10,11; Mark 2.15f.; Luke 5.29f.). 'This man,' complained the Pharisees, 'receives sinners and eats with them' (Luke 15.1). When Jesus invited himself to the house of Zacchaeus, the scandalized exclamation was: 'He has gone in to be the guest of a man who is a sinner' (Luke 19.7). Jesus believed that there is joy in heaven over one sinner who repents and comes home (Luke 5.7,10). The scribes and Pharisees said: 'There is joy before God when those who provoke him perish from the world.'

This attitude coloured the whole relationship of the Pharisees with their fellowmen. The Pharisees regarded ordinary people who did not keep the whole scribal law as unclean. Even to touch the garment of such a person was to be defiled. A Pharisee was forbidden to receive a non-Pharisee as a guest or to be the guest of such a person; a Pharisee would never dream of entering the house of such a person, of sitting at meat with such a person, or of entering into even the remotest fellowship with such a person. Their one aim was to have nothing whatever to do with the sinner; the one aim of Jesus was to get alongside the sinner and to woo him back to God.

Here was another head-on collision. The Pharisees narrowed the love of God until it included only themselves; Jesus widened the love of God until it reached out to all men, saints and sinners alike. There can be no common ground between a religion which sees the sinner as a man to be avoided at all costs and a religion which sees the sinner as a man to be sought out at all costs, between a religion which sees the sinner as a man to be saved and a religion which sees the sinner as a man to be destroyed. The inevitable conclusion of the Pharisaic mind was that Jesus himself was like the company whom he sought out, and that he was making light of, and even encouraging, sin. Once again he seemed to them an evil moral influence, an undoer of the work of God, a character so dangerous to true religion and all that true religion stood for, that he must be immediately eliminated before he could do any more harm.

There is the very stuff of tragedy in this situation. The Pharisees were the spiritual aristocracy of their age; no body of men in history ever took their religion more seriously and in more earnest. As Paul was later to say they had zeal, but not zeal according to knowledge (Rom. 10.2). Because their religion was a religion of legalism they could not understand a religion of love; because Jesus was not one of the group of professional religious experts, they believed that he had no right to speak at all; because he did not keep the petty details of the scribal law, they believed him to be a bad man; because he sought out sinners, they believed him to be a sinner. There was no possible chance of agreement here. The Pharisees in their mistaken zeal for God were determined to eliminate the Son of God.

(ii) Into the opposition to Jesus there entered *the Sadducees.* We often speak of the Pharisees and Sadducees together, as if they jointly formed one group. But in point of fact the Pharisees and the Sadducees were very different, and their beliefs were well-nigh opposite to each other. The Pharisees believed in the resurrection of the body and in judgment to come; the Sadducees did not. On one occasion Paul used this point of difference to throw the Sanhedrin into complete confusion and to set the Pharisees and Sadducees arguing so violently with each other that they almost forgot him (Acts 23.6–10). The Pharisees believed in angels and spirits; the Sadducees did not. The Pharisees believed in the freedom of the will and in individual choice; the Sadducees did not.

But there was one basic difference between the Pharisees and the Sadducees. The scribal or oral law was to the Pharisees the greatest and the most sacred thing in the world. The Sadducees rejected the whole of it. They accepted only what was written in Scripture and would have nothing to do with the scribal elaborations of it; and of Scripture they only accepted the Pentateuch, the first five books of the Old Testament, and did not give any authoritative place either to the prophets or to the writings. 'The Sadducees,' says Josephus, 'say that only what is written is to be esteemed as legal. On the contrary, what has come down to us from the tradition of the fathers need not be observed.'[1] The Sadducees did not accept the mass of rules and regulations on which the Pharisees founded religion and life.

But the distinguishing characteristic of the Sadducees was that they were the aristocrats of the Jews. 'They only gain the well-to-do,' said Josephus, 'they have not the people on their side.' 'This doctrine has reached few individuals, but these are of the first consideration.'[2] Just because of this the Sadducees were the collaborators with Rome; they were well content to cooperate with their Roman masters in the government of Palestine. It is usually among the wealthy that political collaborators are found in any conquered country, because the wealthy have most to lose, and because they are prepared to collaborate in order to keep their comfort, their wealth and their privileges. Such collaboration necessitated frequent association and meetings with the Gentiles which for a Pharisee would have been impossible and unthinkable. The scribal law laid it down: 'Six things are laid down by the rabbis about the man who does not keep the law: "entrust no testimony to him, take no testimony from him, trust him with no secret, do not appoint him

[1] *Antiquities* 13.10.6.
[2] *Antiquities* 13.10.6; 18.1.4.

the guardian of an orphan, do not make him the custodian of any charitable funds, do not accompany him upon a journey." ' The strict Pharisee would never enter the house of a Gentile, or allow a Gentile to enter his. He would not even buy anything from, or sell anything to, a Gentile. For him even ordinary things like bread and milk were unclean, if they were sold, or had been handled, by a Gentile. For a Sadducee all this was quite impossible. The Sadducees would come into frequent contact with the Roman officials, would entertain them in their houses, and would be entertained in theirs. There were even Sadducees who were in sympathy with Greek culture and with the Greek way of life. To a Pharisee a Sadducee would be unclean, and nothing better shows the virulence of the hatred of the Pharisees for Jesus than the fact that they were prepared to enter into a confederacy with the Sadducees to work for the elimination of Jesus.

Why, then, were the Sadducees as eager as the Pharisees to compass the death of Jesus? The real reason for the hatred of the Sadducees lay in the fact that they completely misread Jesus. They looked on Jesus as a political revolutionary ready to raise a rebellion against Rome, or they were at least convinced that it was in such a rebellion that his teaching must end. Luke tells us the charge on which the Jews brought Jesus to Pilate. In their private trial of Jesus the Jewish charge against Jesus was a charge of blasphemy, the charge that he had claimed to be the Son of God (Matt. 26.65; Mark 14.64; Luke 22.71). But that was not the charge on which they brought him to Pilate. When they brought him to Pilate the charge was: 'We found this man perverting our nation, and forbidding us to give tribute to Caesar, and saying that he himself is Christ a king' (Luke 23.2). That was almost certainly a charge concocted by the Sadducees, for they knew that Pilate would never listen to a charge of blasphemy, which would have seemed to him a mere matter of Jewish religion, but that he was bound to listen to a charge of political insurrection. It is further to be noted that the Sadducees did not expect and did not await and pray for a Messiah. Why? The Sadducees knew that the one thing Rome would not tolerate was political unrest and disturbance. Any governing party which allowed any kind of rebellion to arise would receive short shrift from the Roman imperial government and would certainly be speedily evicted from office. The last thing the Sadducees desired was political trouble, for then they would lose their power, their prestige, their comfort, their wealth. It was all in their interests to keep things as they were. For them the coming of the Messiah would be, as they saw it, a disaster. Their thoughts ran like this: 'This man may at any moment put himself at the head of a revolution. Undoubtedly he has unique powers, and undoubtedly the people would follow him. Even if he does not himself do so, his teaching is so explosive that he may raise forces which will erupt even independently of him. If that happens, there will be trouble with the Romans. True, he himself will be crushed. But, if there is trouble, we will lose our jobs in the government and in the administration; our wealth will be confiscated, our place will be lost; our luxury and our comfort will be gone; and that must not happen.'

The hatred of the Sadducees was based entirely on self-interest. In Jesus they saw a threat to their privileges; therefore Jesus must go. The Pharisees hated Jesus because they were men of principle, however misguided their principles were. The Sadducees hated Jesus because they were the complete time-savers. The Pharisees hated Jesus from religious motives, even if these motives were entirely mistaken. The Sadducees hated Jesus for no other reason than worldly and materialistic selfishness. To ensure their own continued comfort and luxury the Sadducees were prepared to do anything to obliterate this perilous and disturbing Jesus of Nazareth.

(iii) There was a third group of people active in the steps which led to the crucifixion of Jesus—*the priests*. Very often in the narrative of the Gospels they are described as *the chief priests*. The chief priests included two kinds of people.

(a) They were ex-High Priests. In the days of Israel's independence the High Priest was appointed for life. But under the Romans the high priesthood became a matter of plots, ambition and intrigues, and the High Priest became a pawn in the political game. It, therefore, happened that High Priests came and went rapidly, as one man after another plotted his way to the supreme office, or as the Roman government substituted one for another to suit its own purposes. Between 37 BC and AD 67 there were no fewer than twenty-eight High Priests. There were, therefore, always ex-High Priests alive; such a man was Annas; and these were included among the chief priests.

(b) Although the high priesthood was not hereditary, the High Priests were drawn from a limited number of aristocratic families. Of the twenty-eight High Priests we have mentioned, all but six came from four families, the families of Phabi, Boethos, Kamith and Annas. These families formed a priestly aristocracy, and their members were known as the chief priests.

At the beginning of Jesus' ministry we do not hear much about the priests, but that is because his early ministry was in Galilee and did not as yet impinge upon the priesthood, which was centralized in the Temple in Jerusalem. By the time of Peter's great discovery and confession at Caesarea Philippi, Jesus was well aware that the priests were his sworn enemies who would be in at the death (Matt. 16.21; 20.18; Mark 8.31; 10.33; Luke 9.22). When we come to the last days and hours of Jesus' life, as we read the narrative of the Gospels, we cannot help feeling that the whole scene is dominated from start to finish by the terrible malignity of the priests. It is true that the elders and the scribes appear on the scene, but the whole impression is that the driving force of the enmity to Jesus was the embittered, malevolent hatred of the priests. When Jesus spoke, they well understood his condemnation of them (Matt. 21.45). They were unhappy and displeased at the welcome Jesus received when he entered Jerusalem (Matt. 21.15). Very naturally they bitterly resented the cleansing of the Temple, and demanded to know what was Jesus' authority for speaking and acting as he did (Matt. 21.23; Mark 11.18,27f.; Luke 20.1). They are continuously shown as plotting to kill Jesus, and seeking a way to eliminate him without arousing the crowd (Matt. 26.3,4; 27.1; Mark 14.1; Luke 19.47; 20.19; 22.2). It was to them that Judas went with the offer of his treachery (Matt. 26.14; Mark 14.10; Luke 22.3f.). It was the priests who were behind the arrest in the Garden, and the Temple police were involved in it (Matt. 26.47; Mark 14.43; Luke 22.52). It was to the house of Caiaphas that Jesus was taken for the mockery of a trial (Matt. 26.57; Mark 14.53; Luke 22.54). The body which tried Jesus was meant to be the Sanhedrin, the supreme council of the Jews; that council contained scribes and

Pharisees, Sadducees, elders and priests; but once again the impression is unavoidable that it was the implacable hostility of the priests which ruled the whole proceedings. They were prepared to hire false witnesses against him (Matt. 26.59; Mark 14.55). The High Priest was the principal cross-examiner of Jesus (Matt. 26.62–65; Mark 14.60–64). It was the priests who delivered Jesus to Pilate (Matt. 27.1,2; Mark 15.1). It was they who were the accusers of Jesus (Matt. 27.12; Mark 15.3; Luke 23.3–5,10). It was they who urged the mob to choose Barabbas and to refuse Jesus (Matt. 27.20; Mark 15.11), and they were the leaders of the shouts which demanded crucifixion for Jesus (Luke 23.23). They flung their mockery at him on the cross (Matt. 27.41; Mark 15.31). Even when he was, as they thought, dead, they could not leave him alone. They urged Pilate to set a special watch on the tomb (Matt. 27.62–66), and they tried to bribe away the evidence for the empty tomb (Matt. 28.11f.). In the last days and the last hours the leaders of the insane fury of hatred were the priests.

Why this enmity? To understand this we must understand the place which the priests held in Jewish religion. The only qualification for the priesthood was unbroken physical descent from Aaron. If a man possessed that descent, nothing could stop him being a priest; if he did not possess that descent, nothing could make him a priest. Moral qualification and spiritual power did not enter into the matter. The only things which could debar a man from exercising the priestly function were certain physical defects (Lev. 21.16–23), of which the later oral law enumerated 142; but even if a man was debarred from exercising the Temple functions of a priest by physical defect, he was still entitled to the perquisites and the emoluments of a priest.

According to Josephus there were 100,000 priests. There were so many of them that they could not possibly serve all at the one time in the Temple. The whole priesthood was on duty only at the festivals of the Passover, Pentecost and Tabernacles. They were divided into twenty-four courses, each of which served for two weeks in the year. This is to say that a priest's working year consisted of no more than five weeks.

The perquisites of the priests were enormous. Of all the sacrifices offered in the Temple, only the burnt-offering was entirely consumed by the fire of the altar. In every other case, only a quite small part of the victim was burned, and of the rest the priests received a very large part. In the case of the sin-offering, which was the offering not for an individual sin but for man as a sinner, only the fat was burned, and all the meat was the perquisite of the priests. It was the same in the case of the trespass-offering, which was the offering for particular sins. In the case of the peace-offering, which was the offering for special occasions of thanksgiving, the fat was burned on the altar; the worshipper received the greater part of the meat; but the priest received the breast and the right shoulder. The one remaining offering was the meat-offering, which was offered along with every other offering. The name is nowadays deceptive, for the meat offering consisted of flour and oil; it is called the 'cereal offering' in the Revised Standard Version. Of it only a small part was burned and the priests received all the rest. With the single exception of the burnt-offering there was no offering of which the priests did not receive a substantial part. No class of the people knew such luxury in food. In Palestine the ordinary working man was more than fortunate if he tasted meat once a week, whereas the priests suffered from an occupational disease consequent on eating too much meat. It is to be noted that even when a priest was not on actual Temple duty, and even if he was debarred from actually officiating at sacrifices because of physical blemish, he still received his full share of the offerings; for by far the greater amount of the meat which fell to the share of the priests need not be consumed in the Temple itself, but could be eaten in any clean place, and could, therefore, be distributed to the non-officiating priests in their own homes.

Nor did the privileges and perquisites of the priests end there. The priests received *the first fruits of the seven kinds* (Ex. 23.19), that is, of wheat, barley, the vine, the fig-tree, the pomegranate, the olive and honey. This offering was meant primarily as an offering to God, but its proceeds were enjoyed by the priests. For the personal support of the priests there was brought to the Temple the *terumah*, which consisted of the choicest fruits of every growing thing (Num. 18.12). One-fiftieth of the crop was the average amount brought to the priests. In addition to this there were the *tithes* (Num. 18.20–22), which consisted of one tenth of everything

which could be used as food. This was for the support of the
Levites, but the priests received their share. Still further, there was
the *challah,* or offering of kneaded dough. The priests were entitled
to one twenty-fourth part of the dough used in any baking.

It can be seen that the priests were a privileged body of men in
a comparatively poor country, living a life of unexampled ease and
luxury at the expense of the people. It is not in human nature that
men should willingly abandon a way of life like that.

Still further, the priests occupied a unique position between man
and God. Since the time of Josiah all local shrines had been forbidden, and the law was that sacrifice could be offered only at the
Temple in Jerusalem, and only through a priest. The priest, therefore, stood between man and God. If a man sinned, and the right
relationship of God was to be restored, sacrifice must be made, and
that sacrifice could be made only through the priest. Seldom can
any body of men have wielded such spiritual power.

All this was true of the priests—and yet one thing was abundantly
and increasingly clear—*if Jesus was right, the priests were wrong.*
If Jesus' view of religion was correct, then the priesthood and all
its functions were a vast irrelevancy. There are not lacking signs
in the religious history of Israel that many times there was a breach
between prophet and priest. Isaiah heard God say:

> 'What to me is the multitude of your sacrifices? . . .
> Bring no more vain offerings;
> incense is an abomination to me' (Isa. 1.11–15).

In face of all the paraphernalia of sacrifice Micah declared:

> 'He has showed you, O man, what is good;
> and what does the Lord require of you but to do justice,
> and to love kindness,
> and to walk humbly with your God?'

God has no use for rivers of oil and thousands of rams; these are
not the offerings he desires (Micah 6.1–8). Again and again the
prophets with their ethical demands challenged the ritual of the
priests. With Jesus the matter had come to a head. 'I will have
mercy and not sacrifice,' he said, quoting Hosea (Matt. 9.13;
12.7; Hosea 6.6).

Here was the supreme challenge. Either Jesus had to go, or the whole sacrificial system had to go. Either the priesthood destroyed Jesus, or Jesus destroyed the priesthood. Beyond a doubt there were priests who loved the Temple service, and who through it sought devotedly to serve God; but, human nature being what it is, the vast majority of the priests must have seen in him a threat to their comfortable way of life, a menace to their spiritual supremacy, the assailant of their vested interests; and they decided that, before Jesus destroyed them, they must destroy him.

It was a queer tangle of human motives which hounded Jesus to the Cross. All the loveliness of his life mattered nothing. The Pharisees honestly and sincerely believed him to be a bad man and an evil influence on other men. The Sadducees wished only to remove a possible threat to their civil and political power and social standing. The priests were determined to eliminate a teacher whose teaching spelt the end of their perquisites and of their spiritual dictatorship. Jesus cut across blind and rigorous orthodoxy, political and social ambition, ritual and spiritual aristocracy; and so men came to the conclusion that he must die.

16

THE RECOGNITION OF JESUS BY MEN

Jesus was well aware of the opposition which was gathering against him, and of the atmosphere of hatred with which he was surrounded, and he knew that, humanly speaking, in the end his enemies would take his life away. He saw ahead, not the possibility, but the certainty of the Cross. This situation confronted Jesus with a question which demanded an answer. Was there anyone who had recognized him? Was there anyone who knew, however dimly and imperfectly, who and what he was? His Kingdom was a kingdom within the hearts of men, and, if there was no one who had enthroned him within his heart, then his Kingdom would have ended before it ever began. But if there was some one who had recognized him and who understood him, even if as yet inadequately, then his work was safe.

To this question Jesus had to find an answer. To find that answer he had for a brief time to disengage and disentangle himself and his little company from the tensions and threats which surrounded them, so that he could be alone with them. To that end he set out for the territory away to the north of Galilee to an area ruled not by Herod Antipas but by Philip the Tetrarch. On the road there was plenty of time for talk in which Jesus could open his heart and mind to the men into whose hands he must commit his work, when the arms of the Cross claimed him. So they came to Caesarea Philippi, and it was against the background of Caesarea Philippi that Jesus asked the most important of all questions and received the greatest of all answers. That background makes the question of Jesus and the answer of Peter all the more astonishing. There could have been few areas with more vivid associations than the area around Caesarea Philippi.

(i) In the ancient days the whole area had been intimately connected with the worship of Baal. It had been, as Sir George Adam Smith says in *The Historical Geography of the Holy Land,* one of the chief dwellings of the Baalim, and may well have been the Baal-gad of which Joshua speaks (Josh. 11.17; 12.7; 13.5). Thomson in *The Land and the Book* enumerates no fewer than fourteen sites of ancient temples of Baal in the near neighbourhood of Caesarea Philippi. Caesarea Philippi was a place where the memory of the ancient gods of Canaan brooded over the scene.

(ii) In Caesarea Philippi the ancient gods of Greece also had their dwelling place. On the hillside there was a grotto or cave with a fountain of waters within it which was said to have been the birthplace of Pan, the god of nature. To this day the inscription 'To Pan and the Nymphs' can be traced in the stone of the grotto. So closely associated was this place with the worship of Pan that its ancient name was Panias, which still survives in the name Banias which is the modern name for the area. The hill, the grotto and the fountain of waters were called Paneion, which means the shrine of Pan. Even to this day the atmosphere of the old Greek gods broods over the place, so that the modern traveller H. V. Morton speaks of 'the eerie grotto'. Sir George Adam Smith describes the place: 'You come to the edge of a deep gorge through which there roars a headlong stream, half stifled by bush. An old Roman bridge takes you over, and then through a tangle of trees, brushwood and fern you break into sight of a high cliff of limestone, reddened by the water that oozes over its face from the iron soil above. In the cliff is a cavern . . . The place is a very sanctuary of waters, and from time immemorial men have drawn near it to worship. As you stand within the charm of it . . . you understand why the early Semites adored the Baalim of the subterranean waters even before they raised their gods to heaven, and thanked them for the rain.' Around Caesarea Philippi there gathered the mystery of the old Greek gods of nature, who were still revered and worshipped when Jesus and his disciples came there.

(iii) Still further, it was within this cavern that the River Jordan was said to have its source and origin. Josephus describes it: 'There is a very fine cave in a mountain, under which there is a great cavity in the earth; and the cavern is abrupt, and prodigiously deep, and full of still water. Over it hangs a vast mountain, and under the cavern arise the springs of the River Jordan.'[1] Much of the history of Israel centered round the Jordan and the Jordan valley, and, therefore, Caesarea Philippi was compassed about with memories of the great things which God had done for his people Israel.

(iv) But there was something even more impressive yet at Caesarea Philippi. In the time of Jesus Caesarea Philippi was one of the most beautiful cities in the East. In 20 BC Augustus had given it as a gift to Herod the Great; and Herod had built on the hill-top a great white temple of gleaming marble with the bust of Caesar in it for the worship of Caesar. 'Herod,' says Josephus in the passage which we have already quoted in part, 'adorned this place, which was already a very remarkable one, still further by the erection of this temple which he dedicated to Caesar.' In another place Josephus again describes the temple and the cave: 'When Caesar had further bestowed on Herod another country, he built there also a temple of white marble, hard by the fountains of Jordan. The place is called Paneion, where there is the top of a mountain which is raised to an immense height, and, at its side, beneath, or at its bottom a dark cave opens itself, within which there is a horrible precipice that descends abruptly to a vast depth. It contains a mighty quantity of water, which is immovable, and when anyone lets down anything to measure the depth of earth beneath the water, no length of cord is sufficient to reach it.' In due time Herod's son Philip inherited the area and the city. He further beautified the already lovely city and the temple, and he changed the name from Panias to Caesarea, 'the City of Caesar', and to the name Caesarea he added his own name Philippi, 'Philip's City of Caesar', to distinguish it from the other Caesarea in the south, which was the seat of the government of Judaea, and where Paul was imprisoned. So, then, at Caesarea all the majesty of imperial Rome and the worship of the Emperor looked down on Jesus and his men. Still later Herod Agrippa was to call Caesarea Philippi by the name Neroneas in honour of the Emperor Nero.

(v) There remains one strange fact to add. It seems that Caesarea Philippi possessed the right of asylum; it was a place

[1] *Antiquities* 15.10.3.

where the fugitive could find shelter and be safe. An inscription describes it as: 'August, sacred, with the rights of sanctuary, under Paneion.' In its history Caesarea Philippi must have sheltered many a fugitive, and it was there that Jesus went for shelter before the breaking of the gathering storm.

The history of Caesarea Philippi is written in the changes of its name. Originally it was Balinas, for it was the centre of the worship of Baal; then it became Panias, for men regarded it as the birthplace of the Greek god Pan; then it became Caesarea, because it was the city where Caesar was worshipped; later it was to become Neroneas, named in honour of Nero; today it has reverted to its ancient name, for it is called Banias, which is the Arabic form of Panias, since Arabic does not have the sound of the letter *p*.

It was here that Jesus asked his greatest question and flung down his greatest challenge, and surely there could be no more dramatic set of circumstances. Here was a wandering Galilaean preacher, who had begun as a carpenter in Nazareth and who had now no place to lay his head. With him there was a little company of men without education, without money and without prestige. At that very moment the orthodox religious authorities were resolved on his death as a dangerous heretic, and he was well on the way to being an outlaw for whom a cross was waiting. He stood in a place surrounded by the memories of the ancient gods of Canaan, a place where men worshipped the gods of Greece, a place around which the memories of the history of Israel gathered, a place where the eye could not miss the white splendour of the temple where men worshipped the majesty of imperial Rome; and there against the backcloth of the world's religions, the world's history and the world's power, Jesus asked the question which demanded the answer that he was the Son of God. It sounds like preposterous madness. But the fact remains that the ancient gods are but a memory. Great Pan is dead. The Empire of Rome is dust. As H. V. Morton says, the great white marble stones of the imperial temple have become building material for the house of an Arab sheik. But Jesus Christ is still gloriously and triumphantly alive. The old faiths died; the old kingdoms fell; but the Kingdom of the homeless Galilaean still stands and still enlarges its borders throughout the world.

So, then, it was here that Jesus asked his all-important question. He began by asking what people were commonly saying about him, and the disciples told him that he was being identified with certain great figures.

Some said that he was *John the Baptizer* come back to life again. That was what Herod Antipas had already surmised (Matt. 14.2). John had made such an impact of greatness upon men that there were still those who felt that death could not have finally defeated him and could not hold him, and that in Jesus he had come again.

Some said that he was *Elijah*. This in its own way was high praise. To the Jewish mind Elijah had two distinctions. First, he was always regarded as supreme among the prophets. Even after the later great prophets had come Elijah was considered as supreme among the prophets as Moses was among the lawgivers. Second, it was the Jewish belief, and it still is, that Elijah would return to earth to be the herald and fore-runner of the Messiah. 'Behold,' Malachi heard God say, 'I will send you Elijah before the great and terrible day of the Lord comes' (Mal. 4.5). If Jesus was to be expressed in human terms at all, he could not have been expressed in higher terms than in terms of Elijah.

Some said that he was *Jeremiah*. It was the belief that, before the Jewish people went into exile, Jeremiah had taken the ark of the covenant and the altar of incense out of the Temple, and had hidden them in a lonely and secret place on Mount Nebo, and that, before the coming of the Messiah, he would return and produce those treasures, and the glory of God would come back to his people (II Macc. 2.1–8). In one of the Old Testament apocryphal books God is represented as saying: 'For thy help I will send my servants Isaiah and Jeremiah' (II Esdras 2.18). Jeremiah was regarded as the forerunner of the Messiah and the champion of the people when they were in need.

Some said he was *one of the prophets*. Even if the people did not identify Jesus with a figure so great as Elijah or Jeremiah, at the very least they regarded him as a prophet, and, therefore, as a man within the confidence of God (Amos 3.7).

Then Jesus asked the crucial question. 'You,' he said, 'who do you say that I am?'" And it was then that Peter made his great discovery and affirmed his faith that Jesus was none other than the Messiah and nothing less than the Son of God. The fact that Jesus did not accept the verdicts of the crowd, and that he pressed for a still deeper answer, tells us certain things about his conception of himself.

(i) It shows us that human terms, even the highest human terms, are inadequate to describe him. To call him Elijah or Jeremiah come back was great, but nevertheless it was not enough. 'I know men,' said Napoleon, 'and Jesus Christ is more than a man.'

(ii) It shows that to Jesus compliments are not enough. When men called Jesus John the Baptizer, or Elijah, or Jeremiah come back to life, they believed that they were paying him a compliment; they intended it as praise. To compliment Jesus and to praise him is not enough; nothing is enough except to worship and adore.

(iii) It shows that the only adequate way in which to think of Jesus is to think of him in terms of God. To say that Jesus is the Son of God is to say that there exists between him and God a relationship which is unique, a relationship which is such that it has never existed, and never will exist, between God and any other person.

(iv) It shows that all this must be a personal discovery. Jesus did not tell his disciples who he was; he encouraged, and even compelled, them to discover it for themselves. True knowledge of Jesus comes not from a text-book, and not even from another person, but from personal confrontation with him.

No sooner had Peter made his great discovery than Jesus made to him a great series of promises. These promises have been the subject of much and embittered controversy, and we must seek to find the mind of Jesus in them.

(i) There is the promise to Peter: 'You are Peter and on this rock I will build my church' (Matt. 16.18). Two things are to be noted. First, here there is a play on names, not reproducible in English. The Greek for 'Peter' is *petros,* and the Greek for rock is *petra*; in Greek there is a change in gender and therefore a change in the ending of the words; but in Aramaic the word play would be even more perfect, for Peter's Aramaic name was *Cephas,* and *cephas* is the word for 'a rock'. Second, whatever the meaning of this is, there is no doubt that it was a very great compliment to Peter. To call a man 'a rock' was high praise. A rabbinic saying says that God said of Abraham: 'Lo, I have discovered a rock on which to found the world.' Abraham, so the rabbis said, was the rock on which the nation was founded, and the rock from which the nation was hewn. The word 'rock', this time in Hebrew *sur,* is again and again applied to God in the Old Testament. 'Who is a rock, except our God?' (Ps. 18.31; II Sam. 22.32). 'The Lord is my rock, and my fortress, and my deliverer' (Ps. 18.2; II Sam. 22.2). There can be no higher tribute than to call a man a rock. To whom, then, or to what does the phrase 'this rock' refer in the saying of Jesus to Peter? Four main suggestions have been made. (*a*) Augustine suggested that the rock in question is Jesus himself, and that Jesus is saying that the Church is founded on him, and that Peter will be honoured in it. (*b*) It is suggested that the rock is Peter's faith, that, to change the metaphor, Peter's initial faith is the spark which kindled the flame and fire of faith which was ultimately to burn in the world-wide Church. (*c*) It is suggested that the rock is the truth that Jesus Christ is the Son of the living God, that this is the bedrock of truth on which the very existence of the Church is founded. (*d*) While we agree that there is truth in all these suggestions, we feel certain that the rock is none other than Peter himself. It is perfectly true that in the ultimate and eternal sense God is the rock on whom the Church is founded; but it is also true that Peter was the first man to discover and publicly to confess who Jesus was; and, therefore, Peter was the first member of the Church of Christ, and, therefore, on him the Church is founded. The meaning is not that the Church *depends* on Peter; the idea is, to use a modern metaphor from the same realm of thought, that Peter is the *founder member* of the Church, because he was the first to experience and to confess the Church's faith in Jesus.

It may be that we will get a better understanding of this saying of Jesus if we in fact avoid the word 'church'; in modern times it has the ideas of denomination, organization, administration, Protestant, Roman Catholic attached to it. It is true that in Greek the word is *ekklēsia,* but in the Greek Old Testament *ekklēsia* regularly translates the Hebrew word *qahal,* which is the word for the congregation, the assembly of the people of Israel, assembled before

God and in his presence. The idea then is that Peter is the founder member of the new Israel, the new people of God, whom Jesus came to create, the company of men and women everywhere who confess that Jesus Christ is Lord. Nothing can take from Peter the honour of being the first stone in the edifice of the new people of God.

(ii) It is then said by Jesus to Peter: 'I will give you the keys of the kingdom of heaven' (Matt. 16.19). The possession of keys always implies very special authority and power. The rabbis for instance had a saying that the keys of birth, and death, and the rain, and the resurrection from the dead belong to God and to God alone. In the New Testament the keys are specially connected with Jesus. It is the Risen Christ who has the keys of death and Hades (Rev. 1.18). It is Jesus who has the key of David and who opens and no man shuts, and shuts and no man opens (Rev. 3.7). These sayings all have a common background. They all go back to Isaiah's picture of the faithful Eliakim who had the key of the house of David on his shoulder, and who alone opened and shut (Isa. 22.22). Now Eliakim was the steward of the house of David; he was the door-keeper who brought people into the presence of the king. So, then, Jesus is saying that Peter is to be *the steward of the Kingdom.* If that be so, *the whole emphasis is on the opening of the door,* for the steward is the person who answers and who opens the door. Peter was to be the man who opened the door of the Kingdom, and indeed he did. At Pentecost it was the preaching of Peter which opened the door to three thousand souls (Acts 2.41). It was Peter who adventurously opened the door of the Kingdom to the Gentile centurion Cornelius (Acts 10). It was Peter who at the Council of Jerusalem gave the decisive witness which flung open the door of the Church to the Gentiles at large (Acts 15.14).

The last thing that Jesus meant when he said that Peter would have the keys of the Kingdom was that Peter would have either the right or the duty to close the door; Jesus meant that in the days to come Peter would be like a faithful steward opening the door of the Kingdom to those who were seeking the King.

(iii) It is then said by Jesus to Peter: 'Whatever you bind on earth shall be bound in heaven, and whatever you loose on earth shall be loosed in heaven' (Matt. 16.19). Here we must note two things First, we must note that it is *whatever* you bind and loose, not *whomever* you bind or loose. This has clearly nothing to do with binding or loosing *people*. Second, the phrase *binding* and *loosing* was very common in Jewish language in regard to rabbinic and scribal decisions about the Law. To *bind* something was to *declare it forbidden;* to *loose* something was to *declare it allowed.* In this context this is the only meaning which these two words can have. Jesus was saying to Peter: 'Peter, in the days to come heavy responsibilities will be laid upon you. You, as leader of the Church, will have to take grave decisions. The guidance and the direction of the young Church is going to fall on you. Will you always remember that the decisions you will be called on to make will affect the lives and souls of men in time and in eternity?' Jesus was not giving Peter some special privilege; he was giving him a grave warning of the almost unbearable responsibility that was going to be laid upon him for the welfare of the Church in the days to come.

Jesus was saying to Peter, and saying with joy: 'Peter, you are the foundation stone of the new community which I came to found, for you are the first man to know me and to confess me. In the days to come you will be the steward of my Kingdom, opening the door to those who seek my presence. In the days to come you will have grave decisions to make, decisions which will affect men's souls. Always remember the duty laid upon you, and your responsibility to men and to me.' This is the natural and inevitable outcome of this whole incident. Jesus took his disciples apart for the all-important purpose of finding out if there was any who understood him. To his joy one man did understand, and Jesus was committing his work into the hands of that man, for that was the very thing he had set out to do.

But there is still something to add to this incident. No sooner had Peter made his great discovery and his great confession than Jesus began to tell his disciples of the suffering, the death, the Cross that lay ahead. And immediately Peter broke out with violence: 'God forbid, Lord! This shall never happen to you!' (Matt. 16.22). Peter's violence was due to two things. First, it is a desperate thing to hear the one you love more than anything else in the world saying that he is going to a cross. Here is the stuff of broken hearts. Second, Peter had just made the great discovery that Jesus was the Messiah, and *the one thing of which the mind of Peter was totally incapable was to connect Messiahship with suffering and death.* He had been taught and trained from his earliest days to think of Messiahship in terms of victory, triumph, glory, conquest, power. A Suffering Messiah was something which had never entered into his mind. Peter's heart had gone out in devotion to Jesus, but Peter had still much to learn, and Jesus had still much to teach.

And here is the explanation to two further things in this incident. First, this is the explanation of why Jesus instructed his disciples to tell no man that he was the Christ (Matt. 16.20). At that moment they were all still thinking in terms of a conquering, fighting, nationalistic Messiah, and, if they had gone out to proclaim Jesus as such, all that would have happened would have been the tragedy of another disastrous and bloody and abortive rising against Rome. They had made the discovery; as yet they did not know what it meant; they must be silent until Jesus could lead them further into the truth that suffering love can do what conquering might can never do.

Second, this is the explanation of Jesus' violent rebuke of Peter. 'Get behind me, Satan, you are a hindrance to me; for you are not on the side of God, but of men' (Matt. 16.23). The truth was that in that moment Peter confronted his Lord with the very same temptation as that with which Satan had confronted him in the wilderness. Jesus too knew the traditional idea of the conquering Messiah; Jesus too had considered that way. No one wishes to die on a cross in agony; but Jesus had deliberately put aside the way of power, which he might well have taken, and had chosen the way of the Cross. Peter in his mistaken love was facing Jesus again with the temptation to take the wrong way, and the temptation was this time all the stronger because it came from the voice of love.

At Caesarea Philippi Jesus had the joy of knowing that his work was safe because there was at least one who understood; but at Caesarea Philippi Jesus knew that he still had the problem of making those who loved him fully understand. But now the way to the Cross was clear, because there was at least one human heart in which he was enthroned.

17

THE RECOGNITION OF JESUS BY GOD

As the drama of the life of Jesus moved onwards towards the tragedy and the triumph of its close, there was a certain inevitability in the pattern of its events. It was inevitable that Caesarea Philippi should be followed by the Mount of Transfiguration. At Caesarea Philippi Jesus put himself to the test of *human recognition;* on the Mount of Transfiguration he put himself to the test of *divine approval.* It was essential that he should find out if there was some one who knew him and recognized him for what he was; but it was still more essential that he should be certain that the course on which he had embarked was in accordance with the will of God.

There were two reasons why Jesus had to be sure that the way he had deliberately chosen was the right way. First, the end of it was death, and, if the end of any course of action is death, a man must be very sure that it is the only way, before he sets out upon it. Second, the reaction of Peter must have sharply reminded Jesus once again that the course that he was following was a flat contradiction of all accepted Jewish messianic hopes and dreams and expectations. The popular expectation was of a day when every nation which would not serve Israel would utterly perish (Isa. 60.12); of a day when the labour of Egypt and the merchandise of Ethiopia, and the Sabaeans, men of stature, would come over to Israel in chains and fall down before her (Isa. 45.14; cp. Zech. 14.17f.). It was a career of conquest which popular thought marked out for the Messiah, not a career whose end was an agony on a cross.

Jesus called himself the Son of Man, and in the Book of Enoch, one of the most influential books between the Testaments, there was a vivid picture of a figure known as that Son of Man. That Son of Man in Enoch was a mighty and divine and supernatural captain, who had existed from all eternity, and who was waiting beside the throne of God for the day when he would be devastatingly and shatteringly unleashed upon the enemies of God. He would arouse the kings and the mighty from their thrones and kingdoms; he would loosen the reins of the strong, and grind to powder the teeth of sinners, he would put down the countenance of the strong and cover them with shame till darkness became their dwelling and worms their bed (Enoch 46.2–7). Before him the enemies of God would be as straw in the fire or lead in the water, and no trace of them would ever again be found (Enoch 48.9). With the word of his mouth he would slay all sinners, and the angels of punishment would be let loose to execute vengeance on them (Enoch 62.6–11). He would destroy the sinners and those who had led the world astray; he would bind them with chains in the assemblage-place of destruction, and the works of sinners would vanish before him from the face of the earth (Enoch 69.27f.). Here was the popular picture of the Son of Man, a figure of irresistible might and power who would blast his enemies from the face of the earth. There could not be a more complete antithesis to the conception that Jesus had of his work.

No wonder Jesus had to be sure. If he went on, he went on to death. If he went on in his way, he was the direct contradiction of all that men expected the Messiah to be. So Jesus sought God, for if God approved, the criticism and the opposition of men were as less than nothing. This is the essence of that event in the life of Jesus which we call the Transfiguration (Matt. 17.1–8; Mark 9.2–8; Luke 9.28–36).

Jesus took Peter and James and John and went up into a mountain to pray (Luke 9.28). Both Matthew and Mark call it a 'high' mountain (Matt. 17.1; Mark 9.2). One tradition identifies the mountain as Mount Tabor, but that is highly unlikely. Tabor is not a very high mountain, for it is not much more than a thousand feet in height. Further, on the top of Tabor there was a fortified city and an armed camp, the ruins of which still exist, which makes it a very unlikely place for the events of the Transfiguration. Still further, Tabor is south of Nazareth and a very considerable distance from Caesarea Philippi, and the Transfiguration took place within a week of the recognition at Caesarea Philippi (Matt. 17.1; Mark 9.2; Luke 9.28).

It is far more likely that the Transfiguration took place on Mount Hermon. Hermon is 9,400 feet above sea-level and 11,000 feet above the level of the Jordan valley. It is easy to climb; Tristram tells how he and his party rode almost to the top of it; but the climber can suffer from the rarefied atmosphere of the summit. Tristram says: 'We spent a great part of the day on the summit, but were before long painfully affected by the rarity of the atmosphere.' Hermon is no more than fourteen miles from Caesarea Philippi, and it was to Hermon and its slopes that Jesus went to meet God.

No one can ever know all that happened on Mount Hermon in this event, for the Gospel narratives are quite clearly attempts to put into words that which is beyond words. When we put the narratives together the story they tell is this. On the mountain top Jesus was transfigured until he became a figure glowing with light (Matt. 17.2; Mark 9.2f.; Luke 9.29). To him there appeared Moses and Elijah (Matt. 17.3; Mark 9.4; Luke 9.30). Matthew and Mark say only that Moses and Elijah talked with Jesus, but Luke says that they spoke with him about the departure which he was to accomplish at Jerusalem (Luke 9.31). It was Peter's instinctive reaction to seek to prolong this precious moment and to seek to remain withdrawn in the glory of the mountain top (Matt. 17.4; Mark 9.5; Luke 9.33). From Luke we gather that the events took place either late in the evening or during the night, for the disciples were overcome with sleep, and it was the next morning when they came down the mountain again (Luke 9.32,37). A cloud overshadowed and enveloped them (Matt. 17.5; Mark 9.7; Luke 9.34); and out of the cloud there came a voice, which was the voice of God, saying: 'This is my beloved Son, with whom I am well pleased,' and bidding them to listen to him (Matt. 17.5; Mark 9.7; Luke 9.35). The whole event is clad in mystery, and yet the meaning and the significance of it for Jesus are clear.

The significant feature of the Transfiguration story is the way in which its every detail either links Jesus with the greatness of the past or nerves him for the challenge of the future.

In Jewish story the mountain tops were always close to God. It was on Mount Sinai that Moses had received the Law from God

(Ex. 31.18); and it was on Mount Horeb that Elijah had had his revelation of the God who was not in the wind, and not in the earthquake, but in the still small voice (I Kings 19.9–12). The very act of going up into Mount Hermon was the act of drawing near to God.

All the Gospels speak of the luminous cloud which enveloped Jesus and his disciples. A curious feature of Mount Hermon, on which travellers comment, is 'the extreme rapidity of the formation of cloud upon the summit. In a few moments a thick cap forms over the top of the mountain, and as quickly disperses, and entirely disappears.' The swift coming and going of the cloud were characteristic of Hermon. But there is more to it than that. All through the history of Israel we find the idea of the *shechinah*. The *shechinah* is the glory of God, and again and again this glory appeared to the people in the form of a cloud. In their journey in the wilderness the pillar of cloud led the people on their way (Ex. 13.21f.). At the end of the building of the Tabernacle there come the words: 'Then the cloud covered the tent of meeting, and the glory of the Lord filled the tabernacle. And Moses was not able to enter the tent of meeting because the cloud abode upon it, and the glory of the Lord filled the tabernacle' (Ex. 40.34f.). It had been in this cloud that God descended to give Moses the law (Ex. 34.5). Once again we find this strange mysterious luminous cloud at the dedication of Solomon's Temple. 'When the priests came out of the holy place, a cloud filled the house of the Lord, so that the priests could not stand to minister because of the cloud; for the glory of the Lord filled the house of the Lord' (I Kings 8.10f.; cp. II Chron. 5.13f.; 7.2). The cloud stands, as it always stood in Jewish thought, for the glory of God settling upon the place. The mountain top is the place of God, and on the Mount of Transfiguration the glory of God was there.

It was Moses and Elijah who appeared to Jesus. These were the two supreme figures of Jewish religion. Moses was the supreme law-giver, and Elijah was the supreme prophet. We have already seen how Jesus must have been very conscious of how his own conception of Messiahship was completely different from the popular conception; but here we see Moses and Elijah encouraging him to go on. It is as if they said to him: 'It is you who are right, and it is the popular teachers who are wrong; it is you in whom there is the fulfilment of all that the law says and all that the prophets foretold. The real fulfilment of the past is not in the popular idea of might and power, but in your way of sacrificial love.' The appearance of these two figures is the guarantee to Jesus that, however he might differ from the teachers of his day, he was none the less the real fulfilment of the message of God's great servants of the past.

But there is more than that. It is a strange thing that Moses and Elijah are the two great Old Testament figures about whose death there is mystery. The death of Moses on the top of Mount Nebo is a strange story. 'So Moses the servant of the Lord died there in the land of Moab, according to the word of the Lord, and he buried him in the valley in the land of Moab opposite Beth-peor, but no man knows the place of his burial to this day' (Deut. 34.5f.). It reads as if the hands of God himself laid his great servant to rest. There can be no burial scene like that in all history. The story of the death of Elijah is equally dramatic. Elijah and Elisha were talking together, 'and as they still went on and talked, behold, a chariot of fire and horses of fire separated the two of them. And Elijah went up by a whirlwind into heaven . . . and he saw him no more' (II Kings 2.11f.). Moses and Elijah both went out in glory. However much they had to suffer as the heralds and representatives of God, in the end, as the old stories had it, they seemed to be too great for death to touch in any ordinary way. They were the great representatives of those who witnessed and suffered for God, and for whom the end was not tragedy but triumph. Here for Jesus was the great encouragement that, if he went on, there would certainly be a cross, but there would equally certainly be the glory.

There is still something else in this event which at one and the same time linked Jesus with the past and sent him forward to the future. As Luke has it, Moses and Elijah spoke with him about the *departure* which he was to accomplish in Jerusalem (Luke 9.31). The Greek word here used for 'departure' is *exodos,* which is transliterated into English as 'exodus'. That word is for ever connected with one of the great adventures of history, the 'going out' of the children of Israel from the land of Egypt to set out on the journey across the desert in order to reach the promised land. They went out into the unknown with nothing but the command and the promise of

God. In the very use of that word it was as if Moses and Elijah said to Jesus: 'Long centuries ago God's people set out upon their *exodus,* that great adventure of faith, which led them in obedience to God across the desert into the promised land. Now you, God's Son, are setting out on your great *exodus,* and it too will lead by way of the cross into the promised land.' The very use of that word *exodos* gave Jesus the certainty that, whatever the agony to come, at the end of it there lay the promised land.

But for Jesus none of these things was the supreme moment of the mountain top. Let us again remember what Jesus was seeking. He had to be very sure that the way which he was taking was the way which God wished him to take. It was for that assurance that he had come to Mount Hermon—and in that moment that assurance came to him. 'This is my beloved Son, with whom I am well pleased'—there spoke the voice of God's approval to Jesus, and the way ahead was clear.

One thing more this story has to say, and this one final thing throws a great illumination on the mind of Jesus. The whole Transfiguration story remains wrapped in mystery, but one thing is quite clear. In it there came to Jesus and to his disciples an experience of God that was unique. To that experience there were two reactions. The reaction of Peter was to take steps to remain as long as possible in the glory of the mountain top, to prepare three booths, and to linger there, and not to come down again (Matt. 17.4; Mark 9.5; Luke 9.33). The reaction of Jesus was to come down from the mountain, to rise, and to enter again into the engagement of life. When Jesus withdrew to pray, when Jesus went up to the mountain top, such action was never for him escape; it was always preparation. The experience of the glory of God did not prompt Jesus to remain withdrawn on the mountain top; it sent him out to walk with an even more certain tread the way that led to Calvary.

On the Mount of Transfiguration Jesus received the assurance that, however much he differed from the popular and orthodox view of the Messiah, it was his view which was the real fulfilment of all that the law and the prophets foretold. On the Mount of Transfiguration Jesus received the approval of God before he went on to his cross and his crown.

18

THE APPEAL OF A ROYAL LOVE

The road to Jerusalem was a road which it was not easy for Jesus to take; no man ever looked forward to death in the agony of a cross. Luke says of him: 'When the days drew near for him to be received up, he set his face to go to Jerusalem' (Luke 9.51). His face looked as if it had been carved in granite; his countenance bore the mark of the inner struggle and determination of his soul. Mark with a vivid touch describes the last journey. 'And they were on the road, going up to Jerusalem, and Jesus was walking ahead of them; and they were amazed, and those who followed were afraid' (Mark 10.32). Jesus was walking out in front of them, and for once there was something about him which made them hesitate to intrude upon that loneliness in which he was enveloped. This was a road which Jesus had to walk alone, and he had to compel himself to walk it.

What awaited him at Jerusalem? In Jerusalem it was Passover time, the time which Jesus had deliberately chosen for the climax and the culmination of his work on earth.

The city was crowded to its utmost capacity; not only from all over Palestine but also from all over the world Jews thronged to keep the Passover. Josephus tells how Nero was contemptuous of the Jewish nation. Cestius, the governor of Palestine during part of Nero's reign, wished to convince him of the importance of the Jews. Cestius, therefore, requested the priests to take a count of the number of Jews who came to Jerusalem to observe the Passover. Every Passover lamb had to be slain and the blood of it sacrificed in the Temple courts. So the priests took their count by counting the number of the Passover lambs. The number of lambs slain was 256,500. The minimum number for a celebration of the Passover was ten, but, as Josephus points out, there could be as many as twenty in a Passover company; so Josephus reckons the number of Passover pilgrims as about 2,700,200 people.[1] It was into a city crowded like that that Jesus came. He could not have chosen to come to Jerusalem at a time when the crowds were greater or the religious feeling more intense.

When Jesus came into Jerusalem, he walked straight into the midst of his enemies. It may well be true that by this time Jesus was an outlaw with a price upon his head. John tells of the ways in which the people discussed whether or not Jesus would come to the Passover, and then goes on to say: 'Now the chief priests and the Pharisees had given orders that if anyone knew where Jesus was, he should let them know, so that they might arrest him' (John 11.56f.). When Jesus came into Jerusalem, he was in the eyes of the authorities a criminal marked down for arrest.

In view of that it would have been common prudence to have stayed away from Jerusalem altogether, or at least to have slipped in unseen and to lie concealed and to keep to the back streets. That is precisely what Jesus did not do. Jesus' decision to come into Jerusalem in such a way that every eye should be focused upon him was no sudden decision of impulse; it was deliberate, and the means to do so had been arranged far ahead. He sent his disciples ahead to find the ass on which he was to ride into the city. This was something which he had long ago arranged with some friend whose name we will never know. If anyone questioned their right to take the animal, they were to say: 'The Lord has need of it," which was clearly a prearranged signal and password (Mark 11.2f.; Luke 19.30f.; Matt. 21.2f.). So they brought the ass, and Jesus came riding into Jerusalem, into the midst of the crowds, and into the hands of the enemies who had determined to destroy him. Even if we were to go no further, we should be bound to say that this entry of Jesus into Jerusalem was an act of supreme courage. There is a courage which is born of the impulse of the moment, a courage born at some sudden emergency in which a man has no time to think, and in which he becomes a hero by a kind of instinctive reaction. But there is an even higher courage, the courage of the man who has had long to think, the courage of the man who sees with complete clarity the terrible things which lie ahead, and who deliberately, of set purpose

[1] *Wars of the Jews* 6.9.3.

and having counted the cost, goes on. That is the highest of all kinds of courage, and that was the courage of Jesus when he entered Jerusalem.

When Jesus rode into Jerusalem, he used a method of action which many a prophet of Israel had used. The prophets had often used the method of dramatic and symbolic action. Men might refuse to listen, but men could hardly fail to see; and again and again the prophets had cast their message into the form of some vivid action, as if to say: 'If you will not listen, you must *see*.' It was thus that Ahijah foretold to Jeroboam that ten tribes would revolt to him and that two would remain with Rehoboam, by tearing the new garment into twelve pieces and handing ten of them to him (I Kings 11.29–40). It was thus that Jeremiah forewarned the people of the slavery that was to fall upon them, by making yokes and wearing them on his neck, and it was thus that the false prophet deceivingly foretold that the slavery would not happen, by taking and breaking the yokes (Jer. 27.1–11; 28.10f.). This method of dramatic and symbolic action was one of Ezekiel's favourite ways of delivering his message (Ezek. 4 and 5). Jesus in his entry into Jerusalem was putting his message into the form of a dramatic, symbolic, meaningful, significant action, for a message can enter by ear-gate when eye-gate is closed, and a message delivered to the eye can reach many more than a message delivered to the ear. What, then, was this message of Jesus?

It was a deliberately made claim to be king. No doubt Jesus was remembering the prophecy of Zechariah which Matthew cites: 'Behold your king is coming to you . . . mounted on an ass' (Zech. 9.9; Matthew 21.5). It is easy for a Western mind completely to misread this action of Jesus. G. K. Chesterton wrote his poem about the donkey:

> When fishes flew and forests walk'd
>   And figs grew upon thorn
> Some moment when the moon was blood
>   Then surely I was born.
>
> With monstrous head and sickening cry
>   And ears like errant wings,
> The devil's walking parody
>   Of all four-footed things.

> The tatter'd outlaw of the earth,
>   Of ancient crooked will;
> Starve, scourge, deride me: I am dumb,
>   I keep my secret still.
>
> Fools! For I also had my hour,
>   One far fierce hour and sweet:
> There was a shout about my ears,
>   And palms before my feet.

It is a magnificent poem, but it is based on a misunderstanding. Nowadays in the West the ass is a beast of caricature and fun; but in the East in the time of Jesus the ass was a noble beast. In the ancient days Jair, who judged Israel, had thirty sons who rode on thirty asses (Judg. 10.4), and Abdon had forty sons and thirty grandsons who rode on seventy asses (Judg. 12.14). The ass was the beast on which kings rode when they came in peace; only in war did they ride upon horses. The entry of Jesus was the claim to be King.

But at the same time it was the claim to be the King of peace. It was upon the ass of peace and not upon the horse of war that Jesus came. He came deliberately refusing the role of the warrior Messiah and claiming to be the Prince of peace. He was appealing for a throne, but the throne was in the hearts of men. In that entry into Jerusalem Jesus, in a dramatic symbolic action which spoke more loudly than any words, was making one last appeal to men, and saying to them: 'Will you not, even now, even yet, accept me as your Lord and King, and enthrone me within your hearts?'

Jesus' entry into Jerusalem was an action of supreme courage; it was an assertion of royalty and an offer of love; it was at one and the same time royalty's claim and love's appeal.

19

THE WRATH OF A PURE LOVE

When Jesus entered Jerusalem, it was natural that the Temple should be the first place to which he should go. His first visit to it was late in the evening. He neither spoke nor acted, but, as Mark has it, he looked round at everything, and then he went out to Bethany with his disciples to spend the night there (Mark 11.11). On the next morning he came back to the Temple, and he proceeded to enact what may well be called the most spectacular event in his whole career, the event which we call the Cleansing of the Temple. He came into the Temple court, and he drove out all those who were selling and buying; he overturned the tables of the money-changers, and the seats of the sellers of victims for the sacrifices (Matt. 21.12; Mark 11.15; Luke 19.45), and, as Mark adds, he would not allow anyone to carry anything through the Temple (Mark 11.16). What was it that so aroused the wrath of Jesus and impelled him to an action of such unparallelled audacity?

Every adult, male, freeborn Jew, who was not a priest, had to pay a yearly Temple tax of half-a-shekel. It is difficult, if not impossible, to give the exact equivalent of any ancient coin; and in seeking to understand money equivalents in terms of modern values, it has to be remembered that the sums have to be multiplied twenty or thirty times to find the equivalent modern purchasing power. However, a shekel is usually said to be equivalent to sixteen cents; but that sum is to be evaluated against the fact that in Palestine a working man's wage for a day's work was about nine cents; and, therefore, the Temple tax was not far short of two days' wages. It is calculated that this Temple tax brought in about $125,000 a year. The extraordinary wealth of the Temple may be seen from the fact that, when Crassus plundered it during his expedition to the East in 54–53 B.C., he took from it money and gold to the value of at least $4,500,000.[1] The payment of the Temple tax was obligatory, and, if it was not paid, it was legally possible for the Temple authorities to distrain upon a defaulter's goods.

Intimation that the Temple tax was due was made on the first day of the month Adar, the month immediately before the month of Nisan in which the Passover fell. On the fifteenth day of Adar, exactly a month before the Passover, stalls were set up in all the towns and villages, and at them the Temple tax could be paid. These stalls remained open until the twenty-fifth day of Adar. Thereafter the Temple tax could be paid only in the Temple itself.

The Temple consisted of a series of courts.[2] There was first the Court of the Gentiles into which anyone of any nation could come, and beyond that court no Gentile could pass on pain of death. Next, there came the Court of the Women, beyond which no woman could pass, unless she was on actual sacrificial business. Next, there was the Court of the Israelites, at the rail of which the offerings of the worshippers were handed over to the priests. Next, there was the Court of the Priests into which only the priests could go, and where the altar of the burnt-offering stood. Finally, at the far end of the Court of the Priests there was the Holy Place, the Temple building proper, and at the west end of this, behind a veil, the Holy of Holies, into which only the High Priest might go, and he only on the Day of Atonement.

In the time of Jesus the Court of the Gentiles had become far more like a crowded, noisy, huckstering market than the approach to the house of God. It was there that the money-changers had their stalls and tables. The necessity for the money-changers lay in the fact that the Temple tax had to be paid in certain kinds of currency and in no others. All kinds of coins of silver, Roman, Greek, Syrian, Phoenician, Persian, Tyrian, were current and valid for all ordinary purposes in Palestine; but the Temple tax had to be paid either in half-shekels of the sacred standard, or in Galilaean shekels. One Galilaean shekel was equal in value to one half-shekel of the sacred standard. The reason why these currencies alone were valid was that they had no king's head stamped on them. Other currencies bore a king's head, and were, therefore, graven images and unclean for

---

[1] Josephus, *Antiquities of the Jews* 14.7.1; *Wars of the Jews* 1.8.8.
[2] Josephus, *Against Apion* 2.8.

sacred purposes. As we have said, for all normal purposes a wide variety of currencies was valid. And, further, Jews came from all over the world from many countries to keep the Passover, bringing with them the money of the country from which they came. The function of the money-changers was to change the money of the pilgrims into the only kinds of coins which were acceptable to the Temple authorities. On the face of it it was a useful enough function; but it had been turned into an imposition and a major financial ramp. For every coin which was changed the money-changers charged a fee of one *maah,* a coin worth about twopence; and, if the coin to be changed was of greater value than a half-shekel, the person who offered it was compelled to pay another *maah* in order to receive the change from it. That is to say, many and many a pilgrim had to pay not only his half-shekel Temple tax, but a sum of fourpence extra in order to get the right coin and his change from his own money. And it must again be remembered that this fourpence has to be evaluated in light of the fact that a working-man's wage for a day's work was about eightpence. It took him half a day's wages to obtain the right coin and to receive his change. This money-changing tax was called *quolbon,* and it has been estimated that it brought in between £8000 and £9000 a year. What was little better than a gigantic financial swindle was being worked on poor pilgrims who could ill afford it. The matter was often complicated by the fact that the silver of the coins offered was worn and the coins were thin; they were then weighed, and there was further grasping and acrimonious dispute as to their true value.

In addition to the money-changers, the sellers of pigeons and doves had their booths in the Court of the Gentiles. A great many pilgrims wished to make an offering of thanksgiving. Apart from the offering of the special thanksgiving a great many routine offerings had to be made. For instance, after childbirth a woman had to offer either a lamb and a pigeon, or, if she was too poor to do so, two pigeons (Lev. 12.6–8). Of course, such offerings could be bought in shops outside the Temple; but the Temple authorities had their official inspectors whose duty it was to inspect all sacrificial victims to see that they were without spot or blemish and fit to be offered. If a victim was bought from an outside shop, it had to be submitted to an inspector, and a fee paid for its examination; and it was to all intents and purposes certain that the inspector would find a flaw, whereas the animals sold within the Temple courts had already been inspected. Again on the face of it it would seem that the booths which sold the animals within the Court of the Gentiles were fulfilling a useful enough purpose; but there had been occasions when a pair of doves cost as little as ninepence outside the Temple and as much as fifteen shillings within the Temple. The booths within the Temple charged prices which were an imposition on the pilgrims and on those who came to sacrifice. Still further, these booths were known as the Bazaars of Annas, and were the private business of the family of Annas, who had once been High Priest.

Mark alone has the addition that Jesus would not allow anyone to carry anything through the Temple (Mark 11.16). On this the Jewish law as contained in the *Mishnah* was quite clear. 'A man may not enter into the Temple mount with his staff or his sandal or his wallet, or with the dust upon his feet, nor may he make of it a short bypath; still less may he spit there' (*Berakoth* 9.5). Quite clearly the Jewish traders were breaking their own law in the way in which they used the Temple Court, and the Temple authorities were actually guilty of encouraging them to do so. And in the time of Jesus it was the common custom to use the Temple Court as a convenient short-cut from the city to the Mount of Olives.

It is not difficult to imagine the uproar, the disturbance, the disputing, the haggling, the bargaining, and the swindling which went on in the Court of the Gentiles. Anything less like the approach to the house of God would be difficult to imagine. What should have been what the prophet called 'a house of prayer for all nations' (Isa. 56.7) had become what Jeremiah called 'a den of robbers' (Jer. 7.11; Matt. 21.13; Mark 11.17; Luke 19.46).

In the action of the cleansing of the Temple the mind of Jesus is clearly revealed to us.

Here Jesus acts as nothing less than the spokesman of God. He did not cleanse the Temple like some church officebearer or official attacking some abuse or cleaning up some evil and improper situation. He cleaned the Temple *as if it belonged to him,* as if it were his own personal house and dwelling-place. In this action and event Jesus did nothing less than identify his own action with the action of God. He does not act like a man dealing with some abuse; he acts like God sweeping the evil from his own house.

Here Jesus acts as nothing less than judge. In the vision of Ezekiel of the days when judgment was to come, the command was: 'Begin at my sanctuary' (Ezek. 9.6). In the action of the cleansing of the Temple Jesus assumed the right of judgment, and that judgment began at the sanctuary. Jesus' consciousness of authority is demonstrated for all to see, in that he was prepared to judge and to condemn those who were responsible for the administration and ordering of what to the Jews was nothing other than the House of God.

Here Jesus acts as nothing less than Messiah. The restoration of the Temple to an even greater glory was a regular part of the visions of the messianic age. The Book of Enoch looks to the day when the old house will be folded up, when its pillars and its ornaments will be carried away, and when a new house greater and loftier than the first will arise (Enoch 90.28f.). The Psalms of Solomon look forward to a day when Jerusalem shall be purged until she shall be holy as of old, and when the Lord shall be glorified in a place to be seen of all the earth (Psalms of Solomon 17.30). It was as if Jesus said: 'The day has come when the House of God shall be purified of those who defile it, for the Messiah has arrived in his own city.'

Jesus' ejection of the money-changers and the sellers of doves demonstrates his passion for social justice. His anger was kindled to a white heat at the sight of simple people cheated, swindled, imposed upon by clever and rapacious scoundrels. Here in this event is the affirmation of the social gospel which regards the exploitation of men as a crime against God.

There is an even deeper condemnation here; there is the condemnation of anything which hinders ordinary people in their search for God. Into the Court of the Gentiles all nations and all people might come. To the Passover there came not only Jews from all over the world, but also people from many other nations, for Jerusalem was one of the wonders of the world, which tourists came from all over to see. Many must have come to the Temple with a sense and hope that perhaps there they might find God; and instead they found a swaying, disputing, bargaining mob, and an atmosphere in which devotion was impossible. The place which should have been, as Mark had it, a house of prayer *for all nations* had become a market-place where avaricious traders swindled and shrewd tourists bargained. There are other ways than that of producing an atmosphere within a church in which it is very difficult for the simple seeker to find God, and any who render the search for God more difficult must face the anger of Jesus.

It may be that buried deep in the heart of this event there lies something which goes far beyond the moment in which it happened, yet something which may well have been in the heart and the mind of Jesus. It may well be that the deep and basic meaning of this event is that it was a condemnation of the whole apparatus of sacrifice and the whole ritual of the Temple. Jesus had long before this quoted God's word to Hosea: 'I desire mercy and not sacrifice' (Matt. 9.13; Hos. 6.6), and the driving of the money-changers and the sellers of victims from the Temple Court may well symbolically mean that all the sacrificial ritual for which they stood was a vast irrelevancy, which had no real place in the House of God. Animal sacrifice could never be a substitute for the offer of the heart's love to God and to man.

It only remains to remember something more simple and more elemental than any of these things. Like the triumphal entry—only, if possible, more so—the cleansing of the Temple was an act of sublime and magnificent courage. It was sheer and utter defiance. It may well be argued that the cleansing of the Temple was the Rubicon in the life of Jesus. In this action he burned his boats forever. He carried the war into the camp of the enemy; yet at the same time, by striking such a blow at the vested interests of trade and religion, humanly speaking, Jesus signed his own death-warrant —and he knew it.

20

THE THREAT OF A DEMANDING LOVE

It is only in the last week of his life that we can follow Jesus from day to day and almost from hour to hour. It was on the Sunday that he came riding into Jerusalem. It was on the Monday that he cleansed the Temple, driving out the money-changers and the sellers of sacrificial victims. The Tuesday was a day of concentrated controversy and teaching. On that day, according to the Gospel narrative, four deputations came to Jesus, each trying to trip and to entangle him in his words. The first demanded to know on what authority he acted as he did (Matt. 22.23–27; Mark 11.27–33; Luke 20.1–8). The second sought to inveigle him into making dangerous statements about the paying of the tribute money to Rome (Matt. 22.15–21; Mark 12.13–17; Luke 20.20–26). The third was the deputation of the Sadducees who sought to entangle him in questions about the life to come (Matt. 22.23–33; Mark 12.18–27; Luke 20.27–38). The fourth demanded that he should tell them which was the greatest of the commandments (Matt. 22.34–40; Mark 12.28–34). In each case Jesus dealt wisely with his questioners and defeated their evil intentions.

It was on this day also that Jesus, as Matthew tells the story, told a series of great parables—the parables of the two sons (Matt. 21.28–32); of the wedding feast (Matt. 22.1–14); of the ten virgins (Matt. 25.1–13); of the talents (Matt. 25.14–30); of the sheep and the goats (Matt. 25.31–46).

But there is one parable of that day which all the three Gospel writers record, the parable of the wicked husbandmen (Matt. 21.33–46; Mark 12.1–12; Luke 20.9–18). In their selection of the material available to them there were things which each of the Gospel writers was willing to omit; but so indelible was the imprint of this parable, and so unforgettable was its effect, that all three without exception record it. And it is right that it should be so, for in that parable is the concentrated essence of the last days of Jesus' life in the flesh upon earth. Seldom did he make so great a claim, fling down so unmistakable a challenge, utter so terrible a threat.

In Palestine men were very familiar with absentee landlords who did with their estates exactly what the owner of the vineyard in the parable did. The owner of the vineyard equipped his vineyard with the best possible equipment—a thickset hedge to keep out the wild beasts, a watchtower to keep guard against the marauders, a wine press where the juice might be extracted from the grapes. He then let it out to cultivators. There were in Palestine three possible arrangements about the payment of rent. The rent might be an agreed sum of money; it might be an agreed and fixed amount of produce; and it might be an agreed proportion of the crop. The time came when the rent for the vineyard fell due, and the owner sent his servants to collect it. One after another the servants were maltreated, injured, beaten, stoned, killed by the cultivators. Finally the owner sent his son, thinking that the cultivators were bound to respect him; but the cultivators took the son and killed him, and planned to seize the vineyard for themselves. Then the owner of the vineyard was compelled to act. He dealt out terrible and deserved punishment to the cultivators and gave the vineyard to others.

We are always rightly warned that we must not turn the parables of Jesus into allegories, that they teach one flashing truth, and that the details are not to be pressed and not to be provided each with a meaning. But in this one parable the case is different, for both the meaning of the whole parable and the meaning of the details are crystal clear. As both the prophets and the Psalmist had it: 'The vineyard of the Lord of hosts is the house of Israel' (Isa. 5.1–7; Jer. 2.21; Ps. 80.8). The vineyard is Israel. The cultivators into whose hands the vineyard was entrusted are the rulers and the leaders of Israel. The owner of the vineyard is God. The messengers are the prophets. It was the lament of Jesus that Jerusalem was the city which killed the prophets and stoned those who were sent unto her (Matt. 23.37). Later Stephen was to confront the Sanhedrin with the demand: 'Which of the prophets did not your fathers persecute?' (Acts. 7.52). The threat of the parable is the threat that

Israel's place of privilege is to be taken from her, and to be given to others—and those who heard the parable well understood it, for their shocked reaction was to say: 'God forbid!' (Luke 20.16). This is a parable which sheds a flood of light upon the mind of Jesus.

(i) Here we find *the claim of Jesus.* In this parable Jesus deliberately removes himself from the succession of the prophets. Each in his day and generation had brought his message, and then had often paid for their loyalty with their lives; but they were *servants,* while he is *the Son.* In this parable Jesus presents himself as the Son of God, come with God's last word, God's final invitation, God's ultimate appeal to Israel. The day of the prophet was past; the day of the Son had come. There were no further lengths to which the appeal and invitation of God could go.

(ii) Here is *the courage of Jesus.* This parable makes it quite clear that Jesus knew that he was to die. His certainty of death to come was not the result of any miraculous foreknowledge; anyone who could read the signs could see what was going to happen. The leaders and the rulers and the orthodox were out for his blood, and he knew it. Escape was still perfectly possible. It was not too late to effect a compromise with the rulers; it was not too late to slip out of Jerusalem and to get away from it all. But neither compromise nor flight ever entered Jesus' mind. Homer makes Achilles say, even when death was certain, 'Nevertheless, I am for going on.'[1] Jesus knew where his chosen pathway was leading—and yet he took it.

(iii) Here is *the threat of Jesus.* The vineyard was to be taken and given to others. Here is a vivid and pictorial way of saying that Israel was to lose her place in God's scheme of things, that all her privilege in the plan of God was to be taken from her. The New Testament is clear that the new Israel is the Church. The Church is the Israel of God (Gal. 6.16). They are not all Israel which are of Israel; the racial descendants of Abraham are not all sons of Abraham in the true sense of the word (Rom. 9.6f.). It is faith, the same faith which Abraham showed, which makes a man a true son of Abraham and an heir of all the promises (Rom. 4.16). A man is not a true Jew who is only a Jew outwardly, and whose circumcision is nothing more than a mark in the flesh; true circumcision is

[1] *Iliad* 18.114.

circumcision of the heart, and the true Jew is the man who is a Jew inwardly (Rom. 2.28f.). It is those who are of faith who are the children of Abraham (Gal. 3.7). If a man is Christ's, then he is a true descendant of Abraham, and all the promises are his (Gal. 3.29). The Jews could never forget that they were the chosen people; but Jesus warned them that they were on their way to losing their position in the plan of God. And so it happened; the Christian Church became the new Israel; and the promises which once belonged to the Jews were transferred to it.

(iv) Here is *the confidence of Jesus*. The end of the parable is the expression by Jesus of the confidence of triumph and vindication to come. For that picture he went to the Psalms. In the Psalms there is the picture of the stone which the builders rejected but which in the end became the head of the corner (Ps. 118.22; cp. Acts 4.11; I Peter 2.4,7). That picture was originally meant to apply to the nation of Israel, but Jesus took it to himself to express his own confidence in his final triumph.

Here in this parable we see Jesus flinging down his challenge. He claims a unique relationship to God. He claims the right to judge and to condemn and to reject Israel. He is aware that the road he is taking will end upon the Cross. But never for one moment does he see the Cross as the end. He goes on in the certainty that beyond the Cross there lies the ultimate triumph.

21

THE ANOINTING OF LOVE

The last week of Jesus' life was lived in a blaze of publicity, and in an atmosphere of conflict. On the Sunday he came riding into Jerusalem; on the Monday he cleansed the Temple, descending on men like the wrath of God; on the Tuesday he had repeatedly to meet those who came to him with questions, not because they were seeking for information and for guidance, but because they were seeking to entrap and to entangle him in his words. But on the Wednesday there came an oasis of sweetness in the desert of bitterness, for on that day there came to him one of the loveliest things which happened to him in all the days of his flesh, and on that day he received one of the last kindnesses which he was to receive at the hands of anyone in the days of his earthly life (Matt. 26.6–13; Mark 14.3–9).

On the Wednesday Jesus did not come into Jerusalem, but remained in the quietness of the village of Bethany. He was invited to a meal by a certain man known as Simon the leper. In Palestine a meal could be a very public occasion. The houses of the well-to-do were built round an open courtyard, in which there was often a garden and a fountain. In the warm weather meals were taken in that courtyard. When a famous and distinguished teacher was sitting at such a meal, people crowded into the courtyard to listen to his conversation and his table-talk, eager to miss no pearl of wisdom that might fall from his lips. It was at such a meal that Jesus was reclining. Into the courtyard there came a woman who loved Jesus for all that he had done for her soul. She had seen the bitterness and the hatred and the hostility in the eyes of his enemies every time they looked at him; she knew that they were venomously plotting to destroy him; and her one desire was to seize this opportunity to demonstrate her love.

Women in Palestine often carried little phials of highly concentrated, very precious perfume, worn on a chain around their necks. These phials could cost as much as £40. The perfume perfumed the whole body, and it was so concentrated and so precious that it was meant to be used one little drop at a time. The woman came as a spectator and a listener at this meal. She did the only thing she could do to show the devotion of her heart; she would give to Jesus the only precious thing which she possessed. She poured, not a single drop, but the whole of her precious phial of perfume on his head, and then broke it. Maybe she broke it because of an eastern custom. In the East, when a very famous and distinguished man came to a meal, after the meal often the goblet from which he had drunk was broken into fragments, so that never again it might be touched by lesser lips.

The reaction of the disciples was shocked astonishment at what they regarded as this fantastic waste. The phial could have been sold for three hundred pence and the proceeds given to the poor (Mark 14.5). The penny in question was a *denarius,* which was worth about ninepence, which in Palestine was a day's wages for a working man. Here was almost a year's wages poured out in waste. At the feeding of the five thousand Philip said that two hundred *denarii* would hardly be enough to feed a crowd like that (John 6.7). The perfume could have been sold for enough to buy a meal for more than five thousand hungry people—and it had been emptied out on Jesus' head.

In answer to the words and thoughts of the disciples Jesus said three things. First, he said that, if a man wished to help the poor, opportunities would never be lacking, for did not the Scriptures say: 'The poor will never cease out of the land'? (Deut. 15.11). Second, he said that the woman had done this against the day of his burial. In Palestine the bodies of the beloved dead were first bathed, and then anointed with perfume, and then the flask which had contained the perfume was broken, and the fragments of it were laid in the tomb with the body. The woman had rendered to him the very service which people rendered to the bodies of those whom they had loved. Third, he said that the story of this lovely deed would go out into all the world, and, so long as the gospel story was told, men would never allow the memory of it to die.

This story tells us a great deal about the love which delights the heart of Jesus.

(i) There is a certain extravagance in love. The alabaster phial of perfume was meant to be used drop by drop; it was meant to last for years, perhaps even for a life-time; but in a moment of utter devotion the woman poured it on the head of Jesus. Love does not stop nicely to calculate the less or more; love does not stop to work out how little it can respectably give. With a kind of divine extravagance love gives everything it has, and never counts the cost. Calculation is never any part of love.

(ii) Love knows well that there are certain moments in life which come and which do not return. There were endless and limitless opportunities to help the poor, but, if that woman had not seized that moment to make known her love to Jesus, the opportunity would never have come again. There are moments in life which do not come a second time. Impulses to devotion, impulses to reformation, impulses to decision enter the heart, and, if they are not acted on at once, they may never return. Love is ever ready to seize the moment to declare itself.

(iii) Love puts into the world a fragrance which time cannot obliterate. To this day the story of that woman's devotion moves the heart. A lovely deed is not only a thing of the moment; it leaves something in the world which time cannot take away. Love adds a permanent legacy of loveliness to life.

This story has light to shed on the mind of Jesus.

(i) Once again it tells us of his consciousness and his claim. In the Old Testament three kinds of people were anointed. *Priests* were anointed. The law runs: 'You shall take the anointing oil, and pour it on his[1] head and anoint him' (Ex. 29.7). *Prophets* were anointed. God's command to Elijah was to anoint Elisha his successor (I Kings 19.16). The prophet whom we call Third Isaiah speaks of himself as having been anointed to preach the good tidings (Isa. 61.1). *Kings* were anointed. It is God's command to Samuel to anoint Saul as king of the people (I Sam. 9.16), and later to anoint David (I Sam. 16.12f.). It was God's command to Elijah to anoint Hazael to be king of Syria (I Kings 19.15f.). Anointing was proper to the priest, the prophet and the king; and

[1] The priest's.

by accepting the action of this woman Jesus implicitly claimed to be the *Prophet* who brought to men the word of God, the *Priest* who built for men the bridge to God, the *King* who claimed from men a throne within their hearts. Even with the shadows closing around him, even amidst the misunderstanding of those closest to him, Jesus never lost the consciousness of his divine destiny.

(ii) Once again we see Jesus perfectly aware of the death and the Cross which lay ahead of him. Anointing was given not only to the living but also to the dead. In the East the bodies of the dead were anointed and embalmed in perfumes and in sweet-smelling spices. It was that very office, as Jesus said, that the woman had performed for him. Humanly speaking, Jesus need never have gone back from Bethany into Jerusalem; he need never have left the circle of his friends to enter the circle of his enemies. Humanly speaking, the way back was still perfectly possible, and the door of escape was still wide open. But Jesus went out knowing that the only arms which would welcome him in Jerusalem were the arms of the Cross.

(iii) Once again we see Jesus confident of his ultimate vindication. It did not occur to him that his work would be obliterated; already he heard the story of the gospel echoing down the corridors of time. He envisaged a day when nothing less than the whole world would know of the lovely thing which this woman had done (Mark 14.9). He knew that men could crucify him, but he also knew that men were powerless to eliminate him from history. He who was on his way to the Cross looked forward to a day when all men would know his name.

22

THE BETRAYAL OF LOVE

It is one of the tragic ironies of the Gospel narrative that, on the very day on which the woman in Bethany poured out upon Jesus the splendour of her love, Judas Iscariot took steps to arrange his betrayal to the leaders of the Jews (Matt. 26. 14–16; Mark 14.10; Luke 22.3–6).

The mind of Judas must always be one of the great enigmas of history. The first three Gospels give us strangely little material about him, for they never so much as mention him between his call by Jesus at the beginning and his betrayal of Jesus at the end. Any information which we do possess comes from the Fourth Gospel, which was the last Gospel to be written, and which naturally tends to darken the picture of the traitor. Let us try, in so far as we can, to reconstruct the mind and the motives of Judas, using the material which the Fourth Gospel supplies.

(i) Judas was *the man whom Jesus called*. From the beginning he was one of the chosen twelve (Matt. 10.4; Mark 3.19; Luke 6.16). That basic fact tells us that Judas might have become great in the service of Jesus—but something went wrong. A certain writer wrote a series of studies on the twelve apostles and entitled it *The Men whom Jesus made,* but when he came to the study of Judas he headed it *The Man whom Jesus could not make.* Jesus never used men as a tradesman uses a tool; Jesus used men as a leader uses his willing followers. If Jesus was to use a man, that man had to consent to be used. Judas was the man whom Jesus called, and the man who refused to be used in Jesus' way.

(ii) Judas was *the man whom Jesus warned*. John tells us of the feeding of the five thousand, and of the consequent movement to make Jesus king, a move which Jesus completely rejected. From that time many were disappointed in him and left him. Jesus thereupon asked his own chosen men if they too were going to leave him, and Peter immediately affirmed his loyalty and the loyalty of his fellow-apostles. Then Jesus said: 'Did not I choose you, the twelve—and one of you is a devil?' (John 6.70). It is quite certain that the rest of the apostles had no suspicion of what was going on in Judas' mind. If they had had any such suspicion, they would have dealt with Judas, even with violence. But Jesus knew, and he was telling Judas to stop in time. Judas was the man whom Jesus warned.

(iii) Judas was *the man to whom Jesus appealed*. There is no doubt that Judas held a leading place in the apostolic company. Jesus appointed Judas their treasurer (John 12.6). When Judas left the Upper Room before the last meal was ended, the disciples were not alarmed, for they thought that he had gone out to deal with the practical arrangements which Passover time necessitated (John 13.29). Often the best way to strengthen a waverer is to give him some special task to do, and often the best way to secure a man's loyalty is to show him that he is trusted. And Jesus tried that way with Judas.

Still clearer is the appeal of Jesus at the last meal together. From the story of that meal it is clear that Judas was in special honour. It was to him that Jesus handed the morsel of food called the sop, for it was thus that a host treated his most favoured guest (John 13.26; Matt. 26.23). The whole story makes it evident that Jesus could speak privately to Judas without the others hearing. Judas must, therefore, have been next to Jesus. In the East guests did not sit at table; the table was a low block and they reclined on couches, leaning on the left elbow, with the right hand free to use, and the feet stretched out behind. The couches usually held three. The place of honour was the place on the right of the host, for whoever was there reclined literally with his head on the breast of the host. That was the place occupied by the beloved disciple, who was most probably John (John 13.23). If Jesus was able to carry on a private conversation with Judas, Judas must have been on Jesus' left, and must have been the third person on the topmost couch. As John's head was on Jesus' breast, so Jesus' head must have been on Judas' breast. It is as if Jesus had deliberately bidden Judas to come and sit beside him that he might make to him a last appeal to halt in his dreadful undertaking. It may be that it was that seating arrangement, that special honour paid to Judas, which roused the strife and argument about precedence about which Luke tells (Luke 22.24–27).

The degeneration of Judas was no sudden affair; it was a long process; and all through it Jesus was making appeal after appeal to Judas in the hope of saving him from his self-chosen way of tragic disaster.

Neither warning nor appeal restrained Judas from his chosen way. The problem, however, was how to arrest Jesus without a riot; the one thing which Rome would never allow was civil disorder; and the Jewish authorities were puzzled to find some way to arrest Jesus without provoking any trouble. It was that problem which Judas was able to solve for them (Matt. 26.14–16; Mark 14.10f.; Luke 22.3–6). Ground was so limited in Jerusalem, the city built on the top of the hill, that there were no private gardens attached to the houses. The well-to-do had their private gardens on the slopes of the Mount of Olives outside the city. Some nameless friend had given Jesus the right to use his garden, and in the evening it was Jesus' custom, when he was in Jerusalem, to retire to that garden for quiet and for prayer. Judas knew this, and it was thither that he proposed to lead the emissaries of the Jews so that the arrest could be carried out without disturbance. And in return for his information they gave him thirty silver pieces, thirty *staters,* the price of a slave, a little less than five pounds (Matt. 26.15).

By this time Judas was completely in the confidence of the authorities, and, when the time came, they gave him a band of men and officers of the Temple police to carry out the arrest. Judas was clearly the commander of the whole engagement. It would be a night of full moon, for it was at the full moon that the Passover took place. There would be light enough to see what must be done; but lest in the milling crowd there might be any mistake, Judas gave them a sign; he would identify Jesus with a kiss (Matt. 26.47–50; Mark 14.43–45; Luke 22.47f.). There would be nothing strange in that, for this was the way in which a disciple always greeted his Rabbi.

So through the agency of Judas Jesus was arrested; and then something very strange happens. Judas for the time being vanishes from the scene. At the beginning of the arrest Judas is obviously the leader of the whole operation; at the end of it he is not even there; and there is no mention of him at the trial, when witnesses against Jesus are being sought. Even as quickly as that something must have happened to Judas.

And then the curtain comes down on tragedy. The New Testament has two accounts of the end of Judas. One says that he went to the priests, tried to give them the money back, and, when they refused it, flung it at their feet, and went out and hanged himself (Matt. 27.3–5). The other account says that he bought a field with the money and there in some dreadful accident was killed (Acts 1.18). No matter which story we accept, the end of the matter for Judas was a broken life and a broken heart.

Such are the external facts of Judas' life as we know them, but what were the facts to his mind? What were the motives which moved him to the greatest act of treachery in history, and which made his name an epitome of all that makes a traitor?

(i) Luke and John both come to the same grim conclusion. Luke writes: 'Then Satan entered into Judas' (Luke 22.3). John writes: 'The devil had already put it into the heart of Judas Iscariot to betray him' (John 13.2). Just as God is looking for hands to use to do his work, so the devil is looking for them too, and the devil found his instrument in Judas. But the fact remains that no man can be used without his own consent. Judas is the man who consented to be used by the devil and by the powers of evil, for Judas could have kept the devil out of his life, and could have shut his heart against the tempter.

(ii) There is an apocryphal book called *The Story of Joseph of Arimathaea*. It has, of course, no claims to be considered as authentic history, but it has an interesting story of Judas. Its story is that Judas was the son of the brother of Caiaphas the High Priest, and that he was persuaded by the Jewish leaders to become a member of Jesus' inner circle with the deliberate intention that he might be a spy and a secret agent. According to this story, Judas was never a loyal or real disciple of Jesus, but was always the enemy agent cunningly inserted into Jesus' inner circle in due time to become the means whereby Jesus could be destroyed. This would mean that from the beginning the one intention of Judas was to find a way to compass the death of Jesus. This much at least is true, that Judas was prepared to become the tool whereby the Jewish authorities found a means to unleash their envenomed hatred upon Jesus.

(iii) One of the features of the first three Gospels is the extraordinary restraint with which they deal with the story of Judas. One might have expected them to paint the picture of Judas in terms of the blackest horror, but in fact they deal with him in silence. But the Fourth Gospel takes things a little further. In John's story of the anointing at Bethany it is Judas who leads the protest against the waste of the money which the sale of the ointment might have procured. But John's stinging comment is that the complaint of Judas was not due to any compassion and care for the poor, but to the fact, as the Authorized Version has it, that he was a thief and had the bag, and '*bare* what was put therein' (John 12.6). The word for 'to bear' is *bastazein*. Colloquially it can be used to mean 'to pilfer', as the Revised Standard Version shows. *Bastazein* is used in Greek as the word 'to lift' is used in Scots; it can be used either in the sense of 'to carry' or 'to pilfer', as in the word 'a shoplifter'. So, then, Judas was a lover of money and a thief. The simplest interpretation of Judas is that in his love for money he betrayed Jesus for no other reason than to gain the promised reward. It may be so, and yet somehow that seems an inadequate motive for the crime of Judas.

(iv) It is most likely that we may find the clue to the mind of Judas in his name. The name *Iscariot* may well be connected with the word *sicarius*. The *sicarii* were literally 'the dagger-bearers'. The *sicarii* were fanatical Jewish nationalists. They believed intensely in the destiny of Israel; they believed that Israel was intended by God to rule the world; but they believed that God would not help Israel until the men of Israel helped themselves. They were therefore pledged to a campaign of murder, assault, assassination, sudden death, directed against the Romans, and they drew their name from the fact that, concealed beneath their robes, they carried daggers with which they were prepared to murder any Roman who gave them any opportunity to do so. They were patriots fanatical almost to the extent of insanity. Such was the flame of their nationalism that they were prepared not only to murder their Roman masters, but also to murder any Jew who would not take their way of violence or who could be suspected of the least collaboration with Rome. They hated any Jew who was lukewarm in what they held to be patriotism almost as much as they hated the Romans.

It is more than likely that Judas was such a man. If he was, two possibilities open out. First, he may have seen Jesus, with his gift of words and with miraculous powers in his hands, as the heaven-sent leader for whom the Jews were waiting, the one who could put himself at the head of the loyalists of Palestine and so sweep the Romans from the land, and begin the campaign which was to lead to world conquest and world power. And then, when bit by bit he began to see that Jesus refused to take that way, in his bitter disillusionment he may have betrayed Jesus into the hands of his enemies. It is the very kind of thing that a disappointed 'dagger-bearer' would have done. But there is something even more likely than that. It may well be that Judas saw in Jesus the leader for whom he and his fellow-fanatics were waiting. Then he began to see that, as he thought, Jesus was wavering in his purpose. Then he took steps to place Jesus in the power of his enemies, not with any intention of compassing his death, but with the intention of placing him in a position in which in his own self-defence he would be bound to act, and bound to launch the long-awaited campaign. It may well be that when Judas said to Jesus: 'Hail, master!' and kissed him that there was no intended treachery, but that Judas was saying: 'Now is your chance to act! Blast them with your power!'

It is this alone which explains Judas' sudden disappearance from the scene, and his reappearance as a haunted man to commit suicide. He had suddenly in one blinding, agonizing moment discovered that his plan had gone wrong, and that he had killed the one he loved—and it may be that in one searing moment of revelation in the eyes of Jesus he had seen that the whole dream on which he had built his life was an error and a delusion.

Judas was the man who tried to make Jesus that which he wished him to be instead of submitting to Jesus, so that he himself might become what Jesus wished him to be.

One tremendous truth the events of this Wednesday in the last week of Jesus demonstrate. On this day the woman at Bethany anointed him in overflowing love; on this day Judas betrayed him either in hate or in expectation. There is no possibility of neutrality in regard to Jesus. A man either desires to enthrone him in his heart or to eliminate him from his life.

23

LOVE'S MEMORIAL

By the Thursday of the last week of his life, time for Jesus was running very short. It was on the Thursday that he ate the last meal in the upper room with the twelve. Out of that meal there has come to the Christian Church that sacrament which is the central act of the Church's worship, and it is, therefore, of special importance to seek the mind of Jesus in it. It so happens that the story of this last meal is beset by problems which are by no means easy of solution, and which yet must at least be faced, if we are to attempt to understand the mind of Jesus.

We may begin by noting one simple fact. For the Jew in the time of Jesus the day ended at sunset, not at midnight. This to our way of thinking has one curious consequence. To the Jew the new day began at 6 p.m. In the case of the Passover, the Passover Feast began on Thursday; that was the first day of the feast of the unleavened bread, or the day of preparation. It was on the Thursday that the lambs which were later to be eaten at the Passover feast were sacrificially slain in the Temple from just before midday until midafternoon. The feast of the Passover was itself in the evening of what we would call Thursday, but of what to the Jews was actually the beginning of Friday, since it was after 6 p.m. By our reckoning the preparation for the Passover, the first day of the feast of unleavened bread and the Passover all fall on Thursday; but to the Jew the first two fell on Thursday, and the third on Friday, because Thursday ended and Friday began at 6 p.m.

We must next face the problem that the first three Gospels and the Fourth Gospel regard the last meal of Jesus and the twelve as different things. There is no real doubt that the first three Gospels all regard the Last Supper as a Passover meal. They note that two days after the events at Bethany the Passover fell to be celebrated

(Matt. 26.2; Mark 14.1; Luke 22.1). Matthew and Mark say that on the first day of the feast of unleavened bread, that is, on the Thursday, Jesus despatched his disciples to Jerusalem to make the necessary preparations (Matt. 26.17; Mark 14.12). It was on that first day that the Passover was killed; that is to say, on that day the Passover lamb was sacrificially slain in the Temple (Mark 14.12; Luke 22.7). Jesus had sent them forward to find the room where he was to eat the Passover, and in accordance with his instructions they made ready the Passover (Matt. 26.19; Mark 14.16; Luke 22.13). When evening came, Jesus sat down with the twelve, and there is no doubt that we are meant to understand that it was the Passover feast at which they sat down together (Matt. 26.20; Mark 14.17; Luke 22.14). The first three Gospels distinctly set the Last Supper in the context of the Passover meal.

On the other hand the Fourth Gospel is just as definite that the crucifixion of Jesus took place *before* the Passover. John's account of that last meal together begins with the direct statement that it took place before the feast of the Passover (John 13.1). John tells us that the Jewish authorities would not enter Pilate's judgment hall, lest they be rendered unclean and so be unable to eat the Passover (John 18.28), and he thereby makes it quite clear that he conceived of the trial of Jesus as taking place before the Passover feast. John gives the day and time of the crucifixion, saying that it took place on the day of the preparation of the Passover at the sixth hour, that is, at twelve noon (John 19.14).

It is on the whole the aim of the writers of the first three Gospels to narrate the facts of the life of Jesus as they knew them; but it is the aim of the writer of the Fourth Gospel to penetrate beyond the immediate fact to the eternal truth of which the immediate fact is a symbol. When we remember that, it is of the greatest importance to note that, as John tells the story, *Jesus was crucified at exactly the same time as the Passover lambs were being sacrificially slain in the Temple.* There can be little doubt that John so tells the story in order to show that Jesus is the Passover lamb of God, whose shed blood brought deliverance to his people.

It is on the whole more likely that in the literal sense the first three Gospels are right, and that John has rearranged the facts to underline the fact that Jesus is the Passover lamb.

One further difficulty must be faced. The Passover lamb was central to the whole Passover feast, and yet in the narrative of the Gospels the lamb does not itself appear, except indirectly in the references to killing the Passover, that is, to sacrificing the Passover lamb and its blood on the afternoon of Thursday, and in the statement that the disciples sent on in advance made ready the Passover (Mark 14.12,16; Luke 22.7,13). But at the feast itself the Gospels do not mention the lamb. If this is felt as a real difficulty, then it is a possible explanation that what the Gospels tell is the story of the Passover Kiddush. *Kiddush* means a 'hallowing', a 'sanctifying', a 'setting apart'. All the great festivals, and in particular the Sabbath, were preceded by a *kiddush,* a hallowing. In the home a table was prepared, and thereon there was placed a cup, a jug of wine, and two loaves of bread. The wine was blessed and poured out; the bread was broken and shared out, the father of the family being the leader of the ceremony. This action was an introduction to the Sabbath, and to all the great festivals. It may be that the part of the Last Supper which is narrated to us is, in fact, not the Passover meal itself but rather the *kiddush* which preceded it. That would explain the absence of all reference to the lamb.

Now we must turn to the narratives to try to see through them the mind of Jesus himself.

The first thing which strikes us in the whole tenor of the narrative is that for Jesus this was no improvisation. From beginning to end he gives the impression of having long ago prepared this, and of being in complete control. He knew precisely where and to whom he was sending on the disciples ahead to make their preparations (Matt. 26.17–19; Mark 14.12–16; Luke 22.7–13). They will find a house with a large upper room. If houses in Palestine had two rooms, the second room was the upper room. The houses were like a large box with a smaller box on top. The smaller box on top was the upper room, and was reached by an outside stair. It was used for storage and as a guest room; but in particular it was used as a place of prayer and as a place where a Rabbi met with his students and disciples to commune with them.

Jesus had already arranged with a nameless friend that such an upper room should be available for him and his disciples that they might keep the Passover. He had even arranged a signal so that his friend might be immediately recognizable. The disciples were to look for a man carrying a water-pot (Mark 14.13; Luke 22.10). Such a man would stand out unmistakably in the crowd. To carry a water-pot on the shoulder was woman's work, something which a man would never do. A man with a water-pot on his shoulder would be as prominent as a man in this country using, let us say, a lady's umbrella on a rainy day. Jesus had left nothing to chance, which shows how important he took this occasion to be.

The disciples went into the city; they found things as Jesus had said; and they made all the necessary preparations for the Passover (Matt. 26.19; Mark 14.16; Luke 22.13). The things necessary for the Passover were as follows. There was the lamb, which had to be killed in the Temple courts, and the blood of which, being the life, had to be poured out as an offering to God. There was the un-leavened bread, to remind the Jews of the bread they had hastily baked without leaven, and had hastily eaten, on the night on which they had escaped from Egypt. There was a bowl of salt water, which stood for the salt tears which they had shed in Egypt, when they were slaves, and for the waters of the Red Sea through which they had escaped. There was the dish of bitter herbs—horse-radish, chicory, endive, horehound—to remind them of the bitterness of slavery. There was the *charosheth*, the paste of apples, nuts and pomegranates, to remind them of the clay with which they had made bricks in Egypt, with sticks of cinnamon running through it, to remind them of the straw which they had used. There was the wine, of which everyone who sat at the Passover must drink the four cups. It must be remembered that the Passover feast was a real meal; the minimum number which constituted a Passover company was ten; but every scrap of the food had to be eaten, and nothing must be left. So all things were prepared, and in the eve-ning Jesus came with the twelve to eat the feast.

As we read the story, the atmosphere is the atmosphere of im-pending disaster; and in particular there were three moments in-stinct with tragedy. There was a strife among the disciples about which of them should be greatest (Luke 22.24–30). Even in the shadow of the Cross personal ambitions and thoughts of personal prestige and envies and jealousies invaded the circle. There was the moment when Jesus declared his knowledge of the traitor in the midst (Matt. 26.21–24; Mark 14.18–21; Luke 22.21–23). It is only Matthew and John who actually identify the traitor as Judas Iscariot (Matt. 26.25; John 13.26–30), and it is quite certain that the other disciples cannot have known the evil purposes of Judas, or they would have attacked him there and then. John speaks of Jesus handing to Judas the morsel, or the sop. About halfway through the feast some of the bitter herbs were placed between two pieces of unleavened bread, dipped in the paste of the *charosheth,* and so eaten, and that was the morsel or sop. So at the Last Supper treachery was there. There was the moment when Jesus foretold the coming denial of which Peter would be so tragically guilty. According to Matthew and Mark it was on the way to Gethsemane (Matt. 26.30–35; Mark 14.26–31) that Jesus gave Peter his warning; but according to Luke it was in the upper room itself (Luke 22.31–34). Peter was sure that not even the threat of death would make him disloyal, but Jesus warned him that his loyalty would not stand the test. So at the Last Supper personal ambition with its attendant bitterness and strife, treachery, disloyalty were all present to drive their nails through the heart of Jesus even before the Cross.

We must now try to see what the mind of Jesus was in that last meal together; and here we have another problem. The words which Jesus spoke are by no means certain. The form of the words which we commonly use in our own celebration and observance of the sacrament is the form which is found, not in the Gospels, but in Paul's First Letter to Corinth. In that form Jesus gives thanks and breaks the bread and says: 'This is my body which is for you. Do this in remembrance of me.' He then takes the cup after the meal, and says: 'This cup is the new covenant in my blood. Do this, as often as you drink it, in remembrance of me' (I Cor. 11.23–26). It may be noted that I Corinthians was in fact written earlier than any of the three Gospels, and that this is in fact the first *written* account of the Last Supper. In Matthew and Mark the best texts omit the word 'new' before the word 'covenant'. Both Matthew and Mark have: 'This is my blood of the covenant which is poured out for many,' to which Matthew alone adds, 'for the forgiveness of sins' (Matt. 26.28; Mark 14.24). In the best text of Luke, Luke 22.19 reads simply: 'And he took bread, and when he had given thanks he broke it and gave it to them, saying, This is my body.' That is to say, the words, 'which is given for you,' and the words, 'This do in remembrance of me,' are not in the best texts of Luke. Further, the best texts of Luke omit Luke 22.20 altogether: 'Likewise the cup after supper, saying: This cup which is poured for you is the new covenant in my blood.' It can, therefore, be seen that the great difference between the account of the Last Supper in the Gospels, if the best text be followed, and the account in I Corinthians is that in the Gospels the idea of the *new* covenant is not so strongly stressed, and the injunction to repeat the actions of the bread and wine is not there at all. In seeking to interpret these words, and in seeking to read the mind of Jesus in them, we must, therefore, be careful to confine ourselves to these ideas and conceptions which are basic to both accounts. What, then, are these ideas?

(i) At the background of the whole meal there lies *the Passover*. This remains true whether or not the meal itself was actually a Passover feast or not. The whole action takes place in the context of the Passover, and with the Passover uppermost in the minds of those who partook of it. Now the basic idea of the Passover is emancipation, deliverance from the bondage and the slavery of Egypt, and safety through the blood of the Passover lamb, smeared on the doorpost of the houses of the children of Israel, when the angel of death slew the firstborn in the land of Egypt (Ex. 12). Jesus is, therefore, setting himself before men in terms of emancipation, liberation, redemption, freedom—and that liberation can only be from sin. Further, he is setting himself before men as the sacrifice for men, for it was the sacrificial blood of the slain lamb which preserved the people in the day of the destruction wrought by the wrath of God. First, then, there is the idea of redemption through sacrifice.

(ii) The second idea which runs through the whole action is the idea of *the covenant*. It does not matter whether the word *new* is inserted or not, the basic idea will remain the same. The essence of a covenant is the establishment of a new relationship between God and man on the initiative of God. But in any event there is an essential difference between the old covenant and the covenant which Jesus claimed to establish. The old covenant was founded and based on, and was dependent on, obedience to the law. Failure to obey the law and to keep the law meant the end of the relationship involved in the covenant (Ex. 24.1–8). But the covenant of which Jesus speaks is established and maintained by his blood, by his life and his death. That is to say, he is claiming that through him, and through his life and his death, a new relationship between God and man has become possible.

These two ideas become one when we remember that the whole sacrificial system of the Jews had as its one aim and object the restoration of the relationship between God and man which breaches of the law had interrupted. Jesus, therefore, was saying that the sacrifice of his life and his death made possible for ever and for ever a relationship between sinful man and holy God, a relationship apart altogether from law, and therefore a relationship of love.

What, then, must this sacrament of the Lord's Supper be to us? It is basic to remember that Jesus was here again using the method of symbolic action which the prophets had so often used, as he did when he came riding into Jerusalem. He was putting a message into dramatic action, the effect of which was meant to be more vivid than any words. If that be so, it is quite certain that in the action of the bread and wine Jesus was seeking to imprint indelibly upon the minds of his men that which he was and that which he had come to do. The Lord's Supper is, then, first and foremost a means of memory. It is the memorial of Jesus. It is meant to act as a stabbing awake of the memory which has become forgetful or lethargic. The human mind forgets; time, as the Greeks said, wipes all things out, as if the mind were a slate and time an erasing sponge; even the most poignant event loses its poignancy as the years go on; so Jesus offered men this action which in the beginning set forth his own claim and which for time to come was to remind them of his claim and of his sacrifice.

But it is necessary to go beyond that. The bare statement that the Lord's Supper is a memorial and a stimulus to memory carries its own inadequacy upon its face. A memory is necessarily a memory of someone or of something who or which is no longer here, but is gone from sight and from life. But Jesus is not the one who is gone; he is the risen Lord; he is the ever-present one in virtue of his risen life and his conquest of death. As it has been vividly put: "No apostle ever *remembered* Jesus.' Jesus is not a memory to be called to mind; he is a presence to be met and a person to be experienced. Therefore, the Lord's Supper must be not only memory; it must be also confrontation. It is confrontation with the risen Lord. This is not even for one moment to say that the Christian cannot meet his Lord anywhere; but at the Lord's Supper everything is prepared to make that confrontation inevitable and deliberately to invite it. It is the compelling of the forgetful memory and the cold heart to become vividly aware of that presence which can otherwise be so easily unrealized and forgotten.

But confrontation must necessarily be to some purpose. Now Jesus in the meeting in the upper room with his disciples, as we have seen, presented himself to them in terms of emancipation, deliverance, redemption into a new relationship with God through the sacrificial love of his life and his death. Therefore, for us the Lord's Supper is not only confrontation; it must also be appropriation. In it we must realize the presence of Jesus Christ and we must appropriate the deliverance, the emancipation, the redemption he offers us, and so enter into the new relationship with God. The Lord's Supper is confrontation with the aim and purpose of appropriation of the saving benefits of Jesus Christ.

It may be that we must still add something to this, and it may be that it is to this end that the tragic incidents of the strife of personal ambition, the tragedy of the traitor, and the heartbreak of disloyalty and denial are fitted into the story. The Lord's Supper must be realization. It must be the realization of the terrible, destructive power of sin, the realization that sin destroys personal relationships, leads a man to betray his Lord and to deny the one he loves, and in the end breaks upon a cross the loveliest of all lives. Therefore, there is a sense in which the Lord's Supper is not only the revelation of the love of God in Jesus Christ, but is also the revelation of the sin of man. The Lord's Supper ought to make him who participates in it realize his own sin, and then it ought to make him avail himself of the one way in which that sin can be conquered and overcome and finally defeated.

There remains one question to be asked. Where is all this to happen? In the narrative of the Gospels we have no word in regard to the continual repetition of the action of the bread and wine, and yet the very fact that that repetition is taken for granted in Paul's account of the Last Supper in I Corinthians shows that, even before the Gospels were written, the Church never doubted that the dramatic and symbolic action of the bread and wine was intended to be repeated. But *what* was intended to be repeated? 'This do in remembrance of me.' Does it mean that this dramatic action was to be re-enacted as each Passover came round, or as each *Kiddush* came week by week? Does it mean that some kind of symbolic action has to be repeated, which is in fact what has happened? The Church, at least in modern times, has made out of the Last Supper not a meal but the symbol of a meal. Can it be that at least in part we have been mistaken as to the intention of Jesus?

It remains a curious fact that in the Gospel narrative there is no definite instruction as to repetition, and from this there emerges a possibility of the greatest significance. We have before stressed the fact that the Passover meal was a real meal, and very far from the taking of a sip of wine and the eating of a fragment, a cube, or a wafer of bread. It remains a very definite possibility that Jesus did not intend to in.titute a symbolic meal, but that he meant that every time bread was broken and eaten, and every time wine was poured out and drunk—that is, at every meal in every house—he was to be remembered. He may well have meant that every meal was a sacrament, that it should be impossible for any Christian at any time to break bread without remembering him. It has been said that we are not fully Christian until Christ has become Lord not only of the communion table but also of the dinner table. It may well be that the symbolic meal became a necessity with the vast growth of the Christian Church and the vast numbers of the Christian fellowship, when great congregations began to be built up; but it remains a real possibility that in the upper room Jesus was not intending to institute a special meal but that he was hallowing and sanctifying every common meal so that every meal might become an experience of his presence.

However that may be, it is the mind of Jesus that in the sacrament of the Lord's Supper we should remember him, we should confront and experience him, we should appropriate his saving work, we should realize the awfulness of sin and the wonder of God's cure for sin; and it is his will that in the end we should become so mindful of him that every common meal should become a sacrament of memory and of experience.

24

THE POINT OF NO RETURN

In every long aeroplane flight there comes the point which the pilot knows as the point of no return. From then on he cannot go back, and he must go on. From that moment he has passed the point when return is possible. Just so, it is true that in every human exploit and undertaking there come the point of no return, the moment when the way back ceases to be possible, and when there is nothing left but to go on. For Jesus that moment came in the Garden of Gethsemane.

The last meal together had ended, and it ended with a hymn of praise. 'When they had sung a hymn, they went out to the Mount of Olives' (Matt. 26.30; Mark 14.26). Part of the ritual of the Passover was the singing of the *Hallel*. The word *Hallel* means 'Praise God'; and the *Hallel* consisted of Pss. 113–118, which are all praising psalms. Two of these psalms were sung midway through the Passover feast, and four of them were sung near the end. Finally, just before the feast came to an end with the blessing, the *Great Hallel* was sung. This was Ps. 136, with its constantly recurring refrain: 'O give thanks to the Lord, for he is good, for his steadfast love endures for ever.' It was with a great cry of praise that Jesus went out to the agony of body, mind and spirit which lay ahead.

Gethsemane means 'the Oil Press'. Jerusalem was built on the strictly circumscribed area on the top of Mount Sion. Because of this there was no space for gardens, and the well-to-do had their gardens on the slopes of the Mount of Olives, which were reached by descending from Jerusalem into the ravine through which the Kidron flowed, and then climbing the slopes of the hill on the other side. Gethsemane must have been such a little enclosed garden on the slopes of the Mount of Olives, and some nameless friend must have given Jesus permission to use it during the Passover week. So out of the upper room into the garden Jesus went. The story of the garden is in Matt. 26.36–46; Mark 14.32–42; Luke 22.40–46, and from it certain things unmistakably emerge.

In the garden we see the *loneliness* of Jesus. He took with him Peter, James and John to share his vigil; but they were so physically exhausted and so emotionally drained that sleep overcame them. Jesus had to take his decision alone. And this is symbolic of all life, for there are certain things which are between a man and God, and which have to be settled in the awful loneliness of a man's own soul.

In the garden we see the *mental agony* of Jesus. There was the sheer physical side of the matter. No man wishes to die at thirty-three, least of all to die in the terrible agony of a cross, for the cross had a lingering agony such as no other form of execution had. There was the mental agony of the situation. Humanly speaking, Jesus was going to death with so little done and so much to do. His supporters were so few, so uncomprehending and ununderstanding, and so unreliable when danger threatened. His opponents were so solidly powerful, for the leaders of orthodox religion were unitedly against him. Humanly speaking, the mission of Jesus seemed to be drawing to its close in failure.

In the garden we see the *spiritual agony* of Jesus. It may be that some will find it impossible to accept the view which we have earlier expressed, but as we read the story of the garden we cannot but feel that the very essence of the matter is that Jesus was accepting that which he did not fully understand. He knew that the Cross was for him the will of God, but at the moment he could not see why it had to be the Cross. He knew that he must drink the cup, but he did not fully know why the cup must be. Unless Jesus knew this acceptance of that which he did not fully understand, he did not enter fully into the deeps of the human situation, for it is precisely this that being a man involves. But we must go further than this.

In the garden we see Jesus *accepting the will of God;* but what is all important is the way in which he accepted it. In Mark's version of the story there is something of infinite beauty and of infinite value. As Mark tells the story Jesus said: '*Abba,* Father, all things are possible to thee; remove this cup from me; yet not what I will, but what thou wilt' (Mark 14.36). The essence of that whole saying lies in the completely untranslatable word *Abba.* As Jeremias points out, Jesus' use of the word *Abba* to God is completely without parallel. That was an address which no one had ever used to God before. Why? Because in Palestine in the time of Jesus *Abba*, as *jaba* is today in Arabic, was the word used in the home circle by a very young child to his father. No English translation can be anything other than grotesque; Jesus in that dark and terrible hour spoke to God as a little child speaks to the father whom he trusts and loves.

Here is the essence of Gethsemane. The whole meaning and significance of the words, 'Thy will be done,' depend on the tone of the voice and the feeling of the heart with which they are spoken. They may be spoken in broken and abject surrender, as by one who is beaten to his knees by some superior and ineluctable force, and has given up the battle. They may be spoken in weary resignation, as by one who has come to see and to admit that further resistance is useless, and who dully and hopelessly gives in. They may be spoken in bitter resentment, as by one who has ceased to struggle but whose whole heart and being are rising up in rebellion against the situation in which he finds himself, as by one who has accepted the inevitable but who still shakes his fist in the face of fate. They may be spoken in utter love and trust, as by one who does not need to understand in order to submit, who knows that a father's hand will never cause his child a needless tear, who knows that he is not the plaything of circumstance or the victim of the blind tyranny of God, or the sport of blind chance and fate, but who is certain that he can take life and leave it in God's hand and be content. Jesus in Gethsemane is the great example of submission to the will of God, even when that will is a mystery, in the certainty that that will is love.

In Gethsemane Jesus passed the point of no return, and passed it in perfect trust in God.

No sooner had Jesus come to his great decision than the quiet of the garden was broken by the trample of feet, the clank of arms, and the shouting of men. The nervous fear of the Jewish authorities is clear in the size of the force which they sent to arrest Jesus, as if he had been a man of violence (Matt. 26.47,55; Mark 14.43, 48; Luke 22.52).

So the drama unfolded itself. First, there was the traitor's kiss (Mark 14.44f.; Matt. 26.48f.; Luke 22.47f.). The tragedy is deepened by the fact that both Matthew and Mark use the Greek word *kataphilein*, which means not only 'to kiss', but 'to kiss tenderly', as a lover might. Then there came Peter's desperate rearguard action, in which he showed himself ready to sell his life dearly in defence of Jesus his Lord and friend (Mark 14.47; Matt. 26.51f.; Luke 22.49–51; John 18.10f.). And finally there came the arrest. In the arrest the action of Jesus makes certain things quite clear.

(i) It is clear that Jesus went voluntarily to death. It is his own saying that he could have called on legions of angels to defend him, had he so willed (Matt. 26.53). As John tells the story, those who came to arrest Jesus were themselves so terrified that Jesus actually had to urge them to do their work (John 18.4–9). No man took Jesus' life from him; willingly he laid it down. Jesus was not the victim of God; he was the servant of God.

(ii) In all this Jesus saw the fulfilment of Scripture (Matt. 26.54; Mark 14.49). This was not an emergency in which affairs and events had got out of control; this was nothing less than an event to which all history had been pointing. Whatever things might look like, God was still in control, and God's redemptive purpose was still being worked out.

(iii) Luke has something which is basic and fundamental to the thought of the New Testament writers. Luke tells us that Jesus said: 'This is your hour, and the power of darkness' (Luke 22.53). All through the New Testament there runs the tremendous paradox of the Cross. The Cross was somehow at one and the same time part of the purpose, the design, the plan of God, and an awful and a dreadful crime at the hands of men. Nowhere does this come out with such absolute clarity as in Peter's sermon at Pentecost. There Peter says: 'This Jesus, being delivered up according to the definite plan and foreknowledge of God, you crucified and killed by the hands of lawless men' (Acts 2.23). Here in this death of Jesus, in the whole drama of the action of the last days, we see fully displayed the sin of man and the love of God.

(iv) As the arrest works itself out, as it becomes clear that Jesus would lift no hand to defend himself, there came the tragic end, for in that moment all the disciples 'forsook him and fled' (Matt.

26.56; Mark 14.50). The end of the road was something which Jesus had to walk alone. There was a part of his work in which no man could help him, and which he had to face in all the loneliness of his soul—until in the end he felt himself forsaken, not only by men, but even by God.

One thing remains. Even when we have set the tragedy of the garden and the arrest at its blackest, its bitterest and its starkest, one indelible impression remains; and that is that in it and through it Jesus was always completely in control. He was never the helpless victim; he was always master of circumstance. Somehow even here there lie beneath the surface the first indications of the final triumph. The story never reads like the arrest of a criminal, unwillingly haled to judgment and to death; the story always reads like the willing sacrifice of one who of his own free will laid down his life for his friends.

25

THE TRIAL OF JESUS

If we would see what the trial of Jesus in fact was, we must begin by seeing what in justice it ought to have been. Here we are in a difficulty. Capital trials of national and supreme religious importance were carried out by the Great Sanhedrin. In the *Mishnah* we have the tractate on the Sanhedrin, and we have the *Tosefta,* or commentary or expansion of it. These set out the jurisdiction, the powers, and the procedure of the Sanhedrin. But it is sometimes argued that the account of the Sanhedrin and its procedure given in the *Mishnah* is highly idealized, and that it is not to be taken as an account of actual practice. It certainly is the fact probably at no time did the Sanhedrin function in the ideal terms of the *Mishnah.* Nevertheless it is still true that the account of the procedure of the Sanhedrin in the *Mishnah* does give us two things. It does give us the broad lines on which the Sanhedrin acted, and it quite certainly gives us the *ideal* of justice, at which the Sanhedrin at least should have aimed in its procedure and in its practice. It is by no means illegitimate to set down the *Mishnah's* account of the Sanhedrin, and to examine the trial of Jesus in the light of it, for, whatever be true of the actual procedure of the trial, very certainly in it the Jewish authorities flouted every ideal of Jewish justice.

The Sanhedrin was the supreme court of the Jews. It was composed of seventy members, for that was the number of elders whom Moses appointed to aid him in his task (Num. 11.16), and its total membership was seventy-one, because it was presided over by the High Priest. In it there were scribes and Pharisees, priests and Sadducees, and elders of the people. It had jurisdiction over every Jew, and in the days of its independence it could impose the death penalty either by stoning, burning, beheading, or strangulation.

The great characteristic of the Sanhedrin was that everything was deliberatedly arranged and ordered to conserve the interests of the man on trial. The rabbinic aim was to exercise 'mercy in judgment'. It was said that the Sanhedrin was only exercising its true function when it acted as 'a counsel for the defence'. Even if there seemed to be no extenuating circumstances, it was the duty of the judges deliberately to try to find some. So much so was this the case that in the tractate Makkoth (1.10) it is laid down that 'the Sanhedrin which condemns to death one man in seven years is accounted murderous', and Rabbi Eleazar ben Azaria would have said, not one man in seven years, but one man in seventy years. Two famous rabbis who lived in the days when the Sanhedrin had ceased to possess the power of carrying out the death penalty declared that, if they had lived in the days when the Sanhedrin possessed that power, no one would ever have been condemned to death. It is almost true to say that ideally the Sanhedrin was organized to defend the man on trial.

Even the production and the examination of witnesses was governed by regulations which were meant to protect the interests of the accused. It was a fundamental principle of Jewish law that the evidence of two witnesses at least was always necessary for condemnation (Deut. 17.6). Salvador, the great Spanish Jewish doctor, laid down the four rules which ought to govern criminal procedure—strictness in the accusation, publicity in the discussion, full freedom granted to the accused, assurance against all dangers or errors in testimony. The procedure of the Sanhedrin was designed to satisfy these demands. The two witnesses were examined separately. The *Mishnah* lays it down that there are seven basic questions which a witness ought to be asked about any event about which he is giving evidence. In what Sabbatic period did it happen? In what year? In what month? On what date of the month? On what day (of the week)? At what hour? Where? Before anything could be done the evidence of the witnesses must exactly agree. One curious feature of legal procedure in the Sanhedrin was that the man involved was held to be absolutely innocent, and, indeed, not even on trial, until the evidence of the witnesses had been stated and confirmed. The argument about the case could only begin when the testimony of the witnesses was given and confirmed. That is the point of the conversation between Jesus and Annas in John 18.19–21. Jesus in that incident was reminding Annas that he had no right to ask him anything until the evidence of witnesses had been taken and found to agree.

Certain people were debarred by law from giving evidence—dice-players, pigeon-fliers, those who traded with the Sabbatic growth (Lev. 25.1ff.), usurers, robbers, herdsmen, extortioners, those who were suspect concerning property—that is to say, any whose honesty was under suspicion. Close relations could not give evidence. A man's friend and his enemy were alike disqualified. His friend was defined as his groomsman, and his enemy defined as 'a man who from hostility had not spoken to his neighbour for three days'.

Witnesses were compelled to appear, not only at the beginning of a trial, but also at the end, and in the case of stoning were under obligation to be the first to cast the stone at the accused, if he was found guilty. In capital cases witnesses were reminded of Gen. 4.10, in which God says to Cain: 'Your brother's blood is now crying to me from the ground.' It was pointed out that in the Hebrew the word *blood* is in the plural and is really *bloods;* and it was argued that the word meant not only the man himself, but also his as yet unborn posterity. So a witness was warned that, if by false witness he compassed the execution of the man on trial, he was no better than the murderer of that man and of his posterity in the sight of God.

The court itself could meet officially only in the Hall of Hewn Stone in the precincts of the Temple. Its members sat in a semi-circle so that each could see, and be seen, by all the others. In front there were two clerks of the court, one to take down the evidence for the prosecution, and one to take down the evidence for the defence. The disciples of the rabbis sat in three rows facing the court, each of them having his own seat. Should a new judge be needed, one from the front row of the disciples joined the court; the rows of the disciples then closed up, and one from the audience was chosen to fill the vacant place. The *Tosefta* gives the curious fact that there were four cubits—that is six feet—between each of the disciples, in order no doubt to put an end to whispered and private discussion. It is also laid down that capital cases could only be tried by judges who were priests, Levites, and Israelites eligible for marriage into priestly families, that is, by those whose lineage was absolutely pure. The *Tosefta* adds the fact that those who had no children and eunuchs could not act as judges in capital cases, which is another way of saying that only married men could act as judges in such cases.

In capital cases there must never be fewer than twenty-three judges. The case always began with the arguments for the acquittal of the prisoner. In non-capital cases a judge could alter either his pleading or his verdict in either direction; but in capital cases one who had pleaded against the prisoner could plead for him, but one who had pleaded for the prisoner could not in any circumstances plead against him, and similarly one who had voted for the condemnation of the prisoner could change his mind and vote for the acquittal of the prisoner, but one who had voted for the acquittal could not change sides and vote for condemnation. In capital cases verdicts had to be given individually, beginning with the youngest member of the court and going on to the eldest. Acquittal required a majority of only one; condemnation required a majority of at least two. Non-capital cases could be tried and ended on the same day; but in capital cases a verdict of acquittal could be given on the same day, and the prisoner immediately released, but a verdict of condemnation could not be finally pronounced until the following day, so that after a night's thought and meditation and prayer there might still be the opportunity to alter the verdict and to set the prisoner free. That was one of the reasons why a capital trial could never take place on the day before the Sabbath or the day before a great festival, for on such days the Sanhedrin could not meet. That is also the reason why capital trials could not be held at night.

One thing further must be noted. It was illegal to put to a prisoner a question by answering which he might condemn himself, and no prisoner could be found guilty on the basis of his own answers. The evidence on which he was found guilty must be the evidence of others who were independent witnesses. Maimonides says: 'Our law condemns no one to death on his own confession.' Bartenora says: 'It is a fundamental principle with us that no one can damage himself by what he says under trial.' To put questions to the accused by answering which he might incriminate himself, and then to condemn him on the strength of his own answers, was a complete reversal of the Jewish ideal of justice.

It is against all this background that we must visualize the trial of Jesus. It is not claimed that all these regulations were ever wholly carried out in practice by the Sanhedrin, although quite certainly many of them were, but it cannot be disputed that these regulations show the ideal at which the practice and procedure of the Sanhedrin aimed.

When we put together the material in the four Gospels we find that within the twelve hours of the night before his crucifixion Jesus underwent a trial that fell into six parts, and that he must have gone through an experience calculated to exhaust a man's body, to benumb his mind, to drain his emotions, and to break his spirit, and that yet in fact he emerged from this terrible ordeal unbroken and unbowed.

(i) First Jesus was brought *before Annas* immediately after his arrest (John 18.13–14). In the days of the independence of the Jews the office of High Priest had been for life; but in the days of Israel's servitude the office of High Priest had become a matter of personal intrigue and political manipulation, so that Tiberius could say that High Priests came and went 'like flies on a sore'. At this time Annas was not High Priest, although some years before he had held office; but since four of his sons had been, or were to be, High Priests, and since Caiaphas was his son-in-law, Annas was very much the power behind the throne. If the stalls in the Temple which Jesus had overturned really were the property of Annas and his family, no doubt Annas used his position to arrange that Jesus should be brought to him first, that he might gloat over the downfall of the presumptuous Galilaean.

(ii) Next, during the night, Jesus was taken to *the house of Caiaphas*, the actual High Priest, and examined there (Matt. 26.57–68; Mark 14.53–65; Luke 22.54,63–65; John 18.19–24). This must have been, not an official meeting of the Sanhedrin, but a kind of preliminary examination, held in order to examine Jesus with a view to formulating a definite charge on which to bring him before the Sanhedrin proper.

(iii) Next, very early in the morning *the Sanhedrin* proper met in order to carry out the official trial and to arrive at the official condemnation (Matt. 27.1f.; Mark 15.1; Luke 22.66–71). In the days of Jewish independence this would have been the end of the matter, but at this time the Jews were under Roman rule; and the *Talmud* tells us that 'forty years before the destruction of the Temple the judgment of capital causes was taken away from Israel'. This necessitated the next step in the trial.

(iv) There was the trial *before Pilate,* the Roman procurator (Matt. 27.2–26; Mark 15.2–15; Luke 23.1–5,13–25). This was the Roman stage of the trial.

(v) There was the trial *before Herod* (Luke 23.6–12). Galilee was not within Pilate's jurisdiction; it was under Herod Antipas, who held his power and enjoyed the courtesy title of king by grace and favour of the Romans. Since Jesus was a Galilaean, Pilate sent him to Herod in order to avoid the responsibility of himself giving a verdict; but Herod sent Jesus back to Pilate with no verdict.

(vi) Lastly there was the completion of the trial *before Pilate,* and the final condemnation.

It is quite true that, when we try to put the narratives of all the Gospels together, there is a certain amount of confusion. Only John tells of the examination before Annas. It seems clear that Matthew and Mark think of the examination of Jesus as happening during the night, while Luke makes it happen early in the morning (Luke 22.66). Matthew and Mark quite clearly thought that the meeting in the house of Caiaphas during the night was an actual meeting of the Sanhedrin (Matt. 26.59; Mark 14.55); and yet all three Gospels make it clear that there was a meeting of the Sanhedrin early in the morning (Matt. 27.1; Mark 15.1; Luke 22.66). But, whatever confusions there may be, and even if it is not possible to make an hour-to-hour time-table of the events of that night, there is no reasonable doubt as to the course the trial took, the treatment Jesus received, and the charges which in the end were levelled against him. On the whole the likeliest sequence of events is the arrest in the garden, the examination before Annas, the preliminary trial in the house of Caiaphas, all during the night of Thursday on our reckoning, but the beginning of Friday by Jewish reckoning; then came the official meeting of the Sanhedrin on the Friday morning and the trial before Pilate, with the despatch of Jesus to

Herod as an interlude. Let us, then, look at the main events of the Jewish part of the trial.

The trial began with a search for witnesses on whose evidence Jesus could be charged. Many false witnesses were prepared to testify, but the story of no two agreed (Matt. 26.59f.; Mark 14.56). According to Mark, no two witnesses agreed to the end of the day (Mark 14.59); according to Matthew, at last two were found whose fabricated evidence did agree (Matt. 26.60f.). The evidence which in the end was produced claimed to prove that Jesus had said that he would destroy the Temple and that he would replace it within three days with a Temple not made with hands (Matt. 26.61f.; Mark 14.58). To this charge Jesus made no answer at all, meeting it with silence (Matt. 26.62f.; Mark 14.60f.). It may well be that this was a twisted version of something which Jesus did say, for the very same thing is referred to in John 2.19–22, and it was on that very charge that Stephen was later to be condemned (Acts 6.14). It may go back to one of two things. Either it may go back to a saying of Jesus about his own death and resurrection, as indeed John explains it (John 2.21), or, and this may well be more likely, it may go back to some statement of Jesus in which he said that the Temple would one day no longer be necessary for the worship of God, as, again according to John, he did say to the woman of Samaria (John 4.21). If that is so, the saying was not a threat against the Temple, but a condemnation of the exclusiveness of Temple worship. In any event, the Jews did not proceed upon that charge, thus tacitly admitting the utter worthlessness of the evidence of their own witnesses.

Then there came the real charge, and the events which led up to a charge of blasphemy. The High Priest asked Jesus the direct question, whether he claimed to be the Messiah (Matt. 26.63; Mark 14.61; Luke 22.67); and Jesus unequivocally replied that he was (Matt. 26.64; Mark 14.62; Luke 22.70). And then he went on: 'I tell you, hereafter you will see the Son of man seated at the right hand of Power, and coming on the clouds of heaven' (Matt. 26.64; Mark 14.62; Luke 22.69).

It is important to understand what Jesus was saying and claiming, for this is a much misunderstood text. Very often this saying of

Jesus is taken as a prophecy of his coming again, although it is to be noted that Luke has it in a form where there is not even a suggestion of the coming again—'But from now on the Son of man shall be seated at the right hand of the power of God' (Luke 22.69). Quite undoubtedly Jesus was quoting from Dan. 7.13f.:

> 'I saw in the night visions,
> and behold,
> there came with the clouds of heaven one like a son of man,
> and he came to the Ancient of Days, and was presented before him.
> And to him was given dominion and glory and kingdom,
> that all peoples, nations and languages should serve him;
> his dominion is an everlasting dominion, which shall not pass away,
> and his kingdom one that shall not be destroyed.'

Now one thing is quite certain—the Daniel passage does not describe an arrival *on earth;* it describes a regal and triumphant arrival *in heaven*. What Jesus was prophesying was his own return to, and enthronement in, glory. He was saying: 'At this moment I may seem to be in your power. At this moment you are gloatingly certain that you are going to eliminate me by having me nailed to a cross. This moment looks like your triumph and my defeat. But the day will come when you will see me again, and I shall be sitting in glory on the throne of God. At this moment you are the judges and I am the judged; the day will come in the heavenly places when I shall be the judge and when you will be on trial for your sins before me. At this moment you think that you are breaking me; the time will come when you will see me as the King of glory.' Here is the expression of the complete confidence of Jesus in his ultimate triumph.

Now, as the Jewish authorities saw it, they had their charge. This was blasphemy, treason against God; and Jesus must die.

If this preliminary trial of Jesus be set against the prescribed procedure of the Sanhedrin, in point after point it breaks the Sanhedrin's own regulations. The witnesses were false witnesses, and, even at that, if Mark is right, no two of them agreed. Jesus was from the beginning assumed to be guilty, even before the evidence of the witnesses was heard, when he should have been regarded as innocent and not even on trial until the evidence of his guilt was certain. He was twice subjected to physical violence (Luke 22.63;

John 18.22). He was asked questions by answering which he was bound to incriminate himself, and he was in the end condemned on evidence which he himself supplied. The Sanhedrin met during the night and during the Passover, when it should not have met, and in the house of Caiaphas, whereas the only place in which it could lawfully meet was the Hall of Hewn Stone. The verdicts were not given in order, as the regulations laid down. It was in fact the case that a *unanimously* unfavourable verdict was illegal.[1] Some one had to take the accused's part. A night did not elapse between the first conviction and the final verdict. The whole spirit of Sanhedrin procedure was broken, for the court acted, not as counsel for the defence, but as counsel for the prosecution, and instead of conserving the rights of the prisoner it systematically destroyed them. Even if we concede that some, or even many, of these regulations were ideal rather than actual, the fact remains that the Jewish authorities were prepared to go to any lengths and to sink to any depths to compass the death of Jesus.

As for Jesus, three things stand out about him. There is his dignity, for all through the scene it is he who seems to be in control. There is his courage, for he gave his answer to the High Priest well knowing that it meant death, and well knowing that he could have temporized, or denied his destiny, and so saved his life. There is his complete confidence in his ultimate triumph, and in the glory beyond the Cross.

As we have seen, in the time of Jesus the Jews, being subject to the Romans, did not possess the power to pass or to carry out sentence of death. The Sanhedrin still possessed a great many of its powers, for it was the policy of the Romans to allow their subject countries to go on using their own laws and their own organization, so long as the country was efficiently governed, and so long as peace and good order were maintained; but clearly the right of passing and carrying out sentence of death is something which any government must keep to itself. For that reason, after the trial before the Sanhedrin, Jesus had to be brought before Pilate, the Roman procurator.

It might have been thought that, even if the Jewish court was

[1] *Mishnah,* Sanhedrin 4.1.

prejudiced, envenomed and embittered, Jesus would at least have received impartial Roman justice from Pilate, but even that was not to be. The Jewish determination to eliminate Jesus at all costs is seen straight away from the fact that they brought Jesus before Pilate on a charge which had never been extracted in the trial and examination before the Sanhedrin, and which they were well aware was a lie. According to the trial before the Sanhedrin, the crime of which Jesus was guilty was the crime of blasphemy, and it is true that that charge did not wholly disappear, for before Pilate the Jews charged Jesus with declaring that he was the Son of God (John 19.7). But the Jewish authorities well knew that, if they brought Jesus before Pilate on a charge of blasphemy, Pilate would refuse to proceed on a charge which to him would seem nothing more than a domestic religious squabble, and even the outcome of misguided superstition. The charge, therefore, which the Jews levelled against Jesus was that he was a political agitator, that he was perverting the nation, that he was forbidding the Jews to pay their taxes to the Roman Emperor, and that he was setting himself up as a king (Luke 23.2), a charge which they were well aware was quite untrue, but a charge which they equally well knew Pilate was bound to investigate, for the one thing which no Roman governor could ever afford to pass over was the possibility of civil disorder and revolution.

In view of this charge, Pilate began his examination of Jesus with a question to which he well knew the answer, for Pilate was an experienced governor, or he would never have been appointed to the explosive province of Palestine; he knew a revolutionary when he saw one, and he knew at once that Jesus was no political insurrectionist. Pilate asked Jesus if he was the king of the Jews, and Jesus accepted the title, although in no worldly and political sense (Matt. 27.11; Mark 15.2; Luke 23.3–5; John 18.33–37). The fact that Pilate made not attempt whatever to follow up this question, or to press home this charge, shows how well aware he was that there was not a grain of truth in it.

In the presence of Jesus Pilate had an almost frightened awareness that he was in the presence of one who was no common man and who had a certain unearthly quality on him. Pilate was astonished at the silence with which Jesus greeted the shouted charges of his enemies (Matt. 27.13f.; Mark 15.3–5), and he was afraid when he knew that the charge was also that Jesus had called himself the Son of God (John 19.8).

Pilate was well aware that it was 'envy', bitter and unreasonable ill-will, and not justice or any desire for justice, which had made the Jews bring Jesus before him (Matt. 27.18; Mark 15.10). Again and again and again he demanded to know what Jesus had done, declared that he had found Jesus guilty of no charge, and insisted that he could find no crime in him (Matt. 27.23f.; Mark 15.14; Luke 23.4,14f.,22f.; John 18.38; 19.4). In the end he called for water and washed his hands as a futile symbol of the fact that, though he gave the Jews their way with Jesus, he disclaimed all personal responsibility for his condemnation (Matt. 27.24).

More and more events made it difficult for Pilate to condemn Jesus, even if it was still more difficult for him to let him go. There came to him a message from his wife, whom tradition calls Procula, saying that she had been warned in a dream that Pilate should refuse to have anything to do with the condemnation of this righteous man (Matt. 27.19). In the apocryphal *Acts of Pilate* it is said that there came a continual stream of witnesses demanding to be allowed to give evidence in favour of Jesus. One man said that he had been an invalid for thirty-eight years and that Jesus had healed him; another said that he had been blind and that Jesus had given him sight; another said that he was bowed and that he had been made straight, another that he had been a leper and that Jesus had cleansed him. And there came a woman called Bernice (Veronica in the Latin), who said that in the crowd she had touched the hem of Jesus' garment and that an issue of blood which had troubled her for ten years was stayed.[1]

Pilate made attempts to release Jesus. He proposed to scourge him, although he had done nothing to deserve scourging, and thus to let him go (Luke 23.16,22). There seems to have been a custom that at the Passover time the Jews had the privilege of having a prisoner released to them at the discretion of the governor. At that time there was in custody a prisoner called Barabbas, a man of violence. *Barabbas* would be from the Aramaic *Bar-Abba,* which

[1] English Translation by M. R. James, *The Apocryphal New Testament,* pp. 101f.

means either 'son of the father' or 'son of the teacher'. According to the lost *Gospel according to the Hebrews* his name was *Bar-rabban*, which means 'son of the Rabbi'. It is certain that Barabbas was no sneak-thief or petty criminal, and it may well be that he was a high-born young man, son of some famous family, who had become a Zealot, a popular nationalistic leader, who had been arrested after a career of murder and of violence in his fanatical patriotism. Pilate gave the Jews the choice between the release of Barabbas and the release of Jesus; the only result was an outbreak of half-crazed shouting for the release of Barabbas and the condemnation and crucifixion of Jesus. The impression we get is that of a mob, whipped up to a very frenzy, shouting for the release of Barabbas, shrieking in an almost insane fury for the death of Jesus (Matt. 27.15–18,23f.; Mark 15.6–15; Luke 23.18–25; John 18.40; 19.6,15).

In connection with Barabbas one interesting point emerges. The Syriac and the Armenian Versions of the New Testament, the Codex Koridethi, one of the great early manuscripts, all call Barabbas by the name Jesus Barabbas, a reading which Origen also knew. In Matt. 23.17 Moffatt puts the reading Jesus Barabbas in his text, and the Revised Standard Version, although not putting the reading in the text, notes that it exists. There is, of course, no doubt that Jesus was a very common name, for 'Jesus' is simply the Greek form of the name 'Joshua'. If this reading is true, and if Jesus was also the first name of Barabbas, two things emerge. First, the cry of the mob is even more dramatic—Jesus Barabbas, not Jesus who is called Christ. Second, it is a strange fact that Jesus Barabbas also may well mean 'Jesus the son of the father'. And the whole incident may well mean, in symbol, that the crowd is always liable to accept the man of violence and war as the son of God rather than the man of gentleness and love, and it would stand for the tragic fact that throughout the centuries men have so often put their trust in war and violence rather than in peace and love to solve the problems of the nation and of the world.

In the apocryphal *Acts of Pilate* there exists what purports to be a report by Pilate to the central government at Rome on the trial and execution of Jesus.

There befell of late a matter of which I myself made trial; for the Jews through envy have punished themselves and their posterity with fearful judgments of their own fault; for whereas their fathers had promised that their God would send out of heaven his holy one who should of right be called their king, and did promise that he would send him upon earth by a virgin; he, then, came when I was governor of Judaea, and they beheld him enlightening the blind, cleansing lepers, healing the palsied, driving devils out of men, raising the dead, rebuking the winds, walking upon the waves of the sea dry-shod, and doing many other wonders, and all the people of the Jews calling him the Son of God: the chief priests, therefore, moved with envy against him, took him and delivered him unto me and brought against him one false accusation after another, saying that he was a sorcerer and did things contrary to their law. But I, believing that these things were so, having scourged him, delivered him unto their will; and they crucified him, and when he was buried they set guards upon him. But while my soldiers watched him he rose again on the third day; yet so much was the malice of the Jews kindled that they gave money to the soldiers, saying: Say ye that his disciples stole away his body. But they, though they took the money, were not able to keep silence concerning that which had come to pass, for they also have testified that they saw him arisen and that they received money from the Jews. And these things have I reported unto thy mightiness for this cause, lest some other should lie unto thee, and thou shouldest deem right to believe the false tales of the Jews.[1]

That letter is quite certainly a fiction, but it is also quite certainly the kind of letter that Pilate might well have written about Jesus. Most revealingly, John says of Pilate that he sought to release Jesus (John 19.12), but in every attempt to release him Pilate came up against the implacable hostility of the Jews. How far that hostility went may be seen from the fact that at the trial of Jesus the Jewish leaders made a statement which it is well-nigh incredible that any Jew should ever have made. When Pilate asked them if they wished him to crucify their king, they answered: 'We have no king but Caesar' (John 19.15). For centuries Jews had been suffering and dying for the very reason that they would give the name king to no earthly person but only to God. In order to get rid of Jesus the Jews were prepared to deny their dearest and their most cherished belief. Nothing that Pilate could do would make them move a fraction of an inch from their irreconcilable hatred of Jesus, and from their grim determination to see him die.

All this is true, but we are compelled to ask one question. Why

---

[1] M. R. James, *The Aprocryphal New Testament*, p. 146.

did Pilate yield to the demands of the Jews? He was the Roman governor. How, then, could he be coerced into condemning one whom he knew to be innocent, and into consciously, though desperately unwillingly, perverting the course of justice? Matthew says that Pilate acted as he did act to avoid a riot, and that is certainly partly true (Matt. 27.24). Mark says that he acted as he did to satisfy the crowd (Mark 15.15), and Luke says that he delivered Jesus to their will (Luke 23.25), which is truer yet. But John says that in the end Pilate was compelled to act as he did, because the Jews said: 'If you release this man, you are not Caesar's friend' (John 19.12). That statement has an atmosphere and flavour of blackmail in it; it is not so much a statement as it is a threat. It is in fact nothing less than an implicit threat to report Pilate to Caesar, for any province could report its governor to the Emperor. The fact is that Pilate had by his conduct laid himself open to precisely this threat.

Palestine was a notoriously explosive province. Pilate became procurator of Palestine in AD 26, with the governor of Syria as his immediate superior. Although we know nothing at all about the life and career of Pilate before he came to Palestine, we can be quite certain that he must have been an experienced soldier and a highly successful administrator or he would never have been appointed to so responsible a position in so difficult a province. From the beginning of his term of office Pilate was in trouble with the Jews, and his actions make it clear that he never understood or even tried to understand them, and that he regarded them with complete contempt.

Josephus tells of his first clash with the Jews. The Roman headquarters in Palestine were not in Jerusalem but in Caesarea. In Jerusalem there was always a detachment of troops to act as guardians of the public peace. They were quartered in the Tower of Antonia which actually overlooked the Temple courts. Roman regimental standards had on them a little metal bust of the reigning Emperor. To the Jews such a bust was anathema, for it was a graven image, and the man whom it represented was held to be a god. The Romans were never unreasonable; they were notably tolerant; and they never looked for trouble. Hitherto, therefore, every Roman commander had marched his troops into Jerusalem without the bust of the Emperor on their standards. Pilate clearly had no intention of pandering to the ridiculous prejudices and superstitions of the Jews, and he marched his troops into Jerusalem with the bust of the Emperor still on their standards, but he did it under cover of night, so that at the moment the Jews did not know that it had happened. The morning came; the Jews awoke to find the Roman standards with the bust of the Emperor in Jerusalem—and in the Tower of Antonia overlooking the very Temple itself. The city was in a turmoil of distress which spread rapidly throughout the whole countryside. Pilate himself was at his headquarters in Caesarea. The Jews sent to Caesarea a deputation humbly beseeching Pilate to remove the standards. Pilate refused. For five days they followed him, prostrating themselves before him; he remained adamant. At last he set up his tribunal, his judgment seat, in the market square, and bade the Jews come at a certain hour, and he would give them an answer. They came. At a given signal they were surrounded by soldiers drawn up three deep, and with their drawn weapons in their hands. Pilate thereupon threatened the Jewish deputation with immediate death, unless they abandoned their entreaties and ceased to disturb him. But they bared their necks and bade the soldiers strike, for they would willingly die rather than see all that they held sacred transgressed. Pilate was baffled by this resolution to keep their laws inviolate; he gave in, and he ordered the standards to be removed. Pilate had recklessly begun by provoking a needless conflict with the Jews—and in the contest of wills he had been worsted. A worse beginning for a governor it would be hard to imagine.[1]

Pilate had not ended his foolishness. His official residence in Jerusalem was the ancient palace of the Herods. In that palace, as Philo tells us, Pilate displayed certain votive shields to the honour of Tiberius the Emperor. The shields had on them in this case no more than the name of Tiberius, to whom they were dedicated, and the name of Pilate, who dedicated them. It was common to attach such shields or tablets with prayers written on them to the knees of the statues of the gods. Now Tiberius was officially a god, and Caesar-worship was almost what might be called the universal religion of the Roman Empire; but never yet had there been any attempt to introduce Caesar-worship into Palestine; the Romans knew Jewish inflexibility far too well to attempt that. This action of Pilate

[1] Josephus, *Antiquities* 18.3.1.; *Wars* 2.9.2f.

seemed to the Jews the thin end of the wedge; here was an attempt to introduce the first beginnings of Caesar-worship. They could not bear to think that there was within the holy city a votive tablet to an Emperor who was held to be a god. They besought Pilate to remove the shields. Even the four sons of Herod, whose loyalty to Rome could not be questioned, joined in the supplication. Pilate stubbornly refused to take the shields away. It was here the Jews made their first threat. They threatened to take the matter up with Tiberius—and Pilate was alarmed, for he feared that an embassy to the Emperor on this matter might go on to other matters—'his corruption, his acts of insolence, his rapine, his habit of insulting people, his cruelty, his continual murders of people untried and uncondemned, his never-ending and gratuitous and most grievous inhumanity', as Philo lists his crimes. In spite of his fear Pilate remained adamant. Very courteously and very humbly the Jewish leaders wrote direct to the Emperor Tiberius; and thereupon Tiberius rebuked Pilate sternly, and ordered him at once to remove the shields from Jerusalem to Caesarea. Once again in a contest of wills with the Jews Pilate was worsted, and this time the Emperor had taken the part of the Jews against him—a dangerous and a threatening precedent.[1]

It seemed curiously impossible for Pilate to treat Jewish principles and feelings with anything other than contempt. The third of his unwise actions concerned the construction of a new aqueduct to improve the water supply of Jerusalem. There could hardly have been a worthier or a more useful undertaking. But to build this aqueduct Pilate raided the resources of the Temple treasury. It may be that Pilate confined his taking of the money to funds which could not in any event have been used for sacred purposes because of the sources from which they had come. But worthy though the object was, and careful as Pilate may have been in his taking it, the Jews were enraged. They congregated in crowds with insistent demands that he should abandon the undertaking; before long the demands turned to violent abuse; and the situation was not far from rioting. To control the situation Pilate surrounded the crowds with soldiers armed, but dressed in civilian clothes, and therefore disguised. They had instructions at a given signal to beat the mob up with staves which they were carrying, but not to use their swords

---

[1] Philo, *The Embassy to Caius* 38.

and daggers and not to kill. As the affair turned out, the soldiers used much more force than Pilate had intended. The people were, of course, quite unarmed and were caught totally unawares. Guilty and innocent were alike beaten up, a great number were slain, and still more were wounded. True, the riot was nipped in the bud, the protests were ended, but Pilate had acquired another black mark in the eyes of the Jews.[1]

We may follow Pilate to the end of his governorship. In AD 35 trouble broke out in Samaria. Samaritan tradition said that the vessels of the Tabernacle had been hidden in Mount Gerizim by Moses. An impostor, who, as Josephus caustically says, 'thought lying a thing of little consequence', emerged, and promised to produce the vessels from where they were hidden. He gained a great following who assembled at the town of Tirabatha, and many of whom were unfortunately bearing arms. Samaria was within Pilate's jurisdiction. He promptly blocked the roads and fell on Tirabatha. Many were immediately slain; many were captured and many of the leaders and the most influential were summarily executed. The Samaritan senate thereupon reported Pilate to his superior, Vitellius, the governor of Syria, accusing him of murdering the prisoners, and pleading that Pilate had used excessive force in a situation in which no rebellion had ever been intended. Vitellius promptly ordered Pilate to Rome to answer to the Emperor Tiberius for the charges made against him; but, before Pilate reached Rome, Tiberius died, and so Pilate vanishes from history with an unfinished story.[2]

There is little doubt that Pilate was blackmailed into giving the Jews their way with Jesus. He was afraid that the Jews would report him for his past misdeeds, as one day the Samaritans were to do, and that he would thus lose his post. Pilate's past rose up before him in the greatest moment of decision in his life. Pilate had to choose between losing his post and abandoning Jesus to the fury of the mob without even a pretence of justice. And Pilate chose to keep his post and to allow Jesus to be murdered.

All through his trial, certain unmistakable things stand out about Jesus.

From the purely human point of view, the most amazing fact of

---

[1] Josephus, *Antiquities* 18.3.2.
[2] Josephus, *Antiquities* 18.4.1.

all is his complete absence of resentment. First from the Jews and then from Pilate he received nothing but the most glaring and intolerable injustice. The laws of his own countrymen and the laws of the Romans were deliberately abrogated to compass his death. In neither court was there even a pretence of justice. Almost anyone else in this world would have bitterly resented such injustice, and would have uttered his resentment in no uncertain terms. Jesus is the supreme example of serenity in the face of injustice.

One of the most extraordinary features of the trial of Jesus is that nowhere in it does he seem to be on trial. At all times he is in control of the situation. In the whole collection of characters there, Jesus alone is in control of himself and the situation. The Jews and their leaders are more than half-crazed with hate; there is in them that which sets a mob on a lynching expedition. Their emotions are out of control. Pilate is the very picture of frustration, like an animal caught in a trap, twisting and turning and quite unable to find any way of escape. Never was any governor less capable of governing, or any ruler more tragically helpless. Alone amidst all the wild, unbalanced hatred and the helpless frustration, Jesus stands serene and calm and in control both of the situation and of himself. The last thing that Jesus ever appears to be is on his defence; rather it is he who stands in judgment.

It is clear that all through the trial Jesus never thought of himself as a victim. There are certain Johannine sayings which, whether they are to be taken as literal and verbatim or not, quite certainly reflect and contain the mind of Jesus. Even before the trial Jesus had said: 'I lay down my life, that I may take it again. No one takes it from me, but I lay it down of my own accord' (John 10.17f.). In this situation Jesus still saw the guiding hand of God. When Pilate sought to remind him that his life was in his hands, Jesus reminded Pilate that he could have possessed no power at all, unless it had been given to him (John 19.10f.). Even amidst that heart-breaking injustice, it was still the conviction of Jesus that he was not the victim of men but the chosen instrument and Servant of God. The happenings of the last days and hours were to Jesus, not fragments in a set of circumstances which were out of control, but events in a drama, whose course and whose culmination were in the hands of God.

26

THE CRUCIFIXION OF JESUS

When we come to think about the Cross, we must indeed put the shoes from off our feet, for the place whereon we stand is holy ground. The extraordinary feature about the narrative of the crucifixion in the Gospels is its reticence. 'When they came to the place that is called The Skull, there they crucified him' (Luke 23.33; see Matt. 27.35; Mark 15.22,24; John 19.17f.). There is no attempt to pile horror on horror and agony on agony; there is no attempt to set out the grim and ghastly details; with a bleak and bare economy of words the Gospel writers simply set down the fact in all its stark simplicity. For them that was enough, for they knew the details and the facts, but for us something more is necessary in order that we may even dimly understand something of what Jesus underwent for us and for all mankind.

Following the verdict of condemnation Jesus was scourged, for scourging was always a prelude to crucifixion (Matt. 27.26; Mark 15.15; Luke 23.16; John 19.1). This was something which Jesus had always foreseen, and which he knew awaited him (Matt. 20.19; Mark 10.34; Luke 18.33). There were few more terrible ordeals than Roman scourging. The victim was stripped, and he was either tied to a pillar in a bent position with his back exposed so that he could not move, or he was stretched rigid upon a frame. The scourge was made of leather thongs studded with sharpened pellets of lead or iron and pieces of bone. It literally ripped a man's back to pieces. Many lost consciousness under the lash; many emerged from the experience raving mad; few were untied from their bonds with spirit still unbroken. This was what Jesus suffered.

He was then handed over to the soldiers that they might make sport of him (Matt. 27.27–29; Mark 15.16–20; John 19.2f.). They made him a crown of thorns and gave him a reed for a sceptre and an old purple cloak for a robe, and mocked him as a king and as a prophet. In the case of the soldiers there was neither malice nor hate; they were simply exercising their right to horse-play with one who was to them a pathetic pretender, a failure who had been condemned to a violent death.

Then there began the procession to Calvary. It always followed the same pattern. The criminal was placed in the centre of a hollow square of four Roman soldiers; in front there walked a herald carrying a board whitened with gypsum with the charge painted in black letters upon it. In the case of Jesus it read: 'This is Jesus, King of the Jews' (Matt. 27.37, but the wording is slightly different in each of the four Gospels; see Mark 15.26; Luke 23.38; John 19.19). According to John, it was written in Hebrew, Latin and Greek, so that all could read it (John 19.20); and it was later to be affixed to Jesus' cross. The criminal was taken to the place of crucifixion by the longest possible way, by the busiest streets, and through as many of them as possible, so that he might be a dreadful warning to any other who might be contemplating some crime; and, as he went, he was lashed and goaded on his way.

The criminal was compelled to carry at least part of his own cross to the place of execution. The upright beam of the cross was called the *stipes;* the cross-beam was called the *patibulum.* If there was a regular place of crucifixion, the upright beam usually stood ready there in its socket, and it was the cross-beam, the *patibulum,* which the prisoner had to carry. Sometimes the *patibulum* consisted of one single beam; more often, perhaps, it consisted of a double beam joined at one end and open at the other, and the prisoner's head was fitted into the space between the two beams. The exhausting experiences of the night of trials and examinations, and the terrible torture of the scourging, had left Jesus so weak that he staggered and fell under the weight of the beam, and Simon of Cyrene, no doubt a pilgrim to the Passover from North Africa, had the grim experience of being all unexpectedly impressed into the Roman service in order to carry the cross (Matt. 27.32; Mark 15.21; Luke 23.26). Palestine was an occupied country, and a Roman officer had only to touch a Jew on the shoulder with the flat of the blade of a spear to compel him to submit to any service, however menial and however repulsive. It is said that they *brought* Jesus to the place called Golgotha (Mark 15.22). In the best manuscripts the word used for 'to bring' is *pherein,* which most naturally means to bear or to carry; and it may well be that Jesus had to be carried and supported to the cross. On the way to the cross there followed Jesus those who had loved him and who mourned for him, and Luke tells how he warned them of still worse things to come (Luke 23.27–31).

When the place of crucifixion was reached, the cross was laid flat on the ground and the criminal was then laid on top of it. At this point it was the custom to give to the victim a drink of medicated wine, which was mercifully prepared by a group of pious women in Jerusalem in obedience to the command of Prov. 31.6: 'Give strong drink to him who is perishing, and wine to those in bitter distress'. The medicated wine was an opiate to dull the pain, but Jesus tasted it and then refused to accept it, for he would meet death at its bitterest and with all his senses at their keenest (Matt. 27.34; Mark 15.23). Half-way up the upright beam of the cross there was a projecting ledge of wood, called the saddle, on which part of the weight of the criminal's body rested, or the weight of his body would have torn the nails clean through his hands. As the criminal was stretched upon the cross, the nails were driven through his hands. Frequently at that moment victims cursed and swore and shrieked and spat at their executioners, but it was then that Jesus prayed: 'Father, forgive them; for they know not what they do' (Luke 23.34). Then in a moment of searing agony the cross was lifted up and set in its socket with the victim hanging on it.

Before the criminal was nailed to the cross—usually only the hands were nailed and the feet were only loosely bound to the upright—the criminal had been stripped save for a loin cloth, which was left to him for decency's sake. The clothes of the criminal were the perquisite of the detachment of four soldiers in charge of the crucifixion. A Jew wore six articles of clothing; there were the belt, the sandals, the girdle, the turban and the tunic, which were of almost equal value, and in the distribution of which there would be no real difficulty. But the main article of clothing was a great robe which served a man as a cloak by day and a blanket by night, and which was so essential an article of clothing that the law laid it down that, even if it was taken for debt, it must be returned to a man at night that he might sleep in it (Ex. 22.26f.). Jesus' robe was specially finely made, for it was woven without seam. Clearly to have cut it up would have been to ruin it, so the soldiers cast lots beneath the cross to see which of them was to have it (Matt. 27.35; Mark 15.24; Luke 23.34; John 19.23f.).

From the cross Jesus was watching. The cross was not high, only from seven to nine feet high at the highest, and he could easily see what was happening. Now there was a Jewish custom in regard to the great outer robe. It was not in shops that clothes were bought in those days; they were made at home. It was the mother who wove the cloth and cut and sewed and shaped it; and usually, before a son left home to go out into the world, his mother's last gift to him was a great outer robe, woven and made with her own hands. No doubt it was Mary who had woven the robe of Jesus, and Jesus' thoughts turned to his mother, and to her loneliness in the days to come. The disciple whom Jesus loved was standing watching there. 'Woman,' said Jesus to Mary, 'behold your son!' And to the beloved disciple he said: 'Behold your mother!' (John 19.26f.).

Not even on the cross would the venom of Jesus' enemies leave him alone. Even there they taunted him. What an end for him who claimed to be the Son of God! What an end for a king! What an end to the would-be destroyer and rebuilder of the Temple! A strange saviour who offered to save others and who was powerless to save himself! (Matt. 27.39–43; Mark 15.29–32; Luke 23.35–37). They came to gloat over the man whom they thought that they were eliminating from life for ever.

On that day Jesus was not the only victim. Two brigands were crucified with him (Matt. 27.38; Mark 15.27; Luke 23.32; John 19.18). Matthew says that they too joined in the mockery. They were not robbers in the sense of petty criminals, or burglars, or sneak-thieves; they were *lēstai,* which means 'brigands', and doubtless they were reckless adventurers and outlaws and men of courage, even if they had taken to a career of crime. But Luke tells us that one of them was fascinated by Jesus even on the cross; he rebuked his fellow-brigand, reminding him that they deserved their fate, while Jesus was guiltless. Then he made one of the most amazing statements in all history. To a broken Galilaean hanging in agony in a cross, mocked by the orthodox among his countrymen, an apparent failure if ever there was one, that brigand said: 'Jesus, remember me when you come in your kingly power.' And back came the calm, strong voice of Jesus: 'Today you will be with me in Paradise' (Luke 23.39–43). It is hardly possible that the world ever saw a less likely candidate for a kingdom, yet in Jesus that brigand saw a king, and Jesus accepted his homage.

It was at 'the third hour'—that is, at nine o'clock in the morning, for, as we have seen, the twelve hours of the Jewish day were counted from 6 a.m. to 6 p.m.—that Jesus had been crucified. When the sun was at its zenith, instead of the brightness of noon there came upon the land a darkness as of midnight, settling on Jerusalem for the next three hours (Matt. 27.45; Mark 15.33; Luke 23.44f.). At three o'clock in the afternoon the most terrible of all cries was wrung from Jesus: 'My God, my God, why hast thou forsaken me?' (Matt. 27.46; Mark 15.34). At that moment Jesus was plumbing unfathomable depths for us men and for our salvation.

And now the drama was coming to its close. Parched by his agony, Jesus said: 'I thirst', and a soldier in a moment of mercy gave him a drink of the rough vinegar wine which was all that the soldiers were allowed to drink when they were on duty (Matt. 27.48; Mark 15.36; John 19.28f.).

The end was very near. Jesus uttered a loud cry (Matt. 27.50; Mark 15.37; Luke 23.46). That cry was neither a cry of pain nor yet a cry of despair. It was a cry of triumph: 'It is finished' (John 19.30), which in Jesus' own tongue was one triumphant word. And then he prayed. He prayed the first prayer that every Jewish boy was taught to pray by his mother before the dark came down; he prayed the prayer that Mary had taught him when he was a little boy: 'Father, into thy hands I commit my spirit' (Luke 23.46; Ps. 31.5). Then he bowed his head and died, and the word which John uses when he says that Jesus *bowed* his head (*klinein*) is the word which would be used for a man peacefully letting his head sink back upon his pillow that he might sleep. And so there came the peace after the long battle, the rest after the bitter toil, the ease after the agony.

At that moment the curtain which veiled the Holy of Holies in the Temple was rent in two (Matt. 27.51; Mark 15.38; Luke 23.45); and at that moment the centurion who was in charge of the crucifixion was kneeling before the cross, breathing out in wonder: 'Truly this was a son of God' (Matt. 27.54; Mark 15.39; Luke 23.47). Jesus, lifted up from the earth, had drawn the first of his captives to himself in the very moment of his death.

In all the agony there was only one mercy. The terror of crucifixion was that it was a lingering death. A man might hang on a cross for days, tortured by the flies, parched with thirst, burned by the sun, frozen by the night frosts, until he died raving mad. If a man refused to die, it was the custom to pound him to death with blows of a mallet. The next day was the Sabbath, and before the Sabbath the bodies must be taken down. At the request of the Jews the soldiers took steps to hasten the end. The brigands were pounded to death; but mercifully Jesus was dead. They plunged a spear into his side and there came out water and blood; so the divine tragedy was ended (John 19.31–35).

We must now go on to look at Jesus on the Cross in order to see what that picture tells us simply and non-theologically about him.

On the Cross we see *the courage of Jesus.* Of all deaths crucifixion is the most terrible. It can involve a man in a death which is a lingering agony. In his article on crucifixion in Smith's *Dictionary of the Bible,* F. W. Farrar quotes from the work of a physician called Richter who wrote a treatise on the physical effects of crucifixion. The unnatural position and the tension of the body made every movement a pain. The fact that the nails were driven through those parts of the hands where the nerves and the tendons are made every movement the most exquisite torture. The wounds of the nails and the weals of the lash very soon became inflamed and even gangrenous. The position of the body hindered the circulation, and caused a pain and tension in the body which is described as more intolerable than death itself. The agony of crucifixion was the worst kind of agony, lingering, gradually but inevitably increasing every moment. And to all this must be added the burning thirst which soon began to torture the victim. These are not pleasant facts, but this was crucifixion—and Jesus knew it. Crucifixion was by no means an uncommon penalty for evil-doers and revolutionaries in Palestine. In the unrest which followed the death of Herod the Great, Varus, the Roman general, captured Sepphoris in Galilee and lined the roads of Galilee with no fewer than two thousand crosses.[1] That was a story that Jesus must often have heard; he must have known well, and may perhaps even have seen, the agony of crucifixion. Jesus knew what crucifixion was like; to the end he might have escaped from it; yet he went steadily on, and in the end he even refused the opiate offered in mercy (Matt. 27.34) that he might endure pain to the uttermost, and that he might meet death with steady eyes and with mind unclouded. It is one kind of courage to do some gallant action on the spur of the moment before there is even time to think. It is another and a far higher kind of courage to know that there is agony and torture at the end of a chosen road, and to go steadily on to meet it.

On the Cross we see *the humanity of Jesus*. There have always been those in the Church who in a false reverence have been unwilling and unable to take the manhood of Jesus seriously. Such people were known as the Docetists, which means, as we might put it, the Seemists. Christianity came into a world in which the body was despised, in which the spirit was all important, and in which a man was held to be able to reach truth and light and God only when he had sloughed off the body. *Sōma sēma* ran the popular saying, the body is a tomb. Plotinus could say that he was ashamed that he had a body. Epictetus could describe himself as a poor soul shackled to a corpse. Seneca could talk of the 'detestable habitation' of the body. The result was that there were those who held that the body of Jesus was only a phantom and an appearance and in no sense a real body. 'The blood of Christ,' said Jerome, 'was still fresh in Jerusalem when his body was said to be a phantasm.'[2] Ignatius continually inveighs against those who held that Jesus only *seemed* to suffer. In the apocryphal *Acts of John* it is said that the feet of Jesus left no print on the ground when he walked, and that his

---

[1] Josephus, *Antiquities* 17.10.10.
[2] *Against the Luciferians* 23.

body was immaterial to the touch. That same book tells how at the very time of the crucifixion Jesus met John on the Mount of Olives, and told him that he only *seemed* to suffer on Calvary, but in reality he was with John.[1] Many of the Gnostic Docetists held that the divine Christ came into the man Jesus at the Baptism and left him before the crucifixion, so that, while the man Jesus did suffer, the divine Christ suffered not at all. Basilides taught that in fact it was not Jesus but Simon of Cyrene who was crucified, although he looked like Jesus, while Jesus stood by and laughed. Jesus was held to have a 'psychic' body, not subject to the laws of matter, not subject to any human desire, passion, or emotion, and quite incapable of feeling pain. It was said that, when his body was taken down from the cross, it was nothing but a 'void'. But the crucifixion narrative in the Gospels unmistakably sets before us the humanity of Jesus. We see Jesus stagger and faint beneath the weight of the beam of the cross; we see him in his human pain and weakness having to be half-carried to Calvary. We hear the human cry: 'I thirst' (John 19.28f.). We hear Pilate's 'Here is the man!' (John 19.5). One of the great aims of the story of the Cross is to show the real and full manhood of Jesus and the complete reality of his sufferings. Here is no phantasm of a body, but quivering human flesh; here is no acted appearance of suffering, but a terrible reality of agony.

On the Cross we see *the identity of Jesus with sinners*. That is symbolically marked in his crucifixion between two criminals (Matt. 27.38; Mark 15.27; Luke 23.33; John 19.18). It was said of the Suffering Servant in Isaiah: 'They made his grave with the wicked . . . He was numbered with the transgressors' (Isa. 53.9,12). Jesus had always been the friend of tax-gatherers and sinners (Matt. 11.19), a friendship which had shocked the orthodox of his day (Matt. 9.10–13). It is symbolic of his whole work that he was crucified between two criminals and identified with sinners in his death.

On the Cross we see *the invincible forgiveness of Jesus*. Even as they drove the nails through him, he prayed: 'Father, forgive them; for they know not what they do' (Luke 23.34). It is as if Jesus said: 'No matter what you do to me, I will still forgive.' If in

[1] *Acts of John* 93, 97.

Jesus we see the mind of God fully displayed, it means that there are no limits to the love, the grace, the forgiveness of God. We see Jesus on the Cross embodying the message of divine forgiveness which he brought to men.

On the Cross we see *the selflessness of Jesus.* Even in his own agony he remembered the sorrow and the loneliness of Mary, and committed her to the care of the disciple whom he loved (John 19.26f.). Nothing is more extraordinary in the whole story of Jesus than his absolute refusal to use his powers for his own gain, his own profit, his own comfort, or his own safety. He thought never in terms of self, and always in terms of others.

On the Cross we see *the depths which Jesus plumbed* in his complete identification with the human situation. 'My God, my God,' he said, 'why hast thou forsaken me?' (Matt. 27.46; Mark 15.34). There are many of Jesus' sayings which are uninventable, but this one is supremely such.

It is sometimes held that when Jesus said that he was beginning to quote Ps. 22, which begins with these very words; and indeed, that Psalm seems inextricably interwoven with the events of the Cross. The Psalmist, describing his own evil case, goes on: 'All who see me mock at me; they make mouths at me, they wag their heads; "He committed his cause to the Lord, let him deliver him; let him rescue him, for he delights in him" ' (vv. 7f.). Still describing his experiences the Psalmist goes on: 'They divide my garments among them, and for my raiment they cast lots' (v. 18). But the Psalm ends not in tragedy but in triumph: 'He has not despised or abhorred the affliction of the afflicted; and he has not hid his face from him, but has heard when he cried to him. From thee comes my praise in the great congregation; my vows I will pay before those who fear him. The afflicted shall eat and be satisfied; those who seek him shall praise the Lord! May your hearts live for ever!' (vv. 24–26). So it has been suggested that this saying of Jesus is not so much, as it were, a personal saying, but that it is rather the beginning of the psalm, which Jesus was quoting to himself to remind himself of the servant of God in the ancient times who had begun in shame and humiliation and who had ended in confidence and glory.

But, as we have said before, it may well be that this is the cry of Jesus caught up in a situation which he knew God intended him to go through, but which he could not understand, that here is Jesus going through the darkness of having to accept that which he did not understand—which is so often an essential part of the human situation. It could never have been claimed that Jesus fully knew the human situation unless he experienced that.

On the Cross we see *the royalty of Jesus*. Again and again we are confronted with the fact that at no time did Jesus seem a broken figure, a victim of circumstances; at all times he carried himself like a king. It was to this man on the cross that the crucified brigand appealed as to a king for a place in his kingdom. John Buchan in his biography of Montrose tells how Montrose was finally captured and brought to Edinburgh for trial and execution. As the procession passed up the Canongate the street was lined with crowds, 'the dregs of the Edinburgh slums, the retainers of the Covenanting lords, ministers from far and near'. The crowds had been deliberately incited, and had even been supplied with ammunition, to stone Montrose as he passed. But the strange thing was that somehow that day in Edinburgh not a voice was raised, not a hand was lifted, not a missile was thrown. The crowd gazed silent and fascinated on one who was treated as a criminal but who looked like a king. 'It is absolutely certain,' wrote one who witnessed the scene, 'that he hath overcome more men by his death in Scotland than he would have done, if he had lived. For I never saw a more sweeter carriage in a man in all my life.' There have always been some men whose kingliness nothing can obscure. Jesus was supremely and uniquely such. Even in the dying criminal on the cross the brigand saw a king.

On the Cross we see *the peace of Jesus*. He died with the child's good-night prayer upon his lips (Luke 23.46; Ps. 31.5). He died as one laying his head upon a pillow to sleep (John 19.30). He died not like a disappointed man with a broken heart, but like one well content that his work was done.

On the Cross we see *the triumph of Jesus*. It is with the cry of victory, 'It is finished,' that he died (John 19.30). His task was accomplished and his work was done, and already in the astonished centurion the Cross had begun its triumphs.

27

LOOKING AT THE CROSS

No one will deny that the Cross is designed to awaken within us not theological disputation but adoring love. It is nevertheless true that the more we think about the Cross and the more we understand it, the greater will be the love and adoration within our hearts. The obligation is, therefore, laid upon us to seek to understand at least something of what happened on the Cross for all mankind and for us. As we read the narrative of the Gospels certain things become unmistakably clear.

(i) It is clear that Jesus went willingly, spontaneously and open-eyed to the Cross. There have been those who saw in Jesus' life 'the Galilaean spring time', a time when men responded to him and when he expected good success. Slowly, it is suggested, Jesus came to see that men would finally and totally reject him, and that there was no other way than the way of the Cross. On that view Jesus went to the Cross because circumstances compelled him to do so, but the Cross was not his original plan. But, if we place any reliance on the story of the Gospels, there never was a time in his earthly life when Jesus was not aware that at the end of the road there stood the Cross. We can trace this consciousness of Jesus backwards through the story.

(a) Towards the very end of his ministry there was the woman who in Bethany anointed Jesus with the very precious ointment. There were those who regarded this act of love as an extravagant waste, but Jesus bade them to let her alone, because she had done it, as it were, to prepare him for burial (Matt. 26.12; Mark 14.8). By this time Jesus had not the slightest doubt that he must die.

(b) Shortly before that incident Jesus had spoken the parable of the wicked husbandmen (Matt. 21.33–46; Mark 12.1–12; Luke 20.9–18). The dramatic culmination of that parable is the murder of the heir by the husbandmen, and it is plain that Jesus was fore-telling what was to happen to himself. Again he was in no doubt that death awaited him, and violent death.

(c) Following upon Peter's great discovery and confession at Caesarea Philippi Jesus repeatedly foretold his own death. 'And he began to teach them that the Son of Man must suffer many things, and be rejected by the elders and the chief priests and the scribes, and be killed, and after three days rise again' (Mark 8.31f.; 9.31f.; 10.33f.; Matt. 16.21; 17.22; Luke 9.22,44). Denney rightly calls attention to the tense of the verbs in Mark 9.31. The verbs for *to teach* and *to say* are both in the imperfect tense (*edidasken* and *elegen*), and that tense expresses repeated, habitual and continuous action. From that time on Jesus repeatedly and openly spoke to his disciples about his coming death on the Cross.

(d) Early in the narrative of the Gospels there is an incident which all three synoptic Gospels relate. The disciples of the Pharisees came asking why the disciples of Jesus did not fast as they did. Jesus' answer was that, so long as the bridegroom was with them, the wedding guests could not fast, but, that a day would come when the bridegroom would be taken away from them, and then they would fast (Matt. 9.14f.; Mark 2.18f.; Luke 5.33f.). Jesus clearly foretold that the joy of fellowship would be followed by the grief of separation.

(e) We can trace the matter even further back than that. At the moment of his baptism the divine voice said to Jesus: 'Thou art my beloved Son; with thee I am well pleased' (Mark 1.11; Matt. 3.17; Luke 3.22). That saying is composed of two quotations from the Old Testament. 'Thou art my beloved Son,' is a quotation of Ps. 2.7. That Psalm is a coronation Psalm, and was always taken as pointing to the triumph and enthronement of the Messiah. 'With thee I am well pleased,' is a quotation from Isa. 42.1, and is part of the description of the Servant of the Lord, whose portrait finds its culmination in the picture of one who was wounded for our trans-gressions and bruised for our iniquities in Isa. 53. This can only mean that from the beginning Jesus thought of himself in terms of the messianic office, but also thought of himself in terms of the Suffering Servant of the Lord.

Here, then, is the first thing which we can say with confidence of the Cross of Jesus. Jesus was not driven to the Cross by force of circumstances. The Cross was not an afterthought when some original hope and plan and scheme had been disappointed. From the beginning Jesus voluntarily and spontaneously thought in terms of the Cross. The Fourth Gospel correctly interprets the mind of Jesus when it pictures him as saying: 'I lay down my life that I may take it again. No one takes it from me, but I lay it down of my own accord' (John 10.17f.).

(ii) Although Jesus voluntarily accepted the Cross, it is also true that he looked on the Cross as an utter necessity. He did not regard his death as the result of some uncontrolled concatenation of circumstances, or as some accidental happening. He regarded it as necessary and essential. 'The Son of Man,' he said, '*must (dei)* suffer many things . . . and be killed' (Mark 8.31; Matt. 16.21; Luke 9.22). 'The Son of Man,' he said, 'goes as it has been determined' (Luke 22.22). To Jesus the Cross was something which was an essential happening from which there was no escape.

(iii) How is it that Jesus could regard the Cross at one and the same time as his own voluntary and spontaneous choice and an utter necessity? The answer is that Jesus was certain that the Cross was part of the eternal will and purpose of God. Gethsemane Jesus was struggling not to discover God's will, but to accept God's will (Matt. 26.36–46; Mark 14.32–42; Luke 22.39–46). Jesus, therefore, did not regard himself as the victim of men, but as the agent and instrument and willing servant of God. He saw the Cross not as the necessity of an iron determinism or an inescapable fate, but as part of the plan and the purpose and the design of God. It was, therefore, something which was at one and the same time voluntary and essential, for the will of Jesus was fully and perfectly and voluntarily identified with the will of God, his Father. In one sense escape lay open to him. He need never have come to Jerusalem. He could have compromised with the orthodox Jewish leaders. Regiments of angels were his for his defence, if he had wished it so (Matt. 26.51–54). But in another sense there was no such thing as escape for him, for there could never be escape from the will of God.

For Jesus, then, the Cross was completely voluntary, absolutely essential, and an integral part of the will and purpose of God.

The meaning of Jesus is something which a man must always

discover for himself. The basic question of Jesus is: 'Who do *you* say that I am?' (Matt. 16.15; Mark 8.29; Luke 9.20). It is not enough to quote what others have said about Jesus. Personal knowledge, personal confrontation, personal discovery and personal decision alone are enough. But, although that is so, we despoil ourselves of something which is of infinite preciousness and value, if we disregard the thoughts and discoveries of those who have gone out on the adventure of thought before us. We will, therefore, do well to see how others have interpreted the Cross and the death of Jesus.

The basic New Testament statement about the death of Jesus and its significance is the saying of Paul: 'Christ died for our sins in accordance with the scriptures' (I Cor. 15.3). It is important to remember what the word *for* means in this statement. The word is *huper*, and it does not mean *because of* or *in place of*. It means *on behalf of, for the sake of*, a fact which only Kenneth Wuest of all the modern translators brings out. The meaning is that Jesus Christ died in order to do something on behalf of our sins. That is to say, our sins and the death of Jesus Christ are indissolubly connected.

The Church in its wisdom has never had any official and orthodox doctrine of the Atonement. Wisely the Church has left every man to find his own way to salvation through the life and death of Jesus. But we can go one step further in company, before the ways diverge. The word atonement is really *at-one-ment*. We may, therefore, go on to say that the death of Jesus has done something which nothing else could ever do to make us *at one* with God. However we go on to interpret these basic statements—and the interpretations of them are many—we must begin with the two great kindred facts that Jesus died on behalf of the sins of men, and the effect of his death is to remove the estrangement between man and God and to make man and God *at one*.

(i) The simplest view of the work of Jesus Christ is that he lived and died to be our example. 'Christ also suffered for you,' wrote Peter, 'leaving you an example, that you should follow in his steps' (I Peter 2.21). The word for example is *hupogrammos*, which is the word for the perfect line of copperplate handwriting at the top of the page of a child's writing exercise-book, the line which he must copy and which he must seek to reproduce. Jesus, then, in his life and death left us an example which we must reproduce. Even in so great a passage as Phil. 2.1–11 in which Paul speaks so lyrically about the self-emptying of Jesus Christ for the sake of men, that self-emptying and that sacrificial obedience are set out as an example of the mind and heart and conduct which should be in the Christian. When Clement of Rome was writing to the warring church at Corinth, he quoted Isa. 53 at length to show what the Servant of the Lord must be like, and then he went on to say: 'You see, beloved, what is the example which is given to us, for, if the Lord was thus humble-minded, what shall we do, who through him have come under the yoke of grace?'[1] When Polycarp was writing to the Philippians, he spoke about the sufferings of Jesus for mankind, and then he went on to say: 'Let us then be imitators of his endurance, and, if we suffer for his name's sake, let us glorify him. For this is the example which he gave us in himself, and this is what we have believed.'[2] Irenaeus speaks of the Christians as 'imitators of his works as well as doers of his words'.[3] Lactantius thinks of Jesus as the perfect teacher, teaching not only by precept but by example. The teacher must practise what he teaches and must 'hold out his hand to one who is about to follow him'. 'It is befitting,' he says, 'that a master and teacher of virtue should most closely resemble man, that by overpowering sin, he may teach man that sin may be overpowered by him.' And if man should answer that the task is impossible, then this Jesus, who was real human flesh and blood, makes answer: 'See, I myself do it.'[4] Augustine in one of his earlier works describes the whole life of Jesus, as H. E. W. Turner translates the phrase, as 'a moral instruction', *disciplina morum*.[5] The idea of the work of Jesus as example is deeply rooted in Christian thought.

Closely allied with the idea of Jesus as the perfect example is the idea of him as the divine bringer of knowledge, the divine illuminer of men, the divine revealer of God and the truth of God. As the New Testament itself has it, we have 'the light of the knowledge of

[1] *I Clement* 16.17.
[2] *To the Philippians* 8.2.
[3] *Against Heresies* 5.1.1.
[4] *Divine Institutes* 4.24.
[5] Augustine, *On True Religion* 16.32; H. E. W. Turner, *The Patristic Doctrine of Redemption*, p. 35.

the glory of God in the face of Christ' (II Cor. 4.6). He brings us the truth and the truth makes us free (John 8.32). He brings life and immortality to light through his glorious gospel (II Tim. 1.10).

The early Church loved to dwell on the thought of the knowledge, the illumination, the revelation which came in Jesus Christ. It is for 'the life and knowledge' which were made known through Jesus that the Eucharistic prayer of the *Didache* gives thanks.[1] Jesus Christ, says Ignatius, is the word of God 'proceeding from silence'.[2] 'Through him,' writes Clement of Rome, 'we fix our gaze on the heights of heaven, through him we see the reflection of his faultless and lofty countenance, through him the eyes of our hearts were opened, through him our foolish and darkened understanding blossoms towards the light, through him the Master willed that we should taste immortal knowledge.'[3] Through him God called us 'from darkness to light, from ignorance to the full knowledge of the glory of his name'.[4] Through Jesus Christ, writes Lactantius, 'the fountain of God, most abundant and most full, is open to all; and this heavenly light rises for all, as many as have eyes'.[5] 'In no other way,' says Irenaeus, 'could we have learned the things of God, unless our Master, existing as the Word, had become man.' In him the invisible becomes visible, the incomprehensible is made comprehensible, the impassible becomes capable of suffering.[6]

In the New Testament itself we have the great picture of Jesus Christ the example, the illuminer, the revealer. Clearly the work of Jesus Christ, the atonement he made, must mean more than that, if for no other reason than that example without the power to follow it, knowledge without the power to put it into practice, revelation without the power to turn it into life, can bring nothing but bitter frustration. And yet it remains true, as H. E. W. Turner writes, of this conception of the work of Jesus that 'No doctrine of the Cross . . . which does not explain how the world is made better by it can claim to represent the fulness of the Christian tradition. Again, any theory which separates the obligation of leading a better

[1] *Didache* 9.3; 10.2.
[2] *To the Magnesians* 8.2.
[3] *I Clement* 36.2.
[4] *I Clement* 59.2.
[5] *Divine Institutes* 3.26.
[6] *Against Heresies* 5.1.1; 3.16.6.

life from the redemption brought by Christ has small claim for acceptance by Christians.'[1]

(ii) Another of the great early Church conceptions of the work of Jesus Christ is expressed in the idea of *recapitulation*. Strange as this conception may now seem to us, it was one of the great basic conceptions of Irenaeus. It finds its biblical basis in three passages. In Eph. 1.10 the aim of God is said to be, as the Authorized Version translates it, 'to gather together all things in Christ'. The Revised Standard Version translates it 'to unite all things in Christ'. The Twentieth Century New Testament translates it 'to make all things centre in Christ'. The word in Greek is *anakephalaiousthai*. Now this word could have another sense; it could mean to summarize, to recapitulate, as it were, to make a *précis* of it. It is in this sense that Irenaeus takes it. The other two Scripture passages which are the basis of this conception are Rom. 5 and I Cor. 15.21f., where there is a close parallel drawn between Adam and Christ. 'As by a man came death, by a man has come also the resurrection of the dead. For as in Adam all die, so also in Christ shall all be made alive.'

To put it very simply, the idea is that Jesus Christ recapitulates, re-enacts, reiterates, repeats the whole course of human history in himself with this crucial difference—that he at all times presents the perfect life and the perfect obedience which man ought to have offered and failed to offer. By so doing Jesus Christ reverses the whole course of human history; he makes it what it ought to be; he cancels out the sins and the failures and the rebellions and the disobediences. He thus by living life as it ought to be redeems man from the consequence of his sins. Jesus Christ repeats human history in the way it ought to have gone.

Jesus Christ, as Irenaeus puts it, became incarnate and was made man, and in himself he recapitulated the long line of human beings . . . so that what we had lost in Adam we recover in Jesus Christ.[2] Jesus Christ recapitulates God's handiwork in himself (4.6.2). By recapitulating things in himself Jesus, as it were, begins a new creation, this time without sin (5.23.2). Jesus Christ recapitulates the disobedience which came from a tree in the Garden of Eden by the obedience of the tree on which he hung on Calvary

[1] *The Patristic Doctrine of Redemption*, p. 46.
[2] *Against Heresies* 3.18.1.

(5.19.1). In the same way Mary recapitulated in obedience the disobedience of Eve, and so becomes what has been called 'a subsidiary champion' of the human race (3.22.4).

The idea is that Jesus Christ recapitulates in himself the whole story and the whole drama of human history; he recapitulates the whole human struggle with temptation and with sin; but there is this vital difference: where in man the story had gone wrong, in Jesus Christ everything is right, and thereby man is redeemed from his sin and from the consequences of it.

In one sense this is a conception which is utterly strange to the modern mind. It depends on the ancient idea of racial solidarity. Because of this idea of solidarity Adam's sin became the sin of the whole human race, and Christ's goodness became the goodness of the whole human race. In another sense this may well be called the most modern of all conceptions of the work of Christ. It could be expressed in modern times in this way. Through man's disobedience the process of the evolution of the human race went wrong, and the course of its wrongness and its error could neither be halted nor reversed by any human means. But in Jesus Christ the whole course of human evolution was perfectly carried out and realized in obedience to the purpose of God; he is the man God meant all men to be. He recapitulates human history, realizing the ideal instead of losing the ideal, and so redeems humanity from its sin.

(iii) One of the great dominant pictures of the work of Jesus Christ in his life and in his death, both in the New Testament and in the thought of the early Church, is the picture of Christ the Victor, the *Christus Victor* theme as it has been called. This is the idea that in his life and in his death and in his resurrection Jesus finally and utterly defeated the evil demonic powers whose aim was to compass the death and destruction of men.

This was a conception of the work of Jesus Christ which was intensely real and vivid to Jew and to Greek, to Christian and to pagan alike, for both alike had no doubt as to the existence of these malignant demons. 'It is not we alone who speak of wicked demons,' wrote Origen to Celsus, 'but it is almost all who acknowledge the existence of demons.'[1]

The ancient world was a haunted world. 'It is hard, perhaps,'

[1] *Against Celsus* 7.69.

says H. E. W. Turner, 'for modern man to realize how hag-ridden was the world into which Christ came.'[1] 'The whole world,' says Harnack, 'and the circumambient atmosphere were filled with devils . . . They sat on thrones, they hovered round cradles. The world was literally a hell.'[2] Plutarch in his treatise *On Superstition* spoke of the craven fear of God 'filling the universe with spectres'.

The Jews believed intensely in demons. The demons were either the spirits of the wicked departed, still malignantly working evil, or they were the descendants of the union of the sinful angels and mortal women in the old story in Gen. 6.4. According to Jewish belief there were tens of thousands of demons, living in unclean places, lurking in tombs and in places where there was no water, howling in the deserts. They ever threatened the lonely traveller, the little child, the woman in childbirth, those newly married. It was the demons who got into a man's body and mind and caused mental and physical illness. There was an Egyptian belief that there were thirty-six parts in the body and any of them might be occupied by a malignant demon.[3] *Mazzikin* they were called, those who work harm.

The Greeks no less believed in demons. Plutarch, writing on the mysteries of Isis, suggested that 'these sinister spirits assert their vast power, and display their malevolence, not only in plague, pestilence and death, and all the desolating convulsions of the physical world, but in the moral perversion and deception of the human race'. He suggested that each of the blessed gods had attached to him an evil demon, who in the god's name perpetrated every kind of enormity, masquerading as a god.[4] For Jew and Greek the world was in bondage to the spirits of evil.

Belief in these demons was part of the faith and even of the instruction of the Christian Church. They are 'the principalities and powers' whom we meet in the New Testament. 'I myself,' writes Ignatius, 'though I am in bonds . . . can understand heavenly things, and the places of the angels and gatherings of the principalities.'[5] It is from fear of the principalities and powers that Christ

---

[1] *The Patristic Doctrine of Redemption,* p. 47.
[2] *The Expansion of Christianity I,* p. 161.
[3] Origen, *Against Celsus* 7.58.
[4] S. Dill, *Roman Society from Nero to Marcus Aurelius,* pf. 431.
[5] *To the Trallians* 5.2.

relieves us (Rom. 8.38). It is against principalities and powers that the Christian soldier wrestles (Eph. 6.12). And then there comes the tremendous triumphant claim of what Christ did on the Cross. 'He disarmed the principalities and powers and made a public example of them, triumphing over them in it' (Col. 2.15). The idea is that on the Cross there was a death grapple between Jesus Christ and the demonic powers of evil, and that once and for all their power was finally defeated and broken. To us this may seem very remote, but to that haunted ancient world there was nothing more wonderful and amazing than to be able to believe that the power of the demons was broken for ever.

H. E. W. Turner[1] summarizes the way in which Martin Werner works out how, not simply the Cross, but every part of Jesus' life was operative in this victory over the powers of evil.

It began at his birth. Ignatius says that by the rising of the wondrous star 'all magic was dissolved, and every bond of wickedness vanished away, ignorance was removed, and the old kingdom was destroyed, when God became manifest as man'.[2] Origen has the idea that it was precisely because their magic and incantations and spells were no longer effective that the Magi knew that there had entered into the world a 'greater manifestation of divinity', by which the powers of the evil spirits were overthrown. They knew that now there had come into the world and there had broken into life some one superior to all the demons.[3]

It is easy to see how the temptation narrative can be used to show the victorious battle of Jesus against the assailing powers of evil.

On the Cross there came the great victorious battle in which the power of the demons was broken for ever. If the 'world rulers', that is, the demons, had known what they were doing, and what they were bringing on themselves, they would not have crucified Christ (I Cor. 2.8). On the Cross Jesus Christ became the slayer of death himself. Cyril of Jerusalem vividly writes: 'Death was struck with dismay on beholding a new visitant descend into Hades, not bound with the chains of that place.'[4]

---

[1] *The Patristic Doctrine of Redemption*, pp. 49–52.
[2] *To the Ephesians* 19.2.
[3] *Against Celsus* 1.69.
[4] *Catechetical Lectures* 14.19.

Clearly this victory becomes even more complete and evident in the event of the Resurrection. 'Through his resurrection,' says Origen, 'he destroyed the kingdom of death, whence it is written that he freed captivity.'[1]

Equally clearly, the descent into Hades is a part of the victorious progress of Jesus Christ. The *Gospel of Nicodemus* 6 (22) describes the arrival of Jesus in Hades. The legion of devils were stricken with terror, and Hades cried out: 'We are overcome! Woe unto us.'[2]

Finally, in the Ascension Jesus burst triumphantly through the demons who encircle the earth (Eph. 4.8), and so returned to glory.

No picture of Jesus is commoner in the thinking of the early Church than the picture of him as *Christus Victor,* the Conquering Christ. It may be that this is one of the pictures which is remote from us, but to a world haunted and hag-ridden by the thought of the demons there can have been nothing in this world so gloriously emancipating as the conviction that the power of the demons was broken. And even if in its particular expression this conception comes from a world of thought which is not our world, it still has this permanent truth that on the Cross a blow was struck which disarmed evil for ever. And it must be remembered that, however strange this idea is to western, civilized, sophisticated man, missionaries repeatedly tell us that for primitive peoples the greatest thrill that Christianity brings is the thrill of knowing that there is one loving God and not a world of hostile spirits and divinities.

(iv) One of the great conceptions of the work of Jesus Christ, which runs through much of early Christian thought, and which is still dominant in the thought of the Greek Orthodox Church, is the idea of the deification of man because of what Jesus Christ has done. The whole idea is summed up in one great saying of Irenaeus, who spoke of the Word of God who, through his transcendent love, 'became what we are to make us what he is.'[3] The idea is that Jesus Christ by taking human nature upon himself freed human nature from the corruptibility which is the consequence of sin and deified it.

The scriptural warrant for any such conception comes from two New Testament passages. I Tim. 6.16 speaks of the Lord Jesus

[1] *Commentary On Romans* 5.1.
[2] M. R. James, *The Apocryphal New Testament,* p. 135.
[3] *Against Heresies,* Preface to the fifth book, the last sentence.

Christ 'who alone has immortality'. Immortality is in the gift of Jesus Christ. II Peter 1.4 tells how Christians through the work of Jesus Christ 'may escape from the corruption that is in the world because of passion, and become *partakers of the divine nature*'.

To us this is a startling idea. Two facts must be noted.

First, this conception does not mean that man becomes identical with God. Sometimes in Greek, when a noun is used without the definite article, it has a kind of adjectival force. To say that man could become *ho theos* would be to say that man can become identical with God, one and the same as God. But to say that a man can become *theos*—using the word without the definite article—is to say that a man can come to have the same kind of life and existence and being as God has, but without becoming identical with God. The conception of deification is that man through Jesus Christ can be lifted out of the life of fallen and corrupt humanity into the very life of God.

Second, startling as this idea may seem to us, it is part and parcel of ancient religious thought long before Christianity came into the world. Mrs Adam wrote: 'Through the course of Greek religious thought a single thread may be traced, the essential unity of man and God.'[1] Seneca writes: 'Why should you not believe that something of divinity exists in one who is a part of God (*dei pars*)?'[2] Aristotle declares that virtue is achieved by man 'through something within him that is divine'. 'We ought,' he says, 'as far as possible to achieve immortality,'[3] Epictetus speaks of the true philosopher as a man 'who has set his heart on changing from a man into a god', and such a man, even when he is in the paltry body of death, has set his purpose 'upon fellowship with Zeus.'[4] Plato talks of the goodness of man 'so long as the inherited nature of God remained strong in him.'[5] He says that when men fix their eyes on God, they are inspired, and they receive from him their habits and their character 'in so far as it is possible for a man to have a part in God'.[6] It was

---

[1] *Greek Ideals of Righteousness*, p. 67.
[2] *Letters* 92.30.
[3] *Nicomachean Ethics* 10.7.8, 1177b, 28,35.
[4] *Discourses* 2.19.27.
[5] *Critias* 120 D - 121 E.
[6] *Phaedrus* 230 A.

due to the gift of Prometheus that man became a partaker of 'a divine portion', and so 'by the nearness of his kin to God' man became the only creature who worships the gods.[1] In *The Laws* he speaks of Lycurgus, the great Spartan law-giver, as 'some man in whom human nature was blended with the divine.'[2] Cicero says that knowledge of the gods makes us 'in no way inferior to the celestials, except in immortality'.[3] The Graeco-Roman world was well acquainted with the idea of the kinship of man and God.

This conception of unity with God came to its peak in the pagan world in the experience of the devotees of the Mystery Religions. The Mystery Religions were mainly based on passion plays, exhibiting the sufferings, the death, and the rising again of some god, played out under such conditions of preparation and emotion that the initiate, watching the play, experienced an actual union between himself and the god. 'I know thee, Hermes,' says the initiate, 'and thou knowest me. I am thou and thou art I.' 'Come to me, Lord Hermes,' he prayed, 'as babes to mothers' wombs.'[4] When Christianity came into the world men were conditioned to accept and to understand the idea of deification in this sense.

In the early Church the conviction that Jesus Christ had done something tremendous to human nature by taking it upon himself was very common. Man by his sin had involved human nature in corruption and death; Jesus Christ by taking that human nature upon himself had reversed the process, and had lifted humanity into deity. Often the idea is that man by himself is neither mortal nor immortal but poised between the two, and in his union with Jesus Christ the potential of immortality is realized.

This belief in the deification of humanity through the work of Christ is most vividly and boldy expressed by the early Christian thinkers. 'By his passion,' said Irenaeus, 'the Lord destroyed death, dissipated error, rooted out corruption, destroyed ignorance, displayed life, showed truth, conferred incorruptibility.'[5] 'He was made man,' said Athanasius, 'that we might become God!'[6] 'The Son of

---

[1] *Plato, Protagoras* 322 A.
[2] *Laws* 691 E.
[3] *On the Nature of the Gods* 2.61.
[4] Samuel Angus, *The Mystery Religions and Christianity*, pp. 110f.
[5] *Against Heresies* 2.32.2.
[6] *On the Incarnation* 54.

God,' said Cyprian, 'suffered to make us sons of God.'[1] 'He was made a sharer in our mortality,' said Augustine. 'He made us sharers in his deity.'[2] Boldest of all is Clement of Alexandria, who was steeped in Greek thought. 'That man,' he writes, 'in whom the Logos dwell . . . that man becomes God, for God so wills it.'[3] 'The Logos of God became man that from man you might learn how man may become God.'[4] The Christian Gnostic, instructed by the Logos, is 'God walking about in the flesh'.[5]

It is clearly to be noted that this process of the deification of human nature was never regarded as automatic. Origen held that it came from contemplation of God in Christ.[6] Frequently the idea is that it comes through the action of the sacraments. Ignatius called the bread of the Eucharist 'the medicine of immortality, the antidote that we should not die, but live for ever in Christ Jesus.'[7] According to Gregory of Nyssa baptism 'deifies the soul', and in the sacrament 'a healing seed is inserted into the body'.[8] A man had to accept Jesus Christ and all that Jesus Christ offers before this tremendous benefit should be his.

Once again we are moving here in a world of ideas which is strange to us. And yet in spite of the strangeness there remains the great, central, inescapable truth. The incarnation and the death and the resurrection of Jesus Christ, the coming of God into humanity in humanity, did something for human nature which cannot be undone. Call it deification, call it what we will, something has happened to manhood because godhead took manhood upon itself.

(v) It may well be that of all the conceptions of the work which Jesus Christ wrought for men that which has been most influential is that of Jesus as the Victim and the Sacrifice for the sin of man. The idea of Jesus as the sacrificial victim for the sin of man may be said to take three forms.

(a) There is the idea that the death of Jesus is the *ransom* price

---

[1] *Letters* 88.6.
[2] *On the Trinity* 4.2.4.
[3] *Paeidagogus* 3.1.1.5.
[4] *Potepticus* 1.8.4.
[5] *Stromateis* 7.16.101.4.
[6] *Commentary on John* 32.37.
[7] *To the Ephesians* 20.2.
[8] *Catechetical Oration* 33-37.

paid for the liberation of man from the bondage in which he was held, and from which he could never free himself.

There is real scriptural basis for this view. 'The Son of Man,' said Jesus, 'came not to be served but to serve, and to give his life as a ransom for many' (Matt. 20.28; Mark 10.45). 'There is one God, and there is no mediator between God and man, the man Christ Jesus, who gave himself as a ransom for all' (I Tim. 2.5f.). 'You know,' wrote Peter, 'that you were ransomed from the futile ways inherited from your fathers, not with perishable things such as silver or gold, but with the precious blood of Christ' (I Peter 1.18f.).

There is a group of New Testament words connected with this picture. There is the word *lutron* (Matt. 20.28; Mark 10.45). In classical Greek it is usually used in the plural *lutra,* and it means 'the price paid for the emancipation or the liberation of any person or thing'. It is used in Homer for the price paid to ransom the body of Hector; it is regularly used in the papyri for the price paid for the freedom of a slave or for the redemption of something which is in pledge or pawn. In the Old Testament it is used of the price which a man must pay, if he is not to suffer the death penalty for something for which he is responsible (Ex. 21.30). It is used for the redemption of the first-born (Num. 3.12,46–49,51; 18.15). It is declared that there is no *lutron* for the life of a murderer (Num. 35.31), and it is used of the ransom price of captives taken in war (Isa. 45.13). Closely connected is the word *antilutron* (I Tim. 2.6). There is the word *lutrousthai* which means 'to ransom' or 'to redeem', to pay the price necessary for liberation. Jesus gave himself that he might *redeem* us from all iniquity (Titus 2.14; I Peter 1.18). There is the word *lutrōsis,* which means 'redemption'. Jesus obtained redemption for us by his own blood (Hebrews 9.12). Commonest of all there is the word *apolutrōsis,* which means 'the act of redeeming', or the 'redemption' won by such an act. We are put into a right relationship with God through the *redemption* that is in Jesus Christ (Romans 3.24). We have *redemption* through the blood of Jesus Christ (Eph. 1.14; 4.30; Col. 1.14; cp. Rom. 8.23; I Cor. 1.30; Heb. 9.15).

All these words describe the paying of the price which is necessary to liberate a man from a bondage or from a situation from which he cannot in any circumstances liberate himself.

Closely connected with this picture and idea there are two other words, *agorazein* and *exagorazein,* which mean 'to buy', 'to purchase', 'to buy out from'. Christians have been *bought* with a price (I Cor. 6.20; 7.23). Christ has *redeemed* us, *bought us out from* the law and its curse (Gal. 3.13; 4.5). These words are specially appropriate for buying a slave out of his slavery into freedom.

There is abundant evidence in the New Testament for the idea of Jesus Christ as the ransom for the sin of man.

Certain things must be said about the interpretation of the work of Jesus Christ in terms of ransom.

First, as David Smith points out in *The Atonement in the Light of History and the Modern Spirit* (pp. 62–64), there can have been few more relevant pictures of the work of Christ, if that work was to be stated in terms contemporary with first-century life. This was the age of brigandage and piracy; the traveller travelled in danger; at any time he might be captured, and held to ransom, and a ransom had to be found, if his freedom was to be regained.

After the Battle of Adrianople in the fourth century, Ambrose, the great Bishop of Milan, spent his all to ransom the captives taken in battle. In the end he even melted down the sacred vessels of the sacrament and turned them into coinage, and, when he was accused of sacrilege, he answered that the souls for which the Lord's blood had been shed were surely more precious than the vessels which contained it.

'Remember them that are in bonds,' says the writer to the Hebrews (Heb. 13.3). It is one of the charges of Ignatius against the false teachers that 'for love they have no care, none for the widow, none for the orphan, none for the distressed, none for the afflicted, *none for the prisoner*'.[1] Clement of Rome in his letter to Corinth prays: 'Save those of us who are in affliction, have mercy on the lowly, raise the fallen, show thyself to those in need, heal the sick, turn again the wanderers of thy people, feed the hungry, ransom the prisoners, raise up the weak, comfort the faint-hearted.'[2]

[1] *To the Smyrnaeans* 6.2.
[2] *I Clement* 59.4.

The prisoners awaiting ransom even found their way into the liturgies. In the *Liturgy of St Mark* we read: 'They that are holden in prisons or in mines or in exile or bitter bondage, pity them all, deliver them all.' The *Liturgy of St James* includes the prayer: 'Remember, O Lord, Christians at sea, on the road, among strangers, those in mines and tortures and bitter bondage, being our fathers and brethren.' In the early days men knew all about the unhappy captive and the need for ransom, for the captives and the prisoners were in their hearts and in their prayers. Here was a picture of the work of Jesus Christ which all men could grasp and understand.

There was another ancient custom which would make the picture of ransom meaningful to earliest Christian thought. There was one way in which it was possible for a Greek slave to gain his freedom. For many years he might save all he could of the very little money which it was possible for him to earn. As he saved the money, he could take it and deposit it in the temple of some god. When after years of saving he had amassed his own purchase price, he could take his master to the temple where the money had been deposited. There the money was handed over to the master and the slave was free. But the idea behind this was that it was *the god* who paid the purchase price; the god bought the slave for himself to be his own. The slave, therefore, became the property of the god, and so free from all human ownership. This is not an analogy which can be overstressed in its details, for it was the slave himself who scrimped and saved to collect his own purchase price, and, therefore, he was freed by the result of his own efforts; but the idea that the god had bought the slave for himself made men familiar with the divine purchase of a man that that man might be freed, liberated, emancipated from the slavery and the bondage in which he was held.

There is no doubt that in the early Church the idea of divine ransom would speak to men's hearts in terms which they knew and understood. There were few ways in which the work of Jesus Christ could be made more vividly real to men.

For the moment we will not discuss or criticize this picture. We must first set beside it, and consider with it, certain kindred and closely connected pictures.

(*b*) There is the idea that the death of Jesus is the *sacrifice* which atones for the sin of man. There are two general things to be said about this idea. First, it is the most universal of all ideas. However a man is going to express this, however he is going to work it out, however, to use a technical term, he is going to conceptualize this, he knows that this is in fact what actually happened in the life and the death of Jesus. Paul spoke of the Son of God who loved him and who gave himself for him (Gal. 2.20), and that is the simplest expression of Jesus as the supreme and availing sacrifice for all mankind. This is not so much one expression of what Jesus did; it is the essential, basic idea behind any possible expression of what Jesus did. Second, it would be next to impossible for a Jew to express his idea of the work of Jesus in any other way. Orthodox Jewish religion was founded on the sacrificial system. It was so founded because it was founded on the law. When God entered into the covenant relationship with Israel, in which he was to be their God and they were to be in a special sense his people, that relationship was founded on the law (Ex. 24.7). It is the dilemma of the human situation that man cannot perfectly keep the law. Were the matter left there, it would mean that the relationship between God and his people must be irretrievably broken. But there enters into the matter the whole sacrificial system, whose aim it is by penitence and by sacrifice to atone for breaches of the law, that is, for sin, and so to restore the broken relationship between God and his covenant people. In Jewish religion it was sacrifice which restored the lost and broken relationship between God and man. Jesus was supremely and uniquely the one who restored the lost relationship between God and man, whose work bridged the gulf which sin had created between God and man, who made it possible for the sinner to receive forgiveness and to enter into the presence of God. How else, then, was it possible for a Jew to express the work of Jesus? Jesus to the Jew must be the supreme sacrifice who brings together again man and God, when man and God were separated, and when man was under condemnation, because of sin.

God put forward Jesus as an expiation (*hilastērion*) by his blood, to be received by faith (Rom. 3.25). Christ our paschal lamb (*pascha*) has been sacrificed (I Cor. 5.7). He is the expiation for our sins (I John 2.2); God sent his Son to be the expiation for

our sins (I John 4.10); in both cases the word is *hilasmos*. Here is
the very basis of the Letter to the Hebrews. The function of the
priest is to offer sacrifice, but the proof that such sacrifices are
unavailing is the unanswerable fact that they have to be made over
and over again every day in life; but Christ offered for all time a
single sacrifice for sins (Heb. 10.11f.). It was not the blood of goats
and calves he took, but his own blood, thus securing an eternal
redemption (Heb. 9.12). He offered himself without blemish to
God (Heb. 9.14).

Here is a picture which stands at the very centre of all Jewish
religion, a picture of the work of Jesus to which the mind and the
heart instinctively respond, and which the human spirit witnesses
to be true. Once again we shall leave the discussion of it, until we
have stated its kindred conceptions.

(*c*) We now turn to one of the most famous of all interpretations
of the work of Jesus Christ, the interpretation which thinks of the
work of Jesus in terms of *satisfaction*. It will be at once seen that
there is no biblical basis at all for the terminology of this theory;
it is expressed in terms and categories which are almost entirely non-
biblical and which are the terms and categories of chivalry and
knighthood; for it was in the age of chivalry that this interpretation
was born. The Satisfaction interpretation of the work of Jesus Christ
was worked out by Anselm in his famous book *Cur Deus Homo*
(*Why God became Man*), which he gave to the public in AD 1098.

Anselm begins by defining sin. Every living creature in the universe, angel and man alike, owes God perfect obedience to God's
law. If that obedience were given, there would be no sin. Sin is
failure to render to God what is owed to God, and that which is
owed to God is perfect submission to his law and will. This is the
one honour which is owed to God and which God desires. To fail
to render this obedience to God is to take away from God what is
his by right, and to 'put God out of his honour'. In an age of chivalry
it was a first principle that he whose honour was belittled or injured
must seek satisfaction, and so, says Anselm, it is with God.

But, even if God's honour is injured and insulted, why cannot
God simply, by an act of grace and pardon and mercy, forgive?
Why is satisfaction necessary? First, God is the moral governor of
the universe, and, if his honour can be insulted with impunity and
without due satisfaction being paid, then the moral government

of the universe is weakened and discredited. To maintain the moral government of the universe, its moral governor must exact satisfaction when his law is broken and his honour insulted. Second, God demands of men that they should unconditionally forgive each other and that they should never exact vengeance. Why does he not do the same himself? The answer is that herein is precisely the difference between man and God. Vengeance belongs to God; man, because he is man, must unconditionally forgive; God, because he is God, has the right to act in vengeance.

The result of this is that man is confronted with an alternative from which there is no escape—satisfaction or punishment—there is no third way. How then can this satisfaction be found? The supreme human dilemma is that it cannot be found by man, for the simple reason that there is nothing which any man can ever do or be which he does not already owe to God. There is nothing *extra,* no work of supererogation which a man can offer to God. That is even true of penitence. If a man sins, penitence is no more than he owes, and satisfaction demands the extra thing. So, then, man is helpless, and in a situation in which he must be punished, because no satisfaction is possible.

It is here that Jesus enters upon the scene. He became man, and in man and for man he offers to God the complete obedience to the will of God and the complete submission to God which alone can satisfy the honour of God. Since Jesus does this in and for man, God can accept this satisfaction, and so can forgive and withhold punishment without compromising his moral authority and without lowering his divine dignity. The complete obedience of Jesus to the law and to the will of God is the offering which satisfies the injured honour of God, and which saves man from the penalty and punishment which his sin had necessitated. Whatever else may be true of Anselm's interpretation of the work of Jesus, this much is certainly true—in Anselm it is *the whole of Jesus* which is important. His work for man is not confined to his death; it extends over his whole life, and his death is simply the ultimate climax and consummation of this life of complete submission to God and perfect service and satisfaction of the honour of God. According to Anselm, Jesus did for man, in his life and death as man, what man could never have done for himself.

Once again there is no doubt that this picture and interpretation of the work of Jesus Christ would speak to the age in which it was first expressed and stated. It was the mediaeval age which thought and lived and acted in terms of knighthood and of chivalry, in which great and knightly tales were told of how honour was injured and honour was vindicated. Once again we shall leave the criticism and evaluation of it until we have examined the last of the great kindred views of the work of Jesus.

(*d*) There is the interpretation of the work of Jesus Christ for men in terms of *substitution*. Before we look at this idea in its wider aspect, we may look at it in its narrower aspect in what has been called its forensic form, which is a form which is specially connected with Reformation thought.

The basic idea behind this is that God is King, Law-giver and Judge. Sin is the breaking of God's law, and the consequence and result of sin is to leave man a criminal under judgment at God's judgment-seat. In such a position there is nothing for which man can look except utter condemnation and consequent punishment. The idea is that Jesus Christ offered himself as a substitute on our behalf and endured the punishment which should have fallen upon us. He is the substitute for sinners; he suffered in our stead. This is the conception which finds such an astonishing foreshadowing in the picture of the Suffering Servant in Isa. 53: 'He was wounded for our transgressions, he was bruised for our iniquities; upon him was the chastisement which made us whole, and with his stripes we are healed. All we like sheep have gone astray; we have turned every one to his own way; *and the Lord has laid on him the iniquity of us all*' (Isa. 53.5f.). As David Smith sums up this idea: 'We lay, by reason of our sin both original and actual, under the wrath and curse of God, sentenced to an eternity of torment; and the doom would have been executed upon us had not Christ offered himself in our room and suffered in our stead the stroke of God's wrath, and thus satisfied his justice and appeased his anger'[1].

David Smith illustrates this by the old children's hymn:

> He knew how wicked men had been
> He knew that God must punish sin;
> So out of pity Jesus said
> He'd bear the punishment instead,

[1] *The Atonement in the Light of History and the Modern Spirit*, p. 103.

and by Mrs Cousin's hymn:

> Jehovah lifted up his rod;
>   O Christ, it fell on thee!
> Thou wast sore stricken of thy God;
>   There's not one stroke for me.
>   Thy tears, thy blood,
>   Beneath it flowed;
> Thy bruising healeth me.
>
> Jehovah bade his sword awake;
>   O Christ, it woke 'gainst thee!
> Thy blood the flaming blade must slake,
>   Thy heart its sheath must be.
>   All for my sake,
>   My peace to make:
> Now sleeps that sword for me.

The substitutionary view of the work of Jesus holds definitely and distinctly that Jesus Christ on his Cross bore the penalty and the punishment for sin which we should have borne, and that he did so as an act of voluntary and spontaneous and sacrificial love.

There is a sense in which this interpretation of the work of Jesus has in modern times fallen into disrepute. It has undergone much criticism, and there are many thinkers who have recoiled from it. But two things have to be said. First, there is the quite general truth that the heart of man witnesses that there is something here which is fundamentally true. John Oxenham has in one of his books an imaginary picture of Barabbas, after he had been set free. Something about Jesus had captured Barabbas and he followed him out to see the end. And, as Barabbas saw Jesus hang upon his Cross, one thought was beating into his mind: 'I should have been hanging there—not he—he saved me!' There is no doubt that that is the reaction of the heart to the Cross. We have only to remember how this idea has captured so many of the great evangelical hymns of the Church to see how it appeals to the human heart. It is there in Henry Williams Baker's hymn:

> In perfect love he dies;
>   For me he dies, for me!
> O all-atoning Sacrifice,
>   I cling by faith to thee.

It is there in Cecil Frances Alexander's hymn:

> There was no other good enough
> To pay the price of sin;
> He only could unlock the gate
> Of heaven, and let us in.

It is there in the hymn of Charles Wesley which has well-nigh become the magnificent anthem of Methodism:

> And can it be, that I should gain
>   An interest in my Saviour's blood?
> Died he for me, who caused him pain—
>   For me who him to death pursued?
> Amazing love! how can it be
> That thou, my God, shouldst die for me?
>
> No condemnation now I dread;
>   Jesus, and all in him, is mine!
> Alive in him, my living Head,
>   And clothed in righteousness divine,
> Bold I approach the eternal throne,
> And claim the crown through Christ my own.

There is no doubt that the idea of Jesus Christ as the great willing substitute who bore the punishment which should have fallen on every sinful man is dear to the Christian heart.

The second general truth is this: this is an interpretation and understanding of the Cross which has existed without break since the beginning of Christian thought. In the New Testament itself we have Paul writing to the Corinthians that God 'made him to be sin who knew no sin, so that in him we might become the righteousness of God' (II Cor. 5.21). We can trace this picture down through patristic thought.

'Who,' said Tertullian, 'ever paid for the death of another by his own except the Son of God?' 'He had come for this purpose that he himself, free from all sin and altogether holy, should die for sinners.'[1] 'Christ,' said Cyprian, 'bore us all in that he bore our sins.'[2] 'The Son of God,' he says, 'did not disdain to take the flesh of man, and, although he was not a sinner, himself to carry the sins of

---

[1] *On Chastity* 22.
[2] *Letters* 62.13.

others.'[1] 'God,' says Hilary, 'aims at the purchase of the salvation of the whole human race by the offering of this holy and perfect victim.'[2] 'He underwent death,' said Ambrose, 'to give satisfaction for those who were under judgment.'[3] 'If man had not sinned,' said Augustine, 'the Son of Man would not have come.'[4] There is no age in Christian thought to which the idea of Jesus Christ as the Saviour, whose death was voluntary, vicarious, sacrificial, substitutionary, has not been dear.

We have now seen the main great interpretations under which the work of Jesus Christ has been understood. How shall we evaluate them? Broadly speaking, they may be grouped under three classes.

(i) There is the interpretation which thinks of the work of Jesus in terms of *ransom*. We have already seen how vivid and meaningful that interpretation must have been to an age in which piracy and brigandage flourished and in which the need for ransom was often a bitter necessity, an age in which life was founded on slavery and in which emancipation was the dearest dream of millions of men and women. But immediately this interpretation is literalised, it runs headlong into one problem—*To whom was the ransom paid?*

There were those like Bernard of Clairvaux who insisted that the ransom was paid to the devil, who had men in his power. 'No one,' he says, 'seeks a Redeemer who does not know himself a captive.' He argues that the devil had power, and just power, over men. Because of man's sin, the devil's power over men was justly permitted by God. Certainly the devil's will and intention were not just but evil; but the fact that he had power over men was just, in that it was permitted by God. 'Man was justly given over, but mercifully delivered.' 'And there was not lacking a certain justice in the very deliverance, since this also concerned the Deliverer's mercy that he should rather employ justice against the assailant than power.'[5] Bernard did not see anything impossible in holding that the ransom was paid to the devil, for it was in the justice of God that man in his

---

[1] *On the Goodness of Patience* 6.
[2] *Commentary on Psalm* 53.13.
[3] *Concerning Flight from the World* VII, 4.
[4] *Sermon* 174.2.
[5] Quoted in David Smith, *The Atonement in the Light of History and the Modern Spirit*, pp. 72, 78, 79.

sin had fallen into the power of the devil, and it befitted God to deal with the devil also in justice.

But there were many more who could not possibly hold that the ransom was paid to the devil, for to conceive of God paying a ransom to the devil is to put the devil on a bargaining equality with God. So Origen writes: 'To whom did Christ give his soul for ransom? Surely not to God. Could it then be to the Evil One? For he had us in his power until the ransom for us should be given to him, even the life of Christ. The Evil One had been deceived and had been led to suppose that he was capable of mastering the soul (of Christ) and did not see that to hold him involved a trial of strength greater than he could successfully undertake.'[1] Here the idea is that in the soul of Christ the devil *thought* that he was receiving the ransom for sinning men, but in actual fact he did not know that he was receiving something which he was quite powerless to hold, and that in the attempt to hold it his power would be broken for ever. So in the same passage Origen goes on: 'Therefore death, though he thought that he had prevailed against him (that is, against Christ), no longer prevails against him, Christ then having become free among the dead and stronger than the power of death and so much stronger than death, that all who will among those who are mastered by death may follow him, death no longer prevailing against him. For everyone who is with Jesus is stronger than death.' Here then the idea is that in the soul of Christ the devil received what he thought was a ransom but what in the end was his destruction.

As time went on, this idea was elaborated, and the elaboration took the line that the Incarnation was a trick or stratagem played on the devil by God. The devil was tricked into thinking that he could master and control the soul of Christ, and in seeking to do so was finally defeated. More than once this was expressed in an almost grotesque metaphor. The human flesh of Christ was said to be the bait which was dangled before the devil; but the deity of Christ was the hook concealed within the bait. So the devil swallowed the bait and was caught by the hook, and his power was destroyed. Gregory of Nyssa says: 'The Deity was hidden under the veil of our nature, that, as is done by greedy fish, the hook of

[1] *Commentary on Matthew* 16.8.

Deity might be gulped down along with the bait of the flesh, and thus, life being introduced into the house of death, and light shining in the darkness, that which is contradictory to light and life might vanish away; for it is not in the nature of darkness to remain where light is present or of death to exist where life is present.'[1] This idea of a trick played on the devil reaches its last word in fantastic grotesqueness in the saying of Peter the Lombard: 'The Cross was a mousetrap (*muscipula*) baited with the blood of Christ.'[2]

So long as the idea of ransom remains a metaphor and a picture, it has real and dramatic value. Whenever the attempt is made to literalize it and to make it a theology, it will not stand the test.

(ii) The method of interpreting the work of Jesus in terms of satisfaction has, as we have already noted, one outstanding value. It gives a very real place to the life of Christ in the work of Christ. It is the obedience of the whole life of Christ and finally of the death of Christ which constitutes that which satisfies the honour of God. But the one insuperable fault in this interpretation is that it regards God as the Moral Governor of the world. And so, of course, he is; but to make the fact that God is the moral governor of the world the one dominating and deciding factor in the whole understanding of the work of Christ is to set out with a view of God which is utterly inadequate. A moral governor's honour may be insulted and injured; but that is strangely different from the breaking of a father's heart.

(iii) When we come to the interpretations of the work of Jesus in terms of sacrifice and of substitution and of vicarious suffering for us, we dare not treat them lightly; still less can we dismiss them contemptuously as is sometimes done. These interpretations must be regarded with real reverence, because it is through them that a great host of people in every age and generation have found peace for their hearts and salvation for their souls. These ideas have always formed the core and essence of evangelical preaching, and in every generation they have been the moving power of conversion. Nonetheless they have great and grave difficulties when they are pressed too far.

In the ransom interpretation of the work of Jesus, the ran-

[1] *Catechetical Oration* 17–23.
[2] *Sentences* 2.19.

som is offered in some sense to the devil; in the sacrifice and sub-stitution interpretations of the work of Jesus the sacrifice is offered to God. The difficulty here is that in some sense God and Jesus are opposed. God demands sacrifice; Jesus gives sacrifice. The result of this is that almost inevitably Jesus is seen in terms of *love,* and God is seen in terms of *justice.* That is why a great many people who have been brought up on these interpretations either con-sciously or unconsciously love Jesus but fear God, and feel at home with Jesus but estranged and remote from God. These interpreta-tions have the effect of setting God and Jesus over against each other.

We may put this in another way—and this is the most serious effect of literalizing the sacrifice and substitution interpretations of the work of Jesus. If we think in terms of sacrifice or in terms of substitution, it almost necessarily means that something that Jesus did changed the attitude of God to men, that before the action of Jesus God could only punish and condemn men and that after the action of Jesus God was able and willing to forgive men. If we think in terms of sacrifice, it means that Jesus offered a sacrifice which made it possible somehow for God to forgive men. If we think in terms of substitution, it means that man was the criminal at the judgment seat of God, and through the action of Jesus God's sen-tence of condemnation was changed into a verdict of acquittal.

There can be no doubt that that is a view which finds no support in Scripture. Nowhere does the New Testament speak of God being reconciled to men; always it speaks of men being reconciled to God. 'We beseech you,' says Paul, 'on behalf of Christ, be reconciled to God' (II Cor. 5.20). It was never the attitude of God to man which had to be changed; it was the attitude of man to God. Still further, the New Testament makes it quite clear that the whole process of salvation finds its initiative in the love of God. It was because God so loved the world that he sent his Son (John 3.16). It is his love for men that God shows in the work which Jesus performed (Rom. 5.8). 'In this is love,' says John, 'not that we loved God, but that he loved us and sent his Son to be the expiation for our sins' (I John 4.10). If one thing is clear, it is that there was no necessity to change the attitude of God to men. That attitude was always love.

An attempt to evade this difficulty is to argue, as Denney did, that it is never right to isolate one attribute of God. It is, therefore, necessary to remember that God is justice *and* love. It is then possible to go on to say that God's justice necessitates the punishment of sin and God's love equally necessitates the forgiveness of sin, and that, therefore, God in his love pays in Jesus Christ the penalty which his justice demands. The hymn would then be right to say of the Cross:

> O trysting-place where heaven's love
> And heaven's justice meet!

We can only speak with hesitating reverence, but it does seem that that view, however logically and neatly and theologically it seems to solve the problem, leaves God for ever a split personality in whom there is eternal tension between justice and love. The work of Christ on this basis would be as much a thing which solved the problem of God as a thing which wrought the salvation of man.

The great problem of all interpretations of the Cross in terms of sacrifice—in the Jewish sense of the term—and in terms of substitution is that they tend to set Jesus in opposition to God, and they must go on to say that something Jesus did in his life, and especially in his death, changed the attitude of God to men, or made it possible for God to treat men in a different way. When they are stated in their crudest way, when the implication is that God laid on Jesus Christ the punishment which should have been laid upon men in order that the divine justice might be maintained, then these interpretations do something even worse. They represent God as protecting his justice by the most monstrous act of injustice the universe has ever seen or ever can see; for he laid on the sinless one the punishment of sin. Even if it be argued that the acceptance by Christ of that situation was absolutely and completely voluntary and spontaneous, the terrible injustice remains.

If then none of the interpretations of the work of Jesus which we have so far examined are such that we can wholly and unreservedly accept them, even if we humbly recognize that which is precious in them and that which they have wrought in the minds and in the hearts and in the lives of men, where are we to turn?

In our examination of the various interpretations of the work of Jesus we omitted one. We omitted that which is attached to the name of Abelard who was born in 1079 and who died in 1142. J. K.

Mozley briefly summarizes the teaching of Abelard: 'Christ died, neither because a ransom had to be paid to the Devil, nor because the blood of an innocent victim was needed to appease the wrath of God, but that a supreme exhibition of love might kindle a corresponding love in men's hearts and inspire them with the true freedom of sonship of God.'[1] This is sometimes called the *moral influence* interpretation of the work of Christ, although Mozley would say that its influence is as much emotional as it is moral.

Abelard had certain basic convictions. He refused to accept any interpretation of Jesus Christ's life and work, and especially of his death, which is based on the idea of ransom. Ransom to the Devil is unthinkable, ransom to God is unnecessary. He based everything on the love of God. The Incarnation of Jesus Christ and the death of Jesus Christ are acts of pure love. Certainly God is righteous, but his righteousness is subordinate to his love, or, even more, his righteousness is his love. The problem, as Abelard saw it, is that sin has separated man from God, and the supreme necessity is to bring man back into a relationship of love and trust to God. There is no necessity for Christ to assuage the wrath of God, because God's attitude to man is not wrath but love. In order to win men back to this relationship to God, Jesus Christ has given to men the highest and the most unanswerable proof of love, a proof of love and an exhibition of love which so moves the hearts of men that they are enabled to enter into the relationship of love with God. The death of Christ on the Cross is not an objective transaction; it is rather the supreme *evidence* of that love which is demonstrated in the life of Christ from the beginning. This love calls forth love, so that we come to love him because he first loved us (I John 4.19, AV).

Abelard did not quite stop there. He went on to say that when this love is awakened in our hearts, God forgives us and reckons the merit of Christ to us, in that Christ is the head of the new humanity which begins in him. But the merit of Jesus does not lie in any accumulation of deeds which he did; the merit of Jesus is his obedience to God, and his service to God and men in utter love.[2]

---

[1] *The Doctrine of the Atonement,* p. 132.

[2] Abelard's views are set out in his own works, the *Commentary on the Epistle to the Romans,* the *Theologia Christiana* 4 (Migne, *PL* 178.1278f.), and the *Sentences* (100.23). Abelard's position is very fairly stated in A. Harnack, *History of Dogma VI,* pp. 78–80.

Abelard also believed that this loving ministry of Christ still goes on in that, as the writer to the Hebrews says, he always lives to make intercession for us (Heb. 7.25).

There is no doubt that there is much that is missing in Abelard's interpretation of the work of Christ, but Harnack is right, when, after making all the necessary criticisms, he says: 'Abelard had too keen a sense of the love of his God, and of the oneness of God and Christ, to entertain the Gnostic thought that God needs a sacrifice or an equivalent, or that for God Christ's death is a benefit.' To put Abelard's position very simply, we may say that he believed that Jesus Christ came to proclaim, to demonstrate and to exhibit the love of God, to say in his life and his death for men, 'God loves you like that.' He came to tell men that they are sinners, but they are already forgiven sinners, if only they will turn to God in response to the love of God. It was Abelard's view that Jesus Christ did nothing to alter the attitude of God, but that he came to tell men in speech and in action, in his life and in his death, what the attitude of God is to men. He came because, as Abelard believed, men had only to see the attitude of God to them, men had only to behold the love of God to answer and to respond to it.

Let us now leave these interpretations of the work of Christ, and turn from his words about giving his life as a ransom to his other great words about his own death. We find these words in the account of the Last Supper. Jesus said of the bread: 'This is my body.' He said of the wine: 'This is my blood of the covenant, which is poured out for many for the forgiveness of sins' (Matt. 26.26–28; Mark 14.22–24). Or, as Paul gives us the words: 'This cup is the new covenant in my blood' (I Cor. 11.25).

What, then, is a *covenant?* A covenant is a special relationship entered into between two people. When God is one of the parties in the covenant relationship, there is a vital difference between such a covenant and a bargain or treaty or agreement in the ordinary sense of the term. In any ordinary agreement the two parties enter into it on level and on equal terms; but in the covenant relationship between God and man the whole initiative is with God; it is in his grace and mercy that he makes this approach to man, and man can only accept or refuse the offer of God. So, then, in the biblical use of the term a covenant is a relationship between God and men.

We read the story of the initiation of the first covenant relationship between God and the nation of Israel in Ex. 24.1–8. That original covenant was entirely dependent on the keeping of the law (Ex. 24.7). So long as Israel kept the law, the covenant relationship remained; when Israel broke the law the covenant relationship was interrupted, broken and destroyed. It was to meet that situation that the whole sacrificial system was designated and intended. A man broke the law; and a sacrifice offered in penitence and contrition was the means whereby the broken covenant relationship, either between an individual or between the nation and God, was restored. The covenant, then, is a special relationship between God and man, entered into solely on the gracious initiative of God, dependent on the keeping of the law of the covenant, and maintained by the institution of sacrifice with penitence, which restored the relationship when it had been broken by rebellion or disobedience.

But already in the Old Testament there are glimpses of a new covenant. Jeremiah heard God say that he would make a new covenant with the people, not like the covenant that he had once made with their fathers. This would be a covenant, not established by an externally imposed law, but written on their hearts and in their inward parts. It would be a covenant in which all men really and truly knew God. 'I will forgive their iniquity,' God said, 'and I will remember their sin no more' (Jer. 31.31–34). Two things stand out about this new covenant; it is a covenant based not on law but on the inward devotion of the heart, and there is no mention of sacrifice at all.

Two things are to be noted in the words of Jesus, as Paul relates them—'This cup is the new covenant in my blood' (I Cor. 11.25). Jeremiah also speaks of the *new* covenant (Jer. 31.31; LXX 38.31). Both in Paul and in the Greek of Jeremiah the word for 'new' is *kainos*. Greek has two words for 'new'. There is *neos,* which is new only in point of time; a thing which is *neos* may simply be the most recent example or specimen of something which has for long existed and for which has for long been produced. But *kainos* means not only new in point of time, but also *new in point of kind or quality*. With a thing which is *kainos* a new quality has entered into life and the world. Since that is so, a *new* (*kainos*) covenant is not simply an old covenant which has been renewed or restated; it is a covenant of a new and different kind. Second, Jesus says of this new covenant that it is *in* his blood. The Greek word for *in* is *en; en* can and does translate the Hebrew word *b͏ᵉ*, which means *at the price of.* It may, therefore, well be that Jesus said that this new and different kind of covenant is made possible only at the cost and at the price of his blood. When we put this together, we see that Jesus said that a new relationship between man and God has become possible through his blood, that is, through his life and his death.

Here, then, we come to the crux and essence of the matter. We have seen that Jesus said that he came to give his life a ransom for many; but we have also seen that that cannot be taken with crude literalness, for, when we ask to whom the ransom was paid, it does not make sense to say that it was paid either to the devil or to God. We have seen that the whole initiative of redemption is in the love of God, and that there can be no question of placating an angry and a hostile God. And yet the fact remains that it is at the cost and price of the life and death of Jesus that this new relationship between man and God, foreshadowed by Jeremiah, alone can come into being. We have further seen that the new covenant foretold by Jeremiah is based neither on law nor on sacrifice, but only on love and on the devotion of the heart.

What, then, was Jesus doing in his life and in his death? The answer must be that in his life and in his death Jesus was demonstrating to men the eternal, unchangeable, unconquerable love of God. He was demonstrating to men that God is the Father who loves undefeatably and whose one desire is that the lost son should come home. When Jesus entered the world, when he healed the sick, comforted the sad, fed the hungry, forgave his enemies, he was saying to men: 'God loves you like that.' When he died upon the cross, he was saying: 'Nothing that men can ever do to God will stop God loving them. There is no limit to the love of God. There is no end beyond which that love will not go. God loves you like that.' That is why nothing less than death on the Cross would do. If Jesus had refused or escaped the Cross, if he had not died, it would have meant that there was some point in suffering and sorrow at which the love of God stopped, that there was some point beyond which forgiveness was impossible. But the Cross is God saying in Jesus: 'There is no limit to which my love will not go and no sin which my love cannot forgive.'

The work of Christ is not something *about which* a man must know; it is something which he must experience in his own heart and mind and life. It is not so much to be understood as it is to be appropriated. For that reason it is not enough to know how others have interpreted it. It is quite true that it would be arrogant and presumptuous folly completely to disregard the great classical interpretations of it; but nevertheless each man must interpret it for himself. But it can only be interpreted from the inside. In the preface to his *Cur Deus Homo,* Anselm said: 'Some men seek for reasons because they do not believe; we seek for them because we do believe.' Any consideration of the work of Christ must be not so much argument as witness. How then are we to interpret it for ourselves?

One thing I know—that because of Jesus Christ and because of what he is and did and does my whole relationship to God is changed. Because of Jesus Christ I know that God is my father and friend. Daily and hourly I experience the fact that I can enter into his presence with confidence and with boldness. He is no longer my enemy; he is no longer even my judge; there is no longer any unbridgeable gulf between him and me; I am more at home with God than I am with any human being in the human world. And all this is so because of Jesus Christ, and it could not possibly have happened without him. But how am I to express this in some kind of personal interpretation of the work of Jesus? We may begin with two general principles.

(i) It is quite wrong to think that one must confine oneself to one of the great classical interpretations and to hold that it expresses the whole truth, to believe that it alone is right and that all the others are wrong, to believe that belief in any one of them is essential for salvation, and to hold that he who believes in any of the others is a heretic and unsaved.

There is a perfect demonstration of this in Nels Ferré's book *Know your Faith.* In one chapter of that book Nels Ferré thinks about the work of Christ and in the compass of three pages (pp. 57–59) he says the following things. 'The Son of God as Son of Man has met sin, law, and death head on and conquered them all. God has assumed our plight, the whole plight, in Jesus Christ, and come off victorious within genuine humanity.' Here is the statement of *Christ the Victor.* 'God as man assumed the burden of our sins that we might know who he is, who we are, and for what he has made us.' Here is Christ *the Sacrifice, the Substitute, the Victim.* 'He shared our whole human experience, becoming the summary and summit of man's history.' Here is the conception of *Recapitulation.* 'The Godman helps us to become Godmen. Paul prays not in vain that we all be filled with the fullness of God.' Here is the conception of *Deification.* 'We are bid to take Jesus Christ as our actual example, "to walk even as he walked", to be perfect even as God is perfect, yes, even to imitate God himself.' Here is the conception of Jesus Christ the perfect *Example.* Within the narrow compass of a few pages this great Christian theologian and man of God has used all the great classical interpretations of Jesus Christ. This is entirely as it should be. Herbert Kelly, founder of Kelham, and one of the great ecumenical influences of our time, once said: 'Is not the cause of all our weakness that what God meant as complementary, men have regarded as antithetical?'[1] The great classical interpretations of the work of Jesus are not antithetical, they are complementary, and to make any one of them a slogan and a test of orthodoxy is profoundly wrong.

(ii) In the evaluation of any interpretation of the work of Jesus we must not test it by the bringing to it proof of texts; we must bring it to, and bring to it, the whole of Scripture. We must test it not by any individual text, however central, but by the whole conception of God which meets us in Jesus Christ. That which divides us perhaps more than anything else is the attempt to erect whole theologies on single texts rather than on the total message of Jesus Christ. Luther dealt with the canon of Scripture with sovereign freedom. His way of accepting some books of the Bible and rejecting others would have branded him as one of the most radical of critics, had he been writing today, and involved him in no little argument in his own day. In regard to this he wrote: "If, in the debates in which exegesis brings no decisive victories, our adversaries press the letter against Christ, we shall insist on Christ against the letter.'[2] The test of any interpretation is harmony or disharmony with the conception of God which Jesus Christ brought to men. Anything

[1] *No Pious Person,* ed. George Every, p. 117.
[2] Quoted in E. Reuss, *History of the Canon of the Holy Scriptures in the Christian Church,* p. 332.

that is unworthy of the God who is the God and Father of our Lord Jesus Christ must be unhesitatingly rejected.

When we bear all this in mind, we can lay it down that there are four great truths which we can affirm about the work of Jesus Christ.

(i) *The work of Christ was a fourfold demonstration.* In Jesus Christ we see *God in his attitude to men.* A word is the expression of a thought and to say that Jesus is the Word of God (John 1.14) is to say that Jesus is the expression of the thought of God. This Jesus who fed the hungry and healed the sick and comforted the sorrowing and was the friend of outcasts and sinners is the expression of the attitude of God to men. The one basic truth with which all Christian thought about God must start out is that God is like Jesus. In Jesus Christ we see *what man ought to be.* Jesus is not, as it were, *less* human than men, he is *more* human than men. In him there is the demonstration of what God intended man to be. In Jesus Christ we see *the perfect demonstration of the love of God.* As we see Jesus in his tenderness to the suffering and the sinning and the sorrowing, we can say: 'God loves me like that.' As we see Jesus on the Cross, we can say: 'God loves me enough to do that for me.' In the events which happened to Jesus Christ we see *the demonstration of the awfulness of sin.* In the death of Jesus Christ we see the wicked hands of men taking and destroying the loveliest life the universe has ever seen, or ever will see. On the Cross we see the terrible destructive power of sin, as it has been called, 'the infinite damnability of sin'. The effect of this must be to impel men to love God and to hate sin and to adore Jesus Christ. In this Abelard is profoundly right; unquestionably there is truth in the Moral Influence interpretation of the work of Jesus Christ, even if it is not the whole truth, and, even if a man never got past that interpretation he would have gone a long way, for he would inevitably be lost in wonder, love, and praise.

(ii) *The work of Christ is sacrificial work.* But that sacrifice was not offered to the devil, for the devil can never be on an equality with God; nor was that sacrifice offered to God, for nothing was ever needed to change the attitude of God to men, or to reconcile God to men. The whole process of which Jesus Christ is the centre and soul begins in the love of God. Wherein then does the sacrifice lie? It lies in this—*it cost the life and the death of Jesus Christ to tell men what God is like*. Without the life and death of Jesus Christ men could never have known what God is like, and could therefore never have entered into a loving relationship with God. It took all that Jesus Christ had to give to enable men to enter into this relationship with God. Only through Jesus Christ can I ever know that God loves me, not because of what I am, but because of what he is.

That sacrifice begins with the Incarnation. He who was rich for our sakes became poor (II Cor. 8.9). It culminates upon the Cross, for Jesus, having loved his own, loved them to the end (John 13.1). But why the death of Christ? The death of Christ was necessary for this reason—if Jesus in his love had stopped short of the Cross, it would have meant that there was somewhere beyond which the love of God would not go, that there was something beyond which God would not forgive. On the Cross God says to us in Jesus Christ: 'Nothing—absolutely nothing that you can do—can stop me loving you.' The Cross is the essential fact in the whole work of Christ.

No interpretation of the work of Christ even begins to be adequate unless it remembers the terrible sacrifice it cost to enable men to see the love of God that they might respond to it. The sacrifice which is in the work of Christ is neither sacrifice to the devil nor sacrifice to God. It is sacrifice *by* God necessitated by his great and gracious act of self-revelation in Jesus Christ.

(iii) *The work of Christ is objective in its character*. It is objective in the sense that it quite definitely produces and achieves something which for ever continues to exist. It is not objective in the sense in which a legal transaction is objective. It is objective in this sense—it produced a completely new situation in regard to the relationship between God and man. It produced a situation which had not existed before, and which, once it had been produced, cannot cease to exist. It produced a situation in which there became possible between man and God a new relationship of intimacy, of confidence, of trust, of love. Prior to the work of Jesus Christ men did not fully know what God was like; between man and God there was the great gulf of ignorance or of semi-knowledge. The power of God, the justice of God, the holiness of God, the

righteousness of God, men did know, but of the marvel of the love
of God they had never dreamed. Men like Hosea glimpsed it, but
in Christ it was fully and for ever displayed. The objective effect
of the work of Jesus Christ is to create a new relationship between
God and man, not by changing the attitude of God to man, but by
revealing to men what the attitude of God to them is.

(iv) *The work of Christ is effective in its dealing with sin.* There
are certain things in this connection about which we must be clear.
The work of Christ is not to be confined to his death, but necessarily
includes that which comes to man through his life and his resurrection. At its lowest and its most obvious, the work of Christ pro-
vides man with the example of the good life. He left us an example
that we should follow in his steps (I Peter 2.21). But the work of
Christ goes far beyond that, or it would be quite unavailing for the
helplessness of man. A fine example can be the most daunting and
depressing thing in the world, if all it does is to convince a man of
the impossibility of following it. Man does not need only *example,*
he also needs *power.* Further, the work of Christ does not deal with
sin in the sense of wiping out the consequences of sin. To be forgiven does not mean to be freed from the consequences of sin. If a
man sins against his body, he will bear the consequences in his body,
even when he is forgiven. If a man's sinning damages himself or
other people, as it must, forgiveness does not remove the damage
that he has done.

It is here that the Resurrection must come in. 'If,' says Paul,
'while we were enemies we were reconciled to God by the death of
his Son, much more, now that we are reconciled, shall we be saved
by his life' (Rom. 5.10). We are not dependent on a Christ who
lived and died, we are dependent on a Christ who lived and died
and who is alive for evermore. Since he is alive, he is here in such
a way that we can draw upon him for power other than our own.

The work of Christ, therefore, enables us to deal effectively
through him with the situations in which sin had rendered us helpless. It enables us to deal with the situation which sin had created
between a man and himself. A man remains a split personality,
poised between goodness and badness, between right and wrong,
between heroism and cowardice, between sainthood and sin, between the ape and the angel, until the power of the Risen Christ

takes possession of him, and makes him a personality integrated by this new centre within it. 'It is no longer I who live,' said Paul, 'but Christ who lives in me; and the life I now live in the flesh I live by faith in the Son of God, who loved me and gave himself for me' (Gal. 2.20). Through the work of Christ a man ceases to be a battle-ground of opposing forces and reaches mature manhood (Eph. 4.13). It enables us to deal with the situation which sin had created *between us and our fellowmen*. One of the great effects of sin is the disturbance of personal relationships; one of the great effects of the work of Christ is the creation of fellowship. It is only in Christ that men can find unity instead of disunity, trust instead of suspicion, love instead of hate. The mutual hostility which is created by sin is defeated by the love which is shed abroad by Christ. It enables us to deal with the situation which sin had created *between us and God*. The work of Christ assures us of the love and of the forgiveness of God, and our desire to hide from God is changed into a great desire to live for ever with God.

The work of Christ is effective, first, in revealing to us the love of God, and, second, in enabling us by his risen power to deal with the tragic and disastrous situations which sin had created in our own lives and in the life of the world.

No man can ever grasp, still less express, all that Jesus Christ has done, but we may be well content to witness with all our hearts that through Jesus Christ we have entered into a relationship with God, which without him would have been utterly impossible, and in him we have entered into a relationship with ourselves and with our fellowmen in which the deadly work of sin can be undone.

28

THE RESURRECTION

It was not long after three o'clock in the afternoon when Jesus died (Mark 15.34). The next day was the Sabbath, and the Sabbath began at 6 p.m. According to the Jewish law a criminal's body might not remain on its cross over the Sabbath day, and therefore the body of Jesus had to be quickly taken down and quickly disposed of. Very often the bodies of crucified criminals were simply left to be the prey of the vultures, the carrion crows, and the pariah dogs. But the followers of Jesus had an influential friend who was able to help them to pay what they thought was their last tribute to their dead Master. His name was Joseph of Arimathaea; he was rich and devout; he was a member of the Sanhedrin, and in secret he was a disciple of Jesus. He went to Pilate and requested the body of Jesus that he might give it decent burial. Pilate was surprised that Jesus had died so soon, but was willing to accede to the request. The tombs of wealthy families in those days were not graves in the ground, but were caves with shelves on which the bodies were laid. Joseph had such a tomb, never hitherto used, in a garden near to Calvary. Nicodemus, John says, came with a gift of spices to embalm the body of Jesus as if it had been the body of a king. So the body of Jesus was wrapped in the grave-clothes, which were like long linen bandages wound round and round the body, and then it was laid on one of the shelves of the rock tomb. Such tombs were not closed with a door, but with a great circular stone like a cartwheel which ran in a groove and which was wheeled up to close the opening. So Jesus was laid in the tomb and the great stone, which one New Testament manuscript, Codex Bezae, says that twenty men could hardly have moved, was rolled up in its groove to close the tomb (Matt. 27.57–60; Mark 15.42–46; Luke 23.50–55; John 19.38–42). And the women who had been there at the foot of the cross marked the place where the body of Jesus was laid (Matt. 27.61; Mark 15.47).

Meanwhile the Jewish authorities had not been idle. Even after they had seen Jesus die on the cross they were still uneasy about him. They went to Pilate and asked that special precautions should be taken, lest the disciples of Jesus should steal his body and claim that he had risen from the dead. Pilate agreed that a guard should be posted and that the stone should be sealed to make things as safe as they could be made (Matt. 27.62–66). The time was to come when the bewildered guards had to report that the tomb was empty, and when they were bribed by the Jewish authorities to say that Jesus' disciples had stolen his body (Matt. 28.11–14).

All the Sabbath day, our Saturday, the body of Jesus lay in the tomb, and the tomb had no visitor, for the Sabbath day was the day of rest, and to have made even the journey from the city to the tomb would have been to break the Sabbath law. Then there came the first day of the week, our Sunday, the first Easter Sunday. It is little wonder that we cannot construct an hour-to-hour time-table of what happened on that day, for its events were so stagger-ing that those who were involved in them must have for ever looked back on them with a kind of incredulous amazement. We can only reconstruct the story as well as we are able.

With the first streaks of dawn, even when it was still dark, the women came to the tomb to give to the body of Jesus their last loving service. There was Mary Magdalene, there was Mary the mother of James and Joses, there was Joanna, and maybe there were others. They were worried about the problem of gaining an entry to the tomb, and could not think how they might be able to move the massive stone which guarded its entrance. But, when they reached the tomb, the stone was rolled away, and there was a mes-senger to tell them that Jesus was risen and had gone before them into Galilee as he had promised that he would do (Matt. 28.1–7; Mark 16.1–8; Luke 24.1–11). As Matthew has it, the risen Jesus himself appeared to them on their way back to the city, and himself repeated the message of the messenger (Matt. 28.8–10).

It would be only natural that the women would rush with the news to the other disciples. Luke tells us that the rest of the disciples flatly refused to believe the news (Luke 24.10f.). But John goes on to tell us more. As he tells the story, Mary Magdalene hurried to tell the story of the empty tomb to Peter and to the disciple whom Jesus loved, but at that time she had not grasped the significance of the empty tomb, but was heart-broken because she thought that someone had taken away the body of Jesus. Peter and the beloved disciple set out for the garden. The beloved disciple saw the empty tomb and the grave-clothes lying in it, but he did not go into it. Then Peter came and went in. 'He saw the linen cloths lying, and the napkin, which had been on his head, not lying with the linen cloths but rolled up in a place by itself.' Then the other disciple also entered the tomb and saw and believed (John 20.6–8). What was it about the grave-clothes and the napkin that was so impressive? There are two possibilities. It may be that the grave-clothes and the napkin were so neatly and tidily laid out and folded that it was quite clear that there had been no hurried theft of the body, but that they had been carefully taken off and laid away. It is just possible that the Greek could mean that the linen grave-clothes and the head-napkin were lying separately, exactly as if the body of Jesus had evaporated out of them and left them lying empty there. So Peter and the beloved disciple returned to Jerusalem with the dawning certainty that Jesus had risen from the dead.

As John tells the story, it is clear that Mary Magdalene did not know what was going on. She lingered sorrowfully in the garden, until, in what some one has called the greatest recognition scene in literature, she suddenly recognized Jesus.

There followed on the same day the special appearance of the risen Jesus to Peter (Luke 24.34; cp. Mark 16.7), and what must have been the scene of reconciliation between Jesus and the disciple who loved him but denied him? There followed still on the same day the appearance of Jesus to the two friends who were walking the road to Emmaus (Luke 24.13–35).

There were still other appearances of Jesus. He appeared to his disciples apparently in the upper room, once when Thomas was absent and refused to believe, and once when Thomas came back to express his worship and his adoration (Luke 24.44–49; John 20.24–29).

These were all appearances in Jerusalem; but Matthew has the story of the appearance of Jesus to his disciples on the hill-top in

Galilee and of his commission to them to go to preach the gospel (Matt. 28.16–20), and John tells of the appearance to the disciples as they were fishing on the seashore of the Sea of Galilee (John 21).

Such, then, is the account of the Resurrection as it appears in the New Testament itself, and it is on this account that the microscope of criticism has been turned; and there is an astonishing diversity in the results. Lives of Jesus such as F. W. Farrar's *Life of Christ* and David Smith's *In the Days of His Flesh* do little more than repeat the New Testament account with placid acceptance. But it is a very different story when we come to the work of the more modern and the more radical New Testament scholars. To read such works as C. Guignebert's *Jesus* (pp. 490–536), M. Goguel's *Jesus the Nazarene* (pp. 216–241), O. Holtzmann's *Life of Jesus* (pp. 492–529), J. Klausner's *Jesus of Nazareth* (pp. 356–359), C. G. Montefiore's *Synoptic Gospels* (I, 397–400), K. Lake's *The Historical Evidence for the Resurrection of Jesus*, J. Weiss's *Earliest Christianity* (I, 14–31, Harper's Torchbooks Edition), is to see how little radical criticism leaves of the New Testament story. And, if we go further back, we will find the work of Strauss and Renan equally devastating. It is necessary that we should at least be aware of the radical attack, for many of its claims and positions have, as it were, vaguely filtered down into popular knowledge, and it is sometimes forgotten that there remains not a little to be said on the other side as, for instance, in A. M. Ramsey's *The Resurrection of Christ*, or, more popularly, in James Martin's *Did Jesus Rise from the Dead?* Let us then see the lines which radical criticism has taken.

In the main it may be said that radical criticism has denied, or cast doubt upon, three facts or sets of facts. It denies the fact of the empty tomb; it denies the Jerusalem appearances of Jesus; it denies the objectivity of these appearances in any real sense of the term. The length to which this denial has gone may be seen from the last sentence of Guignebert's examination of the Resurrection narratives and of the Easter faith. He talks about the centrality of the belief in the Resurrection, but he concludes by saying: 'It is doubtful, however, whether the dogma of the Resurrection, which has so long been the mainstay of Christianity, has not, in our day, become too heavy a burden for it to bear.' Let us then see at what points the attack has been launched.

The source of the evidence has been attacked. Long ago Celsus urged the objection that the evidence for the Resurrection depends very largely on the word of Mary Magdalene, a half-crazed, hysterical woman, out of whom Jesus had cast seven devils.[1] The other main source of the evidence is Peter, a highly suggestible, impulsive, unstable, unbalanced Galilaean fisherman, or Paul, an epileptic with all an epileptic's penchant for seeing visions.

The contradictions within the story have been advanced. No two Gospels list the same women as coming to the tomb. In Mark it is Mary Magdalene, Mary the mother of James, and Salome (Mark 16.1); in Luke it is the two Marys and Joanna (24.10); in Matthew it is simply the two Marys. Mark says that the women came to the tomb very early in the morning, when the sun had risen (16.2); John says that Mary Magdelene came, when it was still dark (20.1); Matthew says that they came, after the Sabbath, toward the dawn of the first day of the week (28.1). The identity of the messenger or messengers in the tomb varies from Gospel to Gospel. In Mark the messenger is a young man clothed in a long white garment (16.5,6); in Luke the news is given by two men in shining garments (24.4–6); in Matthew the messenger is the angel of the Lord (28.2–5); in John the message is delivered by two angels (20.12,13). In Mark and Luke the women simply come to find the stone rolled away from the mouth of the tomb (Mark 16.3,4; Luke 24.2); but in Matthew the stone is miraculously rolled away by an angel of the Lord, who came and sat upon it; and this amazing event together with the earthquake which accompanied it seems to have happened in the sight of the women (Matt. 28.2,3). Only Matthew has the story of the sealing of the tomb and the mounting of a guard upon it (27.62–66), an arrangement of which the women certainly could not have known, or they could have had no hope of entering the tomb.

We may feel, and we may rightly feel, that discrepancies such as we have cited are of little or no importance, but within the Resurrection narratives there does emerge one very real problem, the problem of fitting together the appearances in and around Jerusalem, and the appearances in Galilee.

Mark rightly ends at Mark 16.8, and the concluding verses are no part of the original Gospel, as any modern translation will show.

[1] Luke 8.2; Origen, *Against Celsus* 2.55.

There are in Mark, therefore, no actual Resurrection appearances at all. In Matthew there is a brief appearance to the women as they return to Jerusalem from the tomb (28.9,19), but the central and essential appearance, the appearance to the disciples, is in Galilee (28.16–20). In Luke all the appearances are in or around Jerusalem. There is the appearance on the road to Emmaus (24.13–35), and the appearance where the disciples are gathered together (24.36–49). Luke's narrative is further complicated by the fact that at least at a first reading the Ascension seems to take place on the same day as the Resurrection (24.50–53). But, to make Luke's evidence complete, it must be stated that the words 'and (was) carried up into heaven' in verse 51 are missing from many of the best manuscripts. Weymouth retains them; the RV notes in the margin that they are doubtful; Moffatt and the Twentieth Century New Testament enclose them in square brackets; the RSV omits them, but notes that certain manuscripts do have them. And it is also to be remembered that in Acts Luke says that Jesus was in communication with the disciples for forty days (Acts 1.3). The place of the Ascension in Luke's narrative may be doubtful; it is not doubtful that in Luke the Resurrection appearances all take place in Jerusalem, and there are none recorded in Galilee. The situation in John is also complicated. In John there are Resurrection appearances to Mary in the Garden, and to the disciples, without and with Thomas, in their meeting place in Jerusalem in John 20; but in John 21 there is the appearance of Jesus to the group of disciples by the lakeside in Galilee. But it is generally agreed that John 21 is not part of the original Fourth Gospel, but is in the nature of an appendix by a different hand.

It can at once be seen that there is a problem here. The more radical critics solve the problem by holding that all the Resurrection appearances were in fact in Galilee, and that the Jerusalem appearances are later additions and indeed inventions. How is that conclusion arrived at?

This much certainly is true—the whole New Testament narrative would lead us to expect that the Risen Christ would appear in Galilee. After the last meal together, Jesus and his men went out to the Mount of Olives, and, apparently on the way, Jesus said to them: 'After I am raised up, I will go before you to Galilee' (Mark

14.28). It has been argued, and, as far as the Greek goes, it is perfectly possible that 'go before' does not mean 'precede, go on ahead of you', but rather, 'lead you, put myself at the head of your company and be your leader'. However that may be, it is quite clear that Jesus is, as we might say, making a rendez-vous with his men in Galilee.

The Resurrection narratives would in fact confirm this impression. In Mark the announcement of the messenger at the tomb is: 'He has risen, he is not here; see the place where they laid him. But go, tell his disciples and Peter that he is going before you to Galilee; there you will see him, as he told you' (16.7). With the exception that it omits the message to Peter, Matthew's account is exactly the same (28.7). All this would undoubtedly lead us to expect that the Resurrection appearances would be in Galilee, as indeed in Matthew the great appearance is. It is not entirely irrelevant that the apocryphal Gospel of Peter makes Peter say: 'We, the twelve disciples of the Lord, were weeping and were in sorrow, and each one being grieved for that which had befallen departed unto his own house. But I, Simon Peter, and Andrew my brother, took our nets and went unto the sea; and there was with us Levi the son of Alphaeus' (The Gospel of Peter 13.59,60). It has been suggested that this information of the Gospel of Peter actually comes from the lost ending of Mark's Gospel, if the original of Mark did not actually finish at Mark 16.8.

On the face of it here there is a line of tradition which tells that the disciples fled to Galilee, or that they drifted back to their trade there, and that it was there that the Resurrection appearances of Jesus took place. It is precisely this that many of the radical critics believe took place, and they believe that the Jerusalem appearances as recorded in Luke and John are later inventions, due either to certain happenings which we shall shortly examine, or due to the fact that Christian apologetics desired to have certain appearances of Jesus in the sacred city and near to the tomb where his body had been laid.

There is no doubt at all that a case can be made for the view that the Resurrection appearances did take place in Galilee.

This leads us very naturally to the next great battleground of the Resurrection arguments, the question of the empty tomb. Before

we come to the way in which the Galilaean appearances view and
the question of the empty tomb are connected, there are certain
other things at which we must glance.

Attempts to explain away the empty tomb are as old as Christianity itself. It has been suggested that Jesus did not die on the
Cross but that he swooned, and that in the cool of the tomb he
revived, and then succeeded in making his escape from it. He and
his disciples then claimed that he had risen from the dead, and he
lived on until he died a natural death. The Gospel narratives make
it very clear that Jesus did die on the Cross. The Fourth Gospel tells
of the spear thrust into his side to make assurance of his death
doubly sure (John 19.34). His body was lovingly handled for its
anointing and embalming and any sign of life would certainly have
been noticed. Even if he had only swooned, it is impossible to see
how he could have disentangled himself from the long windings
of the grave-clothes, and how he could have opened the tomb from
the inside and so escaped. If he had escaped, he would have been
a broken and battered figure instead of a figure of glory. And it is
hard to see how Christianity in the end could have survived the
violent anti-climax of a natural death. There are very few who
would nowadays take the swoon theory with any seriousness.

It has been suggested that the Jews took his body away lest the
tomb where he had been laid become a martyr's shrine. But it is
impossible to see how any Jew could ever have conceived it possible
that one who was crucified could ever come to be regarded as a
martyr of God, for the Jewish law pronounced its curse on every one
who hung upon a tree (Deut. 21.23). And yet this suggestion must
have had some currency in the early days, for Tertullian with grim
humour speaks of the story that the gardener removed the body of
Jesus 'lest his lettuces should be trampled on by the throng of
visitors'.[1]

It has been suggested that the disciples removed the body of
Jesus and then claimed that he had risen from the dead. That in
fact is what Matthew says that the Jews feared would happen
(27.63–66), and that is what the late and slanderous Jewish book
the *Tol' doth Yeshu* says did happen. But it is impossible to think
of the whole of Christianity being founded on a lie. It is impossible

[1] *De Spectaculis* 30.

to think of the disciples preaching the Resurrection faith and dying for the Resurrection faith in the full awareness that the whole thing was a deliberate falsehood. As Joseph Klausner, himself a great Jew and scholar, says: 'That is impossible; *deliberate imposture* is not the substance out of which the religion of millions of mankind is created . . . The nineteen hundred years' faith of millions is not founded on deception.'[1]

Guignebert would explain the empty tomb by the fact that Jesus' body was never buried in it at all, but was most likely removed from the Cross by his executioners and flung into the pit into which the bodies of executed prisoners were thrown.[2]

Both Holtzmann and Klausner think it likely that what happened was that Joseph of Arimathaea was unwilling to give the body of Jesus anything but a temporary refuge, and that as soon as the Sabbath was ended, he caused it to be quietly removed and buried in some unknown place.[3]

But by far the most startling explanation of the empty tomb is that of Kirsopp Lake in *The Historical Evidence of the Resurrection of Jesus Christ*. Lake suggests that after the crucifixion the disciples fled to Galilee, and that it was there that they saw the appearance which persuaded them that Jesus was still alive. When they did return to Jerusalem, they found that there was a story that the women had gone to the tomb on the first day of the week and had found it empty. This was, of course, at once seized on as further proof that Jesus was still alive. But it is Lake's suggestion that the story of the women was the result of a misunderstanding. He suggests that they actually visited the wrong grave, and that a young man directed them to the right one with the words: 'He is not here; see the place where they laid him' (Mark 16.6), the words, 'He has risen', being a later addition and insertion into that verse. There can be few more astonishing suggestions than that the story of the empty tomb goes back to a mistake by a company of women which sent them to the wrong tomb, and a misunderstanding of some unknown young man's directions to set them right.

The last argument in the attempt to disprove the story of the

[1] *Jesus of Nazareth* pp. 357, 359.

[2] *Jesus* p. 500.

[3] J. Klausner, *Jesus of Nazareth*, p. 35; O. Holtzmann, *The Life of Jesus*, p. 499.

empty tomb is the fact that it is not mentioned outside the Gospels. It is argued that, if Paul had known of it, he would have cited it as an argument for the Resurrection somewhere in I Corinthians 15, and that, if Peter had really known about it, he would have mentioned it somewhere in the sermon of Acts 2, especially in the section Acts 2.29–36.

The argument is, not that the empty tomb was a factor in the creating of faith in a Risen Lord, but that the appearances of the Risen Lord produced the story of the empty tomb.

We now come to the last of the debated questions in regard to the Resurrection. This is the argument as to what the appearances of Jesus after his death really were. There are three main positions.

(i) There are very few who would deny that something happened, and there are comparatively few who would wish to explain the Resurrection appearances of Jesus in terms of hallucination, but there are many who would say that the alleged appearances of the Risen Christ were subjective visions. That is to say, they were visions seen within the mind, or thought to be seen with the eye, but with no corresponding objective reality. This idea would be explained somewhat as follows.

If we place any belief at all in the Gospel records, the disciples cannot have been entirely unprepared for the Cross, for Jesus forewarned them that it was to come (Mark 8.31; 9.31; 10.33). Yet when it came, it came with such shattering tragedy that faith and hope collapsed. Yet even in the darkest hour the disciples never stopped thinking about Jesus. In Mark 14.27 we read, as the AV has it, that Jesus said to his disciples: 'All ye shall be offended because of me this night.' The RSV translates it: 'You will all fall away.' Lagrange vividly translates it: 'You will all be demoralised.' Demoralised they were, 'for they had hoped that he was the one to redeem Israel' (Luke 24.21). But even in such a condition they were still thinking and talking of this Jesus (Luke 24.15–21).

Now, if this were so, something else was almost bound to follow in the mind of a Jew. All Jewish history showed the saints of God persecuted, oppressed and killed. All Jewish history showed the tale of a series of national disasters and national tragedies. And yet somehow out of every tragedy truth had emerged stronger and faith had burned brighter. Somehow out of the tragedy something fine had come by the action of God, something which had left God, not further away, but nearer. It was almost inevitable that the mind of the disciples should follow along this line in regard to Jesus. When they had had time to think, their whole national history and experience would predispose them to look for the hand of God even in the tragedy.

We may go a step further. The place of Peter in the Resurrection narratives is central. A special message is sent to him (Mark 16.7); one of the first appearances is said to be to him (Luke 24.34); he comes at the head of Paul's list of those by whom Jesus was seen (I Cor. 15.5). So Guignebert writes beautifully about Peter: 'We must think of him as having returned to his home at Capernaum and resumed his fisherman's calling, with the boat which had so often taken Jesus across the lake. Everything there calls up memories of those days of hope and joy. The vision of his Master pursues him and indeed fills his whole life. His entire being centres in the thought that it cannot all be ended, that something will happen and happen through him, that he has not deceived us or forsaken us, he will come back to us. And while his grief at the loss of Jesus grows, and a hope that has no form becomes keener, the expectation of the inevitable miracle surges in his heart. Reason demanded that the miracle should be a personal manifestation of the Crucified. Need we be surprised that Peter saw Jesus?'[1] 'In the inner tension and tumult of his soul,' writes Holtzmann, 'a certain idea possesses Peter unceasingly; in a moment of supreme excitement the same idea presents itself to his mind objectively also.'[2] 'There can be no question,' writes Klausner, 'but that some of the ardent Galilaeans saw their Lord and Messiah in a vision.'[3] It is Renan who puts this most beautifully: 'It was love which resurrected Jesus.'[4]

The idea, and it is a lovely idea, is that the disciples, and especially Peter, thought themselves and loved themselves into seeing a vision of Jesus. But that vision was not objective; it was subjective. It had no objective reality; it was something which happened within their hearts. And once that experience had come to Peter, it spread

[1] *Jesus*, p. 522.
[2] *The Life of Jesus*, p. 503.
[3] *Jesus of Nazareth*, p. 358.
[4] Quoted in A. M. Ramsey, *The Resurrection of Christ*, p. 48.

like an infection and a contagion, because it is characteristic of that kind of experience to repeat itself in others.

No one will deny the beauty of this idea; and yet the line between it and downright hallucination is precariously thin. It is a vision due to a kind of self-hypnotism. The seer of it never for a moment doubted its reality—but nonetheless it was not real, but only a product of the man's own mind.

C. G. Montefiore feels bound to accept this explanation of the Resurrection experiences. Yet, he says, he has a difficulty. Then he goes on: 'It is, perhaps, less a difficulty than a sadness . . . It is hard to be content that great religious results should have had not quite satisfactory causes. The subjective vision was, in one sense, an "illusion". Yet upon this illusion hung the great religious result which we call Christianity.'[1]

Here is exactly the difficulty which anyone must feel. No one questions the reverence of this view; no one questions the beauty of the idea that an undefeatable love within the heart somehow produced its own evidence to enable it to believe that that which it wished to be true was true. But the belief in the Resurrection is the centre of the Christian faith, and, if this idea is correct, there is no escape from the conclusion that Christianity rests on a delusion, however understandable and however emotionally beautiful that delusion may be. An hallucination remains an hallucination, even when it produces the very effect that one wishes to be true. If we hold that the appearances of Jesus Christ after his death were no more than subjective visions, then we can do no other than say, as Strauss said in the original form of his life of Jesus, that the disciples passed from the position, 'He must live!' to the position, 'He does live! He has appeared!'[2] And that is to say that the belief in the Resurrection was no more than self-induced and was without any basis in actual fact.

(ii) The second position is the position of Theodor Keim, which is fully, eloquently, persuasively and reverently stated in his great life of Jesus (*Jesus of Nazara*, VI, 274–365). Keim's position is that the appearances of Jesus were indeed visions, but that they were not subjective visions, but objective visions sent to the disciples by the

[1] *The Synoptic Gospels*, I, 399.
[2] *Life of Jesus*, 4th edition, II, 634ff.

direct action and the direct intervention of God. They were not, to use Keim's own phrases, 'human projections' but rather 'divine manifestations'.

The contention of Keim is that, if Jesus had really ended on a cross, he could never have been accepted as Messiah by any Jew, because the Law is inescapably clear that one who was crucified was under the curse of God (Deut. 21.23). To the Jew this would have been an insuperable barrier to the acceptance of Jesus as the divine vice-regent of God. 'All the evidences go to prove that the belief in the Messiah would have died out without the living Jesus; and by the return of the Apostles to the synagogue, to Judaism, the gold of the words of Jesus would have been buried in the dust of oblivion. The greatest of men would have passed away and left no trace; for a time Galilee would have preserved some truth and fiction about him; but his cause would have begotten no religious exaltation and no Paul.' What was required was, in Keim's famous phrase, 'a telegram from heaven'. 'The evidence that Jesus was alive, the telegram from heaven, was necessary after an earthly downfall which was unexampled, and which in the childhood of the human race would be convincing; the evidence that he was alive was therefore given by his own impulsion and by the will of God.'[1]

On this view the appearances of Jesus were not subjective visions produced by love and meditation and memory; they were divinely sent objective visions. 'Even the corporeal appearance,' says Keim, 'may be granted to those who are afraid of losing everything, unless they have this plastic representation for their thought and their faith.'[2]

There is no doubt of the attraction of this view. It obviates so many difficulties. In particular it solves the difficulty of what happened in the end to the physical body of Jesus, for that physical body of Jesus simply does not enter into the matter at all. Certainly, it leaves the explanation of the empty tomb difficult, and, if the fact of the empty tomb be accepted, this view will mean that the body of Jesus was removed from the tomb by some unknown human hand. But that in many ways is easier to understand than it is to

[1] *Jesus of Nazara*, VI, 362.
[2] *Jesus of Nazara*, VI, 362.

understand what happened to the body of Jesus in the end, if the Resurrection was in some sense a physical event.

But this view encounters one serious difficulty. On this view the appearances of Jesus were purely spiritual with no physical element in them at all. And yet it is true that the narratives of the Resurrection appearances in the Gospels make a great deal of the actual physical character of that event. In Mark there are no actual appearances of Jesus narrated, and so the problem does not arise. In Matthew the problem is very slight. The only physical reference in the Resurrection story in Matthew is the saying that the women returning from the empty tomb met the risen Christ 'and took hold of his feet and worshipped him' (28.9). But the matter is very different in Luke. In Luke in the Emmaus story Jesus takes bread and breaks it with his own hands in the Emmaus house (24.30); in his appearance to the disciples he invites them to touch and handle him, telling them that a spirit has neither flesh nor bones, and thus inferring that he has; and he also shares a meal with them (24.39,41). In John there is a curious double strand of evidence, for there Jesus forbids Mary Magdalene to cling to him, and yet, when he meets the disciples, he shows them his hands and his side, and he invites the hard to convince Thomas actually to touch and handle him, and so to convince himself of the reality of his body and his wounds; and in the last chapter the risen Christ prepares a meal for his disciples, when they disembark from the fishing-boat (John 20.17,20,27; 21.10–13).

In Paul's account of the Resurrection appearances of Jesus (I Cor. 15.3–8) the word that is consistently used is that Jesus *was seen* by the various people involved. (The RSV needlessly and indeed wrongly substitutes *appeared;* the Greek is *ōphthē*). And in Paul there is no suggestion of touching and handling. In fact the suggestion is rather the reverse.

There is real difficulty here. There can be two instinctive reactions to this. There are some who find the continual physical references uncomfortable and unnecessary and who rather shrink from them; and there are some who find them reassuring and necessary. It may well be suggestive that the later the Gospel the more the physical side is stressed; and it may well be that the physical side of the Resurrection came to be elaborated and developed in the interests of underlining and emphasizing the reality of the Resurrection.

In spite of the physical references in the Resurrection narratives as they stand, it would still be possible to accept Keim's interpretation of divinely caused and divinely sent visions, designed and purposed and despatched by God to convince men of the continued and glorified life of Jesus.

(iii) Lastly, there is the view, which is the orthodox view, that the Resurrection of Jesus was in some sense a bodily resurrection, and was in some sense a physical as well as a spiritual event. This is the view that Jesus returned to his disciples in the body.

It is very easy to state this view, but it is not by any means so easy to define what it means. Even if we take the evidence of the Gospels exactly as it is, there remain questions and difficulties. Let us take that evidence and set it down.

(*a*) The appearance of the risen Christ was such as to demand worship. When the women returning from the tomb met him, they took hold of his feet and worshipped him (Matt. 28.9). When the disciples met him on the hilltop in Galilee, when they saw him they worshipped him (Matt. 28.17). The final cry of Thomas is: 'My Lord and my God!' (John 20.28). It may be that the Gospel writers depict the wounds of Christ as still there, yet in spite of that he is no figure of pathos. 'Then the disciples were glad when they saw the Lord' (John 20.20). Whatever may be said of the bodily resurrection of Jesus, the Gospel picture is that he carried the atmosphere of glory with him. The apocryphal Gospel of Peter has a good deal of information of its own about the Passion and the Resurrection— it dates to about AD 150—and it has one significant saying. The words of the messenger in the tomb to the woman are: 'Why have you come? Whom do you seek? Not him who was crucified, for he has risen and gone. But if you do not believe it, look in and see the place where he lay, that he is not here. *For he has risen and gone to the place from which he was sent*' (The Gospel of Peter 13.55,56). Whoever wrote that sentence believed that the risen Christ had returned to his glory; and therefore the Resurrection appearances are appearances of the glorified Christ. This would indeed explain the atmosphere of worship; and it would indeed mean that it is not enough to speak of a bodily and a physical resurrection.

(*b*) One of the curious features of the Resurrection narratives is the number of times when it is stated that Jesus was not recognized. He was not recognized by the two travellers on the way to Emmaus

(Luke 24.16). He was not recognized by Mary Magdalene (John 20.14). It is clear that the disciples by the lakeside were not exactly certain that it was Jesus whom they saw (John 21.4,12). Even in Galilee some worshipped, but some doubted (Matt. 28.17). Here again we seem to come upon a bodily resurrection—and something more.

(*c*) The Gospel narratives seem to indicate that they regard the risen Christ as independent of time and space. He comes and goes, as it were, at will. The end of the Emmaus story is his vanishing from sight (Luke 24.31). The assembled disciples are terrified, thinking that it is a spirit which they see (Luke 24.37). When the doors are shut, suddenly he is in the midst of them (John 20.19,26). Once again, even taking the Gospel narratives as they stand, we seem to be in the presence of a bodily resurrection—and something more.

(*d*) We have already noted the stress on the physical side of the Resurrection appearances. But it has to be remembered that even here there remains something essentially mysterious, for Mary Magdalene is forbidden to touch him (John 20.17), but Thomas is invited to do so (John 20.27).

Let us for the moment leave the matter there, and return to it later. It is enough for the moment to see that the underlying evidence of the Gospels is such as to show that it is not enough simply to talk about a bodily and a physical resurrection of Jesus and to leave it at that. There is something more.

It is worth noting that, if a Jew believed in any kind of resurrection, it would be a physical and bodily resurrection. The Pharisaic belief in the resurrection was crudely physical. In the times of the Maccabees the Jewish martyrs expected to receive back from God these very parts of their bodies which their enemies tortured and mutilated (II Macc. 7.11; 14.46).

In 2 Baruch the hope of the resurrection is that a man will be resurrected in exactly the same form in which he died. Baruch asks God: 'In what shape will those live who live in thy day?' The answer is: 'The earth will then assuredly restore the dead, which it now receives, in order to preserve them, making no change in their form, but as it has received, so it will restore them, and as I delivered them unto it, so also will it raise them' (2 Baruch 49.2–4). The hope is the hope of a physical resurrection in exactly the form in which a man died, after which will come the judgment. So far was this belief carried that it was sometimes held that a man would rise wearing exactly the same clothes as the clothes in which he had been laid in his tomb,[1] and there were many cases of dying Rabbis who gave minute and detailed instructions regarding the clothes in which they were to be buried.[2]

In view of this it is not difficult to see that the whole tendency would be to make the Resurrection of Jesus as physical as possible; the physical side of it would tend to be exaggerated.

Let us return to the radical criticism of the Resurrection narratives of the Gospels.

These narratives are attacked on the ground of their discrepancies and their inconsistencies. We already noted that many of the discrepancies are quite trifling and unimportant. It might well be argued that the discrepancies are the best proof of the sincerity of the writers. No two people will ever give precisely the same account of any event. If they do, the indication is not so much an indication of truth-telling as it is of collaboration, not to say collusion. Collin Brooks tells how on one occasion he and the famous banker Sir James Hope Simpson had to provide some specimen signatures on little cards for the block-makers to use. As Sir James signed the little cards, he turned to Collin Brooks and said: 'Brooks, if ever you want to compare two signatures, and you hold one over the other against a window or a light, and they coincide exactly—one is a forgery.'[3] Exact correspondence either of signatures or narratives tends to prove the reverse of what it is intended to prove. Even if the discrepancies are large, as, for instance, the discrepancies between the appearances in Jerusalem and in Galilee might be said to be, it is to be remembered that secular history can easily parallel this. It is a notorious fact of ancient history that Polybius, the Greek historian, and Livy, the Latin historian, represent Hannibal in his invasion of Italy crossing the Alps by completely different routes, routes which can by no stretch of imagination be harmonised, yet no one doubts that Hannibal most certainly arrived in Italy. The discrepancy is there—but so is the quite undeniable fact. Discrepan-

[1] *Sanhedrin* 90 b.
[2] W. O. E. Oesterley, *The Doctrine of the Last Things,* p. 141.
[3] *More Tavern Talk,* p. 70.

cies in the accounts of the Resurrection cannot be used as evidence
to prove that the Resurrection did not take place.

It is further to be noted that it was not necessary to wait until
the nineteenth and twentieth centuries to find men of common sense,
and acute minds, and reputable scholarship reading the New Testament. The men who wrote the New Testament were not fools. They
were quite as able to recognize a discrepancy as we are! And yet they
left them there, thereby showing that they certainly did not seem to
them to invalidate the fact of the Resurrection.

Let us next look at the 'subjective vision' interpretation of the
Resurrection. In this case it is absolutely necessary to examine the
mental and emotional condition of the men who were alleged to
have had these subjective visions. Beyond a doubt the women were
on their way to the tomb to anoint and to pay the last tributes to the
body of a dead man (Luke 24.1,3; Matt. 28.1; Mark 16.1; John
20.2). The Gospel of Peter makes them say: 'Even if we were not
able to weep and to lament him on that day whereon he was
crucified, yet let us now do so at his tomb' (The Gospel of Peter
12.52). It was a dead body for which Mary was looking (John
20.13–15). For the disciples hope was dead, despair was in their
hearts, and fear had them in its grip. They had hoped that Jesus
would have been the one to redeem Israel—but no (Luke 24.21).
The doors of the place where they were meeting were locked and
barred for fear (John 20.19,26). The reaction of the women was
total amazement (Mark 16.8; Matt. 28.8). The news of the empty
tomb came to the disciples as an empty tale beyond belief (Luke
24.11). At the sight of Jesus they were not so much overjoyed as
terrified (Luke 24.37). The news seemed to them far too good to
be possibly true (Luke 24.41). They were prostrate with sorrow.
The Gospel of Peter makes Peter say: 'But I with my fellows was
in grief, and we were wounded in our minds, and would have hid
ourselves' (The Gospel of Peter 7.26). The Gospel of Peter shows
us the disciples weeping and grieved and going back to the boats
because there was nowhere else to go and nothing else to do, a situation which is very probably reflected in John 21 (The Gospel of
Peter 13.59,60; John 21.3).

Now in view of all this it is perfectly possible that given time,
given some weeks or even months of memory and of reflection, the

disciples might well have worked themselves into a state in which they read the lesson of Jewish history and saw God's purpose in disaster, but it is not possible that they should think themselves into that state overnight. If we are willing to spread the Resurrection events over, say, a year, as Renan in fact does, then the subjective vision interpretation is possible and even likely; but, if we accept the chronology of the Gospels and see the whole matter happening over a weekend, it is impossible. The subjective vision interpretation is an attempt to rationalise by a method that is itself unreasonable.

We may note one further significant fact. The Gospel narratives are far from deliberately spectacular and are far from piling wonder upon wonder. They are in fact astonishingly reticent and amazingly restrained. We can see how restrained the canonical Gospels are when we turn to the apocryphal Gospels and Acts. In the Acts of Pilate the rolling away of the stone takes place at midnight in the presence of the women and the terrified guard dazzled and blinded by the angelic lightning (Acts of Pilate 23). In the Gospel of Peter the guards pitch a tent and keep watch and there is a description of the actual event of the Resurrection. There was a great sound in heaven and two men descended from heaven, clothed in dazzling light, and approached the tomb. The stone was rolled away and knocked over on its side and the men entered the tomb. Then 'three men came out of the tomb, two of them sustaining the other, and a cross following after them. And of the two they saw that their heads reached unto heaven, but of him that was led by them that it overpassed the heavens.' And all this took place in the very presence of the terrified guards (The Gospel of Peter 9.35–42). The Latin manuscript Codex Bobbiensis (*k*) inserts an account of the event of the Resurrection between Mark 16.3 and 4. But suddenly at the third hour of the day there was darkness over the whole circle of the earth, and the angels descended from the heavens and rising in the glory of the living God they ascended with him, and straightway it was light.'

It is clear that we no sooner enter into the world of the apocryphal Gospels than we enter into the world of legend. We no sooner read them than we begin to see the reticence and the restraint of the canonical Gospels. Taken all in all, the narrative of the Gospels does not read like fiction or legend, and certainly does not pile wonder upon wonder. There are no doubt elaborations in it but its general atmosphere is an atmosphere of credibility.

What conclusions are we then to come to regarding the Resurrection of Jesus and regarding the form in which it took place?

That something happened is certain beyond all doubt; and the proof that something happened is the existence of the Christian Church. Had the disciples not been convinced that Jesus was not dead, but that he had conquered death and was alive for evermore, there would be no Christian Church today. After the crucifixion we see a company of hopeless, frightened, disappointed men, terrified that they would be involved in the same fate as him who had been their master, and with nothing but the desire to escape back to Galilee and to get back to their old jobs and forget. Fear, despair, flight—these were the things which filled the horizon of the disciples after the event of Calvary. This was their condition at the Passover time. Seven weeks later Pentecost came and we see these same men filled with a blazing hope and confidence, with a courage which defied the Sanhedrin and the mob alike. Every effect must have an adequate cause. And the only possible explanation of this astonishing change is that the disciples were firmly convinced that Jesus was alive. Seven weeks before they had been prepared to go away and forget—in which case there would have been no Christian Church. But now they are prepared to take on the impossible task of winning a world for Jesus Christ—and therefore the Church was born. And it all happened because something or some series of things had happened which convinced them that Jesus was still alive. We have only to contrast the picture of Peter denying his Master in his craven determination to save his own skin (Mark 14.66–72) with the picture of this same Peter two months later bidding the Sanhedrin to do its worst (Acts 4) to see this astonishing change epitomised; and the cause of that change was the conviction that Jesus had risen from the dead.

Acts has justly been called The Gospel of the Resurrection, and there is not a sermon in it in which the Resurrection is not at the centre of the preacher's message (Acts 2.24,32; 3.15,26; 4.10,33; 5.30; 10.40; 13.30–34; 17.31). The Resurrection, as it has been put, had become the star in the firmament of Christianity.

It is beyond dispute that the existence of the Church is due to the conviction of the disciples that Jesus had risen from the dead. It would be very difficult to believe that the beginning of the Church and the continued existence of the Church are based either on an hallucination or on an imposture. In view of the existence of the Church it is more difficult not to believe in the Resurrection than it is to believe in it.

But we must still ask one question—even although we know before we ask it that we can never answer it fully and completely. What was the nature of these appearances of Jesus which meant so much both to those who first received him and to the history of the Church, and, therefore, to the history of the world? Have we any evidence, any guidance, which will enable us to glimpse something of the character of these appearances?

The first list of Resurrection appearances is that given by Paul in I Corinthians 15.3–8, for I Corinthians was almost certainly written before the earliest of the Gospels. For the purposes of our present quest by far the most significant thing in that list is *the occurrence of Paul's name in it*. 'Last of all,' writes Paul, 'as to one untimely born, he appeared also to me' (I Cor. 15.8). Now this is to say that Paul in no way distinguished the appearance of Jesus to him from Jesus' appearance to Peter, to the twelve, to the five hundred and to James. 'Have I not seen Jesus our Lord?' he demands (I Cor. 9.1). This appearance to Paul took place about three years after the crucifixion, and, therefore, about three years after the other appearances which are cited. If that be so, it certainly was not a bodily and physical appearance of Jesus. The impression which the narratives of Paul's conversion on the Damascus road leave is two-fold (Acts 9.1–9; 22.1–16; 26.13–19). First, it was a manifestation of blinding light and of a voice, but not a physical appearance of Jesus. Second, it was private to Paul, for the travelling companions of Paul clearly did not know what was going on (Acts 9.7). The appearance of Jesus to Paul was a quite unmistakable manifestation that Jesus was triumphantly alive, but it was not a bodily appearance of Jesus, and yet it is included without question with the other appearances.

No sooner have we begun on this line of thought than another question arises. If Paul does not distinguish the appearance of Jesus Christ to him on the Damascus road from the appearances of Jesus as related in the Gospels, wherein do the appearances in the Gospels differ from the appearance to Stephen (Acts 7.55); the appearance to Ananias with the instructions regarding the reception of Paul (Acts 9.10–16); the later appearance when Jesus appeared to Paul in Ephesus to cheer and comfort his heart (Acts 18.9,10); the still later appearance in which the Lord appeared to Paul and assured him that he would yet reach, and preach in, Rome (Acts 23.11)? What is the difference between the appearances of Jesus as narrated in the Gospels and these appearances as related in Acts?

What is the difference between what we might call the original appearances of Jesus and the appearances to the saints in all ages? Take the case of Francis of Assisi. In his unsettlement and his unhappiness and his dissatisfaction with the fashionable life of earthly gallantry which he led, he was faced with the leper on the road. G. K. Chesterton describes the incident. 'Francis Bernardone saw his fear coming up the road towards him; the fear that comes from within and not without; though it stood white and horrible in the sunlight. For once in the long rush of his life his soul must have stood still. Then he sprang from his horse, knowing nothing between stillness and swiftness, and rushed on the leper and threw his arms round him. It was the beginning of a long vocation among many lepers, for whom he did many services; to this man he gave what money he could and mounted and rode on. We do not know how far he rode or with what sense of the things around him; *but it is said that when he looked back, he could see no figure on the road.*' And since then many have believed—as Francis believed—that it was Jesus Christ who appeared to him in that leper that day. Wherein does this differ from the appearances of the first days?

A. J. Gossip used to have two stories which he loved to tell and which none of his ex-students are likely to forget. The first was of Ramon Lull who lived at the turn of the thirteenth century, and who was once a courtier and a steward of kings, and who became a Franciscan, a defender of the faith and a missionary to the Moslems in North Africa. Ramon Lull would tell how he became what he became. Christ came to him once, carrying his Cross, and tried to place it in Ramon Lull's hands, saying: 'Carry this for me!' But Ramon Lull pushed him and his Cross away. A second time Christ came; a second time he tried to lay his Cross in Ramon Lull's hands, saying: 'Carry this for me!' and a second time Ramon Lull refused. A third time Christ came, and as Ramon Lull said: 'He took his Cross, he said no word, but with a look he left it in my hands. What could I do but take it up and carry it on?' Wherein, if in anything, does Ramon Lull's experience of Jesus Christ in person differ from the experiences which the New Testament records?

A. J. Gossip's second story was about himself, and Gossip was a saint of God. One week he had had a very busy week; time for preparation for Sunday had been very scarce, but to the best of his ability he had done what he could. On that Sunday morning, as he mounted the stairs of his pulpit in St Matthew's Church in Glasgow, as he rounded the bend in them, clearly and unmistakably he met Christ. And Christ said to him looking at the sermon in his hands: 'Is this the best that you could do?' Knowing of the week that lay behind, humbly yet sincerely Gossip said: 'Lord, it is.' And that Sunday that hastily prepared sermon became in his hands and by the grace of God a trumpet. No one who ever heard Gossip tell that story could doubt the reality of it. Wherein does an appearance of Christ like that differ from the appearances recorded in the Gospels?

We may put the question we are asking in another form: What, if any, is the difference between the risen Christ and the ever-living Christ? I do not think that in kind there is any difference, although I think that there is a difference in purpose. The first appearances of Jesus to his own were *evidential.* They were utterly necessary to convince his disciples that the Cross was not the end but the beginning, that he was still victoriously alive. Ever since, the appearances of the risen and ever-living Christ have been *sustaining, strengthening, renewing;* but the Christ who appears is the same.

We would not say that the way of the appearance is the same. At the very first the appearances were visible to those who loved him —and only to them with the single exception of Paul who was fighting against love—although whatever happened to the physical body of Jesus his resurrection body was more than physical. In the later days it was to the eye of faith and love that he appeared, but he did appear and still he does appear. The closing words of Albert Schweitzer's *The Quest of the Historical Jesus* still ring true: 'He comes to us as One unknown, without a name, as of old, by the lakeside, he came to those men who knew him not. He speaks to us the same word: "Follow thou me!" and sets us to the tasks which he has to fulfil for our time. He commands. And to those who obey him, whether they be wise or simple, he will reveal himself in the toils, the conflicts, the sufferings which they shall pass through in his fellowship, and, as an ineffable mystery, they shall learn in their own experience who he is.'[1]

The risen Christ and the ever-living Christ are one and the same. To the risen Christ the Church owed its beginning; to the ever-living Christ it owes its continued existence. That is why for the Christian the Resurrection is not so much an event in history, not even the greatest event in history, as a reality which has to be appropriated. And we shall find help for this act of personal appropriation, if we look at the Resurrection events, simply as the Gospels tell them, along three lines—what the risen Christ offered, where the risen Christ showed himself, and to whom the risen Christ appeared.

When the risen Jesus appeared to his followers, he offered them certain things.

(i) He offered them a *commission*. 'Go into all the world,' he said, 'and preach the gospel to the whole creation' (Mark 16.15). 'Go and make disciples of all nations' (Matt. 28.19). The commission of the risen Jesus is to go out and to make the kingdom of the world into the Kingdom of God.

(ii) He offered them a *task*. 'You shall be my witnesses,' he said, 'in Jerusalem and in all Judaea and Samaria and to the end of the earth' (Acts 1.8). The task of the Christian is to be by word and by life the witness of Jesus.

(iii) He offered them a *message*. They were to preach repentance and the remission of sins (Luke 24.47). They were to awaken men to the realization of the depth and urgency of their need, and then they were to point and lead them to the one in whom that need could be met.

(iv) He offered them *an explanation*. He opened the Scriptures to them, and showed them how these Scriptures pointed to himself (Luke 24.27, 44–46). Jesus opened the eyes of his people to the meaning of history and to the culmination of history in himself.

(v) He offered them a *promise*. 'Lo,' he said, 'I am with you

[1] *The Quest of the Historical Jesus,* 3rd edition, 1954, p. 401.

always, to the close of the age' (Matt. 28.20). 'You shall receive power,' he said, 'when the Holy Spirit has come upon you' (Acts 1.8). With the commission and the task he gave the power to carry them out.

We must now look at the places where the risen Jesus showed himself to men.

(i) He showed himself to men in the garden *beside the empty tomb* (Matt. 28.1–8; Mark 16.1–8; Luke 24.1–9; John 20.1–18). Beside that same tomb in which they had laid Jesus with broken hearts in the bitterness of death he appeared to them in the new-born radiance of glory. And by his appearing he turned death into victory and the shadows of the night into the joy of the morning.

(ii) He showed himself to them *as they travelled on the road* (Luke 24.13–30). When he met them, they were travelling in disillusionment; when he left them they were travelling in wonder. The road that led to nowhere became with the risen Jesus the road that led to glory. John Drinkwater wrote:

> Shakespeare is dust, and will not come
> To question from his Avon tomb,
> And Socrates and Shelley keep
> An Attic and Italian sleep.
>
> They see not. But, O Christians, who
> Throng Holborn and Fifth Avenue,
> May you not meet, in spite of death
> A traveller from Nazareth?

(iii) He showed himself to men *in the cottage home* (Luke 24.28–31). It was in the breaking of bread, not a sacramental service, but in a village house that he was known to them. 'Where two or three are gathered in my name,' he said, 'there am I in the midst of them' (Matt. 18.20). And it has been beautifully suggested that the two or three are father, mother and child. The fact of the risen Jesus turns every common house into a temple.

(iv) He showed himself *on the lakeside to men who were at their fishing* (John 21). Not in the Temple, not in the synagogue, not in any so-called holy place or sacred shrine, but in the day's work he came to them. There is a saying of Jesus, not in the gospels but surely genuine: 'Cleave the wood and you will find me, raise the stone and I am there.' The meaning is that when the carpenter is working with the wood and the mason with the stone Jesus is there. Because of the risen Christ all work has become worship.

(v) He showed himself to men *in the upper room,* where they were sitting in sheer terror and in bleak despair (Mark 16.14; Luke 24.36–39; John 20.19–29). He came when they had lost their courage and when they had lost their faith, and by his coming the fear was turned into confidence and the despair into hope. But one thing is to be noted—they were waiting *together* and they were waiting, as we may assume, in the *upper room* where they had companied with Jesus. We are likeliest of all to meet the risen Christ when we wait in fellowship, and when we wait in some place which has been consecrated by his presence.

The risen Jesus by his appearances banished the sorrow of death, turned every common road into the road to glory, sanctified the home, consecrated work, and defeated despair.

Finally, we must see to whom the risen Jesus appeared, and it may well be that we shall find this study the most illuminating of all.

(i) He appeared to *love.* The accounts of the Crucifixion and of the Resurrection may differ in detail in the different Gospels, but in the centre of the picture of every one of them stands Mary Magdalene. She was there at the foot of the cross (Matt. 27.56; Mark 15.40; John 19.25). She was there when they laid Jesus in the tomb (Matt. 27.61; Mark 15.47). She was the first to be there on the Resurrection morning even before the first streaks of dawn had come (Matt. 28.1; Mark 16.1; Luke 24.10; John 20.1). In Mary Magdalene is personified the love and the devotion of one who owed everything to Jesus, and who knew it. It is of the greatest significance that the first appearance of Jesus was to one whose only claim was love.

(ii) He appeared to *sorrowing penitence.* As far as we can work it out, the second appearance of Jesus was to Peter (Luke 24.34; I Cor. 15.5; cp. Mark 16.7). There is no shame of penitence so bitter and so deep in all the New Testament as there was in that moment when Peter after his denial of his Lord flung himself out and wept his heart out (Matt. 26.75; Mark 14.72; Luke 22.62). The astonishing thing is that Peter was there with his fellow-disciples at all. A man of lesser moral fibre would never have been able to meet the eyes of his fellow-men. Jesus appeared to Peter to save him from too much self-torture, from too much self-hatred, from too much despair. Here is enshrined the precious truth that Jesus makes a personal visit of forgiveness and of reconciliation to every penitent heart.

(iii) He appeared to *bewildered seeking*. He appeared to the two on the road to Emmaus when they were talking of the things which had happened in Jerusalem, and when they were seeking to find some explanation for the tragedy for which there seemed to be no explanation (Luke 24.14–21). This story must be read with great care to find the full meaning of it. At first it sounds like a story of sheer despair. He in whom they had set their hopes as the redeemer and deliverer of Israel had been hounded to a cross, and it seemed that all their hopes were dust and ashes. But the whole point of the story is that *they were still talking about Jesus*. Bewildered they might be, but they could not forget. Shattered their world might be, but somewhere at the heart of it there was still this Jesus. There are times when a man cannot understand; there are times when life is a dark mystery and when there are problems which are so immense that they defy all solution; there are times when in face of this distracted world the work of Jesus seems failure. But if at the heart of our personal world there still remains this Jesus, if he is still quite unforgettable, if he refuses to be banished from the mind and from the heart, then in the end he comes—and the darkness becomes light.

(iv) He appeared to *utter despair and to desperate fear*. That was the attitude of the disciples in the upper room, when Jesus came back to them (Luke 24.36–41; John 20.19). Their nerves were in such a jangle of terror that they were even terrified when he appeared to them (Luke 24.37). They had reached the ultimate depths of fear and hopelessness and despair. But, as Neville Talbot put it, 'When you get to the bottom, you find God.' They had reached bottom, but they were still thinking about Jesus, they were still haunted by Jesus, he was somehow still the centre of their lives. Jesus still comes to those who even in fear and despair cannot help remembering and cannot stop loving him.

(v) He came to *doubt*, for Jesus appeared specially for the sake of Thomas (John 20.24–29). There is doubt and doubt. There is a kind of clever doubt which takes a pride in its scepticism; there is a kind of intellectual society in which it is rather discreditable to profess anything other than agnosticism. There is a kind of comfortable agnosticism which enjoys a twilight of not unpleasant uncertainty. But there is also a doubt which is a desperate and a passionate thing, a doubt which is an agony of spirit, because it matters so much to be sure, a doubt which is a matter of life and death. That was the state of Thomas. The doubt of Thomas did not spring from the intellectual superiority which prefers not to commit itself, but from the desperate need and desire to believe. At such a time if a man continues to ask his questions, if he continues his desperate struggle for certainty, the risen Jesus will come back to him.

(vi) He appeared to two men *who were fighting a last ditch battle against him*. He appeared to James, one of his brothers who did not believe in him (John 7.5; I Cor. 15.7); and, above all, he appeared to Paul (I Cor. 15.8; Acts 9.1–9; 22.1–11; 26.1–18). There is nothing so very surprising about this. James and especially Paul took Jesus seriously enough to hate him. Here was no vague neutrality, no serene indifference; here was flaming opposition to some one who had to be taken with immense and enormous seriousness. So long as a man takes Jesus seriously, even if he opposes Jesus to the last ditch, there always remains the chance that Jesus will break in upon him. Against indifference little or nothing can be done; but, if a man disbelieves intensely, there is still the possibility that he may yet believe equally intensely. The man who takes Jesus seriously can never tell when the risen Jesus will at last confront him and break the barriers down.

(vii) Lastly, Jesus appeared to *the assembled disciples* (Acts 1.4–8). We may well say that this was his first appearance to his Church. When men are assembled for worship and for prayer, it is then that the risen Jesus can always appear among them.

There are few better attested facts in history than the Resurrection of Jesus. And what the risen Jesus once did, he still does. He comes in answer to love; he comes with forgiveness to the heart in penitence and shame; he comes to the bewildered yet still seeking mind; he comes when despair and fear have reached the bottom, and have still not succeeded in forgetting him; he comes when doubt is agonizing because the need of certainty is so imperative; he comes to the man who takes him seriously, even if that man hates him; he comes to his own worshipping people in his own Church.

29

THE ASCENSION

It may be said that there is no incident in the life of Jesus at one and the same time so beset with difficulties and so essential as the Ascension.

The actual New Testament evidence for the Ascension is very meagre. The only unquestioned evidence for it is in Acts 1.1–12. It is briefly mentioned in Mark 16.19: 'So the Lord Jesus, after he had spoken to them, was taken up into heaven, and sat down at the right hand of God.' But it is quite certain that Mark 16.9–20 is not an original part of Mark's Gospel, and, therefore, cannot be taken as first-hand evidence for the Ascension. In Luke 24.51 the Authorized Version reads: 'And it came to pass, while he blessed them, he was parted from them, and carried up into heaven.' But it is a matter of considerable uncertainty whether or not the phrase 'and was carried up into heaven' is part of the original text. The Revised Version notes that it is doubtful; Moffatt encloses it in brackets; and the Revised Standard Version relegates it to a footnote. Even if Luke 24.51 was unquestionably accepted as evidence for the Ascension, the difficulty would still remain that on any natural reading of the whole chapter it seems to place the Ascension on the same day as the Resurrection and not forty days after it as Acts 1.1–12 does.

It is further strange that in certain semi-credal passages of the New Testament the Ascension is omitted, and the impression left is that Jesus passed straight from Resurrection to exaltation. In Rom. 8.34 Paul speaks of Christ Jesus who *died*, who was *raised* from the dead, and who *is at the right hand of God*. In I Cor. 15.3–5 Paul speaks of Christ who *died* for our sins, was *buried*, and was *raised* on the third day, and *appeared* to Cephas and to the

others. In these passages, where we would expect a clear reference
to the Ascension, we do not in fact find one.

It is nevertheless quite clear that this is one of the many occasions
when it would be quite wrong to place any weight on the argument
from silence. The rest of the New Testament makes it quite clear
that the Ascension was an integral part of Christian belief. In the
Fourth Gospel Jesus says: 'What if you were to see the Son of man
ascending where he was before?' (John 6.62). In the same Gospel
Jesus says to Mary Magdalene: 'Do not hold me, for I have not yet
ascended to the Father; but go to my brethren and say to them, I
am ascending to my Father and your Father, to my God and your
God' (John 20.17). In the New Testament letters there are unmistakable references to the Ascension. In Ephesians we read: 'He who
descended is he who also ascended far above all the heavens, that
he might fill all things' (Eph. 4.10-10). The writer to the Hebrews
speaks of Jesus as 'a great high priest who has passed through the
heavens' (Heb. 4.14); he speaks of Jesus as 'exalted above the
heavens' (Heb. 7.26). Peter speaks of Jesus who has 'gone into
heaven and is at the right hand of God' (I Peter 3.22). In I Timothy
there is part of a very early Christian hymn which says of Jesus:

> He was manifested in the flesh,
> vindicated in the Spirit,
> seen by angels,
> believed on in the world
> taken up in glory (I Tim. 3.16).

There is no lack of evidence that the Ascension was an essential
part of the Christian picture of Jesus.

There is another series of passages which fit into this picture.
These are the passages which speak of Jesus as being *at the right
hand of God*. Jesus himself quoted Ps. 110.1, which is the basis of
all these passages:

> 'The Lord said to my Lord,
> Sit at my right hand,
> till I put thy enemies under thy feet'
>   (Matt. 22.44).

This is again quoted in Peter's sermon in Acts 2.33f.; cp. 3.21; 5.31;
7.56. Paul speaks of God highly exalting Jesus (Phil. 2.9), and of

God setting Jesus Christ at his own right hand in the heavenly places (Eph. 1.20). He speaks of Christ sitting on the right hand of God (Col. 3.1), and of Christ as risen and at the right hand of God (Rom. 8.34). The writer to the Hebrews says of Jesus that, after he had completed his earthly work, he sat down on the right hand of the Majesty on high (1.3); he speaks of him as being crowned with glory and honour (2.9); he speaks of Jesus as the high priest who is set on the right hand of the throne of the Majesty in heaven (8.1); he speaks of Jesus enduring the cross and despising the shame, and being set down at the right hand of the throne of God (12.2). The John of the Revelation speaks of Jesus as sharing the throne of God (Rev. 3.21). It is the warning of Jesus to his accusers that they will see the Son of Man sitting on the right hand of Power (Mark 14.62). It is easy to see that there is no stratum of New Testament thought which does not picture the exaltation of Jesus, and the exaltation necessarily involves the Ascension.

We may finally note that the Ascension is clearly a part of the creed of the early Church. It is embedded in the Apostles' Creed, which may well have expressed the baptismal confession of faith in the Roman Church in the second century. Aristides says of Jesus that he went up into the heavens;[1] Irenaeus declares that it is the belief of the Church throughout the world that the flesh of Jesus was taken up into heaven;[2] Tertullian declares that it was his own belief and the belief of the Church that he who rose from the dead was carried up or taken back into heaven.[3]

However brief and meagre the direct evidence for the Ascension may be, it is certain that the Ascension is an integral part of the New Testament picture of Jesus and an essential part of the belief of the early Church.

There is still another point in which there has been difference in the interpretation of the narrative. According to the narrative in Acts there were forty days between the death of Jesus and his final Ascension (Acts 1.3). In the arrangement of the Christian year this forty days is taken quite literally, and Ascension Day falls on the sixth Thursday after Easter. But it must be remembered that

[1] *Apology* 2.
[2] *Against Heresies* 1.10.1.
[3] *Against Praxeas* 2.

in Hebrew terminology *forty days* is a phrase which is not intended
to be arithmetically accurate, but which simply describes a considerable period of time. In English we use the two phrases *ten days*
and *a month* to express a longer or a shorter period without con-
fining ourselves to actual calendar accuracy. In the Bible the phrase
'forty days' is used of the period of the flood (Gen. 7.12,17); of the
stay of Moses in Mount Sinai to receive the law (Ex. 24.18); and of
the time of Jesus' temptations in the wilderness (Matt. 4.2). The
phrase 'forty days' simply means some considerable time. In the
days of the early Church the Valentinians held that there were
eighteen months between the Resurrection and the Ascension; the
Ophites held that there were eleven or twelve years; Eusebius men-
tions the belief that the length of Jesus' ministry after the Resurrection was the same as the length of his ministry before the Resurrection. We may simply say that Jesus spent a considerable length of
time with his disciples between his Resurrection and his Ascension.

To the modern mind one of the greatest difficulties in the Ascension is the word 'ascension' itself. In Acts 1.11 the Ascension is described by the word *analambanein,* which means 'to take up'; in
Acts 1.9 it is described by the word *epairein,* which means 'to lift up';
although the words are different, the picture is the same. The modern objection to this is that these words come from a belief which
thinks of a three-storey universe, in which the earth is in the middle, heaven above the sky and therefore literally upwards, Hades
beneath the earth and therefore literally downwards. It is significant
to note that this very word *analambanein* is used in the Greek Old
Testament about two men whose deaths were strange and mysterious. It is used of Elijah, who went up by a whirlwind into heaven
(II Kings 2.11); and in Ecclesiasticus it is used of both Elijah and
Enoch, who were taken up from the earth (Ecclus. 48.9; 49.14).
The fact is that no one writing in either Old Testament or New
Testament times would think in any other way. If anyone in those
days wished to describe a mysterious ending to a life which was victorious over death, there is no other way of speaking which he could
use. We do not need to literalize this picture; we do not know what
actually happened at the time of the Ascension. It is not the picture
which is important but the truth behind the picture. The picture
is only the symbolic envelope of the truth. Let us, then, after facing

all the difficulties, try to think positively about the meaning of the Ascension.

It must be clear that the Ascension was an absolute necessity. It was in the first place necessary that Jesus should remain visibly with his disciples for some time after his Resurrection. That was necessary in order that they might be truly and fully convinced that he was alive, that his legacy to them was not, as some one has put it, 'dead and inoperative information', but a living presence. It was necessary, as Denney says, that there should be a time in which Jesus instructed his disciples in the Christian meaning of the Old Testament, in the universality of the gospel, and in the promise of the Spirit. But it is equally clear that it was absolutely necessary that that period should come to an end. Jesus could not go on making personal appearances to his men, for that would have meant that, though he truly belonged to the spiritual world, he was still limited to visible, personal appearances. Nor would it have been right that such appearances should become fewer and fewer, and so drift indeterminately and undecidedly to a close. This special time must definitely *end,* and not fade out. Some quite definite end to the interim period after the Resurrection was necessary; and Denney is right when he calls the Ascension 'a point of transition'.

Still further, something which could only be called an Ascension had to happen. A. J. Maclean points out that Jesus could not remain for ever visibly with his disciples, that clearly he could not die all over again, and that therefore the end had to come in *glorification* and not in *dissolution.* However we look at this, some terminating event had to happen, and that event is the Ascension.

From all this it is clear that the right place for the Ascension is not at the end of the story of the Gospels but at the beginning of the Acts. In one sense the Ascension closes a chapter, but in another and an even greater sense it begins a new chapter, for the Ascension is the necessary prelude to the events of Pentecost and to the coming of the Holy Spirit. The Ascension is the necessary conclusion of one part of Jesus' ministry and the equally necessary introduction to the next and even greater part of that ministry.

Still further, the Ascension is the *enthronement* of Jesus. It was, as Denney puts it, his enthroning 'in reality and not in imagination'.

Jesus ascended in order to reign. As Paul has it: 'He must reign until he has put all his enemies under his feet' (I Cor. 15.25). He was raised 'far above all rule and authority and power and dominion, not only in this age, but in that which is to come' (Eph. 1.21). Jesus had to ascend into heaven to begin his universal rule and kingdom and dominion.

So far we have looked at the Ascension, as it were, from the point of view of Jesus. For him it was the transition from his ministry upon earth to his glory in heaven. It was the end of one stage and the beginning of another. It was his final enthronement after the humiliation of the Cross and the triumph of the Resurrection. But there is something in the Ascension of infinite preciousness for us also. It is the consistent belief of the New Testament that Jesus ascended to make intercession for us. It is Christ who is at the right hand of God who indeed intercedes for us (Rom. 8.34). He always lives to make intercession for us (Heb. 7.25). He appears in the presence of God on our behalf (Heb. 9.24). In him we have an advocate in the presence of God (I John 2.1). He is the mediator who stands between man and God to bring man and God together, and he continues that mediating work in the presence of God (Heb. 8.6; 12.24; I Tim. 2.1,5). Jesus ascended, not to end his work for men, but to continue his work for men, that in this or in any other world he may still carry on his ministry of intercession and mediation for men.

There remains still one other consequence of the Ascension which it may be that we can only dimly grasp and understand. It is the great truth of Christianity that the Christian shares in all the experiences of his Lord. In the Ascension the manhood of Jesus was taken up into the heavenly places, and, therefore, our manhood will also be so taken up. As Denney finely says, the Ascension is the proof that manhood is destined for heaven and not for the grave, that manhood is destined, not for dissolution but for glory. Here is the answer to the hope which Tennyson expressed:

> Thou wilt not leave us in the dust;
> Thou madest man, he knows not why;
> He thinks he was not made to die;
> And Thou hast made him; Thou art just.

It may be that we may end our study of the Ascension by remembering a hint and a suggestion which certain writers have reverently made. It may be that the days between the Resurrection and the Ascension were necessary for Jesus too, that it was for him a time of the increasing spiritualization of his earthly body until he could ascend to the glory of God. The Authorized Version translates John 20.17: '*I ascend* unto my Father and your Father, unto my God and your God.' But the Revised Standard Version translates it perfectly correctly: '*I am ascending* to my Father and your Father, to my God and your God.' *I am ascending*—it may well be that this means that the Ascension was not so much an event, as a process reaching to a culmination. Of this conception we can only say that we do not know whether or not it is true, but maybe we may see in it the foretaste and example of that which life should be for everyone of us—a long development through grace until in the end we too are taken up to God. It may be that we may think of this in terms of Charles Wesley's lines:

> Changed from glory into glory,
>   Till in heaven we take our place,
> Till we cast our crowns before Thee
>   Lost in wonder, love, and praise.

30

JESUS CHRIST IS LORD

It is the experience of life that we have to live long with a person before we can know him in any real sense of the term. It is also the experience of life that the most valuable people in life are not the shallow people who carry all their goods in the shop window, but the people whose character and kindness, whose personality and wisdom grow more and more precious the longer we know them. This was necessarily the experience of the Christian Church and of the individual Christian in regard to Jesus Christ. The longer men think about Jesus the greater he becomes; and the longer they live with him the more they know that no human categories can contain him.

One of the great practical problems of the early Church was to find a name and a title for Jesus which would at least in some sense sum up what they held him to be. 'Son of Man' is an obscure title only intelligible after a study of Jewish intertestamental literature. 'Son of David' and 'Messiah' are titles immediately intelligible to a Jew, but meaningless to a Greek without a long course of preliminary instruction. 'Son of God' was a title too liable to be read in terms of Greek mythology, and too suggestive of the Greek demigods and of the Greek heroes who were the children of the unions of immortal gods with mortal men. But in the end the Church did find its great title for Jesus Christ, and that title is the title LORD, in Greek *kurios*. The word *kurios* occurs in the New Testament well over six hundred times, and, of these six hundred odd times, more than three hundred occur in the writings of Paul.

The application of this title to Jesus was a growth and a development. It may be said as a general rule that Jesus did not become known as *kurios*, Lord, until after his Resurrection, and that after his Resurrection *kurios* became the great Christian title for him.

It is unfortunate that this is a fact which the Authorized Version very badly obscures. We shall very soon go on to study the meanings of the word *kurios;* when we do so, we shall find that *kurie,* the vocative case of the word, that is, the case used in addressing other people, is the commonest of all Greek expressions of respect, and is used as 'Sir' is used in English. Many and many a time in the Gospels Jesus is addressed as *kurie,* but the meaning is far nearer 'Sir' or 'Master' than 'Lord'; and any modern translation will show this in the Gospels. To take an example, both the Syro-Phoenician woman and the Samaritan woman address Jesus as *kurie* (Mark 7.28; Matt. 15.27; John 4.11), but it is quite obvious that, meeting Jesus for the first time, they cannot be using the word in the same sense as Paul uses it after years of living with the risen Christ.

The really significant use of *kurios* is not so much when it is used in address to Jesus, in which case it need mean no more than 'Sir', but when it is used of him in narrative, when he is referred to as 'the Lord' by the person who is writing or speaking of him. This use occurs hardly at all in Mark and Matthew; it is beginning to occur in Luke and in John; but in Paul it is regular and constant. For Paul, and for the early Church in its wider aspect, Jesus is distinctively and characteristically 'the Lord'.

So much so is this the case that 'Jesus Christ is Lord' became nothing less than the creed of the early Church. It is Paul's dream, and Paul believes that it is God's dream, that a day will come when every tongue will confess that Jesus Christ is Lord (Phil. 2.11). The confession that Jesus Christ is Lord, and the belief in the Resurrection, are necessary elements in salvation (Rom. 10.9). It is only in and through the Holy Spirit that a man can say that Jesus Christ is Lord (I Cor. 12.3). Paul does not preach himself but Jesus Christ as Lord (II Cor. 4.5). There is one Lord, Jesus Christ (I Cor. 8.6). There is one Lord, one faith, and one baptism (Eph. 4.5). The Christian in his heart must reverence Christ as Lord (I Peter 3.15). The Christian Church distilled its experience of Jesus Christ in the word Lord. The word Lord became a one-word creed, a one-word summary of belief. It is clearly an imperative duty to investigate the meaning of this word which to the Christian Church became the distinctive title of Jesus Christ. *Kurios* is a word with a wide and ascending range of meanings.

(i) *Kurios* is the normal word of respect and courtesy in address to other people. It is the exact Greek equivalent of the English Sir, the French *Monsieur,* and the German *Herr.* In the Parable of the Two Sons the superficially polite, but actually disobedient, son answers his father's request by saying: 'I go, sir,' and the word for 'sir' is *kurios* (Matt. 21.30). This is the commonest of all uses of the word *kurios.*

(ii) In letters *kurios* is used much as in English we use the phrase 'My dear'. The soldier Apion begins his letter to his father Epimachus with greetings to 'his father and lord' (*kurios*), as we would say in English 'My dear father'.[1] Apollinarius begins his letter home with many greetings to 'his mother and lady' (*kuria*), as we would say in English, 'My dear mother'.[2] There is one possible example of this usage in the New Testament. II John begins: 'The elder to the elect lady.' *Lady* is *kuria,* and this is most likely the same kind of address. In English it would be, 'My dear elect one'. *Kurios* is the word of affectionate and respectful greeting.

(iii) *Kurios* very commonly means 'owner'. It is used of the owner of the vineyard and the owner of the colt (Matt. 20.8; 21.40; Mark 12.9; Luke 19.33; 20.13,15).

(iv) *Kurios* is the regular word for 'master' in contradistinction to servant or slave. No man can serve two masters, two *kurioi* (Matt. 6.24). Earthly masters (*kurioi*) are warned of their duty to the servants and the slaves over whom they have authority, and must treat others in the constant awareness that Christ is their *kurios* (Eph. 6.5,9; Col. 3.22; 4.1).

(v) *Kurios* is the regular word for 'the head of the household'. No one, says Epictetus, can come into a well-ordered household from the outside and proceed to issue orders; if he does the *kurios,* the head of the house, will speedily have him ejected.[3] The father's authority over his daughter is expressed by calling him *kurios.*[4]

(vi) In Greek legal agreements and contracts entered into by a woman, the woman is regularly accompanied and represented by her *kurios,* who is her 'guardian'. In a marriage contract Thermion, daughter of Apion, has with her her guardian Apollonius.[5] In a

---

[1] A. S. Hunt and G. C. Edgar, *Select Papyri* vol. i, p. 304.
[2] *Select Papyri* vol. i, p. 302.
[3] Epictetus, *Discourses* 3.22.3.
[4] Aristotle, *Rhetoric* 2.24.8 (1042a 1).
[5] *Select Papyri* vol. i, p. 10.

deed of divorce Thaesis has with her as her guardian Onnophris her step-father.[1] The *kurios* is the guardian and the protector of those whose helplessness needs protection, if their rights are to be conserved.

(vii) It can be seen from these usages of the word that *kurios* is specially and particularly the word of *authority*. It is used of those who have the right to make military decisions and to despatch troops in war.[2] It is used of the magistrate who has the authority to impose the death penalty.[3] It describes a law which cannot be broken, a decision which is valid and binding, a decree which is authoritative, a treaty which has been ratified.[4] It is so used when it is said that the Son of Man is lord (*kurios*) of the Sabbath (Mark 2.28). The word *kurios* is a word which has the atmosphere of authority around it and about it.

Even if the meaning of the word *kurios* went no further than the stage to which we have reached, *kurios* would be a great word, but there are still three further meanings of the word.

(viii) *Kurios* became through time the standard title of the Roman Emperor. This was the process of a growth. In the West people were hesitant to use the word of the Emperor, and the Emperor was hesitant to permit it and still more hesitant to demand it. The reason was that in the West, at least in theory, the Empire remained a democracy, and the word *kurios* had too much of the suggestion of the relationship of master and slave to be palatable. In the East it was very different. There the relationship between king and subject had always been much that of master and slave, and there the word *kurios* was early used of the Emperor. But as time went on, and in particular as the Emperor came to be regarded as a god, the use of the word *kurios* spread more and more widely, until by the time of Domitian, towards the end of the first century AD, *kurios* was the regular title of the Emperor. It was the title which appeared at the head of laws, edicts and decrees, and which appeared on coins. It becomes very common on legal papyri in dates. An edict is dated in such and such a year—the number is

[1] *Selected Papyri* vol. i, p. 24.
[2] Thucydides 4.20; 5.63; 8.5.
[3] Plato, *Critias* 120 D.
[4] Aristotle, *Politics* 1286a 24; Plato, *Crito* 50 B; Demosthenes 24.1; Lysias 18.15.

missing—of Hadrianus Caesar the lord. A complaint is dated 'year 33 of Aurelius Commodus Caesar the lord'. A census return is dated 'the ninth year of Antoninus Caesar the lord'.[1] *Kurios* grew to be the accepted title of imperial majesty.

(ix) *Kurios* came to be the word and title regularly prefixed to the names of gods and goddesses. Apion the Roman recruit writes to his father Epimachus: 'I thank the lord Serapis that when I was in danger on the sea he straightway saved me.'[2] An invitation to dinner runs: 'Chaeremon invites you to dine at the table of the lord Serapis in the Temple of Serapis tomorrow.'[3] *Kurios* became more and more the word of divinity, the word which was the title of a god.

(x) So *kurios* comes to its final step. In the Septuagint, the Greek version of the Hebrew Old Testament, *kurios* is the word which is regularly used to translate the name of God, Yahweh or Jehovah, and so *kurios* became nothing less than the name of God. In the New Testament it is so used at least one hundred and fifty times (e.g. Luke 2.9; 4.18).

Deissmann is right when he says of *kurios* that it was 'a divine predicate intelligible to the whole eastern world'.

It is now plain to see what a man ought to mean when he calls Jesus Lord, or when he speaks of the Lord Jesus, or the Lord Jesus Christ. When I call Jesus Lord, I ought to mean that he is the absolute and undisputed owner and possessor of my life, and that he is the Master, whose servant and slave I must be all my life long. When I call Jesus Lord, it ought to mean that I think of him as the head of that great family in heaven and in earth of which God is the Father, and of which I through him have become a member. When I call Jesus Lord, it ought to mean that I think of him as the help of the helpless and the guardian of those who have no other to protect them. When I call Jesus Lord, it ought to mean that I look on him as having absolute authority over all my life, all my thoughts, all my actions. When I call Jesus Lord, it ought to mean that he is the King and Emperor to whom I owe and give my constant homage, allegiance and loyalty. When I call Jesus Lord, it ought to mean that for me he is the Divine One whom I must for ever worship and adore.

[1] *Select Papyri* vol. ii, pp. 110, 276, 336.
[2] *Select Papyri* vol. i, p. 304.
[3] M. David and B. A. van Groningen, *Papyrological Primer*, p. 155.

When we remember what this word Lord means, and what we ought to mean when we take it upon our lips, we must feel something very like horror at the glib unthinking way in which it is so often used, and we must hesitate and shrink to take it on our lips, lest the speaking of it is for us nothing less than a lie. When we remember the meaning of this word Lord, and when we remember how irreverently and unthinkingly it is bandied about in the Church, then there comes a new meaning into the saying of Jesus which Matthew hands down: 'Not every one who says to me, "Lord, Lord", shall enter the kingdom of heaven, but he who does the will of my Father who is in heaven' (Matt. 7.21).

The word Lord is a one-word creed, a one-word expression of complete devotion, a one-word expression of reverence and adoration. There is little wonder that it was the word in which the Church summed up its belief in Jesus Christ, and one of the Church's most clamant needs today is the rediscovery of its meaning, and the cessation of the empty use of the greatest name of Jesus Christ.

So then the early Church summed up and affirmed its faith and belief in Jesus in the phrase 'Jesus Christ is Lord'. From this there emerges a question which it was entirely natural that thinking men should ask. When did Jesus become Lord? When did he enter into his Lordship? Or, to put it in a wider and more comprehensive way, when did Jesus enter into that unique relationship with God which made him Lord? To that question more than one answer was given, and to look at the various answers is to see how the reverence of the Church for Jesus increased more and more, and to see how the Church struggled to find some way in which that reverence could be not entirely inadequately stated and expressed.

(i) Sometimes the Lordship of Christ is connected with the Resurrection. Paul speaks of Jesus as being 'designated Son of God in power according to the Spirit of holiness by his resurrection from the dead' (Rom. 1.4). Here the idea is that it was the Resurrection which gave Jesus the supreme right to the title of Son of God and Lord; it was the Resurrection which above all proved and attested and guaranteed what he was.

(ii) Sometimes the special relationship of Jesus to God is, as we might put it, dated from his baptism. At the baptism the voice which came to Jesus said: 'Thou art my beloved Son; with thee I am well pleased' (Mark 1.11; Luke 3.22; Matt. 3.17). But in Luke certain manuscripts, Codex Bezae in the Greek and Codex Vercellensis and Veronensis in the Old Latin, and certain of the early Fathers record that the words of the divine voice were: 'Thou art my beloved Son; today I have begotten thee', which indeed makes the whole saying a quotation from the coronation Psalm (Ps. 2.7). If we were to accept this reading, it would mean that Jesus was a man specially prepared and trained and equipped by God throughout the years, a man who had proved himself, and disciplined himself throughout the years, until the time had come when he was ready and fit to be specially *adopted* by God to be in a unique sense his son, and in a unique sense to do his work. This is in fact the foundation of what is known as adoptionist Christology. The basic idea is that for thirty years the man Jesus was trained and equipped by God, that for thirty years the man Jesus proved himself in the life and work of the world, so that at the moment of the baptism he could be specially adopted by God as his Son to carry out his purposes. That is in fact a view of Jesus which has always attracted some thinkers.

(iii) Some have held that Jesus entered into his special relationship with God when he was a boy of twelve in the Temple. He stayed behind and listened to the wise men. Joseph and Mary sought him worried and anxious; they found him. Then Mary said to him: 'Son, why have you treated us so? Behold, your father and I have been looking for you anxiously.' And Jesus answered: 'How is it that you sought me? Did you not know that I must be in my Father's house?' (Luke 2.48f.). There, it is said, Jesus very gently but very firmly took the name of father from Joseph and gave it to God, for in the experience of those days he had entered into his own unique relationship with God. It would not be argued that at that time his experience of God was complete; but it would be argued that it was at that time that Jesus first discovered it.

(iv) But instinctively men sought to push further and further back this special relationship of Jesus with God. This is the whole point of the story and the doctrine of the Virgin Birth. The aim of that story is to say that Jesus did not achieve his special relationship to God, but that he was born with it.

It is worth while to list the difficulties which a literal interpretation of the story of the Virgin Birth involves.

(*a*) Both the genealogies of Jesus (Matt. 1.1–17; Luke 3.23–38) trace the lineage of Jesus through Joseph and not through Mary. It is quite clear that the compilers of these genealogies were seeking to prove that Jesus was the son of David because he was the son of Joseph. In these genealogies Mary is never even mentioned, other than to say that Joseph was her husband (Matt. 1.16).

(*b*) If the Virgin Birth story be taken literally, it is difficult, if not impossible, to hold that Jesus was the son of David, for Mary was the kinswoman of Elisabeth, the mother of John the Baptizer (Luke 1.36), and Elisabeth was 'of the daughters of Aaron' (Luke 1.5). If Jesus was the son of Mary alone, he was of Aaronic and not of Davidic descent.

(*c*) The New Testament writers freely speak of Joseph and Mary as Jesus' parents (Luke 2.27; 2.41). They speak of Jesus' father and mother (Luke 2.33). It is to be noted that the later and less good manuscripts change *father and mother* in Luke 2.33 into *Joseph and his mother,* and change *his parents* in Luke 2.43 into *Joseph and his mother* as the difference between the Authorized Version and the Revised Standard Version in these passages show. The changes are due to the desire of the later scribes to maintain the Virgin Birth and to avoid calling Joseph the father of Jesus. But the early writers had no such scruples. 'Is not this the carpenter's son?' is the question of the people of Nazareth (Matt. 13.55). 'Is not this Joseph's son?' (Luke 4.22). John can write about Philip calling Jesus, 'Jesus of Nazareth, the son of Joseph' (John 1.45). 'Is not this Jesus, the son of Joseph,' the people say, 'whose father and mother we know?' (John 6.42). In Mark 3.21,31–35 we find Jesus' friends and Mary among them coming to bring Jesus home because they regarded him as mad. Is it really likely that Mary would say: 'Your father and I have been looking for you anxiously', if she know that Joseph was in no sense the father of her son? (Luke 2.48). The Gospel writers speak so very naturally about Joseph as the father of Jesus that it is difficult to think that they meant anything else than what they were saying.

(*d*) When we study the text of the New Testament, we find under the immediate surface a strong strand of thought which was at least unaware of the Virgin Birth.

There are three passages in the birth stories where this becomes clear. The Syriac Version is one of the earliest of all the versions of the New Testament, and in Matt. 1.16 it reads: 'Joseph, to whom was bethrothed Mary the Virgin, begat Jesus, who is called the Christ.' The Old Latin fifth-century manuscript, Codex Veronensis, entirely omits Luke 1.34: 'And Mary said to the angel: "How can this be, since I have no husband?" ' and substitutes in its place Luke 1.38: 'And Mary said: "Behold, I am the handmaid of the Lord; let it be to me according to your Word." ' This substitution completely excises the Virgin Birth from the narrative of Luke. In Luke 2.5 the reading of most of the manuscripts is that Joseph went to Bethlehem 'with Mary his *betrothed* who was with child'. But the Sinaitic Syriac, and four Old Latin manuscripts, Codex Vercellensis (fourth century), Codex Veronensis (fifth century), Codex Colbertinus (twelfth century), and Codex Corbeiensis II (fifth century), all read, not *betrothed,* but *wife.* All this is to say that in the background, and in the very early background, there is a strand of tradition which does not include the Virgin Birth.

(*e*) There is no mention of the Virgin Birth outside Matthew and Luke. There is no mention of the Virgin Birth in Paul. It is sometimes claimed that Paul does speak of the Virgin Birth in Gal. 4.4–5., where he says: 'But when the time has fully come, God sent forth his Son, born of woman, born under the law, to redeem those who were under the law.' But the fact is that the phrase 'born of a woman' is the regular phrase for a mortal man. 'Man that is born of a woman,' we read in Job, 'is of few days and full of trouble' (Job 14.1). 'How then can man be righteous before God? How can he who is born of woman be clean?' (Job 25.4). The phrase 'born of a woman' has nothing to do with the Virgin Birth. The fact that neither Paul's letters nor his recorded sermons in Acts ever mention the Virgin Birth is no proof that Paul did not know of it, still less that he did not accept it; but it very definitely is proof that, even if Paul did know of it and did accept it, he did not set it in the forefront of his gospel, and did not regard knowledge of it and belief in it as in any way necessary for salvation.

There is no mention of the Virgin Birth in John. Again there is a question here. Nearly all the manuscripts of the New Testament in John 1.12f. read: 'But to all who received him, who believed in his name, he gave power to become children of God; who were born, not of blood nor of the will of the flesh nor of the will of man, but of God.' But there is one manuscript, the Old Latin manuscript Codex Veronensis, which reads not 'who were born,' but 'who was born'. The second half of the passage then becomes a reference not to the rebirth of the Christian but to the Virgin Birth of Jesus. It is not possible to set the weight of one manuscript against the weight of practically all the manuscripts; but we shall nevertheless see that this is a very significant reading.

(*f*) It may finally be pointed out that a Virgin Birth would have very serious effects on the doctrine of the total incarnation, or, as Nels Ferré calls it, the 'enmanning' of Jesus Christ; for, if Jesus was born by the special action of God in a virgin, apart altogether from the natural processes of birth, then he entered into the world in a way in which no other man entered into the world, or at least in an extremely abnormal way, and, therefore, it would no longer be possible to say that he was like us in all things. This is an argument which will have different weight with different people, but it does seem that the Virgin Birth would affect the complete manhood of Jesus.

In spite of all this the idea of the Virgin Birth appears in all the early Fathers and is lodged immovably in the earliest of the creeds.

We have set out all difficulties and the problems and the contradictions which a literal belief in the Virgin Birth entails. And now one thing emerges—*these difficulties and problems and contradictions must have been every bit as apparent to the writers of the New Testament as they are to us.* We are not the first generation to have any intelligence; the New Testament writers, and the early thinkers, were quite as intelligent as we are—*and yet they allowed these contradictions to stand.* The most vivid illustration of this is the Old Latin manuscript Codex Veronensis. Let us remember its readings. It is Veronensis which omits Luke 1.34 and substitutes for it Luke 1.38 and so erases the Virgin Birth from Luke. Veronensis is one of the manuscripts which call Mary Joseph's wife instead of his betrothed in Luke 2.5. And yet it is Veronensis alone which in John 1.13 reads the singular 'who was born' and so is the only manuscript out of thousands to make that verse into a reference to the Virgin Birth!

There seems to be only one possible conclusion. The New Testament writers were not primarily concerned with the Virgin Birth as a literal and historic fact; they were concerned with it as a symbolic way of saying that from his very first entry into the world Jesus was in a special and unique relationship to God. I do not think that we are intended to take the Virgin Birth literally; I think that if we were intended so to do the writers of Scripture and the compilers of the New Testament would have reconciled the inconsistencies and would have harmonised the divergences. I think that we are clearly intended to take the story of the Virgin Birth as a parabolic, symbolic, pictorial, metaphorical method of carrying the unique relationship with God back to the very birth of Jesus, quite irrespective of whether that birth was a virgin birth or a normal birth like the birth by which all men enter into the world.

(v) But we have not yet come to the end of this purpose. We have seen how the special relationship of Jesus to God is connected with the Resurrection, with the baptism, with his experience in the Temple as a boy of twelve, with his birth. Then comes the Fourth Gospel, and the Fourth Gospel pushes the unique relationship of Jesus with God back to a time before time began. It takes it completely out of time and lodges it in the forevers of eternity. 'In the beginning was the Word, and the Word was with God, and the Word was God' (John 1.1). In the Fourth Gospel we have the culmination of the whole process, the great leap of human thought, the great vision in response to revelation, in which the relationship of Jesus Christ the Son to God the Father is something which was before time began, which is now while time shall run, and which shall be when time has come to an end. In Jesus Christ we see the very essence and being of God in human flesh—and that is the final reason why Jesus Christ is Lord.

And so in the end we come beyond theology to wondering adoration. Our minds realize the utter inadequacy of all our thinking, but our hearts cry out with Thomas in his great discovery: 'My Lord and my God!' (John 20.28).

INDEX